HUMAN NATURE
IN ITS FOURFOLD STATE

THOMAS BOSTON

★

HUMAN NATURE
IN ITS FOURFOLD STATE

OF PRIMITIVE INTEGRITY
ENTIRE DEPRAVITY
BEGUN RECOVERY AND
CONSUMMATE HAPPINESS
OR MISERY

THE BANNER OF TRUTH TRUST

THE BANNER OF TRUTH TRUST
3 Murrayfield Road, Edinburgh EH12 6EL
PO Box 621, Carlisle, Pennsylvania 17013, USA

*

© The Banner of Truth Trust 1964
Reprinted 1989
Reprinted 1997
ISBN 0 85151 559 2

*

Printed and bound by The Bath Press, Bath

CONTENTS

[5]

IV: THE ETERNAL STATE

BIOGRAPHICAL INTRODUCTION

REV GEORGE H. MORRISON, M.A.[1]

The little town of Duns is pleasantly situated on the skirts of the
Lammermuirs. The neighbourhood is rich in Covenanting
memories, and on the summit of Duns Law, which rises to the
north of the town, are still to be seen the vestiges of a camp,
occupied by General Leslie and the Covenanters in 1639, under
the threatened invasion by King Charles. Tradition has it that
John Duns Scotus, the mediæval doctor subtilis, was a native of
the parish. Nor has it been without distinguished sons in modern
times. It is the birthplace of an Oxford professor, famous enough
in his day; of the biographer of Melville and of Knox; and of at
least one noteworthy and beloved minister of the Presbyterian
Church.

Here on the 17th March 1676 – three years before the country
rang with the death of Archbishop Sharp – Thomas Boston was
born, in a tenement in Newtown Street which is still shown.
Fraser of Brea was then a man of thirty-seven. Thomas Haly-
burton was a child of two. And four years were to elapse before
the birth of Ebenezer Erskine – three men who, like Boston,
served and suffered much, and like him have enriched our literature with imperishable memoirs.

The Boston stock, which came originally from Ayr, was
staunchly Presbyterian, and sometime about 1680 John Boston,
Thomas's father, had been cast into the Duns prison for non-
conformity. Here Boston kept his father company for one night
at least. And in the after days, when he himself had strong forebodings of imprisonment, on his refusal to sign the Abjuration

---

[1] This is the original introduction to the new edition of *Memoirs of
the Life, Time, and Writings of the Rev Thomas Boston*, written by
himself, published in 1899, and edited with notes by Rev George H.
Morrison, M.A., Dundee, and a Recommendatory Note by Dr Alexander
Whyte.

Oath, these childish memories of the jail revived with peculiar vividness.

About his schooldays we have little information. He learned to read in a dame's school, kept in the upper storey of his father's house. He attended the Duns grammar school, and made rapid progress from the age of eight till he was thirteen. He was a quiet and somewhat timorous boy, unduly eager, as the timorous often are, to finish any task once started; of no great physical strength, and more fond of reading than of sport. From the first he seems to have had a retentive memory – a priceless possession for one whose books were to be few till late in life. And how he used and trained his memory will be most apparent to those who are best acquainted with the amazing wealth of scriptural quotation in his works. No system of commonplacing, however perfect, could furnish the apt and beautiful citations that abound everywhere in his books.

It was at the age of eleven that Boston was spiritually awakened, under the ministry of one whose family name was yet to rank among the most honoured in Scottish religious history. The Rev Henry Erskine,[1] father of Ebenezer and Ralph Erskine, had been ejected from his charge at Cornhill just across the border, by the Act of Uniformity of 1662, and from that time onward he had resided mostly at Dryburgh, his native town. But in 1687, when Boston was a lad, King James granted the Presbyterians liberty to worship in their own way in private houses and chapels, and almost immediately the Presbyterians of Whitsome, a parish a few miles to the south-east of Duns, gave Mr Erskine a call to come and minister to them. John Boston was not the man to listen to the curate in the parish church of Duns when a sufferer and a saint like Henry Erskine was preaching four miles from his door. And we can see him yet, as he steps out on Sabbath mornings with his sons, and not a few of the more earnest townsfolk in their company, for the hamlet of Rivelaw in Whit-

---

[1] Memoir, prefixed to 1831 edition of Fraser, *Life of Ebenezer Erskine*.

some, where Mr Erskine preached. It was at these meetings, and under that preaching, that Thomas Boston was awakened. And twelve years afterwards, when penning his noble soliloquy on Man-Fishing, he has not forgotten the skill that cast the line so cunningly in Whitsome. 'Little wast thou thinking, O my soul,' he writes, 'on Christ, heaven, or thyself, when thou went to the Newton of Whitsome to hear a preaching, when Christ first dealt with thee; there thou got an unexpected cast.'[1]

John Boston had doubtless by this time resolved that his youngest son should be a minister, and the son himself, before his schooldays were well over, had secretly set his heart on the same calling. But there were difficulties in the way. The Bostons were not rich, and a three-years' college course involved no little outlay. So hopeless indeed at one time did the prospects seem, that young Boston seriously thought of turning to a trade; but his father – to his honour be it told – would not hear of it. At length, after two anxious years, spent partly in the office of the Duns notary, and partly in study in the malt-loft, the way opened, and Boston entered Edinburgh University in 1691. Of his life there we know but little. He studied unweariedly, and seldom went into company. He passed through the regular curriculum. He learned shorthand, and had lessons in music. Ever fearful of exhausting his father's slender purse, he practised an economy that is notable even in a Scottish student, for when he graduated in 1694, his college expenses – fees, maintenance, and all – had only mounted up to some £11.[2] We cannot wonder that he often swooned, nor that he suffered much from melancholy.

In the summer of 1694 Boston received the bursary of the Presbytery of Duns, and after an autumn spent in the private study of divinity, he entered on his theological course in Edinburgh at the beginning of 1695. One short session there was all that he enjoyed. It was allowable, and at that time not uncommon, for a student who had taken one session of theology with credit,

---

[1] *A Soliloquy on the Art of Man-Fishing*, III, 4; *Works*, Vol. V, p. 11.
[2] One has, of course, to bear in mind the altered value of money.

and who desired to support himself by teaching, to complete his studies under the superintendence of the Presbytery within whose bounds he lived. For economic reasons Boston determined on this course. And after a month's unhappy experience in the beautiful parish of Glencairn, he found himself settled, early in 1696, as tutor to the stepson of Lieut-Col Bruce of Kennet, at the salary of a hundred merks per annum.

The estate of Kennet, within a mile of Clackmannan, has been for more than five hundred years in the possession of the Bruces of Kennet, a branch of the Bruces of Clackmannan, who are of royal lineage. The last Bruce of Clackmannan died about the beginning of the nineteenth century, but Bruce of Kennet still remains, hidden under the name of Lord Balfour of Burleigh. With this family Boston lived about a twelvemonth, and no part of the Memoir is richer in spiritual interest than the narrative of the trials and triumphs of that memorable year. Boston learned much at Kennet that no class lectures could have taught him. And the house of Kennet had many a lesson from Boston that had never been mentioned in the bond. Sometimes the youth of twenty was indiscreet. And sometimes the military household fretted and chafed at this embodied conscience. But it is clear that by the time he left, Boston had inspired all with a deep respect for him. And in the ancient house of a distinguished soldier, it is not every student of divinity, of humble birth and naturally timid, who could do that. Above all else there was ample leisure and there were quiet spots at Kennet for intercourse with God. And to the end Boston looked back upon the year there as a thriving time for his soul. He left Kennet in February 1697, and on the 15th June of the same year was licensed by the united Presbytery of Duns and Chirnside.

Reading the story of his inward life, we do not wonder that his preaching soon began to attract attention. There was a force and freshness in it that arrested the common people. There were gleams of vision in it such as are only granted to those who daily are near God. There was a grip in it that no preacher wins who is a stranger to his own heart. And there was in it a scriptural fulness that nothing but passionate devotion to the Bible gives. Everywhere Boston preached, the word came with power. And if at first he dealt too largely in denunciation, and here and there was roundly abused as a railer, he was soon to find, as many a noble preacher besides Boston has found, that the thunders of Sinai are not so mighty against abounding sin as is the sweeter message of the cross. How lofty his conceptions of the preacher's art and office were, is evident in the *Soliloquy on the Art of Man-Fishing* – that scribble, as he calls it – which he wrote in 1699.

One would have thought that such a preacher would have been settled soon. And if the people's voice had been determinative, Boston would not have been long without a charge. As a matter of fact, he was a probationer over two years. These were the times when heritors were still all-powerful, and Boston had no liberty of conscience to bring pressure to bear upon the heritors. He would not court them. He would not bow to them from the pulpit. He would not spend the Sabbath evening with them. And he knew well that his preaching strain could never be acceptable to such of them as had sat and slept under the curates' homilies. At Foulden, at Dollar, at Clackmannan, among other places, his hopes were dashed when things seemed ripening to a call. And how he bore himself under these disappointments, and turned his deepening experience to noble uses, is familiar to every reader of his Memoirs. At length, in 1699, the people and heritor of one small parish were found to be agreed. And on Thursday 21st September, Boston was ordained to the ministry in the parish of Simprin.

The parish of Simprin has long ceased to exist. In the autumn of 1761 it was united to the adjacent parish of Swinton, and from that date onwards the united flocks have worshipped God in the old and beautiful parish church at the east end of Swinton village, where sleep not a few of those gallant Swinton knights, whose line runs back unbroken to the times of the Heptarchy. About a mile and a half southwards from Swinton village, and so about eight miles south-east of Duns, nestling in a clump of elm and ash trees, and surrounded by a graveyard not a few of whose stones carry us back to Boston's time, are the ruins of the little church of Simprin where Boston preached. It would be difficult to picture a sweeter situation for any house of God. To the north the eye catches the slopes of the Lammermuirs. Southward the country rolls away, by Flodden field, into the heights of Cheviot. A few miles off rise the towers and battlements of Twizel Castle; while all around is the rich country of the Merse, with here a farm and there a manor-house, 'bosomed high mid tufted trees'. Of the church itself little is standing to-day but the east gable. The roof is gone. The walls are crumbling away. Nettles and thorns, with here and there the seedling of a plane tree, ramble and root among the corner-stones. And the whole structure is on a scale so diminutive, that five short paces carry one from wall to wall, and twenty from end to end. When we remember that on his first round of visitation Boston discovered but eighty-eight examinable persons; and when we find that in 1751 the total population of the parish was 143, we cease to wonder at the modest proportions of the ruined sanctuary.

Readers of the Memoirs will recall that for the first three years of his ministry in Simprin, Boston tenanted an old house at the west end of the farm-town. It was not till 1702 that a new manse was built; and this new manse, so hallowed in the after years by prayer, may probably be identified with a very humble dwelling, still to be seen a few yards westwards from the church, and still inhabited.[1] When the manse was finished, Boston tells us, he formed a large garden and built the dyke. And between this cottage and the churchyard still stretches a piece of garden ground, bounded by a wall, and pierced by an old gateway that would afford immediate access to the church.

The first few years of any ministry are always years of large

[1] Rev Mr Macdonald informs me that old inhabitants of Swinton village used to hear this called 'Boston's house' in their childhood. A ruined dwelling hard by may well have been the *old* manse.

significance. And it is not difficult to see that the pastorate in Simprin was the formative period in Boston's life. It was in the quiet of that secluded charge, and in the exercise of his calling among his handful – as he often terms his flock – that he first found how different are the stern realities of ministering from all anticipative dreams, and first formed those habits of public work and private study from which he never deviated till the end. Before the first year had run, his little parish was thoroughly organised. There was a forenoon and an afternoon sermon every Sabbath, with a lecture on the chapter at the former diet, and an address by way of preface to the whole. There was a Sabbath evening meeting for the study of the catechism. Every Tuesday evening in the manse there was a friendly gathering for praise and prayer. And every Thursday, in winter in the evenings, and in summer in the daytime, there was a week-day service. Diets of catechising were held at stated intervals throughout the parish. Every household was regularly visited. And these pastoral offices were fulfilled, not lightly, but with a faithfulness which is one of the quietest and noblest of all heroisms. All this, be it remembered, in a parish that could furnish but eighty-eight examinable persons and where for some considerable time strange faces were of the rarest. No wonder Boston had long periods of deep dejection. A shallower man would have scamped his work. Boston deliberately gave his best to his handful. And what a noble best it was, Scotland was yet to know, when the substance of it, reset and rich with the prayer of after years, was given to the world in the *Fourfold State.*

Nor were those years less memorable for their influence upon Boston himself. In the interior life every man comes to his own through manifold experiment. And before Boston left Simprin for Ettrick his chief experiments had been made, and his methods of devotion and study fashioned for good. It was here he found how the tone of the week is lowered by plunging into worldly business on the Monday morning, and it was here he formed the lifelong habit of spending the first hours of every Monday in prayer. It was here that he first systematically prepared himself for family worship, and expounded the chapter that was read in the ordinary course at night. At Simprin, too, began those family fasts that played a part in his household economy until the end. And above all, perhaps, it was at Simprin Boston awoke to the sanctifying power of dogged work. It shames us yet to read of his passion for study, that no broken weeks and no scarcity of books could quench. He struggled through the psalms in Hebrew. He set himself to master French from a paper of rules lent by a neighbouring tutor. With little help from any summa or commentary, he faced some of the stiffest questions in theology, and answered them with a surprising depth and fulness. A life like that is bound to tell. No pulpit work won by such prayer and fasting and study can long be powerless. Nor was it powerless in the Merse. We trace in the pages of the Memoir a growing interest and widening response, until at last the little church was quite unable to accommodate the throngs who crowded, especially on Communion seasons, to hear the gospel preached by the young minister of Simprin.

Here, too, first fell on Boston's life the lights and shadows of the home. In 1697, when on the point of leaving Kennet, he first met Catherine Brown of Barhill, in Culross. The meeting was but momentary, and Catherine was some two years the elder; but we may fairly gather from the guarded expressions in the diary, that it was a genuine instance of love at first sight. 'Whenever I saw her,' says Boston, 'a thought struck through my heart about her being my wife.' And 'both of us were in great distress'. For the next year the two saw nothing of each other. But when in the spring of 1698 Boston returned to the Presbytery of Stirling, and took a lodging with Catherine's brother-in-law, the acquaintance-ship of a day was soon renewed, and speedily ripened into a pledge of loving companionship for life. Perhaps neither thought that two years must elapse before they could be married. They had not laid their reckoning with stubborn heritors, nor with the miserable stipend at Simprin. And it is easy to see the sore perplexities of both in carrying the matter of their engagement rightly. At length, on the 17th July 1700, they were married at Culross, by Mr Mair, and Boston brought his bride home to Simprin. It was the beginning of a wedded life that was to be chequered by the sorest griefs. Of the five children born at Simprin two were soon laid in the churchyard. In later years Mrs Boston fell under a mysterious and racking disorder of the intellect. Yet Boston felt to the end that his marriage was of God. Two years before his death, writing his narrative, and looking backwards through the sunshine and the storm of the two-and-thirty years since they first met, Boston recorded of his wife one of the tenderest and noblest tributes wherewith a wife was ever honoured, and blessed God that he had been made acquainted with her. So enriched by love and sorrow, and so sanctified by fellowship with God and work, was Thomas Boston, when on the 1st of May 1707, in the thirty-second year of his age, he was translated from Simprin to the parish of Ettrick, where the remainder of his life was to be spent.

The parish of Ettrick,[1] in Selkirkshire is a large one. It stretches about ten miles every way, and embraces the upper courses of the Ettrick River, taking within its sweep the tributaries of Tima and Rankleburn on the south, and crossing the hills northward to the Loch of the Lowes in Yarrow. From Simprin to Ettrick church is only some forty-five miles, as Boston would have ridden it; but to pass from one parish to the other is like passing from the Lowlands into the midst of Highland scenery. Around the little church of Simprin lie the rich lands of Berwickshire. The towns of Coldstream, of Kelso, and of Duns are none of them far away. But the church and manse of Ettrick nestle at the foot of lofty hills, where they begin to draw together with increasing height and grandeur towards the valley-head. And Ettrick River, springing from the rushes between two of these

---

[1] The Forest, as Boston often calls his parish, was a name originally applied to the valleys of Yarrow and Tweed, as well as to that of the Ettrick.

highest Fells, and falling like a thread of silver into the valley, will have good eighteen miles to travel past Ettrick church before it reach the county town of Selkirk. Across the hills to the north lies the valley of the Yarrow – that chosen home of song and legend. And though Ettrick can never match its famous sister in the spell it casts on the poet's imagination and the people's heart, it too is rich in legend, and has not been entirely unsung. It has inspired some of the finest of the older ballads. It teems with romantic memories of the Border feuds. One of its loneliest cleuchs has given the title to the ducal family of Buccleuch. Here Michael Scott, the wizard, had his last home. And here, within a stone-cast of the church, the Ettrick Shepherd – that true interpreter of Border wizardry – was born thirty-eight years after Boston's death.

It is not easy to determine what the population of Ettrick was in Boston's time. To-day in the whole valley there are about a thousand people, and in the parish itself about four hundred, and we have really no valid ground for holding that the population was much larger two centuries ago. It is true that here and there, as on the south side of the river opposite the church, may be traced the ruins of considerable hamlets where now there is not one house; but the earliest statistics of the parish – of the date 1755 – give the population at 397, a number slightly less than that of the present day.

But if the population has been stationary, and if the green hills look down on farms and homesteads still bearing the names familiar to lovers of these Memoirs, the Ettrick of to-day is different in many ways from the Ettrick where Thomas Boston wrought. The upper valley must always be a lonely region, and now as then the snow will sometimes lie for weeks upon the hills. But the good roads that stretch away from the church door, and the line of telegraph that threads the valley, and the daily post that brings the news of the great world without, all make it hard for us to realise the isolation of Thomas Boston's Ettrick. So late as 1792 the writer of the Statistical Account supplies a somewhat doleful description of his parish. 'This parish,' he says, 'possesses no advantages. The roads are almost impassable.[1] The only road that looks like a turnpike is to Selkirk, but even it in many places is so deep as greatly to obstruct travelling. The snow also, at times, is a great inconvenience; often for many months we can have no intercourse with mankind. Another great disadvantage is the want of bridges. For many hours the traveller is obstructed on his journey when the waters are swelled. In this parish there are twelve ploughs and twenty carts, but no carriages or waggons.' Such, then, was Ettrick – a parish possessing no advantages. It was for Boston to discover what might be done through work and prayer in this disadvantageous spot.

For a long time it looked as if nothing could be done. Work and prayer seemed to be well-nigh powerless. Amid that sea of hills, as Ettrick has been called, Boston had taken arms against a sea of troubles, and nothing but the deep conviction that his call had been of God could have upheld him through his earlier ministry. The little flock at Simprin had been ignorant, but, at least, they had received with meekness the engrafted word. Ettrick was very liberal to its poor, and very hospitable to the passing stranger; but it was full of pride, and self-assurance, and conceit – the frequent offspring of an isolated life; and how that self-assurance and conceit hampered the work of ministering, and how it plagued the minister, is frankly told in these truly human Memoirs. And then it was a sorely broken parish. The smouldering discontent with the Revolution Settlement had been fanned into a flame by Cameronians from the west. Every hamlet in the upper valley had its separatist. The common talk was all of separation, and of the lawfulness of attending service in the parish church; till Boston, ever eager to get to personal dealing with his people, was like to be wrestled out of breath with them,

---

[1] 'At the beginning of this century it was common to see a driver going before his horses with a spade in his hands to fill up the ruts.' – Angus, *Ettrick and Yarrow*, 3. Cf. Scott's 'Up *pathless* Ettrick and on Yarrow.'

and almost dreaded his pastoral visiting. Nor were things better on the Sabbath. A four years' vacancy had wrought its natural effects. Men had grown careless. They had lost the art of decent attention during service. They gossiped and chaffered so noisily in the churchyard in time of sermon, that one of the elders had to be told off to keep order there.[1] Worse, too, than any inattention was the so lax morality. The vice of swearing was widespread. And one has but to turn the pages of the old Session Records to be ashamed at the prevalent uncleanness. No wonder Boston was made to go with a bowed-down back. No wonder that after eight years of it he said to his wife, 'My heart is alienated from this place.' At times he was filled with the longing to be gone. And it is characteristic of his large and loyal heart, that nothing so speedily subdued that longing as the thought of the sad plight of Ettrick if he went.

But in the long-run, faith and prayer and study will tell. And as they had told in Simprin they were to tell in Ettrick too. It is not every minister who grows and deepens amid an unsympathetic people. It is not every father who abounds in thankfulness when called to meet the bitterest sorrows of the home. Boston did both. And the artless story of his study and his preaching and his daily wrestling with God, surrounded and shadowed as he was, is one of the noblest records that was ever penned. Slowly and surely his influence grew. Gird as they would, men felt the thrust and power of his preaching, and knew the Holy Ghost was in it. One of his action sermons had been published, and word began to steal into the valley that it was making a deep impression in Edinburgh. Strange faces became common in the church. Then came the inevitable calls. And Ettrick grew convinced at last – and the conviction had taken ten years to ripen – that in losing Boston they would lose an incomparable minister. It is touching to note the outbreakings of a rough affection, and to find a congregational fast appointed by the Session, when in 1716 Boston came under call to Closeburn. It is touching, too, and something

[1] Session Minutes, 1707.

more, when we remember what the past had been, to mark how Boston, in Presbytery and Synod and Assembly, battled against the call, and how at last he won. It was the turning-point in the parish life. Henceforth he was to minister with a new authority, and to be the instrument of far larger blessing.

How these ten years of difficulty enriched Boston it is not hard, reading the Memoirs, to see. Nor is it hard to see how they enriched the world. It is to them we owe the *Fourfold State*. The substance of that work had been already preached at Simprin. In 1708 and 1709 it was recast and amplified, and given from the Ettrick pulpit. And when, some two years later, Boston was urged by his beloved physician, Dr Trotter, to publish, it was these notes that seemed the likeliest venture. But Boston dared not move till he was certain of the call of God. And of all the signs that pointed to a call, none was more patent than his divided parish. These sermons had been greatly blessed to those who heard them. When printed, might they not reach the many who never darkened Ettrick kirk? Boston would almost have been content with that. It was a lowly prospect, but it determined him. He did not know what scattered multitudes were to be found and fed by the reading of the *Fourfold State*.

And if ever a book was steeped in prayer, it was that *Fourfold State*. From the Tuesday in January 1712 when Boston first put pen to paper for the final draft, it was daily spread before a throne of grace, and found its place in every family fast. At times it looked as if the book would never see the light. It was delayed by the Rebellion of the '15. It was almost strangled in the birth by the well-meant meddling of an Edinburgh Treasurer – one of the most amazing and ludicrous incidents in the whole history of literature. And it was not till November 1720 that Boston handled a bound copy of his work. Almost immediately it took a hold. New editions were called for, and testimonies of its usefulness came pouring in. It was discussed in Edinburgh drawing-rooms. The shepherd read it on the hills. It made its way into the Highland crofts, where stained and tattered copies of the earlier editions may still be found. For more than a hundred years its influence upon the religious life of Scotland was incalculable. And though the interests and the outlook are very changed to-day, and the book itself is very little read, there are great parts of Scotland in which one cannot move among the people, and catch the accent of their more serious talk, and listen to their prayers, without perceiving, howsoever dimly, that the influence of Boston's masterpiece is unexhausted yet. Nor need one wonder at the power of it. It is so orderly and clear, so rich in just and beautiful citation, so searching, and here and there so softening; it is so strong in its appeals, so full, for all its doctrine, of warmth and human life; it is so couched in language of the homeliest and truest ring, rising at times into unquestionable eloquence, that the secret of its acceptance is not far to seek. And yet to Boston himself that was not all the secret. 'When I have considered the acceptance that book met with,' he writes in 1730, 'I could not but impute it to an over-ruling hand of kind Providence, that would needs have it so.'

Boston was no ecclesiastic. He makes the quaint confession that he was defective in ecclesiastical prudence. One could scarcely conceive a greater contrast than that between the author of the *Fourfold State* – the leader of the people's thought, and the courtly Carstares – the leader of the people's church. Still, when the question in church courts was one of principle or doctrine, Boston was always ready to declare himself. And at three points especially he touched the larger church life of his day.

The first was in that now forgotten controversy that raged around the Abjuration Oath. Early in 1712 the British Parliament had passed an Act,[1] imposing the Oath of Abjuration upon all the ministers of Scotland. The title of that oath explains itself.

---

[1] 'An Act to prevent the disturbing of those of the Episcopal communion in Scotland, in the exercise of their religious worship.' – Struthers, *History of Scotland* I, p. 154.

It was an oath abjuring the Pretender. It aimed at the safeguarding of the Queen, and made the Protestant succession to the crown secure.

So far, however offensive were the circumstances of its imposition, there might be little real objection to the oath, for certainly no men in Scotland were more eager to repudiate King James the Eighth, with all his spurious rights and titles, than were the Presbyterian ministers. Unhappily, the oath made mention of, and indeed was based upon, two Acts of the English Parliament, that had been passed before the Union, and in these Acts it was expressly stipulated that the reigning sovereign should belong to the communion of the Church of England. This was the rock of stumbling. It was impossible for Presbyterian ministers to pledge themselves to the upholding of Episcopacy. It was unjust, and wholly inconsistent with the Treaty and Articles of Union, to force upon them any such acknowledgment, on pain of extraordinary penalties if they refused. Once perhaps the Church of Scotland would have risked the inevitable charges of disloyalty, and scorned subscription. But the Assembly of 1712 had lost the faith and daring of an older day, and it was left to individual ministers to take the oath or not at their discretion.

It is hard for us, after the long interval of years, to realise how deeply this matter of the oath moved the whole Church. It brought her to the verge of a disruption. It broke old friendships, and became a term of ministerial communion. In numberless cases it impaired, and in not a few entirely dissolved, that so unique and sacred tie that binds the pastor and his flock together. Perhaps no subscription in the long history of the Church was ever the cause of such abounding bitterness. Some signed without a scruple. Many – and in their number not a few of the saintliest and wisest – complied under a sorrowful protest. But some three hundred refused to sign on any terms, and among these was Boston. It was no light thing to incur a fine greater than all the stipend he had ever handled.[1] It was no easy thing to hold com-

---

[1] £500. The penalty was never enacted, though often threatened.

munion with his jurant friends when it set all Ettrick snarling.[1] But Boston was convinced, and his convictions in the matter never changed. Seven years later the oath was reimposed. It was so altered then, and freed from all reference to the objectionable Acts, that the great body of non-jurors signed at last. Boston had still no liberty to sign, and he remained a 'Non' until the end. It is a noble instance, at the very least, of how a naturally timid man, set in a lonely parish, and far from the quickening inter-course of kindred souls, may school himself into the heroism of high moral courage.

Boston's position in this matter of the oath was shared by many. He was not solitary in his sustained defiance of the Government. But shortly after the first imposition of the oath a case began deeply to agitate the Church, and this time, at one stage in the proceedings, Boston was to stand alone. It was the case of Professor Simson.

Readers of Wodrow's *Letters* – that very precious and some-times very tedious correspondence – grow painfully familiar, before they close the last of the three bulky volumes, with the name of Simson. The conscientious minister of Eastwood was in the habit of writing daily letters from the Assembly to his wife, and he was present, though not always as a member, at every Assembly in which the Simson case came up. One would have thought that Mrs Wodrow might have been furnished with livelier news from Edinburgh than these interminable wranglings. But my Lord Pollok of Eastwood was at home, too frail to come up to the Assembly now, but just as keenly interested in its work as ever, and the daily letters directed to the manse were doubt-less intended for the castle too. Whether or not, Wodrow so narrowly watched the Simson case, and followed it so closely

---

[1] 'My father was very tenacious of what he judged truth, while at the same time he could love, esteem, and honour his brethren who differed from him, and very freely hold communion with them.' – T. Boston, junr. Preface to his father's sermon on *Schism*.

through all its windings to the end, that we have no ampler commentary on the relative portions of this diary, than these so circumstantial letters.

John Simson was Professor of Divinity at Glasgow, and if he was not an inspiration to his students, for fifteen years at any rate he was an irritation to his Church. He was a keen and subtle thinker, with his chief interest in metaphysics. But he was an unsettled and ill-balanced man, with little depth or dignity of character. And he conspicuously lacked the comprehensive mind that is so needful for a teacher of theology.

First he was charged with teaching Arminian doctrine, and after much debate and much delay was very gently reprimanded. Nine years later the cry got up that he was tainted with the heresies of Dr Clarke, and that he was inculcating Arian tenets now – impugning the accepted doctrine of the Trinity, and denying the necessary existence of our Lord Jesus Christ. No charges could be graver, but to prove the charges was supremely difficult. The lectures complained of had been in Latin. The nicest terms may be equivocal. And the Professor not only was a master in the art of teaching heresy orthodoxly,[1] but was so feverishly eager to concede, and to reiterate his adherence to the standards, that honest men, who had no learning to dispute his doctrine, began instinctively to doubt his character. Through four Assemblies, and countless meetings of committee and of Presbytery, the matter was debated. Side issues caused delay. The finest points were argued at unconscionable length, and with a mighty show of learning. And it was not till the Assembly of 1729 that the case was finally disposed of. The charges were found proven. Would, then, the culprit be excommunicated? or would he be deposed? or would he be merely suspended from the work of teaching? Professor Simson was perpetually suspended, still to enjoy the emoluments, without fulfilling the duties, of the chair.

[1] The phrase is Lord Grange's. Wodrow, *Letters*, III, p. 261.

And it was then that Boston, like Athanasius *contra totum orbem*, stood alone. Boston was clear that if the charges had been proven, Simson should be deposed. He could not tolerate the unfaithful gentleness of the Assembly. When the report of the committee recommending the suspension was brought in, the house was crowded. The case was drawing to a close at last, and the great strain was nearly over. The Act was read; the Moderator asked if the Assembly acquiesced in it, and for a moment there was profound stillness. Then Boston rose. 'Moderator,' he said, 'I dissent in my own name, and in the name of all that shall adhere to me;' then looking round the house, 'with an air of majesty,' as an eye-witness has it, 'that I shall never forget,' and finding none had risen, he added, 'and for myself alone if nobody shall adhere.' 'Sir,' said the Moderator, a very solemn, grave man, 'will you tear out the bowels of your mother?' 'If that were the tendency of this,' said Boston, pointing to the paper in his hand, 'rather would I take it, and tear it in a thousand pieces.' At length, in the sole interest of the Church's peace, Boston agreed not to insist on the recording of his protest, and the Simson case was at an end. Boston had acted with a quiet and courageous dignity that made a deep impression on the house, and greatly raised his reputation in the Church. And it was all wonderful to him. In his whole management of the affair he traced a higher wisdom than his own. He was a richer man, in things more heavenly than reputation, when he turned his horse's head out of the crowded Edinburgh street and made towards the solitude of Ettrick.

The Abjuration question and the Simson case, however engrossing in their day, have long been forgotten. But there was one other controversy of the time, which may not have commanded the intense interest of the others, but which was destined to be far more powerful for good. The echoes of it have not yet died away. The influences of it are still not altogether indiscernible. It was the Marrow controversy. And among all the ministers so honourably concerned in that, none was more deeply engaged than Boston.

At the commencement of his ministry, Boston, like many another regenerate and able preacher, was still intellectually groping in no little darkness towards right uptakings of the grace of God. Trained in the covenant theology, he was soon face to face with the tremendous difficulties which that theology offers to the thinker. And it is characteristic of the man that he made no attempt to shirk these difficulties. He preached according to his knowledge, and out of his growing experience of Christ. But always, with abounding prayer, he was studying, comparing, writing, and longing for the breaking of a fuller light.

And if that saying of Duncan Matheson's – that we aye get what we gang in for – was ever true, it was true in Boston's case. Some time in 1700, sitting in an old soldier's cottage at Simprin, he spied above the window-head two little books. One proved to be a work by Saltmarsh, that Boston did not relish. The other was titled *The Marrow of Modern Divinity*. It was a new name to Boston. Neither at Kennet nor in the Merse had he ever heard a whisper of the book. It is not likely that any minister of his acquaintance had ever seen it, save Fraser of Brea,[1] and he had never mentioned it. But it so suited Boston's case and met his difficulties, so cleared him in the matter of the covenants, and gave him boldness in his full offers of salvation, that it became, and to the end remained, the choicest volume on his not-overburdened shelf. 'It speedily gave a tincture to my preaching,' says Boston; but it did more than that. Little could he foresee what consequences for himself and for his church were still to flow from that bookish glance at the old soldier's window-head.

And what, then, was this book? It was a little treatise by an English gentleman, Edward Fisher, M.A., of Brazenose College,

---

[1] Fraser had been helped by the *Marrow*. See *Memoirs* (1891, Inverness), p. 232.

Oxford, and it first saw the light in 1646,[1] the memorable year
of the Westminster Confession. As its name indicates, it does
not claim originality. It is a gathering together of the most
marrowy passages of the acknowledged masters of divinity. But
the selection is so skilful, and the progress of the argument so
clear, and the whole is thrown into such an interesting form,
that the book is far from being a mere catena. Students of the
religious history of England are well aware of the countless sects
and heresies that sprang up during the Civil War. They know,
too, that among all the questions in debate, none were more
eagerly pursued in press and pulpit than those which turn on
the relationships of law and grace. It was in these that Fisher
was most deeply interested. Like a clean English gentleman, he
saw and scorned the unworthy licence that men were calling the
liberty of Christ. On the other hand, he had himself, for twelve
weary years, been fettered by a legal spirit, and ignorant of the
secret of free grace. And when he found the light, and grasped,
through conference and prayer and most exhaustive reading, the
mutual bearings of the older law and of the newer liberty, nothing
would serve but he must tell the news. So came the *Marrow*. It
is no dry compend of theology. It is the earnest effort of a
Christian and a scholar to solve some of the problems of his time.
It is the endeavour of a 'middle man' to take the 'middle path,'
and the middle path – the only path to heaven, says Boston in his
note – was Jesus Christ truly received by faith, and walked in
answerably by holiness of heart and life.

To some who read these pages it may seem not a little strange
that such a thesis should ever call for vindication. They must
remember that they were never trained to think in terms of that
noble system of covenant theology. Every theology has its point

[1] Strictly, this applies only to the first part of the *Marrow*. A second
part, dealing with the Ten Commandments, was published in 1648.
Boston's edition contains both parts; but it was the first part only that
he found at Simprin, and the first part that was edited by Hog, and
excepted against by the Assembly. In general references to the *Marrow*,
it is the first part that is commonly intended.

[26]

of strain. And in the covenant-system, so rich in intellectual satisfaction, one point of strain must always be the inter-relations of the covenants. Was the moral law the covenant of works? What, then, is the standing of the moral law in the covenant of grace? Was the covenant between God and Christ the very same as that between God and Adam? And does the believer accept the moral law out of the hand of God the Creator or God the Redeemer? Such questions seem very far away to us. They sound unpractical. They speak a language we hardly understand. But sooner or later they must be asked and answered by every student of the covenant theology. And they were never better answered than by Fisher. At times his expressions are not a little harsh; and there are paragraphs that lend themselves most admirably to misrepresentation. But how a Scottish Assembly could condemn the book, as it was yet to be condemned, and could deliberately find in it an antinomian bias, must surely remain a mystery for ever.

Boston had been a student of the *Marrow* for a score of years, before the book began to make a stir in Scotland. And all the stir, though Boston did not know it at the time, sprang from his find on the Simprin window-head. In 1717, when the first case against Simson had been closed, the Assembly was called upon to give its judgment on the famous Auchterarder Creed. This so-called creed was a proposition framed by the Presbytery of Auchterarder, and put to a student when applying for licence, and it ran in these terms : 'It is not sound and orthodox to teach that we must forsake sin in order to our coming to Christ, and instating us in covenant with God.' That certainly has got an ugly sound. We cannot wonder that it was widely misinterpreted. To those who could receive it, it was but the harsh expression of the thought –

'Just as I am, and waiting not
To rid my soul of one dark blot,
O Lamb of God, I come.'

but to many it seemed a direct incentive to a lawless life, and as such it was condemned by the Assembly.

Now it was just on points like these that Boston had been so aided by the *Marrow*. And it was of the *Marrow* that Boston's mind was full during the progress of that Auchterarder diet. He did not speak in the debate, but he did better. He spoke of the *Marrow* to his neighbour in the house. His neighbour – the minister of Crieff – searched through the Edinburgh bookshops until he got a copy. It passed from his hands into those of Mr Webster. From Mr Webster it was hurried on to James Hog, minister of Carnock. And early in 1718 Hog published a new edition of the book.

And then the stir began. Following so hard upon the first Simson case, and on the question of the Auchterarder Creed, the book became at once the source of violent debate. It was attacked in Synod sermons. It was defended in explanatory pamphlets. It was complained of to the next Assembly. A committee of the Commission sat in judgment on it. And the end of all the scrutiny was this, that by an Act of Assembly of 20th May 1720 the *Marrow* was condemned.[1]

That year Boston was not a member. But we can well conceive how sorely he was wounded when he heard of the ban upon his precious *Marrow*. Had he owed little to the book, he might have had a day of fasting for the condemning Act, and let things be. But the *Marrow* had come to him with the countersign of God, and it was impossible for Boston to be silent. At Presbytery and in Synod he sought redress in vain. Nothing was left but to petition the Assembly. And it was that petition, drawn up by Boston, and perfected by the counsels and the prayers of eleven likeminded ministers, that was laid before the Assembly of 1721, and is known in history as the Representation.[2] It is a lengthy

---

[1] See the full text of the Act in Struthers, *History of Scotland*, I, p. 480: Brown's *Gospel Truth* (1831), p. 171.
[2] Full text in Struthers, *History of Scotland*, I, p. 498: Brown's *Gospel Truth* (1831), p. 176.

document, rebutting the several charges of the Act, and here and there, in the homely vigour of its style, betraying the hand that drafted it. And it was handed in to the Committee of Bills by Mr Kid of Queensferry, 'a man of singular boldness,' on Friday, 12th May 1721.

But if the Representers hoped that the Assembly would take action, their hopes were doomed to disappointment. John, Earl of Rothes, was the King's Commissioner; and the day before the Assembly met we have Wodrow writing to his wife that the Commissioner is not well. The following Tuesday 'the Commissioner is really ill; he has a most violent cough, and is blue and ill-coloured. . . . Some think him a-dying, and that we will rise to-morrow.' And this the Assembly actually did. On Wednesday the 17th it was dissolved, and the Representation was referred to the Commission.

And how the Commission dealt with the twelve Marrowmen, and how it wearied them and worried them, students of the Memoirs will discover. But students will pardon the Commission everything for the one service it rendered to theology. It set the Marrowmen twelve posing questions. It gathered up the points at issue into a dozen queries, and bade the petitioners answer them in writing. And the answers, submitted to the March Commission, form one of the noblest pieces of theology that ever enriched the English tongue. One would fain trace the hand of Boston in them, but it cannot be. They were begun by Ebenezer Erskine, and perfected by Gabriel Wilson, minister of Maxton. We do not wonder that the latter was Boston's dearest friend, nor that the former bears a venerated name, if this was the manner of their handiwork. Every votary of the queen of sciences would be a debtor to the Marrow controversy, if it had left us nothing but these so strong and luminous replies.[1]

But neither the answers of the Marrowmen, nor the awakening interest of the common people, moved the Commission. Its

---

[1] They are appended in full to many editions of the *Marrow*: as in *Works*, VII, p. 466. Also in Brown's *Gospel Truth* (1831), p. 189.

overture was adverse. And on the 21st of May 1722 the General Assembly ratified the overture, and admonished and rebuked the Representers. 'I received the rebuke,' says Boston, 'as an ornament, being for the cause of truth.' A Protest, drawn by Boston and signed by all, was handed in. It was received, but was not read. And so the Marrow controversy ended. Four years later, spite of the prohibition of his Church, Boston put forth a new edition of the *Marrow* with very ample notes. And spite of the prohibition of the Church, or perhaps in part because of it, the book had a rapid and extensive sale.

It would be an interesting, though by no means an easy task, to trace the influences of the *Marrow*, and of the Marrow controversy, upon religious Scotland. Weighted with the authority of saintly names, and rich in the added interests of church debate, the book was read by multitudes, and proved to many 'a light struck up in darkness.' It was interpreted in some of Boston's most familiar writings. Men caught the echoes of it in the preaching of George Whitefield.[1] It was a silent witness against the dry morality of countless pulpits. And if the nation was at all in readiness for the evangelical revival of the succeeding century, directly and indirectly the *Marrow* had played its part in that. But there was more than that. It was in the Marrow controversy, for the first time since the Revolution, that the country saw a little band of venerated ministers united to oppose the Church's will, for conscience' sake. And though that controversy issued without rupture, it made the strained relationship so evident, and brought the possibilities of separation so home to ministers and people, that none were wholly unprepared for the notable secessions of the next forty years.

The Marrow controversy over – 'that plunge into public affairs that filled both my head and my hands' – Boston was free to resume his parish work, and to ply his beloved and sorely broken studies. His health was frail, and his wife's case was yearly becoming more tragical. He had a presentiment that the end was

[1] Cf. Thomson's *History of the Secession Church* (1848), p. 16 *note*.

[30]

not very far away. We might have thought that one so prematurely old, and so afflicted in his wife's affliction, had earned a little rest. But Boston could not rest . No period of his life is stored with labours like these last ten years. 'The little that is done,' says Goethe, 'seems nothing, when we look forward and see how much we have yet to do.'

His duties of catechising were resumed. His stated meetings with the young were continued till very near the end. He visited the sick in the remotest corners of the parish, not seldom fighting his way to them through storm and under grievous bodily distress. He wrote his treatise on the Covenant of Grace; prepared an Explanation of the first part of the Catechism; completed his admirable Memorial on Fasting; translated and annotated a great part of Genesis. And all the time his pulpit was his throne. His preaching was never more fragrant nor more full than in that last decade. It was then he delivered those notable discourses on the *Mystery of Christ in the Form of a Servant*. It is to that period we owe the sermons that were published posthumously as the *Crook in the Lot*. And nothing could give a better idea of the compass, and the intellectual power, and the comforting strength of Boston's later ministry, than these examples of his pulpit work. We cannot wonder that such work was owned. Preaching like that will win its way and draw its audience even among the hills of Ettrick. In 1710 Boston for the first time had dispensed the Sacrament in Ettrick, and some sixty persons had partaken. In 1731 he celebrated his last Communion, and the tokens distributed numbered 777.

But that decade was memorable for another study to which a pathetic interest attaches. As a student of divinity in Edinburgh, Boston had learned the rudiments of Hebrew, and as a young minister at Simprin he had begun his study of the Hebrew Bible. That study he plied, with all his wonted enthusiasm, till the last; and there can be little question that in the course of years he wrought himself into one of the profoundest Hebraists in Scotland.

But it is one thing to understand the Hebrew text and another thing to understand the Hebrew accents – those mystical scatterings of dots and dashes that variegate the Hebrew page. These accents are guides to the pronunciation, and form a kind of commentary on the true sense and recitation of the text, and scholars tell us that they were invented by the Jewish doctors in the earlier centuries of our era. They form no part of the original Hebrew text; they are not found in the Old Testaments of the Jewish synagogue, nor in the citations of the first Christian Fathers. All this we know now, but much of it was unknown to Boston. And an eager mind like his could never rest while every page of his beloved Hebrew was intricate with mysteries like these.

It was in 1713 that Boston began the study of the accents, and for three years he groped and stumbled in Cimmerian darkness. He read, and wrote, and prayed, and meditated, but the perplexities remained. Most men would have given over. Most ministers would have found it all telling adversely on their public work. Boston held on, and by abounding prayer sanctified both his accents and himself. After three years of wandering, the light began to break. The meaning of the accents became plainer; they settled down into something of function and of law; until at last they threw such a flood of light upon the sacred text, and gave him such an insight into debated passages, that Boston grew convinced the accents were divine, and the true key to the genuine sense of Scripture. It was a great discovery to Boston. It came to be his passion. It took possession of him, heart and soul. He had been called to preach the everlasting gospel, and he would preach it to the end. But next to that the greatest business of his life must be his work on the Accentuation.

And how that work progressed, and how he wrestled with its difficulties, and how the publication of it baffled him – all this is one of the touching passages in these Memoirs. It took him three years to write his book. It cost him the labour of another year to turn it into Latin. Lord Grange was interested. Sir

Richard Ellys was ready to befriend. The Ettrick messenger brought letters in his wallet from famous scholars at continental universities. But the difficulties in the way of publication were insuperable, and Boston died with his hope unrealised. The book was published in 1738 at Amsterdam. It bears the title *Tractatus Stigmologicus*, and has a Latin dedication to Sir Richard Ellys, written by Boston's son. And surely it is the most curious and recondite work that ever issued from a Scottish manse. We do not find that it influenced Hebrew scholarship. The divine authority of the accents was a dream. Yet he who knows how the world has progressed through its errors, and he who has learned the matchless discipline of exact and unremitting toil, will be the last to deplore Boston's beloved study. It is not often that the writers of a people's books bear honoured names among the learned. It has never been a very common thing to find in the evangelical minister the ripened scholar. And Scotland has not been ignorant of popular theologians, who would have been far less popular if they had been truer students. It is something then to know, and it is worthy of remembrance, that the evangelical minister of Ettrick, whose works were treasured by the cottar and the herd, was welcomed as an equal by the finest Hebrew scholars in the world.

Boston was never a robust man, although he sets it down with thankfulness that he never spent a silent Sabbath through ill-health. Early in life he feared consumption, and all his life he seems to have been troubled with a painful binding in the breast. In 1724 he had a first attack of gravel. Two years later he noticed a palsied shaking of the head, which spread in time to his whole body. With the New Year of 1732 it became plain that his work was nearly done. His sufferings had increased. His strength was very low. He could not think to leave off preaching while it was possible to preach at all; but he was forced to sit during the delivery of the short discourse. When April came, with its message of the returning life of spring, he was too feeble to make out the pulpit. But on the first two Sabbaths he preached from the manse window, choosing most characteristically – the ruling passion strong in death – the theme of self-examination. These were his last discourses to his people. In great weakness he lingered for a little, and on the 20th of May, a Saturday – the day he commonly rested from his studies – he died, at the age of fifty-six.

He was buried in the beautiful churchyard of Ettrick, that had so often echoed with his communion-message of eternal life. Until the beginning of this century the spot was marked by a small stone, on one half of which was graven his name, and on the other half his wife's. But in 1806 a monument was erected to his memory, and it still stands unharmed by the storm and sunshine of these ninety years.[1] On every side, graven in stone, we read the names that have grown familiar in these Memoirs. Bryden and Biggar and Linton, Crosslie and Thirlstane, all are here. Here rest the children Boston baptized. There sleeps a wandering sheep who gave his minister many a weary hour. And yonder is the grave of one who for conscience' sake could never enter Ettrick church. But all have come to the one quiet church-yard. The separations are forgotten here. In death and in the dust pastor and people are at last united, until the day break and the shadows flee away.

[1] The first proposal for this monument was made in the *Monitor*, April 1804. An interesting letter by Rev Wm Brown of Eskdalemuir (who wrote the inscription) giving full particulars of the erecting will be founded in the 1827 *Life of Boston* (Oliphant), p. 281.

I
THE STATE OF INNOCENCE

MAN'S ORIGINAL RIGHTEOUSNESS

Lo, this only have I found, that God hath made man
upright; but they have sought out many inventions.
ECCLESIASTES 7.29

There are four things very necessary to be known by all that would see heaven: 1. What man *was* in the state of innocence, as God made him. 2. What he *is* in the state of corrupt nature, as he hath unmade himself. 3. What he *must be* in the state of grace, as created in Christ Jesus unto good works, if ever he be made a partaker of the inheritance of the saints in light. 4. What he *will be* in his eternal state, as made by the Judge of all, either perfectly happy, or completely miserable, and that for ever. These are weighty points, that touch the vitals of practical godliness, from which most men, and even many professors, in these dregs of time, are quite estranged. I design, therefore, under the divine conduct, to open these things, and apply them.

I begin with the first of them, namely, the *State of Innocence:* that, beholding man polished after the similitude of a palace, the ruins may the more affect us; we may the more prize that matchless Person whom the Father has appointed the repairer of the breach; and that we may, with fixed resolves, betake ourselves to that way which leads to the city that has immovable foundations.

In the text we have three things:

1 : The state of innocence wherein man was created. 'God hath made man upright.' By 'man' here we are to understand our first parents; the archetypal pair, the root of mankind, the compendized world, and the fountain from whence all generations have streamed; as may appear by comparing Gen 5.1,2, 'In the day that God created man, in the likeness of God made he him:

[37]

male and female created he them; and blessed them, and called their name Adam.' The original word is the same in our text. In this sense, man was made right (agreeable to the nature of God, whose work is perfect), without any imperfection, corruption, or principle of corruption, in his body or soul. He was made 'upright,' that is, straight with the will and law of God, without any irregularity in his soul. By the set it got in its creation, it directly pointed towards God, as his chief end; which straight inclination was represented, as in an emblem, by the erect figure of his body, a figure that no other living creature partakes of. What David was in a gospel sense, that was he in a legal sense; one 'according to God's own heart,' altogether righteous, pure, and holy. God made him thus: He did not first make him, and then make him righteous, but in the very making of him, He made him righteous. Original righteousness was created with him; so that in the same moment he was a man, he was a righteous man, morally good; with the same breath that God breathed into him a living soul, He breathed into him a righteous soul.

2: Here is man's fallen state: 'But they have sought out many inventions.' They fell off from their rest in God, and fell upon seeking inventions of their own, to mend their case; and they quite marred it. Their ruin was from their own proper motion: they would not abide as God had made them; but they sought out inventions, to deform and undo themselves.

3: Observe here the certainty and importance of these things; 'Lo, this only have I found.' Believe them, they are the result of a narrow search, and a serious inquiry, performed by the wisest of men. In the two preceding verses, Solomon represents himself as in quest of goodness in the world; but the issue of it was, he could find no satisfying end of his search after it; though it was not for want of pains, for he counted one by one, to find out the account. 'Behold, this have I found, saith the preacher' – to wit, 'That,' as the same word is read in our text, 'yet my soul seeketh, but I find not.' He could make no satisfying discovery of it, which might stay his inquiry. He found the good very rare, one

[38]

as it were among a thousand. But could that satisfy the grand query, 'Where shall wisdom be found?' No it could not: and if the experience of others in this point run counter to Solomon's, as it is no reflection on his discernment, it can as little decide the question, which will remain undetermined till the last day. But, amidst all this uncertainty there is one point found out and fixed – 'This have I found.' You may depend upon it as a most certain truth, and be fully satisfied in it. 'Lo this;' fix your eyes upon it, as a matter worthy of most deep and serious regard; namely, that man's nature is now depraved: but that depravity was not from God, for He 'made man upright,' but from themselves, 'they have sought out many inventions.'

DOCTRINE: *God made man altogether righteous*

This is that state of innocence in which God placed man in the world. It is described in the holy Scripture with a running pen, in comparison of the following states; for it was of no continuance, but passed away as a flying shadow, by man's abusing the freedom of his will. I shall,

I : Inquire into the righteousness of this state wherein man was created.
II : Lay before you some of the happy concomitants and consequences thereof.
III : Apply the whole.

I : Man's Original Righteousness

As to the righteousness of this state, consider, that as uncreated righteousness, the righteousness of God is the supreme rule; so all created righteousness, whether of men or angels, has respect to a law as its rule, and is a conformity thereto. A creature can no more be morally independent of God in its actions and powers, than it can be naturally independent of Him. A creature, as a creature, must acknowledge the Creator's will as its supreme law;

for as it cannot exist without Him, so it must not be but for Him, and according to His will; yet no law obliges, until it is revealed. And hence it follows, that there was a law which man, as a rational creature, was subjected to in his creation; and that this law was revealed to him.

'God made man upright.' This supposes a law to which he was conformed in his creation; as when any thing is made regular, or according to rule, of necessity the rule itself is pre-supposed. Whence we may gather that this law was no other than the eternal, indispensable law of righteousness, observed in all points by the second Adam, opposed by the carnal mind, and some notions of which remain yet among the Pagans, who, 'having not the law, are a law unto themselves' (Rom 2.14). In a word, this law is the very same which was afterwards summed up in the ten commandments, and promulgated, on mount Sinai, to the Israelites, called by us the moral law; and man's righteousness consisted in conformity to this law or rule. More particularly, there is a twofold conformity required of a man; a conformity of the powers of his soul to the law, which you may call habitual righteousness; and a conformity of all his actions to it, which is actual righteousness. Now, God made man habitually righteous; man was to make himself actually righteous. The former was the stock which God put into his hand; the latter was the improvement he should have made of it. The sum of what I have said is, that the righteousness wherein man was created, was the conformity of all the faculties and powers of his soul to the moral law. This is what we call Original Righteousness, which man was originally endued with. We may take it up in these three things:

1 : Man's understanding was a lamp of light. He had perfect knowledge of the law, and of his duty accordingly: he was made after God's image, and consequently could not want knowledge, which is a part thereof (Col 3.10). 'The new man is renewed in knowledge, after the image of Him that created him.' And indeed this was necessary to fit him for universal obedience; seeing no obedience can be according to the law, unless it proceed from

a sense of the commandment of God requiring it. It is true, Adam had not the law written upon tables of stone, but it was written upon his mind, the knowledge thereof being created with him. God impressed it upon his soul, and made him a law to himself, as the remains of it among the heathens do testify (Rom 2.14,15). And seeing man was made to be the mouth of the creation, to glorify God in His works, we have ground to believe he had naturally an exquisite knowledge of the works of God. We have proof of this in Adam's giving names to the beasts of the field, and the fowls of the air, and these such as express their nature. 'Whatsoever Adam called every living creature, that was the name thereof' (Gen 2.19). The dominion which God gave him over the creatures, soberly to use and dispose of them according to his will (still in subordination to the will of God), seems to require no less than a knowledge of their natures. And, besides all this, his perfect knowledge of the law proves his knowledge in the management of civil affairs, which, in respect of the law of God, 'a good man will guide with discretion' (Psa 112.5).

2: His will in all things was agreeable with the will of God (Eph 4.24). There was no corruption in his will, no inclination to evil; for that is sin, properly and truly so called: hence the apostle says (Rom 7.7), 'I had not known sin, but by the law; for I had not known lust, except the law had said, Thou shalt not covet.' An inclination to evil is really a fountain of sin, and therefore inconsistent with that rectitude and uprightness which the text expressly says he was endued with at his creation. The will of man then was directed and naturally inclined to God and goodness, though mutable. It was disposed, by its original make, to follow the Creator's will, as the shadow does the body. It was not left in an equal balance to good and evil: for at that rate he had not been upright, nor habitually conformed to the law; which in no moment can allow the creature not to be inclined towards God as his chief end, any more than it can allow man to be a god to himself. The law was impressed upon Adam's soul: now this, according to the new covenant, by which the image of God is

THE STATE OF INNOCENCE

repaired, consists in two things: 1. Putting the law in the mind, denoting the knowledge of it. 2. Writing it in the heart, denoting inclinations in the will, answerable to the commands of the law (Heb 8.10). So that as the will, when we consider it as renewed by grace, is by that grace naturally inclined to the same holiness, in all its parts, which the law requires; so was the will of man, when we consider him as God made him at first, endued with natural inclinations to every thing commanded by the law. For if the regenerate are partakers of the divine nature, as undoubtedly they are, for so says the Scripture (2 Pet 1.4); and if this divine nature can import no less than the inclination of the heart to holiness, then surely Adam's will could not want this inclination; for in him the image of God was perfect. It is true, it is said (Rom 2.14,15), 'That the Gentiles show the work of the law written in their hearts;' but this denotes only their knowledge of that law, such as it is: but the apostle to the Hebrews, in the text cited, takes the word heart in another sense, distinguishing it plainly from the mind. And it must be granted, that, when God promises, in the new covenant, 'to write his law in the hearts of his people,' it imports quite another thing than what heathens have: for though they have notions of it in their minds, yet their hearts go another way; their will has got a set and bias quite contrary to that law. Therefore the expression suitable to the present purpose must needs import, besides these notions of the mind, inclinations of the will going along therewith; which inclinations, though mixed with corruption in the regenerate, were pure and unmixed in upright Adam. In a word, as Adam knew his Master's pleasure in the matter of duty, so his will inclined to what he knew.

3: His affections were orderly, pure, and holy; which is a necessary part of that uprightness wherein man was created. The apostle has a petition (2 Thess 3.5), 'The Lord direct your hearts into the love of God;' that is, 'The Lord straighten your hearts,' or make them lie straight to the love of God: and our text tells us that man was made straight. 'The new man is created in righteousness and true holiness' (Eph 4.24). Now this holiness, as it is distinguished from righteousness, may import the purity and good order of the affections. Thus the apostle (1 Tim 2.8), will have men to 'pray, lifting up holy hands, without wrath and doubting:' because, as troubled water is unfit to receive the image of the sun so the heart filled with impure and disorderly affections is not fit for divine communications. Man's sensitive appetite was indeed naturally carried out towards objects grateful to the senses. For seeing man was made up of body and soul, and God made man to glorify and enjoy Him, and for this end to use His good creatures in subordination to Himself, it is plain that man was naturally inclined both to spiritual and sensible good; yet to spiritual good, the chief good as his ultimate end. Therefore his sensitive motions and inclinations were subordinate to his reason and will, which lay straight with the will of God, and were not in the least contrary to the same. Otherwise he would have been made up of contradictions; his soul being naturally inclined to God, as the chief end, in the superior part thereof; and the same soul inclined to the creature, as the chief end, in the inferior part thereof, as they call it; which is impossible, for man, at the same instant, cannot have two chief ends. Man's affections, then, in his primitive state, were pure from all defilement, free from all disorder and distemper, because in all their motions they were duly subjected to his clear reason, and his holy will. He had also an executive power answerable to his will; a power to do the good which he knew should be done, and which he was inclined to do, even to fulfil the whole law of God. If it had not been so, God would not have required of him perfect obedience; for to say that 'the Lord gathereth where he hath not strawed,' is but the blasphemy of a wicked heart against so good and bountiful a God (Matt 25.24–26).

From what has been said, it may be gathered, that the original righteousness explained was universal and natural, yet mutable.

1 : It was universal, both with respect to the subject of it, the whole man, and the object of it, the whole law. Universal, I say, with respect to the subject of it; for this righteousness was diffused

through the whole man: it was a blessed leaven, that leavened the whole lump. There was not a wrong pin in the tabernacle of human nature, when God set it up, however shattered it is now. Man was then holy in soul, body, and spirit; while the soul remained untainted, its lodging was kept clean and undefiled; the members of the body were consecrated vessels, and instruments of righteousness. A combat between flesh and spirit, reason and appetite, nay, the least inclination to sin, or lust of the flesh in the inferior part of the soul, was utterly inconsistent with this uprightness in which man was created; and has been invented to veil the corruption of man's nature, and to obscure the grace of God in Jesus Christ; it looks very much like the language of fallen Adam, laying his own sin at his Maker's door (Gen 3.12), 'The woman whom thou gavest to be with me, she gave me of the tree, and I did eat.' But as this righteousness was universal in respect of the subject, because it spread through the whole man; so also it was universal in respect of the object, the holy law. There was nothing in the law but what was agreeable to his reason and will, as God made him, though sin has now set him at odds with it; his soul was shapen out in length and breadth to the commandment, though exceeding broad; so that his original righteousness was not only perfect in its parts, but in degrees.

2 : As it was universal, so it was natural to him, and not supernatural, in that state. Not that it was essential to man, as man, for then he could not have lost it, without the loss of his very being, but it was natural to him; he was created with it, and it was necessary to the perfection of man, as he came out of the hand of God, necessary to his being placed in a state of integrity. Yet,

3 : It was mutable; it was a righteousness that might be lost, as is manifested by the doleful event. His will was not absolutely indifferent to good and evil. God set it towards good only, yet he did not so fix and confirm its inclinations, that it could not alter. No, it was moveable to evil, and that only by man himself, God having given him a sufficient power to stand in this integrity, if he had

[44]

pleased. Let no man quarrel with God's work in this; for if Adam had been unchangeably righteous, he must have been so either by nature or by free gift: by nature he could not be so, for that is proper to God, and incommunicable to any creature; if by free gift, then no wrong was done to him in withholding what he could not crave. Confirmation in a righteous state is a reward of grace, given upon continuing righteous through the state of trial, and would have been given to Adam if he had stood out the time appointed for probation by the Creator; and accordingly is given to the saints upon account of the merits of Christ, who 'was obedient even unto death.' And herein believers have the advantage of Adam, that they can never totally nor finally fall away from grace.

Thus was man made originally righteous, being created in 'God's own image' (Gen 1.27), which consists in the positive qualities of 'knowledge, righteousness, and true holiness' (Col 3.10; Eph 4.24). All that God made was very good, according to their several natures (Gen 1.31). And so was man morally good, being made after the image of Him who is 'good and upright' (Psa 25.8). Without this, he could not have answered the great end of his creation, which was, to know, love, and serve his God, according to His will; nay, he could not be created otherwise, for he must either be conformed to the law in his powers, principles, and inclinations, or not: if he was, then he was righteous; and, if not, he was a sinner; which is absurd and horrible to imagine.

11: I shall lay before you some of those things which accompanied or flowed from the righteousness of man's primitive state. Happiness is the result of holiness; and as this was a holy, so it was a happy state.

1: Man was then a very glorious creature. We have reason to suppose, that as Moses' face shone when he came down from the mount, so man had a very lightsome and pleasant countenance, and beautiful body, while as yet there was no darkness of sin in him at all. But seeing God Himself is 'glorious in holiness' (Exod

15,11), surely that spiritual comeliness which the Lord put upon man at his creation, made him a very glorious creature. O how did light shine in his holy conversation, to the glory of the Creator! while every action was but the darting forth of a ray and beam of that glorious unmixed light which God had set up in his soul, while that lamp of love, lighted from heaven, continued burning in his heart, as in the holy place; and the law of the Lord, put in his inward parts by the finger of God, was kept by him there, as in the most holy. There was no impurity to be seen without; no squint look in the eyes after any unclean thing; the tongue spoke nothing but the language of heaven; and, in a word, the King's son was 'all glorious within,' and his 'clothing of wrought gold.'

2: He was the favourite of Heaven. He shone brightly in the image of God, who cannot but love His own image, wherever it appears. While he was alone in the world, he was not alone, for God was with him. His communion and fellowship were with his Creator, and that immediately; for as yet there was nothing to turn away the face of God from the work of His own hands, seeing sin had not as yet entered, which alone could make the breach.

By the favour of God he was advanced to be confederate with heaven in the first covenant, called the covenant of works. God reduced the law, which he gave in his creation, into the form of a covenant, whereof perfect obedience was the condition: life was the thing promised, and death the penalty. As for the condition, one great branch of the natural law was that man should believe whatsoever God revealed, and should do whatsoever He commanded; accordingly, God making this covenant with man, extended his duty to the 'not eating of the tree of knowledge of good and evil;' and the law, thus extended, was the rule of man's covenant obedience. How easy were these terms to him who had the natural law written on his heart; and that inclining him to obey this positive law, revealed to him, it seems, by an audible voice (Gen 2.16,17), the matter whereof was so very easy! And indeed it was highly reasonable that the rule and matter of his

[46]

covenant obedience should be thus extended, that which was added being a thing in itself indifferent, where his obedience was to turn upon the precise point of the will of God, the plainest evidence of true obedience; and it being in an external thing, wherein his obedience or disobedience would be most clear and conspicuous.

Now, upon this condition, God promised him life, the continuance of natural life, in the union of soul and body, and of spiritual life, in the favour of his Creator. He promised him also eternal life in heaven, to have been entered into when he should have passed the time of his trial upon earth, and the Lord should see meet to transport him into the upper paradise. This promise of life was included in the threatening of death, mentioned (Gen 2.17). For while God says, 'In the day thou eatest thereof, thou shalt surely die;' it is, in effect, 'If thou do not eat of it, thou shalt surely live.' And this was sacramentally confirmed by another tree in the garden, called therefore, 'The Tree of Life,' which he was debarred from when he had sinned (Gen 3.22,23); 'Lest he put forth his hand, and take also of the tree of life, and eat, and live for ever; therefore the Lord God sent him forth from the garden of Eden.' Yet it is not to be thought that man's life and death did hang only on this matter of the forbidden fruit, but on the whole law; for so says the apostle (Gal 3.10), 'It is written, Cursed is every one that continueth not in all things which are written in the book of the law to do them.' That of the forbidden fruit was a revealed part of Adam's religion, and so was necessary expressly to be laid before him; but as to the natural law, he naturally knew death to be the wages of disobedience, for the very heathens were not ignorant of this, 'knowing the judgment of God, that they which commit such things are worthy of death' (Rom 1.32). Moreover, the promise included in the threatening, secured Adam's life, according to the covenant, as long as he obeyed the natural law, with the addition of that positive command; so that he needed nothing to be expressed to him in the covenant but what concerned the eating of the forbidden fruit.

That eternal life in heaven was promised in this covenant, is plain from this, that the threatening was of eternal death in hell, to which, when man had made himself liable, Christ was promised, by his death, to purchase eternal life. And Christ Himself expounds the promise of the covenant of works, of eternal life, while He proposes the condition of that covenant to a proud young man, who, though he had not Adam's stock, yet would needs enter into life in the way of working, as Adam was to have done under this covenant (Matt 19.17), 'If thou wilt enter into life' (namely, eternal life, by doing, ver 16), 'keep the commandments.'

The penalty was death (Gen 2.17), 'In the day that thou eatest thereof, thou shalt surely die.' The death threatened was such as the life promised was, and that most justly; namely, temporal, spiritual, and eternal death. The event is a commentary on this; for that very day he did eat thereof he was a dead man, in law, but the execution was stopped because of his posterity, then in his loins, and another covenant was prepared. However, that day his body got its death-wound, and became mortal. Death also seized his soul; he lost his original righteousness, and the favour of God; witness the pangs of conscience which made him hide himself from God. And he became liable to eternal death, which would have actually followed of necessity, if the Mediator had not been provided, who found him bound with the cords of death, as a malefactor ready to be led to execution. Thus you have a short description of the covenant into which the Lord brought man in the state of innocence.

And does it seem a small thing unto you, that earth was thus confederate with heaven? This could have been done to none but him whom the King of Heaven delighted to honour. It was an act of grace, worthy of the gracious God whose favourite he was; for there was grace and free favour in the first covenant, though the exceeding riches of the grace, as the apostle calls it (Eph 2.7), were reserved for the second. It was certainly an act of grace, favour, and admirable condescension in God, to enter into a covenant, and such a covenant, with His own creature. Man was not at his own, but at God's disposal, nor had he any thing to work with but what he had received from God. There was no proportion between the work and the promised reward. Before that covenant, man was bound to perfect obedience, in virtue of his natural dependence on God; and death was naturally the wages of sin, which the justice of God could and would have required, though there had never been any covenant between God and man. But God was free; man could never have required eternal life as the reward of his work, if there had not been such a covenant. God was free to have disposed of His creature as He saw meet. If he had stood in his integrity to the end of time, and there had been no covenant promising eternal life to him upon his obedience, God might have withdrawn His supporting hand at last and so have made him creep back into nothing, whence almighty power had drawn him forth. And what wrong could have been in this, for God would have only taken back what He freely gave? But now, the covenant being made, God becomes debtor to His own faithfulness: if man will work, he may crave the reward on the ground of the covenant. Well might the angels, then, upon his being raised to this dignity, have given him that salutation – 'Hail! thou that art highly favoured, the Lord is with thee.'

3: God made him lord of the world, prince of the inferior creatures, universal lord and emperor of the whole earth. His Creator gave him dominion over the fish of the sea, and over the fowl of the air, over all the earth, yea, and every living thing that moveth on the earth; he 'put all things under his feet' (Psa 8.6–8). He gave him a power, soberly to use and dispose of the creatures in the earth, sea, and air. Thus man was God's deputy governor in the lower world, and this his dominion was an image of God's sovereignty. This was common to the man and to the woman: but the man had one thing peculiar to him, namely, that he had dominion over the woman also (1 Cor 11.7). Behold how the creatures came unto him, to own their subjection, and to do him homage as their lord, and quietly stood before him till he put names on them as his own (Gen 2.19). Man's face struck an awe upon them; the stoutest creatures stood astonished, tamely and quietly owning him as their lord and ruler. Thus was man 'crowned with glory and honour' (Psa 8.5). The Lord dealt most liberally and bountifully with him, 'put all things under his feet;' only he kept one thing, one tree in the garden, out of his hands, even the tree of knowledge of good and evil.

But you may say, And did He grudge him this? I answer, Nay; but when He had made him thus holy and happy, He graciously gave him this restriction, which was in its own nature a prop and stay to keep him from falling. And this I say upon these three grounds: 1. As it was most proper for the honour of God, who had made man lord of the lower world, to assert His sovereign dominion over all, by some particular visible sign; so it was most proper for man's safety. Man being set down in a beautiful paradise, it was an act of infinite wisdom, and of grace too, to keep him from one single tree, as a visible testimony that he must hold all from his Creator as his great landlord; that so, while he saw himself lord of the creatures, he might not forget that he was still God's subject. 2. This was a memorial of his mutable state given to him from heaven, to be laid up by him for his greater caution. For man was created with a free will to good, which the tree of life was an evidence of: but his will was also free to evil, and the forbidden tree was to him a memorial thereof. It was, in a manner, a continual watchword to him against evil, a beacon set up before him, to bid him beware of dashing himself to pieces on the rock of sin. 3. God made man upright, directed towards God as his chief end. He set him, like Moses, on the top of the hill, holding up his hands to heaven: and as Aaron and Hur stayed up Moses' hands (Exod 17.10–12), so God gave man an erect figure of body, and forbade him the eating of this tree to keep him in that posture of uprightness wherein he was created. God made the beasts looking down towards the earth, to shew that their satisfaction might be brought from thence; and accordingly it does afford them

[50]

what is suited to their appetite: but the erect figure of man's body, which looks upward, shewed him that his happiness lay above him, in God: and that he was to expect it from heaven, and not from earth. Now this fair tree, of which he was forbidden to eat, taught him the same lesson; that his happiness lay not in enjoyment of the creatures, for there was a want even in paradise: so that the forbidden tree was, in effect, the hand of all the creatures, pointing man away from themselves to God for happiness. It was a sign of emptiness hung before the door of the creation, with the inscription, 'This is not your rest.'

4: As he had a perfect tranquility within his own breast, so he had a perfect calm without. His heart had nothing to reproach him with; conscience then had nothing to do, but to direct, approve, and feast him: and without, there was nothing to annoy him. The happy pair lived in perfect amity; and though their knowledge was vast, true, and clear, they knew no shame. Though they were naked, there were no blushes in their faces; for sin, the seed of shame, was not yet sown (Gen 2.25). And their beautiful bodies were not capable of injuries from the air: so they had no need of clothes, which are originally the badges of our shame. They were liable to no diseases nor pains: and, though they were not to live idle, yet toil, weariness, and sweat of the brows, were not known in this state.

5: Man had a life of pure delight and unalloyed pleasure, in this state. Rivers of pure pleasures ran through it. The earth, with the product thereof, was now in its glory; nothing had yet come in to mar the beauty of the creatures. God placed him, not in a common place of the earth, but in Eden, a place eminent for pleasantness, as the name of it imports; nay, not only in Eden, but in the garden of Eden – the most pleasant spot of that pleasant place; a garden planted by God Himself, to be the mansion-house of this His favourite. When God made the other living creatures, He said, 'Let the waters bring forth the moving creature' (Gen 1.20), and, 'Let the earth bring forth the living creature' (verse 24). But when man was to be made, He said, 'Let us make man' (verse 26). So, when the rest of the earth was to be furnished with herbs and trees, God said, 'Let the earth bring forth grass' (verse 11). But of paradise it is said that God planted it (Gen 2.8), which cannot but denote a singular excellence in that garden, beyond all other parts of the then beautiful earth. He was provided with every thing necessary and delightful; for there was 'every tree that is pleasant to the sight, and good for food' (verse 9). He knew not those delights which luxury has invented for the gratification of lust, but his delights were such as came out of the hand of God, without passing through sinful hands, which always leave marks of impurity on what they touch. So his delights were pure, his pleasures refined. Yet may I show you a more excellent way: wisdom had entered into his heart; surely then knowledge was pleasant unto his soul. What delight do some find in their discoveries of the works of nature, by those scraps of knowledge they have gathered! but how much more exquisite pleasure had Adam, while his piercing eyes read the book of God's works, which God laid before him, to the end he might glorify Him in the same; and therefore had certainly fitted him for the work! But, above all, his knowledge of God, and that as his God, and the communion which he had with Him, could not but afford him the most refined and exquisite pleasure in the innermost recesses of his heart. Great is that delight which the saints find in those views of the glory of God, which their souls are sometimes let into, while they are compassed about with many infirmities: and much more may well be allowed to sinless Adam, who no doubt had a peculiar relish of these pleasures.

6: He was immortal. He would never have died if he had not sinned; it was in case of sin that death was threatened (Gen 2.17), which shows it to be the consequence of sin, and not of the sinless human nature. The perfect constitution of his body, which came out of God's hand very good, and the righteousness and holiness of his soul, removed all inward causes of death; nothing being prepared for the grave's devouring mouth, but the vile body (Phil 3.21), and those who have sinned (Job 24.19). And God's special care of His innocent creature secured him against outward violence. The apostle's testimony is express (Rom 5.12), 'By one man sin entered into the world, and death by sin.' Behold the door by which death came in! Satan wrought with his lies till he got it opened, and so death entered; therefore is he said to have been 'a murderer from the beginning' (John 8.44).

Thus have I shown you the holiness and happiness of man in this state. If any should say, What is all this to us, who never tasted of that holy and happy state? – they must know, it directly concerns us, as Adam was the root of all mankind, our common head and representative, who received from God our inheritance and stock, to keep it for himself and his children, and to convey it to them. The Lord put all mankind's stock, as it were, in one ship; and, as we ourselves would have done, He made our common father the pilot. He put a blessing in the root, to have been, if rightly managed, diffused into all the branches. According to our text, making Adam upright, He made man upright; and all mankind had that uprightness in him; for, 'if the root be holy, so are the branches.' But more of this afterwards. Had Adam stood, none would have quarrelled with the representation.

III: The Doctrine of the State of Innocence applied

Use 1: For information. This shows us, 1. That not God, but man himself was the cause of his ruin. God made him upright; his Creator set him up, but he threw himself down. Was the Lord's directing and inclining him to good the reason of his woeful choice? or did heaven deal so sparingly with him, that his pressing wants sent him to hell to seek supply? Nay, man was, and is, the cause of his own ruin. 2. God may most justly require of men perfect obedience to His law, and condemn them for their not obeying it perfectly, though now they have no ability to keep it. In so doing, He gathers but where He has sown. He gave man ability to keep the whole law; man has lost it by his own fault; but his sin could never take away that right which God has to exact perfect obedience of His creature, and to punish in case of disobedience. 3. Behold here the infinite obligation we lie under to Jesus Christ the second Adam, who with His own precious blood has bought our freedom, and freely makes offer of it again to us (Hos 13.9), and that with the advantage of everlasting security, that it can never be altogether lost any more (John 10.28,29). Free grace will fix those whom free will shook down into a gulf of misery.

Use 2: This conveys a reproof to three sorts of persons: 1. To those who hate religion in the power of it, wherever it appears; and can take pleasure in nothing but in the world and in their lusts. Surely such men are far from righteousness: they are haters of God (Rom 1.30), for they are haters of His image. Upright Adam in paradise would have been a great eyesore to all such persons; as he was to the serpent, whose seed they prove themselves to be, by their malignity. 2. It reproves those who put religion to shame, and those who are ashamed of religion, before a graceless world. There is a generation who make so bold with the God who made them, and can in a moment crush them, that they ridicule piety, and make a mock of seriousness. 'Against whom do ye sport yourselves? against whom make ye a wide mouth, and draw out the tongue?' (Isa 57.4). Is it not against God Himself, whose image, in some measure restored to some of His creatures, makes them fools in your eyes? But, 'be ye not mockers, lest your bands be made strong' (Isa 28.22). Holiness was the glory which God put on man when He made him; but now the sons of men turn that glory into shame, because they themselves glory in their shame. There are others that secretly approve of religion, and in religious company will profess it, who, at other times, to be neighbour-like, are ashamed to own it; so weak are they, that they are blown over with the wind of the wicked's mouth. A broad laughter, an impious jest, a scoffing jeer out of a profane mouth, is to many an unanswerable argument against religion and seriousness; for, in the cause of religion, they are as silly doves without heart. O that such would consider that weighty sentence, 'Whosoever therefore shall be ashamed of me, and of my words, in this adulterous and sinful generation, of him also shall the Son of man be ashamed, when he cometh in the glory of his Father, with the holy angels' (Mark 8.38)! 3. It reproves the proud self-conceited professor, who admires himself in a garment of rags which he has patched together. There are many who, when once they have gathered some scraps of knowledge of religion, and have attained to some reformation of life, swell big with conceit of themselves; a sad sign that the effects of the fall lie so heavy upon them that they have not as yet come to themselves (Luke 15.17). They have eyes behind, to see their attainments, but no eyes within, no eyes before, to see their wants, which would surely humble them: for true knowledge makes men to see, both what once they were, and what they are at present, and so is humbling, and will not suffer them to be content with any measure of grace attained, but inclines them to press forward, 'forgetting the things that are behind' (Phil 3.13). But those men are such a spectacle of commiseration, as one would be who had set his palace on fire, and was glorying in a cottage which he had built for himself out of the rubbish, though so very weak, that it could not stand against a storm.

Use 3: Of lamentation. Here was a stately building; man carved like a fair palace, but now lying in ashes: let us stand and look on the ruins, and drop a tear. This is a lamentation, and shall be for a lamentation. Could we avoid weeping if we saw our country ruined, and turned by the enemy into a wilderness? if we saw our houses on fire, and our property perishing in the flames? But all this comes far short of the dismal sight – man fallen as a star from heaven. Ah, may we not now say, 'O that we were as in months past!' when there was no stain in our nature, no cloud on our minds, no pollution in our hearts! Had we never been in better case, the matter had been less, but they that were brought up in scarlet do now embrace dunghills. Where is our primitive glory now? Once no darkness in the mind, no rebellion in the will, no disorder in the affections. But ah! 'How is the faithful city become an harlot! – Righteousness lodged in it; but now murderers. Our silver is become dross, our wine mixed with water.' That heart which was once the temple of God, is now turned into a den of thieves. Let our name be Ichabod, for the glory is departed. Happy wast thou, O man! who was like unto thee? no pain nor sickness could affect thee, no death could approach thee, no sigh was heard from thee, till these bitter fruits were plucked from the forbidden tree. Heaven shone upon thee, and earth smiled: thou wast the companion of angels, and the envy of devils. But how low is he now laid, who was created for dominion, and made lord of the world! 'The crown is fallen from our head: woe unto us, that we have sinned!' The creatures that waited to do him service, are now, since the fall, set in battle-array against him, and the least of them, having commission, proves too hard for him. Waters overflow the old world; fire consumes Sodom; the stars in their courses fight against Sisera; frogs, flies, lice, &c. become executioners to Pharaoh and his Egyptians; worms eat up Herod: yea, man needs a league with the beasts; yea, with the very stones of the field (Job 5.23), having reason to fear, that every one that findeth him will slay him. Alas! how are we fallen! how are we plunged into a gulf of misery! The sun has gone down on us, death has come in at our windows; our enemies have put out our two eyes, and sport themselves with our miseries. Let us then lie down in the dust, let shame and confusion cover us. Nevertheless, there is hope in Israel concerning this thing. Come then, O sinner, look to Jesus Christ, the second Adam: quit the first Adam and his covenant; come over to the Mediator and Surety of the new and better covenant; and let your hearts say, 'Be thou our ruler, and let this breach be under thy hand.' Let your 'eye trickle down, and cease not, without any intermission, till the Lord look down, and behold from heaven' (Lam 3.49,50).

II
THE STATE OF NATURE

THE SINFULNESS OF
MAN'S NATURAL STATE

God saw that the wickedness of man was great in the
earth, and that every imagination of the thoughts of
his heart was only evil continually.   GENESIS 6.5

We have seen what man was, as God made him; a lovely and
happy creature. Let us view him now as he has unmade himself;
and we shall see him a sinful and a miserable creature. This is
the sad state we are brought into by the fall; a state as black and
doleful as the former was glorious; and this we commonly call
'The State of Nature,' or 'Man's Natural State'; according to
that of the apostle (Eph 2.3), 'And were by nature the children of
wrath, even as others.' – And herein two things are to be considered: 1. The *sinfulness* 2. The *misery* of this state, in which
all the unregenerate live. I begin with the *sinfulness* of man's
natural state, whereof the text gives us a full, though short,
account.

The scope and design of these words is, to clear God's justice
in bringing the flood on the old world. There are two particular
causes taken notice of in the preceding verses: 1. Mixed marriages (verse 2), 'The sons of God,' the posterity of Seth and
Enos, professors of the true religion, married with 'the daughters
of men,' the profane, cursed race of Cain. They did not carry the
matter before the Lord, that He might choose for them (Psa
48.14), but without any respect to the will of God, they chose, not
according to the rules of their faith, but of their fancy; they 'saw
that they were fair;' and their marriage with them occasioned
their divorce from God. This was one of the causes of the deluge,
which swept away the old world. Would to God that all professors
in our day could plead not guilty. But though that sin brought on

the deluge, yet the deluge has not swept away that sin, which as of old, so in our day, may justly be looked upon as one of the causes of the decay of religion. It was an ordinary thing among the Pagans, to change their gods, as they changed their condition into a married lot: many sad instances the Christian world affords of the same; as if people were of Pharaoh's opinion, That religion is only for those who have no other care upon their heads (Exod 5.17). 2. Great oppression (verse 4), 'There were giants in the earth in those days;' men of great stature, great strength, and monstrous wickedness, 'filling the earth with violence' (verse 11). But neither their strength, nor treasures of wickedness, could profit them in the day of wrath. Yet the gain of oppression still causes many to forget the terror of this dreadful example. Thus much for the connexion, and what particular crimes that generation was guilty of. But every person that was swept away by the flood could not be guilty of these things; and 'shall not the Judge of all the earth do right?' Therefore, in my text, there is a general indictment drawn up against them all, 'The wickedness of man was great in the earth,' and clearly proved, for God saw it. Two things are here laid to their charge:

1: Corruption of life, *wickedness, great wickedness*. I understand this of the wickedness of their lives; for it is plainly distinguished from the wickedness of their hearts. The sins of their outward conversation were great in the nature of them, and greatly aggravated by their attendant circumstances: and this not only among those of the race of cursed Cain, but those of holy Seth; the wickedness of man was great. And then it is added, 'in the earth:' 1. To vindicate God's severity, in that He not only cut off sinners, but defaced the beauty of the earth, and swept off the brute creatures from it, by the deluge; that as men had set the marks of their impiety, God might set the marks of His indignation, on the earth. 2. To shew the heinousness of their sin, in making the earth, which God had so adorned for the use of man, a sink of sin, and a stage whereon to act their wickedness, in defiance of heaven. God saw this corruption of life: He not only knew it, and took notice of it, but He made them to know that He took notice of it, and that He had not forsaken the earth, though they had forsaken heaven.

2: Corruption of nature: *Every imagination of the thoughts of his heart was only evil continually.* All their wicked practices are here traced to the fountain and spring-head: a corrupt heart was the source of all. The soul, which was made upright in all its faculties, is now wholly disordered. The heart that was made according to God's own heart, is now the reverse of it, a forge of evil imaginations, a sink of inordinate affections, and a storehouse of all impiety (Mark 7.21,22). Behold the heart of the natural man, as it is opened in our text. The mind is defiled; the thoughts of the heart are evil; the will and affections are defiled: the imagination of the thoughts of the heart, that is, whatsoever the heart frames within itself by thinking, such as judgment, choice, purposes devices, desires, every inward motion; or rather the frame of the thoughts of the heart, namely the frame, make, or mould of these (1 Chron 29.18), is evil. Yea, and every imagination, every frame of his thoughts, is so. The heart is ever framing something, but never one right thing: the frame of thoughts in the heart of man is exceedingly various; yet are they never cast into a right frame. But is there not, at least, a mixture of good in them? No, they are only evil; there is nothing in them truly good and acceptable to God: nor can any thing be so, that comes out of the forge where, not the Spirit of God, but 'the prince of the power of the air' works (Eph 2.2). Whatever changes may be found in them, are only from evil to evil; for the imagination of the heart, or frame of thoughts in natural men, is evil continually, or every day. From the first day to the last day, in this state, they are in midnight darkness; there is not the glimmering of the light of holiness in them; not one holy thought can ever be produced by the unholy heart. O what a vile heart is this! O what a corrupt nature is this! The tree that always brings forth fruit, but never good fruit, whatever soil it be set in, whatever pains be taken with it, must naturally be an evil tree: and what can that heart be, whereof every imagination, every set of thoughts, is only evil, and that continually? Surely that corruption is ingrained in our hearts, interwoven with our very natures, has sunk into the marrow of our souls, and will never be cured but by a miracle of grace. Now such is man's heart, such is his nature, till regenerating grace change it. God that searches the heart saw man's heart was so. He took special notice of it: and the faithful and true Witness cannot mistake our case; though we are most apt to mistake ourselves in this point, and generally do overlook it.

Beware that there be not a thought in your wicked heart saying, What is that to us? Let that generation of whom the text speaks, see to that. For the Lord has left the case of that generation on record, to be a looking-glass to all after generations, wherein they may see their own corruption of heart, and what their lives would be too, if he restrained them not: for 'as in water face answereth to face, so the heart of man to man' (Prov 27.19). Adam's fall has framed all men's hearts alike in this matter. Hence the apostle (Rom 3.10–18), proves the corruption of the nature, hearts, and lives of all men, from what the psalmist says of the wicked in his day (Psa 14.1–3; Psa 5.9; Psa 140.3; Psa 10.7; Psa 36.1); and from what Jeremiah says of the wicked in his day (Jer 9.3), and from what Isaiah says of those that lived in his time (Isa 57.7,8), and concludes (verse 19), 'Now we know that what things soever the law saith, it saith to them who are under the law; that every mouth may be stopped, and all the world may become guilty before God.' Had the history of the deluge been transmitted unto us, without the reason thereof in the text, we might thence have gathered the corruption and total depravity of man's nature: for what other quarrel could the holy and just God have with the infants that were destroyed by the flood, seeing they had no actual sin? If we saw a wise man, who having made a curious piece of work, and heartily approved of it when he gave it out of his hand, as fit for the use it was designed for, rise up in wrath and break it all in pieces, when he looked on it afterwards; should we not thence conclude that the frame of it had been quite marred since it came out of his hand, and that it does not serve for the use it was at first designed for? How much more, when we see the holy and wise God destroying the work of His own hands, once solemnly pronounced by Him very good, may we not conclude that the original frame thereof is utterly marred, that it cannot be mended, but must needs be new made, or lost altogether? (Gen 6.6,7), 'And it repented the Lord that he had made man on the earth, and it grieved him at his heart; and the Lord said, I will destroy man,' or blot him out; as a man doth a sentence out of a book, that cannot be corrected by cutting off some letters, syllables, or words, and interlining others here and there, but must needs be wholly new framed. But did the deluge carry off this corruption of man's nature? did it mend the matter? No, it did not. God, in His holy providence, 'that every mouth may be stopped,' and all the new 'world may become guilty before God,' as well as the old, permits that corruption of nature to break out in Noah, the father of the new world, after the deluge was over. Behold him, as another Adam, sinning in the fruit of a tree (Gen 9.20,21), 'He planted a vineyard, and he drank of the wine, and was drunken, and he was uncovered within his tent.' More than that, God gives the same reason against a new deluge, which he gives in our text for bringing that on the old world: 'I will not,' saith he, 'again curse the ground any more for man's sake; for the imagination of man's heart is evil from his youth' (Gen 8.21). Whereby it is intimated, that there is no mending of the matter by this means; and that if He should always take the same course with men that He had done, He would be always sending deluges on the earth, seeing the corruption of man's nature still remains. But though the flood could not carry off the corruption of nature, yet it pointed at the way how it is to be done; namely, that men must be 'born of water and of the Spirit,' raised from spiritual death in sin by the grace of Jesus Christ, who came by water and blood; out of which a new world of saints arise in regeneration, even as the new world of sinners out of the waters, where they had long lain buried, as it were, in the ark. This we learn from 1 Pet

[63]

3.20,21, where the apostle, speaking of Noah's ark, says, 'Wherein few, that is, eight souls, were saved by water. The like figure whereunto even baptism doth also now save us.' Now the waters of the deluge being a like figure to baptism, it plainly follows, that they signified, as baptism does, 'the washing of regeneration, and renewing of the Holy Ghost.' To conclude then, those waters, though now dried up, may serve us still for a looking-glass, in which we may see the total corruption of our nature, and the necessity of regeneration.

From the text, thus explained, this weighty point of doctrine arises, which he that runs may read in it, namely:

DOCTRINE: *Man's nature is now wholly corrupted*

There is a sad alteration, a wonderful overturning in the nature of man: where, at first, there was nothing evil, now there is nothing good. In treating on this doctrine, I shall,

I: Confirm it.
II: Represent this corruption of nature in its several parts.
III: Shew you how man's nature comes to be thus corrupted.
IV: Apply this doctrine.

I: I shall confirm the doctrine of the corruption of nature.

I shall hold the glass to your eyes, wherein you may see your sinful nature; which, though God takes particular notice of it, many quite overlook. Here we shall consult the Word of God, and men's experience and observation.

For Scripture proof, let us consider,

1: How the Scripture takes particular notice of fallen Adam's communicating his image to his posterity (Gen 5.3), 'Adam begat a son in his own likeness, after his image, and called his name Seth.' Compare with this the first verse of that chapter, 'In the day that God created man, in the likeness of God made he him.' Behold here, how the image after which man was made, and the image after which he is begotten, are opposed. Man was created

[64]

in the likeness of God; that is, the holy and righteous God made a holy and righteous creature, but fallen Adam begat a son, not in the likeness of God, but in his own likeness; that is, corrupt sinful Adam begat a corrupt sinful son. For as the image of God bore righteousness and immortality in it, as was shewn before; so this image of fallen Adam bore corruption and death in it (1 Cor 15.49,50, compare verse 22). Moses, in that fifth chapter of Genesis, giving us the first bill of mortality that ever was in the world, ushers it in with this, that dying Adam begat mortals. Having sinned, he became mortal, according to the threatening; and so he begat a son in his own likeness, sinful, and therefore mortal. Thus sin and death passed on all. Doubtless he begat both Cain and Abel in his own likeness, as well as Seth. But it is not recorded of Abel, because he left no issue behind him, and his falling the first sacrifice to death in the world, was a sufficient document of it: nor of Cain, to whom it might have been thought peculiar, because of his monstrous wickedness; and besides, his posterity was drowned in the flood: but it is recorded of Seth, because he was the father of the holy seed; and from him all mankind since the flood have descended, and fallen Adam's own likeness with them.

2: It appears from that text of Scripture (Job 14.4), 'Who can bring a clean thing out of an unclean? Not one.' Our first parents were unclean, how then can we be clean? How could our immediate parents be clean? how can our children be so? The uncleanness here referred to, is a sinful uncleanness; for it is such as makes man's days full of trouble: and it is natural, being derived from unclean parents: 'Man is born of a woman' (verse 1), 'And how can he be clean, that is born of a woman?' (Job 25.4). The omnipotent God, whose power is not here challenged, could bring a clean thing out of an unclean, and did so in the case of the man Christ: but no other can. Every person that is born according to the course of nature is born unclean. If the root be corrupt, so must the branches be. Neither is the matter mended, though the parents be sanctified ones; for they are but holy in part, and that by grace, not by nature, and they beget their children as men, not as holy men. Wherefore, as the circumcised parent begets an uncircumcised child, and after the purest grain is sown, we reap chaff with the corn; so the holiest parents beget unholy children, and cannot communicate their grace to them, as they do their nature; which many godly parents find true, in their sad experience.

3: Consider the confession of the psalmist David (Psa 51.5), 'Behold, I was shapen in iniquity, and in sin did my mother conceive me.' Here he ascends from his actual sin, to the fountain of it, namely, corrupt nature. He was a man according to God's own heart, but from the beginning it was not so with him. He was begotten in lawful marriage: but when the lump was shapen in the womb, it was a sinful lump. Hence the corruption of nature is called the 'old man;' being as old as ourselves, older than grace, even in those that are sanctified from the womb.

4: Hear our Lord's determination of the point (John 3.6), 'That which is born of the flesh is flesh.' Behold the universal corruption of mankind – all are flesh! Not that all are frail, though that is a sad truth too: yea, and our natural frailty is an evidence of our natural corruption, but that is not the sense of the text. The meaning of it is – all are corrupt and sinful, and that naturally. Hence our Lord argues that because they are flesh, therefore they must be born again, or else they cannot enter into the kingdom of God (verses 3–5). And as the corruption of our nature shows the absolute necessity of regeneration, so the absolute necessity of regeneration plainly proves the corruption of our nature; for why should a man need a second birth, if his nature were not quite marred in his first birth?

5: Man certainly is sunk very low now, in comparison of what he once was. God made him but a 'little lower than the angels:' but now we find him likened to the beasts that perish. He hearkened to a brute, and is now become like one of them. Like Nebuchadnezzar, his portion in his natural state is with the beasts, 'minding only earthly things' (Phil 3.19). Nay, brutes, in some sort, have the advantage of the natural man, who is sunk a degree below them. He is more negligent of what concerns him most, than the stork, or the turtle, or the crane, or the swallow, in what is for their interest (Jer 8.7). He is more stupid than the ox or ass (Isa 1.3). I find him sent to school to learn of the ant, which has no guide or leader to go before her; no overseer or officer to compel or stir her up to work; no ruler, but may do as she lists, being under the dominion of none; yet 'provideth her meat in the summer and harvest' (Prov 6.6–8); while the natural man has all these, and yet exposes himself to eternal starving. Nay, more than all this, the Scriptures hold out the natural man, not only as wanting the good qualities of these creatures, but as a compound of the evil qualities of the worst of the creatures; in whom the fierceness of the lion, the craft of the fox, the unteachableness of the wild ass, the filthiness of the dog and swine, the poison of the asp, and such like, meet. Truth itself calls them 'serpents, a generation of vipers;' yea, more, even 'children of the devil' (Matt 23.33; John 8.44). Surely, then, man's nature is miserably corrupted.

6: 'We are by nature the children of wrath' (Eph 2.3). We are worthy of, and liable to, the wrath of God; and this by nature: therefore, doubtless, we are by nature sinful creatures. We are condemned before we have done good or evil; under the curse, before we know what it is. But, 'will a lion roar in the forest when he hath no prey?' (Amos 3.4); that is, will the holy and just God roar in His wrath against man, if he be not, by his sin, made a prey for His wrath? No, He will not; He cannot. Let us conclude then, that, according to the Word of God, man's nature is a corrupt nature.

If we consult experience, and observe the case of the world, in those things that are obvious to any person who will not shut his eyes against clear light, we shall quickly perceive such fruits as discover this root of bitterness. I shall propose a few things that may serve to convince us in this point:

1: Who sees not a flood of miseries overflowing the world?

[67]

Whither can a man go where he shall not dip his foot, if he go not over head and ears, in it? Every one at home and abroad, in city and country, in palaces and cottages, is groaning under some one thing or other, distasteful to him. Some are oppressed with poverty, some chastened with sickness and pain, some are lamenting their losses, every one has a cross of one sort or another. No man's condition is so soft, but there is some thorn of uneasiness in it. At length death, the wages of sin, comes after these its harbingers, and sweeps all away. Now, what but sin has opened the sluice of sorrow? There is not a complaint nor sigh heard in the world, nor a tear that falls from our eye, but it is an evidence that man is fallen as a star from heaven; for 'God distributeth sorrows in his anger' (Job 21.17). This is a plain proof of the corruption of nature: forasmuch as those who have not yet actually sinned, have their share of these sorrows; yea, and draw their first breath in the world weeping, as if they knew this world at first sight to be a Bochim, the place of weepers. There are graves of the smallest, as well as of the largest size, in the churchyard; and there are never wanting some in the world, who are, like Rachel, weeping for their children because they are not (Matt 2.18).

2: Observe how early this corruption of nature begins to appear in young ones. Solomon observes, that 'even a child is known by his doings' (Prov 20.11). It may soon be discerned what way the bias of the heart lies. Do not the children of fallen Adam, before they can go alone, follow their father's footsteps? What a vast deal of little pride, ambition, sinful curiosity, vanity, wilfulness, and averseness to good, appears in them? And when they creep out of infancy, there is a necessity of using the rod of correction, to drive away the foolishness that is bound in their hearts (Prov 22.15), which shows that, if grace prevail not, the child will be as Ishmael – 'a wild ass-man,' as the word is (Gen 16.12).

3: Take a view of the manifold gross outbreakings of sin in the world: the wickedness of man is yet great in the earth. Behold the bitter fruits of the corruption of our nature (Hos 4.2). 'By swearing, and lying, and killing, and stealing, and committing adultery, they break out (like the breaking forth of waters), and blood toucheth blood.' The world is filled with filthiness, and all manner of lewdness, wickedness, and profanity. From whence comes the deluge of sin on the earth, but from the breaking up of the fountains of the great deep, the heart of man? out of which proceed evil thoughts, adulteries, fornications, murders, thefts, covetousness, &c. (Mark 7.21,22). You will, it may be, thank God with a whole heart, that you are not like these other men; and indeed you have more reason for it than, I fear, you are aware of; for 'as in water face answereth to face, so the heart of man to man' (Prov 27.19). As, looking into clear water, you see your own face; so, looking into your heart, you may see other men's there; and, looking into other men's, in them you may see your own. So that the most vile and profane wretches that are in the world, should serve you for a looking-glass, in which you ought to discern the corruption of your own nature: and if you were to do so, you would, with a heart truly touched, thank God, and not yourselves, indeed, that you are not as other men in your lives; seeing the corruption of nature is the same in you as in them.

4: Cast your eye upon those terrible convulsions which the world is thrown into by the lusts of men! Lions make not a prey of lions, nor wolves of wolves: but men are turned lions and wolves to one another, biting and devouring one another. Upon how slight occasions will men sheath their swords in one another! The world is a wilderness, where the clearest fire that men can carry about with them will not frighten away the wild beasts that inhabit it (and that because they are men and not brutes); but one way or other they will be wounded. Since Cain shed the blood of Abel, the earth has been turned into a slaughter-house; and the chase has been continued since Nimrod began his hunting; on the earth, as in the sea, the greater still devouring the lesser. When we see the world in such a ferment, every one attacking another with words or swords, we may conclude there is an evil spirit among them. These violent heats among Adam's sons show the

[69]

whole body to be distempered, the whole head to be sick, and the whole heart to be faint. They surely proceed from an inward cause (James 4.1), 'lusts that war in our members.'

5: Consider the necessity of human laws, guarded by terrors and severities; to which we may apply what the apostle says (1 Tim 1.9), that 'the law is not made for a righteous man, but for the lawless and disobedient, for the ungodly and for sinners.' Man was made for society; and God Himself said of the first man, when He had created him, that it was 'not meet he should be alone;' yet the case is such now, that, in society, he must be hedged in with thorns. And that from hence we may the better see the corruption of man's nature, let us consider: 1. Every man naturally loves to be at full liberty himself; to have his own will for his law; and, if he were to follow his natural inclinations, he would vote himself out of the reach of all laws, divine and human. Hence some, the power of whose hands has been answerable to their natural inclination, have indeed made themselves absolute, and above laws; agreeably to man's monstrous design at first, to be as gods (Gen 3.5). 2. There is no man that would willingly adventure to live in a lawless society: therefore even pirates and robbers have laws among themselves, though the whole society casts off all respect to law and right. Thus men discover themselves to be conscious of the corruption of nature; not daring to trust one another, but upon security. 3. How dangerous soever it is to break through the hedge, yet the violence of lust makes many daily adventure to run the risk. They will not only sacrifice their credit and conscience, which last is lightly esteemed in the world; but for the pleasure of a few moments, immediately succeeded with terror from within, they will lay themselves open to a violent death by the laws of the land wherein they live. 4. The laws are often made to yield to men's lusts. Sometimes whole societies run into such extravagances, that, like a company of prisoners, they break off their fetters, and put their guard to flight; and the voice of laws cannot be heard for the noise of arms. And seldom is there a time, wherein there are not some persons so great and daring, that the laws dare not look their impetuous lusts in the face; which made David say, in the case of Joab, who had murdered Abner, 'These men, the sons of Zeruiah, be too hard for me' (2 Sam 3.39). Lusts sometimes grow too strong for laws, so that the law becomes slack, as the pulse of a dying man (Hab 1.3,4). 5. Consider what necessity often appears of amending old laws, and making new ones; which have their rise from new crimes, of which man's nature is very fruitful. There would be no need of mending the hedge, if men were not, like unruly beasts, still breaking it down. It is astonishing to see what a figure the Israelites, who were separated unto God from among all the nations of the earth, make in their history; what horrible confusions were among them, when there was no king in Israel, as you may see from the eighteenth to the twenty-first chapter of Judges: how hard it was to reform them, when they had the best of magistrates! and how quickly they turned aside again, when they got wicked rulers! I cannot but think, that one grand design of that sacred history, was to discover the corruption of man's nature, the absolute need of the Messiah, and His grace; and that we ought, in reading it, to improve it to that end. How cutting is that word which the Lord has to Samuel, concerning Saul (1 Sam 9.17), 'The same shall reign over' – or, as the word is, *shall restrain* – 'my people'! O the corruption of man's nature! the awe and dread of the God of heaven restrains them not; but they must have gods on earth to do it, 'to put them to shame' (Judges 18.7).

6: Consider the remains of that natural corruption in the saints. Though grace has entered, yet corruption is not expelled: though they have got the new creature, yet much of the old corrupt nature remains; and these struggle together within them, as the twins in Rebekah's womb (Gal 5.17). They find it present with them at all times, and in all places, even in the most retired corners. If a man has a troublesome neighbour, he may remove; if he has an ill servant, he may put him away at the term; if a bad yoke-fellow, he may sometimes leave the house, and be free from molestation that way: but should the saint go into a wilderness, or set up his

[71]

tent on some remote rock in the sea, where never foot of man, beast, or fowl had touched, there will it be with him. Should he be with Paul, caught up to the third heaven, it will come back with him (2 Cor 12.7). It follows him as the shadow does the body; it makes a blot in the fairest line he can draw. It is like the fig-tree on the wall, which however closely it was cut, yet still grew, till the wall was thrown down: for the roots of it are fixed in the heart, while the saint is in the world, as with bands of iron and brass. It is especially active when he would do good (Rom 7.21), then the fowls come down upon the carcases. Hence often, in holy duties, the spirit of a saint, as it were, evaporates; and he is left before he is aware, like Michal, with an image in the bed instead of a husband. I need not stand to prove to the godly the corruption of nature in them, for they groan under it; and to prove it to them, were to hold out a candle to let them see the sun: as for the wicked, they are ready to account mole-hills in the saints as big as mountains, if not to reckon them all hypocrites. But consider these few things on this head: 1. 'If it be thus in the green tree how must it be in the dry?' The saints are not born saints, but made so by the power of regenerating grace. Have they got a new nature, and yet the old remains with them? How great must that corruption be in others, in whom there is no grace! 2. The saints groan under it, as a heavy burden. Hear the apostle (Rom 7.24), 'O wretched man that I am! who shall deliver me from the body of this death?' What though the carnal man lives at ease and quiet, and the corruption of nature is not his burden, is he therefore free from it? No, no; it is because he is dead, that he feels not the sinking weight. Many a groan is heard from a sick bed, but never any from a grave. In the saint, as in the sick man, there is a mighty struggle; life and death striving for the mastery: but in the natural man, as in the dead corpse, there is no noise, because death bears full sway. 3. The godly man resists the old corrupt nature; he strives to mortify it, yet it remains; he endeavours to starve it, and by that means to weaken it, yet it is active. How must it spread then, and strengthen itself

[72]

in that soul, where it is not starved, but fed! And this is the case of all the unregenerate, who make 'provision for the flesh, to fulfil the lusts thereof.' If the garden of the diligent afford him new work daily, in cutting off and rooting up, surely that of the sluggard must needs be 'all grown over with thorns.'

7: I shall add but one observation more, and that is, that in every man, naturally, the image of fallen Adam appears. Some children, by the features and lineaments of their face, do, as it were, father themselves: and thus we resemble our first parents. Every one of us bears the image and impression of the fall upon him: and to evince the truth of this, I appeal to the consciences of all, in these following particulars:

1: Is not sinful curiosity natural to us? and is not this a print of Adam's image? (Gen 3.6). Is not man naturally much more desirous to know new things, than to practise old known truths? How much like old Adam do we look in this eagerness for novelties, and disrelish of old solid doctrines? We seek after knowledge rather than holiness, and study most to know those things which are least edifying. Our wild and roving fancies need a bridle to curb them, while good solid affections must be quickened and spurred on.

2: If the Lord, by His holy law and wise providence, puts a restraint upon us, to keep us back from any thing, does not that restraint whet the edge of our natural inclinations, and make us so much the keener in our desires? And in this do we not betray it plainly, that we are Adam's children? (Gen 3.2–6). I think this cannot be denied, for daily observation evinces, that it is a natural principle, that 'stolen waters are sweet, and bread eaten in secret is pleasant' (Prov 9.17). The very heathens were convinced that man was possessed with this spirit of contradiction, though they knew not the spring of it. How often do men let themselves loose in those things, in which, had God left them at liberty, they would have bound up themselves! but corrupt nature takes a pleasure in the very jumping over the hedge. And is it not a repeating of our father's folly, that men will rather climb for forbidden fruit, than gather what is shaken off the tree of good providence to them, when they have God's express allowance for it?

3: Which of all the children of Adam is not naturally disposed to hear the instruction that causeth to err? And was not this the rock our first parents split upon? (Gen 3.4–6). How apt is weak man, ever since that time, to parley with temptations! 'God speaketh once, yea twice, yet man perceiveth it not' (Job 33.14), but he readily listens to Satan. Men might often come fair off, if they would dismiss temptations with abhorrence, when first they appear; if they would nip them in the bud, they would soon die away, but, alas! though we see the train laid for us, and the fire put to it, yet we stand till it runs along, and we are blown up with its force.

4: Do not the eyes in our head often blind the eyes of the mind? And was not this the very case of our first parents? (Gen 3.6). Man is never more blind than when he is looking on the objects that are most pleasing to sense. Since the eyes of our first parents were opened to the forbidden fruit, men's eyes have been the gates of destruction to their souls; at which impure imaginations and sinful desires have entered the heart, to the wounding of the soul, wasting of the conscience, and bringing dismal effects sometimes on whole societies, as in Achan's case (Joshua 7.21). Holy Job was aware of this danger from these two little rolling bodies, which a very small splinter of wood can make useless; so that, with the king who durst not, with his ten thousand, meet him that came with twenty thousand against him (Luke 14.31,32), he sendeth and desireth conditions of peace, 'I made a covenant with mine eyes' (Job 31.1).

5: Is it not natural to us to care for the body, even at the expense of the soul? This was one ingredient in the sin of our first parents (Gen 3.6). O how happy might we be, if we were but at half the pains about our souls, that we bestow upon our bodies! If that question, 'What must I do to be saved?' (Acts 16.30), ran but near as often through our minds as these questions do, 'What shall we eat? what shall we drink? wherewithal shall we be clothed?' (Matt 6.31), then many a hopeless case would become very hopeful. But the truth is, most men live as if they were nothing but a lump of flesh: or as if their soul served for no other use, but, like salt, to keep their body from corrupting. 'They are flesh' (John 3.6); 'they mind the things of the flesh' (Rom 8.5); 'and they live after the flesh' (verse 13). If the consent of the flesh be got to an action, the consent of the conscience is rarely waited for: yea, the body is often served, when the conscience has entered a protest against it.

6: Is not every one by nature discontented with his present lot in the world, or with some one thing or other in it? This also was Adam's case (Gen 3.5,6). Some one thing is always wanting; so that man is a creature given to changes. If any doubt this, let them look over all their enjoyments; and, after a review of them, listen to their own hearts, and they will hear a secret murmuring for want of something; though perhaps, if they considered the matter aright, they would see that it is better for them to want than to have that something. Since the hearts of our first parents flew out at their eyes, on the forbidden fruit, and a night of darkness was thereby brought on the world, their posterity have a natural disease which Solomon calls, 'The wandering of the desire,' or, as the word is, 'The walking of the soul' (Eccl 6.9). This is a sort of diabolical trance, wherein the soul traverses the world; feeds itself with a thousand airy nothings; snatches at this and the other created excellency, in imagination and desire; goes here, and there, and every where, except where it should go. And the soul is never cured of this disease, till conquering grace brings it back to take up its everlasting rest in God through Christ: but till this be, if man were set again in paradise, the garden of the Lord, all the pleasures there would not keep him from looking, yea, and leaping over the hedge a second time.

7: Are we not far more easily impressed and influenced by evil counsels and examples, than by those that are good! You will see this was the ruin of Adam (Gen 3.6). Evil example, to this day, is one of Satan's master-devices to ruin men. Though we have, by nature, more of the fox than of the lamb; yet that ill property which some observe in this creature, namely, that if one lamb skip into a water, the rest that are near will suddenly follow, may be observed also in the disposition of the children of men; to whom it is very natural to embrace an evil way, because they see others in it before them. Ill example has frequently the force of a violent stream, to carry us over plain duty, but especially if the example be given by those we bear a great affection to; our affection, in that case, blinds our judgment; and what we should abhor in others, is complied with, to humour them. Nothing is more plain, than that generally men choose rather to do what the most do, than what the best do.

8: Who of all Adam's sons needs be taught the art of sewing fig-leaves together, to cover their nakedness? (Gen 3.7). When we have ruined ourselves, and made ourselves naked to our shame, we naturally seek to help ourselves by ourselves: many poor contrivances are employed, as silly and insignificant as Adam's fig-leaves. What pains are men at, to cover their sin from their own conscience, and to draw all the fair colours upon it that they can! And when once convictions are fastened upon them, so that they cannot but see themselves naked, it is as natural for them to attempt to cover it by self-deceit, as for fish to swim in water, or birds to fly in the air. Therefore the first question of the convinced is, 'What shall we do?' (Acts 2.37). How shall we qualify ourselves? What shall we perform? Not considering that the new creature is God's own workmanship or deed (Eph 2.10), any more than Adam considered and thought of being clothed with the skins of sacrifices (Gen 3.21).

9: Do not Adam's children naturally follow his footsteps, in hiding themselves from the presence of the Lord? (Gen 3.8). We are quite as blind in this matter as he was, who thought to hide himself from the presence of God amongst the shady trees of the garden. We are very apt to promise ourselves more security in a secret sin, than in one that is openly committed. 'The eye of the adulterer waiteth for the twilight, saying, no eye shall see me'

(Job 24.15). Men will freely do that in secret, which they would be ashamed to do in the presence of a child; as if darkness could hide from the all-seeing God. Are we not naturally careless of communion with God; aye, and averse to it? Never was there any communion between God and Adam's children, where the Lord Himself had not the first word. If He were to let them alone they would never inquire after Him; 'I hid me' (Isa 57.17). Did he seek after a hiding God? Very far from it: 'He went on in the way of his heart.'

10: How loth are men to confess sin, to take guilt and shame to themselves? Was it not thus in the case before us? (Gen 3.10). Adam confesses his nakedness, which could not be denied; but says not one word of his sin: the reason of it was, he would fain have hid it if he could. It is as natural for us to hide sin, as to commit it. Many sad instances thereof we have in this world, but a far clearer proof of it we shall get at the day of judgment, the day in which 'God will judge the secrets of men' (Rom 2.16). Many a foul mouth will then be seen which is now 'wiped, and saith, I have done no wickedness' (Prov 30.20).

11: Is it not natural for us to extenuate our sin, and transfer the guilt upon others? When God examined our guilty first parents, did not Adam lay the blame on the woman? and did not the woman lay the blame on the serpent? (Gen 3.12,13). Now Adam's children need not be taught this hellish policy; for before they can well speak, if they cannot get the fact denied, they will cunningly lisp out something to lessen their fault, and lay the blame upon another. Nay, so natural is this to men, that in the greatest sins, they will lay the fault upon God Himself; they will blaspheme His holy providence under the mistaken name of misfortune or ill luck, and thereby lay the blame of their sin at heaven's door. And was not this one of Adam's tricks after his fall? 'And the man said, The woman whom thou gavest to be with me, she gave me of the tree, and I did eat' (Gen 3.12). Observe the order of the speech. He makes his apology in the first place, and then comes his confession: his apology is long,

[77]

but his confession very short; it is all comprehended in one word, 'and I did eat.' How pointed and distinct is his apology, as if he was afraid his meaning should have been mistaken! 'The woman,' says he, or 'that woman', as if he would have pointed the Judge to His own works, of which we read (Gen 2.22). There was but one woman then in the world, so that one would think he needed not to have been so nice and exact in pointing at her: yet she is as carefully marked out in his defence, as if there had been ten thousand. 'The woman whom thou gavest me:' here he speaks, as if he had been ruined with God's gift. And, to make the gift look the blacker, it is added to all this, 'thou gavest to be with me,' as my constant companion, to stand by me as a helper. This looks as if Adam would have fathered an ill design upon the Lord, in giving him this gift. And, after all, there is a new demonstrative here, before the sentence is complete; he says not, 'The woman gave me,' but 'the woman, she gave me,' emphatically; as if he had said, *she*, even *she*, gave me of the tree. This much for his apology. But his confession is quickly over, in one word, as he spoke it, 'and I did eat.' There is nothing here to point out himself and as little to show what he had eaten. How natural is this black art to Adam's posterity! he that runs may read it. So universally does Solomon's observation hold true (Prov 19.3), 'The foolishness of man perverteth his way; and his heart fretteth against the Lord.' Let us then call fallen Adam, father; let us not deny the relation, seeing we bear his image.

To shut up this point, sufficiently confirmed by concurring evidence from the Lord's Word, our own experience, and observation; let us be persuaded to believe the doctrine of the corruption of our nature; and look to the second Adam, the blessed Jesus, for the application of His precious blood, to remove the guilt of our sin; and for the efficacy of His Holy Spirit, to make us new creatures; knowing that 'except we be born again, we cannot enter into the kingdom of God.'

1: I proceed to inquire into the *corruption of nature* in the several parts thereof. But who can comprehend it? who can take

[78]

the exact dimensions of it, in its breadth, length, height, and depth? 'The heart is deceitful above all things, and desperately wicked; who can know it?' (Jer 17.9). However, we may quickly perceive as much of it as may be matter of deepest humiliation, and may discover to us the absolute necessity of regeneration. Man in his natural state is altogether corrupt: both soul and body are polluted, as the apostle proves at large (Rom 3.10–18). As for the soul, this natural corruption has spread itself through all the faculties thereof; and is to be found in the *understanding*, the *will*, the *affections*, the *conscience*, and the *memory*.

1 : *The Corruption of the Understanding*

The *understanding*, that leading faculty, is despoiled of its primitive glory, and covered over with confusion. We have fallen into the hands of our grand adversary, as Samson into the hands of the Philistines, and are deprived of our two eyes. 'There is none that understandeth' (Rom 3.11). 'Mind and conscience are defiled' (Titus 1.15). The natural man's apprehension of divine things is corrupt. (Psa 50.21), 'Thou thoughtest that I was altogether such an one as thyself.' His judgment is corrupt, and cannot be otherwise, seeing his eye is evil: therefore the Scriptures, to show that man did all wrong, says, 'every one did that which was right in his own eyes' (Judges 17.6; and 21.25). And his imaginations, or reasonings, must be cast down by the power of the Word, being of a piece with his judgment (2 Cor 10.5). But, to point out this corruption of the mind or understanding more particularly, let these following things be considered:

1 : There is a natural weakness in the minds of men with respect to spiritual things. The apostle determines concerning every one that is not endued with the graces of the Spirit, 'That he is blind, and cannot see afar off' (2 Pet 1.9). Hence the Spirit of God in the Scriptures clothes, as it were, divine truths with earthly figures, even as parents teach their children, using similitudes (Hosea 12.10). This, though it does not cure, yet it proves

THE STATE OF NATURE

this natural weakness in the minds of men. But there are not wanting plain proofs of it from experience. As, 1. How hard a task is it to teach many people the common principles of our holy religion, and to make truths so plain as they may understand them? There must be 'precept upon precept, precept upon precept; line upon line, line upon line' (Isa 28.10). Try the same persons in other things, they will be found 'wiser in their generation than the children of light.' They understand their work and business in the world as well as their neighbours; though they are very stupid and unteachable in the matters of God. Tell them how they may advance their worldly wealth, or how they may gratify their lusts, and they will quickly understand these things; though it is very hard to make them know how their souls may be saved, or how their hearts may find rest in Jesus Christ. 2. Consider those who have many advantages beyond the generality of mankind; who have had the benefits of good education and instruction; yea, and are blessed with the light of grace in that measure wherein it is distributed to the saints on earth; yet how small a portion have they of the knowledge of divine things! What ignorance and confusion still remain in their minds! How often are they perplexed even as to practical truths, and speak as children in these things! It is a pitiful weakness that we cannot perceive the things which God has revealed to us; and it must needs be a sinful weakness, since the law of God requires us to know and believe them. 3. What dangerous mistakes are to be found amongst men, in concerns of the greatest weight! What woeful delusions prevail over them! Do we not often see those, who in other things are the wisest of men, the most notorious fools with respect to their souls' interest? (Matt 11.25), 'Thou hast hid these things from the wise and prudent.' Many that are eagle-eyed in the trifles of time, are like owls and bats in the light of life. Nay, truly, the life of every natural man is but one continued dream and delusion, out of which he never awakes, till either, by a new light darted from heaven into his soul, he come to himself (Luke 15.17), or, 'in hell he lift up his eyes' (Luke 16.23). Therefore, in Scripture account, be he never so wise, he is a fool, and a simple one.

2: Man's understanding is naturally overwhelmed with gross darkness in spiritual things. Man, at the instigation of the devil, attempting to break out a new light in his mind (Gen 3.5), instead of that, broke up the doors of the bottomless pit, so as, by the smoke thereof, he was buried in darkness. When God first made man, his mind was a lamp of light, but now, when He comes to make him over again, in regeneration, He finds it darkness; 'Ye were sometimes darkness' (Eph 5.8). Sin has closed the windows of the soul, darkness is over all the region: it is the land of darkness and the shadow of death, where the light is as darkness. The prince of darkness reigns there, and nothing but the works of darkness are framed there. We are born spiritually blind, and cannot be restored without a miracle of grace. This is your case, whoever you are, who are not born again. That you may be convinced in this matter, take the following proofs of it:

Proof 1: The darkness that was upon the face of the world, before, and at the time when Christ came, arising as the Sun of Righteousness upon the earth. When Adam by his sin had lost that primitive light with which he was endued at his creation, it pleased God to make a glorious revelation of His mind and will to him, as to the way of salvation (Gen 3.15). This was handed down by him, and other godly fathers, before the flood: yet the natural darkness of the mind of man prevailed so far against that revelation, as to carry off all sense of true religion from the old world, except what remained in Noah's family, which was preserved in the ark. After the flood, as men multiplied on the earth, the natural darkness of the mind prevailed again, and the light decayed, till it died away among the generality of mankind, and was preserved only among the posterity of Shem. And even with them it had nearly set, when God called Abraham from serving other gods (Joshua 24.15). God gives Abraham a more full and clear revelation, which he communicates to his family (Gen 18.19); yet the natural darkness wears it out at length, save that it was preserved among the posterity of Jacob. They being carried down into Egypt, that darkness so prevailed, as to leave them very little sense of true religion; and there was a necessity for a new revelation to be made to them in the wilderness. And many a cloud of darkness got above that, now and then, during the time from Moses to Christ. When Christ came, the world was divided into Jews and Gentiles. The Jews, and the true light with them, were within an enclosure (Psa 147.19,20). Between them and the Gentile world, there was a partition wall of God's making, namely, the ceremonial law: and upon that was reared up another of man's own making, namely, a rooted enmity betwixt the parties (Eph 2.14,15). If we look abroad without the enclosure – and except those proselytes of the Gentiles, who by means of some rays of light breaking forth upon them from within the enclosure, having renounced idolatry, worshipped the true God, but did not conform to the Mosaical rites – we see nothing but 'dark places of the earth, full of the habitations of cruelty' (Psa 74.20). Gross darkness covered the face of the Gentile world, and the way of salvation was utterly unknown among them. They were drowned in superstition and idolatry, and had multiplied their idols to such a vast number, that above thirty thousand are reckoned to have been worshipped by the men of Europe alone. Whatever wisdom was among their philosophers, 'the world by' that 'wisdom knew not God' (1 Cor 1.21), and all their researches in religion were but groping in the dark (Acts 17.27). If we look within the enclosure, and except a few that were groaning and 'waiting for the consolation of Israel,' we shall see gross darkness on the face of that generation. Though 'to them were committed the oracles of God,' yet they were most corrupt in their doctrine. Their traditions were multiplied; but the knowledge of those things, wherein the life of religion lies, was lost. Masters of Israel knew not the nature and necessity of regeneration (John 3.10). Their religion was to build on their birth-privileges, as children of Abraham (Matt 3.9), to glory in their circumcision, and other external ordinances (Phil 3.2,3), and to 'rest in the law' (Rom

[82]

2.17), after they had, by their false glosses, cut it so short, as they might outwardly go well nigh to the fulfilling of it (Matt 5).

Thus was darkness over the face of the world, when Christ, the true light, came into it; and so is darkness over every soul, till He, as the day-star, arises in the heart. The latter is an evidence of the former. What, but the natural darkness of men's minds, could still thus wear out the light of external revelation, in a matter upon which eternal happiness depends? Men did not forget the way of preserving their lives: but how quickly they lost the knowledge of the way of salvation of their souls, which are infinitely more weight and worth! When the teaching of patriarchs and prophets was ineffectual, it became necessary for them to be taught of God Himself, who alone can open the eyes of the understanding. But that it might appear that the corruption of man's mind lay deeper than to be cured by mere external revelation, there were but very few converted by Christ's preaching, who spoke as never man spoke (John 12.37,38). The great cure remained to be performed, by the Spirit accompanying the preaching of the apostles, who according to the promise (John 14.12), were to do greater works. And if we look to the miracles wrought by our blessed Lord, we shall find, that by applying the remedy to the soul, for the cure of bodily distempers, as in the case of 'the man sick of the palsy' (Matt 9.2), he plainly discovered that his main errand into the world was to cure the diseases of the soul. I find a miracle wrought upon one that was born blind, performed in such a way, as seems to have been designed to let the world see in it, as in glass, their case and cure (John 9.6), 'He made clay, and anointed the eyes of the blind man with the clay.' What could more fitly represent the blindness of men's minds, than eyes closed up with earth? 'Shut their eyes;' shut them up by anointing or 'casting them with mortar,' as the word will bear (Isa 6.10). And (chap 44.18), 'He hath shut their eyes:' the word properly signifies, he hath plastered their eyes; as the house in which the leprosy had been, was to be plastered (Lev 14.42). Thus the Lord's Word discovers the design of that strange work; and by it shows us, that the eyes of our understanding are naturally shut. Then the blind man must go and wash off this clay in the pool of Siloam: no other water will serve this purpose. If that pool had not represented Him, whom the Father sent into the world to open the blind eyes (Isa 42.7), I think the evangelist had not given us the interpretation of the name which, he says, signifies *sent* (John 9.7). So we may conclude, that the natural darkness of our minds is such as there is no cure for, but from the blood and Spirit of Jesus Christ, whose eye-salve only can make us see (Rev 3.18).

Proof 2: Every natural man's heart and life is a mass of darkness, disorder, and confusion, how refined soever he may appear in the sight of men. 'For we ourselves also,' says the apostle Paul, 'were sometimes foolish, disobedient, deceived, serving divers lusts and pleasures' (Tit 3.3); and yet, at the time which this text refers to, he was blameless, 'touching the righteousness which is in the law' (Phil 3.6). This is a plain evidence that 'the eye is evil, the whole body being full of darkness' (Matt 6.23). The unrenewed part of mankind is rambling through the world, like so many blind men, who will neither take a guide, nor can guide themselves; and therefore are falling over this and the other precipice, into destruction. Some are running after their covetousness, till they are pierced through with many sorrows; some sticking in the mire of sensuality; others dashing themselves on the rock of pride and self-conceit: every one stumbling on some one stone of stumbling or other: all of them are running themselves upon the sword-point of justice, while they eagerly follow whither unmortified passions and affections lead them: and while some are lying along in the way, others are coming up, and falling headlong over them. Therefore, 'woe unto the (blind) world because of offences' (Matt 18.7). Errors in judgment swarm in the world because it is 'night, wherein all the beasts of the forest do creep forth.' All the unregenerate are utterly mistaken in the point of true happiness: for though Christianity hath fixed that matter in point of principle, yet nothing less than overcoming

[84]

grace can fix it in the practical judgment. All men agree in the desire of being happy; but, amongst the unrenewed men, concerning the way to happiness, there are almost as many opinions as there are men; they being 'turned every one to his own way' (Isa 53.6). They are like the blind men of Sodom, about Lot's house; all were seeking to find the door; some grope one part of the wall for it, some another, but none of them could certainly say, he had found it; so the natural man may stumble on any good but the chief good. Look into your own unregenerate heart, and there you will see all turned upside down: heaven lying under, and earth at top. Look into your life, there you may see how you are playing the madman, snatching at shadows, and neglecting the substance: eagerly flying after that which is not, and slighting that which is, and will be for ever.

Proof 3: The natural man is always as a workman left without light; either trifling or doing mischief. Try to catch thy heart at any time thou wilt, and thou wilt find it either weaving the spider's web, or hatching cockatrice' eggs (Isa 59.5), roving through the world, or digging into the pit; filled with vanity, or else with vileness; busy doing nothing, or what is worse than nothing. A sad sign of a dark mind.

Proof 4: The natural man is void of the saving knowledge of spiritual things. He knows not what a God he has to do with: he is unacquainted with Christ, and knows not what sin is. The greatest graceless wits are blind as moles in these things. Aye, but some such can speak of them to good purpose; so might those Israelites of the temptations, signs, and miracles, which their eyes had seen (Deut 29.3); to whom nevertheless, the Lord had 'not given a heart to perceive, and eyes to see, and ears to hear, unto that day' (verse 4). Many a man that bears the name of a Christian may make Pharaoh's confession of faith (Exod 5.2), 'I know not the Lord,' neither will he let go what He commands them to part with. God is with them, as a prince in disguise among his subjects, who meets with no better treatment from them than if they were his fellows (Psa 50.21). Do they know Christ, or see His glory, and any beauty in Him, for which He is to be desired? If they did, they would not slight Him as they do: a view of His glory would so darken all created excellence, that they would take Him for and instead of all, and gladly close with Him, as He offers Himself in the gospel (John 4.10; Psa 9.10; Matt 13.44–46). Do they know what sin is, who nurse the serpent in their bosom, hold fast deceit, and refuse to let it go? I own, indeed, that they may have a natural knowledge of these things, as the unbelieving Jews had of Christ, whom they saw and conversed with; but there was a spiritual glory in Him, perceived by believers only (John 1.14), and in respect of that glory, 'the world knew him not' (verse 10). The spiritual knowledge of them they cannot have; it is above the reach of the carnal mind (1 Cor 2.14). 'The natural man receiveth not the things of the Spirit of God, for they are foolishness unto him; neither can he know them, for they are spiritually discerned.' He may indeed discourse of them, but in no other way than one can talk of honey or vinegar, who never tasted the sweetness of the one, nor the sourness of the other. He has some notions of spiritual truths, but sees not the things themselves that are wrapt up in the words of truth (1 Tim 1.7). 'Understanding neither what they say, nor whereof they affirm.' In a word, natural men fear, seek, confess, they know not what. Thus you may see man's understanding is naturally overwhelmed with gross darkness in spiritual things.

3: There is in the mind of man a natural bias to evil, whereby it comes to pass, that whatever difficulties it finds while occupied about things truly good, it acts with a great deal of ease in evil, as being in that case in its own element (Jer 4.22). The carnal mind drives heavily on in the thoughts of good, but furiously in the thoughts of evil. While holiness is before it, fetters are upon it; but when once it has got over the hedge, it is as a bird got out of a cage, and becomes a freethinker indeed. Let us reflect a little on the apprehension and imagination of the carnal mind, and we shall find incontestable evidence of this woeful bias to evil.

Proof 1: As when a man by a violent stroke on the head loses his sight, there arises to him a kind of false light whereby he seems to see a thousand airy nothings, so man, being struck blind to all that is truly good for his eternal interest, has a light of another sort brought into his mind, his eyes are opened, knowing evil, and so are the words of the tempter verified (Gen 3.5). The words of the prophet are plain – 'They are wise to do evil, but to do good they have no knowledge' (Jer 4.22). The mind of man has a natural dexterity to devise mischief; there are not any so simple as to want skill to contrive ways to gratify their lusts, and ruin their souls, though the power of every one's hand cannot reach to put their devices in execution. No one needs to be taught this black art, but, as weeds grow up of their own accord in the neglected ground, so does this wisdom which is earthly, sensual, devilish (Jas 3.15), grow up in the minds of men by virtue of the corruption of their nature. Why should we be surprised with the product of corrupt wits, their cunning devices to affront Heaven, to oppose and run down truth and holiness, and to gratify their own and other men's lusts? They row with the stream, no wonder they make great progress; their stock is within them, and increases by using it, and the works of darkness are contrived with the greater advantage, because the mind is wholly destitute of spiritual light. If this light were in them in any measure it would so far mar the work (1 John 3.9), 'Whosoever is born of God doth not commit sin;' he does it not as by art, wilfully and habitually, for 'his seed remaineth in him.' But, on the other hand, 'It is as sport to a fool to do mischief: but a man of understanding hath wisdom' (Prov 10.23). 'To do witty wickedness nicely', as the words import, 'is as sport or play to a fool;' it comes off with him easily; and why, but because he is a fool, and has not wisdom, which would mar the contrivances of darkness! The more natural a thing is, the more easily it is done.

Proof 2: Let the corrupt mind have but the advantage of one's being employed in, or present at, some piece of service for God, that so the device, if not in itself sinful, yet may become sinful by its unseasonableness, it will quickly fall upon some device or expedient, by its starting aside, which deliberation, in season, could not produce. Thus Saul who knew not what to do before the priest began to consult God, is quickly determined when once the priest's hand was in; his own heart then gave him an answer, and would not allow him to wait an answer from the Lord (1 Sam 14.18,19). Such a devilish dexterity has the carnal mind in devising what may most effectually divert men from their duty to God.

Proof 3: Does not the carnal mind naturally strive to grasp spiritual things in imagination, as if the soul were quite immersed in flesh and blood, and would turn every thing into its own shape? Let men who are used to the forming of the most abstracted notions look into their own souls, and they will find this bias in their minds, whereof the idolatry which did of old, and still does, so much prevail in the world, is an incontestable evidence. For it plainly shews that men naturally would have a visible deity, and see what they worship, and therefore they 'changed the glory of the incorruptible God into an image' (Rom 1.23). The reformation of these nations (blessed be the Lord for it) has banished idolatry, and images too, out of our churches; but heart-reformation only can break down mental idolatry, and banish the more subtle and refined image worship, and representations of the Deity, out of the minds of men. The world, in the time of its darkness, was never more prone to the former than the unsanctified mind is to the latter. Hence are horrible, monstrous, and mis-shapen thoughts of God, Christ, the glory above, and all spiritual things.

Proof 4: What a difficult task is it to detain the carnal mind before the Lord! how averse is it to entertain good thoughts, and dwell in the meditation of spiritual things! If a person be driven, at any time, to think of the great concerns of his soul, it is not harder work to hold in an unruly hungry beast, than to hedge in the carnal mind, that it get not away to the vanities of the world again. When God is speaking to men by His word, or they are speaking to Him in prayer, does not the mind often leave them before the Lord, like so many 'idols that have eyes, but see not, and ears, but hear not.' The carcase is laid down before God, but the world gets away the heart. Though the eyes be closed, the man sees a thousand vanities; the mind, in the mean time, is like a bird got loose out of a cage, skipping from bush to bush, so that, in effect, the man never comes to himself till he is gone from the presence of the Lord. Say not, it is impossible to get the mind fixed – it is hard, indeed, but not impossible; grace from the Lord can do it (Psa 108.1), agreeable objects will do it. A pleasant speculation will arrest the minds of the inquisitive; the worldly man's mind is in little hazard of wandering, when he is contriving his business, casting up his accounts, or counting his money; if he answers you not at first, he tells you he did not hear you, he was busy, his mind was fixed. Were we admitted into the presence of a king to petition for our lives, we should be in no hazard of gazing through the chamber of presence. But here lies the case; the carnal mind, employed about any spiritual good, is out of its element, and therefore cannot fix.

Proof 5: But however hard it is to keep the mind on good thoughts, it sticks like glue to what is evil and corrupt like itself (2 Pet 2.14), 'Having eyes full of adultery, and that cannot cease from sin.' Their eyes cannot cease from sin (so the words are constructed), that is, their hearts and minds, venting by the eyes what is within, are like a furious beast, which cannot be held in when once it has got out its head. Let the corrupt imagination once be let loose on its favourite object, it will be found hard work to call it back again, though both reason and will are for its retreat. For then it is in its own element, and to draw it off from its impurities is like drawing a fish out of the water, or rending a limb from a man. It runs like fire set to a train of powder, that rests not till it can get no further.

Proof 6: Consider how the carnal imagination supplies the want of real objects to the corrupt heart, that it may make sinners happy, at least in the imaginary enjoyment of their lusts. Thus the corrupt heart feeds itself with imagination-sins, the unclean person is filled with speculative impurities, 'having eyes full of adultery.' The covetous man fills his heart with the world, though he cannot get his hands full of it; the malicious person with delight acts his revenge within his own breast; the envious man, within his own narrow soul, beholds with satisfaction his neighbour laid low; and every lust finds the corrupt imagination a friend to it in time of need. This the heart does, not only when people are awake, but sometimes even when they are asleep, whereby it comes to pass, that those sins are acted in dreams, which their hearts pant after when they are awake. I am aware that some question the sinfulness of these things, but can it be thought they are consistent with that holy nature and frame of spirit which was in innocent Adam, and in Jesus Christ, and should be in every man? It is the corruption of nature, then, that makes filthy dreamers condemned (Jude, verse 8). Solomon had experience of the exercise of grace in sleep; in a dream he prayed, in a dream he made the best choice; both were accepted of God (1 Kings 3.5–15). And if a man may, in his sleep, do what is good and acceptable to God, why may he not also, when asleep, do that which is evil and displeasing to God? The same Solomon would have men aware of this, and prescribes the best remedy against it, namely, 'the law upon the heart' (Prov 6.20,21). 'When thou sleepest,' says he (verse 22), 'it shall keep thee,' to wit, from sinning in thy sleep, that is, from sinful dreams: for a man's being kept from sin, not his being kept from affliction, is the immediate proper effect of the law of God impressed upon the heart (Psa 119.11). And thus the whole verse is to be understood, as appears from verse 23. 'For the commandment is a lamp, and the law is light, and reproofs of instruction are the way of life.' Now, the law is a lamp and light, as it guides in the way of duty, and instructing reproofs from the law are the way of life, as they keep from sin; they guide not into the way of peace, but as they lead into the way of duty; nor do they keep a man out of trouble, but as they keep him from sin. Remarkable is the particular which Solomon instances, namely, the sin of uncleanness, 'to keep thee from the evil woman,' &c. (verse 24, which is to be joined to verse 22, enclosing the 23rd in a parenthesis, as some versions have it). These things may suffice to convince us of the natural bias of the mind to evil.

4: There is in the carnal mind an opposition to spiritual truths, and an aversion to receive them. It is as little a friend to divine truths, as it is to holiness. The truths of natural religion, which do, as it were, force their entry into the minds of natural men, they hold prisoners in unrighteousness (Rom 1.18). As for the truths of revealed religion, there is an evil heart of unbelief in them, which opposes their entry; and there is an armed force necessary to captivate the mind to the belief of them (2 Cor 10.4,5). God has made a revelation of His mind and will to sinners, concerning the way of salvation; He has given us the doctrine of His holy Word, but do natural men believe it indeed? No, they do not; 'for he that believeth not on the Son of God, believeth not God,' as is plain from 1 John 5.10. They believe not the promises of the Word; they look on them, in effect, only as fair words, for those who receive them are thereby made 'partakers of the divine nature' (2 Pet 1.4). The promises are as silver cords let down from heaven, to draw sinners unto God, and to waft them over into the promised land, but they cast them from them. They believe not the threatenings of the Word. As men travelling in deserts carry fire about with them, to frighten away wild beasts, so God has made His law a fiery law (Deut 33.2), surrounding it with threats of wrath: but men are naturally more brutish than beasts themselves and will needs touch the fiery smoking mountain, though they should be thrust through with a dart. I doubt not but most, if not all of you, who are yet in the black state of nature, will here plead, Not Guilty; but remember, the carnal Jews in Christ's time were as confident as you are, that they believed Moses (John 9.28,29). But He confutes their confidence, roundly telling them (John 5.46), 'Had ye believed Moses, ye would have believed Me.' If you believe the truths of God, you dare not reject, as you do, Him who is truth itself.

The very difficulty you find in assenting to this truth, discovers that unbelief which I am charging you with. Has it not proceeded so far with some at this day, that it has steeled their foreheads with impudence and impiety, openly to reject all revealed religion? Surely it is 'out of the abundance of the heart their mouth speaketh.' But, though you set not your mouth against the heavens, as they do, the same bitter root of unbelief is in all men by nature, and reigns in you, and will reign, till overcoming grace brings your minds to the belief of the truth. To convince you in this point, consider these three things:

Proof 1: How few are there who have been blessed with an inward illumination, by the special operation of the Spirit of Christ, leading them into a view of divine truths in their spiritual and heavenly lustre! How have you learned the truths of religion, which you pretend to believe? You have them merely by the benefit of external revelation, and by education; so that you are Christians, just because you were born and bred not in a Pagan, but in a Christian country. You are strangers to the inward work of the Holy Spirit, bearing witness by and with the Word in your hearts, and so you cannot have the assurance of faith, with respect to the outward divine revelation made in the Word (1 Cor 2.10–12); therefore you are still unbelievers. 'It is written in the Prophets, They shall be all taught of God. Every man, therefore, that hath heard, and hath learned of the Father cometh unto me,' says our Lord (John 6.45). Now, you have not come to Christ, therefore you have not been taught of God: you have not been so taught, and therefore you have not come; you believe not. Behold the revelation from which the faith, even of the fundamental principles in religion, springs (Matt 16.16,17), 'Thou art Christ, the Son of the living God. – Blessed art thou, Simon Bar-jona; for flesh and blood hath not revealed it unto thee, but my Father which is in heaven.' If ever the Spirit of the Lord take you in hand, to work in you that faith which is of the operation of God, it may be, that as much time will be spent in razing the old foundation, as will make you find the necessity of the working of His mighty power, to enable you to believe the very foundation-principles, which now you think you make no doubt of (Eph 1.19).

Proof 2: How many professors have made shipwreck of their faith, such as it was, in time of temptation and trial! See how they fall, like stars from heaven, when Antichrist prevails! (2 Thess 2.11–12), 'God shall send them strong delusion, that they should believe a lie; that they all might be damned, who believed not the truth.' They fall into damning delusions because they never really believed the truth, though they themselves, and others too, thought they did believe it. That house is built on the sand, and that faith is but ill-founded, that cannot stand, but is quite overthrown, when the storm comes.

Proof 3: Consider the utter inconsistency of most men's lives with the principles of religion which they profess; you may as soon bring east and west together, as their principles and practice. Men believe that fire will burn them, and therefore they will not throw themselves into it, but the truth is, most men live as if they thought the Gospel a mere fable, and the wrath of God, revealed in His Word against their unrighteousness and ungodliness, a mere scarecrow. If you believe the doctrines of the Word, how is it that you are so unconcerned about the state of your souls before the Lord? how is it that you are so little concerned about this weighty point, whether you be born again or not? Many live as they were born, and are likely to die as they live, and yet live in peace. Do such persons believe the sinfulness and misery of a natural state? Do they believe that they are children of wrath? Do they believe that there is no salvation without regeneration, and no regeneration but what makes a man a new creature? If you believe the promises of the Word, why do you not embrace them, and seek to enter into the promised rest? What sluggard would not dig for a hid treasure, if he really believed that he might so obtain it? Men will work and toil for a maintenance, because they believe that by so doing they shall get it, yet they will be at no tolerable pains for the eternal weight of glory!

[93]

why, but because they do not believe the word of promise? (Heb 4.1,2). If you believe the threatenings, how is it that you live in your sins; live out of Christ, and yet hope for mercy? Do such persons believe God to be the holy and just One, who will by no means clear the guilty? No, no; none believe; none, or next to none, believe what a just God the Lord is, and how severely He punishes.

5: There is in the mind of man a natural proneness to lies and falsehood, which favours his lusts: 'They go astray as soon as they be born, speaking lies' (Psa 58.3). We have this, with the rest of the corruption of our nature, from our first parents. God revealed the truth to them, but through the solicitation of the tempter, they first doubted, then disbelieved it, and embraced a lie instead of it. For an incontestable evidence hereof, we may see the first article of the devil's creed, 'ye shall not surely die' (Gen 3.4), which was obtruded by him on our first parents, and by them received, naturally embraced by their posterity, and held fast, till light from heaven obliges them to quit it. It spreads itself through the lives of natural men who, till their consciences are awakened, walk after their own lusts, still retaining the principle, 'That they shall not surely die.' And this is often improved to such perfection, that man says, in the face of the pronounced curse, 'I shall have peace, though I walk in the imagination of my heart, to add drunkenness to thirst' (Deut 29.19). Whatever advantage the truths of God have over error, by means of education or otherwise, error has always, with the natural man, this advantage against truth, namely, that there is something within him which says, 'O that it were true!' so that the mind lies fair for assenting to it. And this is the reason of it: the true doctrine is, 'the doctrine that is according to godliness' (1 Tim 6.3), and the truth which is after godliness' (Titus 1.1). Error is the doctrine which is according to ungodliness; for there is not an error in the mind, nor an untruth vented in the world, in matters of religion, but has an affinity with one corruption of the heart or another; according to that saying of the apostle (2 Thess 2.12), 'They

[94]

believed not the truth, but had pleasure in unrighteousness.' So that truth and error, being otherwise attended with equal advantages for their reception, error, by this means, has most ready access into the minds of men in their natural state. Wherefore, it is not strange that men reject the simplicity of Gospel truths and institutions, and greedily embrace error and external pomp in religion, seeing they are so agreeable to the lusts of the heart, and the vanity of the mind of the natural man. Hence also it is, that so many embrace atheistical principles, for none do it but in compliance with their irregular passions, none but those whose advantage it would be that there were no God.

6: Man is naturally high-minded; for when the Gospel comes in power to him, it is employed in 'casting down imaginations, and every high thing that exalteth itself against the knowledge of God' (2 Cor 10.5). Lowliness of mind is not a flower that grows in the field of nature; but is planted by the finger of God in a renewed heart, and learned of the lowly Jesus. It is natural to man to think highly of himself, and what is his own: for the stroke which he has got by his fall in Adam, has produced a false light, whereby mole-hills about him appear like mountains, and a thousand airy beauties present themselves to his deluded fancy. 'Vain man would be wise,' so he accounts himself, and so he would be accounted by others, 'though man be born like a wild ass's colt' (Job 11.12). His way is right, because it is his own: for 'every way of a man is right in his own eyes' (Prov 21.2). His state is good, because he knows none better; he is alive without the law (Rom 7.9), and therefore his hope is strong, and his confidence firm. It is another tower of Babel, reared up against heaven; and it will not fall while the power of darkness can hold it up. The Word batters it, yet it stands; one while breaches are made in it, but they are quickly repaired; at another time, it is all made to shake, but still it is kept up, till either God Himself by His Spirit raises a heart-quake within the man, which tumbles it down, and leaves not one stone upon another (2 Cor 10.4,5), or death batters it down, and razes the foundation of it (Luke 16.23).

And as the natural man thinks highly of himself, so he thinks meanly of God, whatever he pretends (Psa 50.21), 'Thou thoughtest that I was altogether such an one as thyself.' The doctrine of the Gospel, and the mystery of Christ, are foolishness to him, and in his practice he treats them as such (1 Cor 1.18, and 2.14). He brings the Word and the works of God, in the government of the world, before the bar of his carnal reason, and there they are presumptuously censured and condemned (Hosea 14.9). Sometimes the ordinary restraints of Providence are taken off, and Satan is permitted to stir up the carnal mind: and, in that case, it is like an ants' nest, uncovered and disturbed; doubts, denials, and hellish reasonings crowd in it, and cannot be overcome by all the arguments brought against them, till a power from on high subdue the mind, and still the mutiny of the corrupt principles.

Thus much of the corruption of the understanding, which, although the half be not told, may discover to you the absolute necessity of regenerating grace. Call the understanding now, 'Ichabod; for the glory is departed from it' (1 Sam 4.21). Consider this, you that are yet in the state of nature, and groan out your case before the Lord, that the Sun of Righteousness may arise upon you, lest you be shut up in everlasting darkness. What avails your worldly wisdom? What do your attainments in religion avail, while your understanding lies wrapt up in its natural darkness and confusion, utterly void of the light of life? Whatever be the natural man's gifts or attainments, we must, as in the case of the leper (Lev 13.44), 'pronounce him utterly unclean, his plague is in his head.' But that is not all, it is in his heart too; his will is corrupted, as I shall soon shew.

II : *The Corruption of the Will*

The Will, that commanding faculty, which at first was faithful and ruled with God, is now turned traitor, and rules with and for the devil. God planted it in man, 'wholly a right seed;' but now it is 'turned into the degenerate plant of a strange vine.' It was originally placed in due subordination to the will of God, as was shewn before; but now it is wholly gone aside. However some magnify the power of free-will, a view of the spirituality of the law, to which acts of moral discipline in no wise answer, and a deep insight into the corruption of nature, given by the inward operation of the Spirit, convincing of sin, righteousness, and judgment, would make men find an absolute need of the power of free grace, to remove the bands of wickedness from off their free-will. To open up this plague of the heart, I offer these following things to be considered:

1: There is, in the unrenewed will, an utter inability for what is truly good and acceptable in the sight of God. The natural man's will is in Satan's fetters, hemmed in within the circle of evil, and cannot move beyond it, any more than a dead man can raise himself out of his grave (Eph 2.1). We deny him not a power to choose, pursue, and act what, as to the matter, is good; but though he can will what is good and right, he can will nothing aright and well (John 15.5). Christ says, 'Without me' that is, separate from Me, as a branch from the stock, as both the word and context will bear, 'ye can do nothing;' which means, nothing truly and spiritually good. His very choice and desire of spiritual things is carnal and selfish (John 6.26). 'Ye seek me – because ye did eat of the loaves and were filled.' He not only does not come to Christ, but 'he cannot come' (verse 44). And what can he do acceptable to God, who believeth not on Him whom the Father has sent? To prove this inability for good in the unregenerate, consider these two things:

Proof 1: How often does the light so shine before men's eyes, that they cannot but see the good which they should choose, and the evil which they should refuse; and yet their hearts have no more power to comply with that light, than if they were arrested by some invisible hand! They see what is right, yet they follow, and cannot but follow, what is wrong. Their consciences tell them the right way, and approve of it too, yet their will cannot be brought up to it: their corruption so chains them, that they cannot embrace it, so that they sigh and go backward, not-withstanding their light. If it be not thus, how is it that the Word and way of holiness meet with such entertainment in the world? How is it that clear arguments and reason on the side of piety and a holy life, which seem to have weight even with the carnal mind, do not bring men over to that side? Although the existence of a heaven and a hell were only probable, it were sufficient to determine the will to the choice of holiness, were it capable of being determined thereto by mere reason: but men, 'knowing the judgment of God, that they who commit such things are worthy of death, not only do the same, but have pleasure in them that do them' (Rom 1.32). And how is it that those who magnify the power of free-will, do not confirm their opinion before the world, by an ocular demonstration in a practice as far above others in holiness, as the opinion of their natural ability is above that of others? Or is it maintained only for the protection of lusts, which men may hold fast as long as they please; and when they have no more use for them, throw them off in a moment, and leap out of Delilah's lap into Abraham's bosom? Whatever use some make of that principle, it does of itself, and in its own nature, cast a broad shadow for a shelter to wickedness of heart and life. It may be observed, that the generality of the hearers of the Gospel, of all denominations, are plagued with it, for it is a root of bitterness, natural to all men, from whence spring so much fearlessness about the soul's eternal state, so many delays and excuses in that weighty matter, whereby much work is laid up for a deathbed by some, while others are ruined by a legal walk, and neglect the life of faith, and the making use of Christ for sanctification; all flowing from the persuasion of sufficient natural abilities. So agreeable is it to corrupt nature.

Proof 2: Let those, who, by the power of the spirit of bondage, have had the law opened before them in its spirituality, for their conviction, speak and tell, if they found themselves able to incline their hearts toward it, in that case; nay, whether the more that light shone into their souls, they did not find their hearts

[98]

more and more unable to comply with it. There are some who have been brought unto 'the place of the breaking forth,' who are yet in the devil's camp, who from their experience can tell, that light let into the mind cannot give life to the will, to enable it to comply therewith; and could give their testimony here, if they would. But take Paul's testimony concerning it, who, in his unconverted state, was far from believing his utter inability for good, but learned it by experience (Rom 7.8–13). I own, the natural man may have a kind of love to the letter of the law: but here lies the stress of the matter, he looks on the holy law in a carnal dress, and so, while he embraces the creature of his own fancy, he thinks that he has the law; but in very deed he is without the law, for as yet he sees it not in its spirituality. If he did, he would find it the very reverse of his own nature, and what his will could not fall in with, till changed by the power of grace.

2: There is in the unrenewed will an aversion to good. Sin is the natural man's element; he is as unwilling to part with it as fish are to come out of the water on to dry land. He not only cannot come to Christ, but he *will not come* (John 5.40). He is polluted, and hates to be washed (Jer 13.27), 'Wilt thou not be made clean? when shall it once be?' He is sick, yet utterly averse to the remedy; he loves his disease so, that he loathes the Physician. He is a captive, a prisoner, and a slave, but he loves his conqueror, his jailor, and master: he is fond of his fetters, prison, and drudgery, and has no liking to his liberty. For proof of the aversion to good in the will of man, I will instance in some particulars:

Proof 1: The untowardness of children. Do we not see them naturally lovers of sinful liberty? How unwilling are they to be hedged in! How averse to restraint! The world can bear witness, that they are 'as bullocks unaccustomed to the yoke:' and more, that it is far easier to bring young bullocks tamely to bear the yoke, than to bring young children under discipline, and make them tamely submit to be restrained in sinful liberty. Everybody may see in this, as in a glass, that man is naturally wild and

[99]

wilful, according to Zophar's observation (Job 11.12), that 'man is born like a wild ass's colt.' What can be said more? He is like a colt, the colt of an ass, the colt of a wild ass. Compare (Jer 2.24), 'A wild ass used to the wilderness, that snuffeth up the wind at her pleasure; in her occasion who can turn her away?'

Proof 2: What pain and difficulty do men often find in bringing their hearts to religious duties! and what a task is it to the carnal heart to abide at them! It is a pain to it, to leave the world but a little to come before God. It is not easy to borrow time from the many things, to spend it upon the one thing needful. Men often go to God in duties, with their faces towards the world; and when their bodies are on the mount of ordinances, their hearts will be found at the foot of the hill 'going after their covetousness' (Ezek 33.31). They are soon wearied of well-doing, for holy duties are not agreeable to their corrupt nature. Take notice of them at their worldly business, set them down with their carnal company, or let them be enjoying a lust, time seems to them to fly, and drive furiously, so that it is gone before they are aware. But how heavily does it pass, while a prayer, a sermon, or a Sabbath lasts! The Lord's day is the longest day of all the week with many; therefore they must sleep longer that morning, and go sooner to bed that night, than ordinarily they do; that the day may be made of a tolerable length: for their hearts say within them, 'When will the Sabbath be gone?' (Amos 8.5). The hours of worship are the longest hours of that day: hence, when duty is over, they are like men eased of a burden, and when sermon is ended, many have neither the grace nor the good manners to stay till the blessing is pronounced, but, like the beasts, their head is away, so soon as a man puts his hand to loose them; and why? because, while they are at ordinances, they are, as Doeg, 'detained before the Lord' (1 Sam 22.7).

Proof 3: Consider how the will of the natural man rebels against the light (Job 24.13). Light sometimes enters in, because he is not able to keep it out: but he loves darkness rather than light. Sometimes, by the force of truth, the outer door of the understanding is broken up; but the inner door of the will remains fast bolted. Then lusts rise against light: corruption and conscience encounter, and fight as in the field of battle, till corruption getting the upper hand, conscience is forced to turn its back; convictions are murdered, and truth is made and held prisoner, so that it can create no more disturbance. While the Word is preached or read, or the rod of God is upon the natural man, sometimes convictions are darted in upon him, and his spirit is wounded in greater or lesser measure: but these convictions not being able to make him fall, he runs away with the arrows sticking in his conscience, and at length, one way or other, gets them out, and makes himself whole again. Thus, while the light shines, men, naturally averse to it, wilfully shut their eyes, till God is provoked to blind them judicially, and they become proof against His Word and providences too. So, go where they will, they can sit at ease; there is never a word from heaven to them, that goes deeper than their ears. (Hos 4.17), 'Ephraim is joined to idols: let him alone.'

Proof 4: Let us observe the resistance made by elect souls, when the Spirit of the Lord is at work, to bring them from 'the power of Satan unto God.' Zion's King gets no subjects but by stroke of sword, 'in the day of his power' (Psa 110.2,3). None come to Him, but such as are drawn by a divine Hand (John 6.44). When the Lord comes to the soul, He finds the strong man keeping the house, and a deep peace and security there, while the soul is fast asleep in the devil's arms. But 'the prey must be taken from the mighty, and the captive delivered.' Therefore the Lord awakens the sinner, opens his eyes, and strikes him with terror, while the clouds are black above his head, and the sword of vengeance is held to his breast. Now, he is at no small pains to put a fair face on a black heart, to shake off his fears, to make head against them, and to divert himself from thinking on the unpleasant and ungrateful subject of his soul's case. If he cannot so rid himself from them, carnal reason is called in to help, and urges, that there is no ground for such great fear; all may be well enough yet; and if it be ill with him, it will be ill with many. When the sinner is beat from this, and sees no advantage in going to hell with company, he resolves to leave his sins, but cannot think of breaking off so soon; there is time enough, and he will do it afterwards. Conscience says, 'To-day if ye will hear his voice harden not your hearts:' but he cries, 'To-morrow, Lord; to-morrow, Lord;' and 'just now, Lord;' till that now is never like to come. Thus, many times he comes from his prayers and confessions, with nothing but a breast full of sharper convictions; for the heart does not always cast up the sweet morsel as soon as confession is made with the mouth (Judges 10.10–16). And when conscience obliges him to part with some lusts, others are kept as right eyes and right hands, and there are rueful looks after those that are put away; as it was with the Israelites, who with bitter hearts remembered 'the fish they did eat in Egypt freely' (Num 11.5). Nay, when he is so pressed, that he must needs say before the Lord that he is content to part with all his idols, the heart will be giving the tongue the lie. In a word, the soul, in this case, will shift from one thing to another, like a fish with the hook in its jaws, till it can do no more, for power is come to make it yield, as 'the wild ass in her month' (Jer 2.24).

3: There is in the will of man a natural 'proneness to evil,' a woeful bent towards sin. Men naturally are 'bent to backsliding from God' (Hos 11.7). They hang, as the word is, towards back-sliding; even as a hanging wall, whose breaking 'cometh suddenly at an instant'. Set holiness and life upon the one side, sin and death upon the other. Leave the unrenewed will to itself, it will choose sin, and reject holiness. This is no more to be doubted, than that water poured on the side of a hill will run downward, and not upward; or that a flame will ascend, and not descend.

Proof 1: Is not the way of evil the first way which the children of men go? Do not their inclinations plainly appear on the wrong side, while yet they have no cunning to hide them? In the first opening of our eyes in the world, we look a-squint, hell-ward, not heaven-ward. As soon as it appears that we are rational creatures, it appears that we are sinful creatures (Psa 58.3), 'The wicked are estranged from the womb; they go astray as soon as they be born.' (Prov 22.15), 'Foolishness is bound in the heart of a child: but the rod of correction shall drive it far from him.' Folly is bound in the heart, it is woven into our very nature. The knot will not unloose; it must be broken asunder by strokes. Words will not do it, the rod must be taken to drive it away; and if it be not driven far away, the heart and it will meet and knit again. Not that the rod of itself will do this: the sad experience of many parents testifies the contrary; and Solomon himself tells you (Prov 27.22), 'Though thou shouldest bray a fool in a mortar among wheat with a pestle, yet will not his foolishness depart from him;' it is so bound in his heart. But the rod is an ordinance of God, appointed for that end, which, like the Word, is made effectual, by the Spirit's accompanying His own ordinance. This, by the way, shows that parents, in administering correction to their children, have need, first of all, to correct their own irregular passions, and look upon it as a matter of awful solemnity, setting about it with much dependence on the Lord, and following it with prayer for the blessing, if they would have it effectual.

Proof 2: How easily are men led aside to sin! The children who are not persuaded to good, are otherwise simple ones, easily wrought upon: those whom the Word cannot draw to holiness, are 'led by Satan at his pleasure.' Profane Esau, that cunning man (Gen 25.27), was as easily cheated of the blessing as if he had been a fool or an idiot. The more natural a thing is, the more easy it is; so Christ's yoke is easy to the saints, in so far as they are partakers of the divine nature, and sin is easy to the unrenewed man. But to learn to do good is as difficult as for the Ethiopian to change his skin, because the will naturally hangs towards evil, and is averse to good. A child can cause a round thing to run, when he cannot move a square thing of the same weight; for the roundness makes it fit for motion, so that it goes with a touch. Even so, men find the heart easily carried towards sin, while it is as a dead weight in the way of holiness. We must seek for the reason of this from the natural set and disposition of the heart, whereby it is prone and bent to evil. Were man's will, naturally, but in equal balance to good and evil, the one might be embraced with as little difficulty as the other, but experience testifies it is not so. In the sacred history of the Israelites, especially in the Book of Judges, how often do we find them forsaking Jehovah, the mighty God, and doting upon the idols of the nations about them! But did ever any one of these nations grow fond of Israel's God, and forsake their own idols? No, no; though man is naturally given to changes, it is but from evil to evil, not from evil to good. (Jer 2.10,11), 'Hath a nation changed their gods, which are yet no gods? But my people have changed their glory, for that which doth not profit.' Surely the will of man stands not in equal balance, but has a cast to the wrong side.

Proof 3: Consider how men go on still in the way of sin, till they are stopped, and that by another hand than their own (Isa 57.17), 'I hid me, and he went on forwardly in the way of his heart.' If God withdraw His restraining hand, and lay the reins on the sinner's neck, he is under no doubt what way to choose; for, observe it, the way of sin is the way of his heart, his heart naturally lies that way, it hath a natural propensity to sin. As long as God suffers them, they walk in their own way (Acts 14.16). The natural man is so fixed in his woeful choice, that there needs no more to show he is off from God's way, than to say he is upon his own.

Proof 4: Whatsoever good impressions are made on him, they do not last. Though his heart be firm as a stone, yea, harder than the nether-millstone, in point of receiving of them, it is otherwise unstable as water, and cannot keep them. It works against the receiving of them, and, when they are made, it works them off, and returns to its natural bias (Hos 6.4), 'Your goodness is as a morning cloud, and as the early dew it goeth away.' The morning cloud promises a heavy shower, but, when the sun arises, it vanishes: the sun beats upon the early dew, and it evaporates, so the husbandman's expectation is disappointed. Such is the goodness of the natural man. Some sharp affliction, or piercing conviction, obliges him, in some sort, to turn from his evil course: but his will not being renewed, religion is still against the grain with him, and therefore this goes off again (Psa 78.34–37). Though a stone thrown up into the air may abide there a little while, yet its natural heaviness will bring it down again: so do unrenewed men return to their wallowing in the mire, because, though they washed themselves, yet their swinish nature was not changed. It is hard to cause wet wood to take fire, hard to make it keep alight, but it is harder than either of these to make the unrenewed will retain attained goodness, which is a plain evidence of the natural bent of the will to evil.

Proof 5 : Do the saints serve the Lord now, as they were wont to serve sin, in their unconverted state? Very far from it (Rom 6.20), 'When ye were the servants of sin, ye were free from righteousness.' Sin got all, and admitted no partner; but now, when they are the servants of Christ, are they free from sin? Nay, there are still with them some deeds of the old man, showing that he is but dying in them; and hence their hearts often misgive them, and slip aside unto evil, 'when they would do good' (Rom 7.21). They need to watch, and keep their hearts with all diligence; and their sad experience teaches them, 'That he that trusteth in his own heart is a fool' (Prov 28.26). If it be thus in the green tree, how must it be in the dry?

4 : There is a natural contrariety, direct opposition, and enmity, in the will of man, to God Himself, and His holy will (Rom 8.7), 'The carnal mind is enmity against God; for it is not subject to the law of God, neither indeed can be.' The will was once God's deputy in the soul, set to command there for Him; but now it is set up against Him. If you would have the picture of it in its natural state, the very reverse of the will of God represents it. If the fruit hanging before one's eye be but forbidden, that is sufficient to draw the heart after it. Let me instance in the sin of profane swearing and cursing, to which some are so abandoned that they take a pride in it, belching out horrid oaths and curses,

as if hell opened with the opening of their mouths; or larding their speeches with minced oaths; and all this without any manner of provocation, though even that would not excuse them. Pray, tell me: 1. What profit is there here? A thief gets something for his pains; a drunkard gets a belly-full; but what do you get? Others serve the devil for pay; but you are volunteers, who expect no reward but your work itself, in affronting Heaven; and if you repent not, you will get your reward in full measure; when you go to hell, your work will follow you. The drunkard shall not have a drop of water to cool his tongue there; nor will the covetous man's wealth follow him into the other world! You may drive on your old trade there, eternity will be long enough to give you your heart's fill of it. 2. What pleasure is there here, but what flows from your trampling on the holy law? Which of your senses does swearing and cursing gratify? If it gratify your ears, it can only be by the noise it makes against the heavens. Though you had a mind to give up yourselves to all manner of profanity and sensuality, there is so little pleasure can be strained out of these sins, that we must needs conclude, your love to them in this case is a love to them for themselves, a devilish unhired love, without any prospect of profit or pleasure from them otherwise. If any shall say, these are monsters of men: be it so; yet, alas! the world is full of such monsters, they are to be found almost everywhere. Allow me to say, they must be admitted as the mouth of the whole unregenerate world against heaven (Rom 3.14), 'Whose mouth is full of cursing and bitterness.' (Verse 19), 'Now we know, that what things soever the law saith, it saith to them who are under the law, that every mouth may be stopped, and all the world may become guilty before God.'

I have a charge against every unregenerate man and woman, young and old, to be proved by the testimony of Scripture, and their own consciences; namely, that whether they be professors or profane, seeing they are not born again, they are heart-enemies to God, to the Son of God, to the Spirit of God, and to the law

[106]

of God. Hear this, you careless souls, that live at ease in your natural state.

(1) You are enemies to God in your mind (Col 1.21). You are not as yet reconciled to Him; the natural enmity is not as yet slain, though perhaps it lies hid, and you do not perceive it. 1. You are enemies to the very being of God (Psa 14.1), 'The fool hath said in his heart, there is no God.' The proud man wishes that none were above himself; the rebel, that there were no king; and the unrenewed man, who is a mass of pride and rebellion, that there were no God. He saith it in his heart, he wisheth it were so, though he is ashamed and afraid to speak it out. That all natural men are such fools, appears from the apostle's quoting a part of this psalm, 'that every mouth may be stopped' (Rom 3.10–19). I own, indeed, that while the natural man looks on God as the Creator and Preserver of the world, because he loves his own self, therefore his heart rises not against the being of his Benefactor: but his enmity will quickly appear when he looks on God as the Governor and Judge of the world, binding him, under the pain of the curse, to exact holiness, and girding him with the cords of death because of his sin. Listen in this case to the voice of the heart, and you will find it to be, 'No God.' 2. You are enemies to the nature of God (Job 21.14), 'They say unto God, Depart from us, for we desire not the knowledge of thy ways.' Men set up to themselves an idol of their own fancy, instead of God, and then fall down and worship it. They love Him no other way than Jacob loved Leah, while he took her for Rachel. Every natural man is an enemy to God, as He is revealed in His word. The infinitely holy, just, powerful, and true Being, is not the God whom he loves, but the God whom he loathes. In fact, men naturally are haters of God (Rom 1.30); if they could, they certainly would make Him otherwise than what He is. For, consider it is a certain truth, that whatsoever is in God, is God; therefore His attributes or perfections are not any thing really distinct from Himself. If God's attributes be not God Himself, He is a compound Being, and so not the first Being, to say which is blasphemous; for the

parts compounding, are before the compound itself; but He is Alpha and Omega, the first and the last.

Now, upon this I would, for your conviction, propose to your conscience a few queries. 1. How stand your hearts affected towards the infinite purity and holiness of God? Conscience will give an answer to this, which the tongue will not speak out. If you be not partakers of His holiness you cannot be reconciled to it. The Pagans finding that they could not be like God in holiness, made their gods like themselves in filthiness; and thereby they showed what sort of a god the natural man would have. God is holy; can an unholy creature love His unspotted holiness? Nay, it is the righteous only that can 'give thanks at the remembrance of his holiness' (Psa 97.12). God is light; can creatures of darkness rejoice therein? Nay, 'every one that doeth evil hateth the light' (John 3.20). 'For what communion hath light with darkness?' (2 Cor 6.14). 2. How stand your hearts affected to the justice of God? There is not a man who is wedded to his lusts, as all the unregenerate are, but would be content, with the blood of his body, to blot that letter out of the name of God. Can the malefactor love his condemning judge? or an unjustified sinner, a just God? No, he cannot (Luke 7.47), 'To whom little is forgiven, the same loveth little.' Hence, as men cannot get the doctrine of His justice blotted out of the Bible, it is such an eye-sore to them, that they strive to blot it out of their minds: they ruin themselves by presuming on His mercy, while they are not careful to get a righteousness, wherein they may stand before His justice; but 'say in their heart, The Lord will not do good, neither will he do evil' (Zeph 1.12). 3. How stand you affected to the omniscience and omnipresence of God? Men naturally would rather have a blind idol, than the all-seeing God; therefore they do what they can, as Adam did, to hide themselves from the presence of the Lord. They no more love the all-seeing, every-where present God, than the thief loves to have the judge witness to his evil deeds. If it could be carried by votes, God would be voted out of the world, and closed up in heaven; for the language of the carnal heart is,

'The Lord seeth us not; the Lord hath forsaken the earth' (Ezek 8.12). 4. How stand you affected to the truth and veracity of God? There are but few in the world who can heartily subscribe to this sentence of the apostle (Rom 3.4), 'Let God be true, but every man a liar.' Nay, truly, there are many who, in effect, hope that God will not be true to His Word. There are thousands who hear the gospel, that hope to be saved, and think all safe with them for eternity, who never had any experience of the new birth, nor do at all concern themselves in the question, Whether they are born again, or not? a question that is likely to wear out from among us at this day. Our Lord's words are plain and peremptory, 'Except a man be born again, he cannot see the kingdom of God.' What are such hopes, then, but real hopes that God – with profoundest reverence be it spoken – will recall His word, and that Christ will prove a false prophet? What else means the sinner, who, 'when he heareth the words of the curse, blesseth himself in his heart, saying, I shall have peace, though I walk in the imagination of mine heart?' (Deut 29.19). 5. How stand you affected to the power of God? None but new creatures will love Him for it, on a fair view thereof; though others may slavishly fear Him upon account of it. There is not a natural man, but would contribute, to the utmost of his power, to the building of another tower of Babel, to hem it in. On these grounds I declare every unrenewed man an enemy to God.

(2) You are enemies to the Son of God. That enmity to Christ is in your hearts, which would have made you join the husbandmen who killed the heir, and cast him out of the vineyard, if ye had been beset with their temptations, and no more restrained than they were. 'Am I a dog?' you will say, that I should so treat my sweet Saviour? So did Hazael ask in another case; but when he had the temptation, he was a dog to do it. Many call Christ their dear Saviour, whose consciences can bear witness that they never derived as much sweetness from Him as from their sweet lusts, which are ten times dearer to them than their Saviour. He is no other way dear to them, than as they abuse His death and

sufferings, for the peaceable enjoyment of their lusts; that they may live as they please in the world, and when they die, be kept out of hell. Alas! it is but a mistaken Christ that is sweet to you, whose souls loathe that Christ who is the 'brightness of the Father's glory, and the express image of His person.' It is with you as it was with the carnal Jews, who delighted in Him, while they mistook His errand into the world, fancying that He would be a temporal deliverer to them (Mal 3.1). But when He 'sat as a refiner and purifier of silver' (verses 2, 3), and rejected them as reprobate silver, who thought to have had no small honour in the kingdom of the Messiah, His doctrine galled their consciences, and they had no rest till they imbrued their hands in His blood. To open your eyes in this point, which you are so averse to believe, I will lay before you the enmity of your hearts against Christ in all His offices.

First, Every unregenerate man is an enemy to Christ in His prophetical office. He is appointed of the Father the great Prophet and Teacher; but not upon the call of the world, who, in their natural state, would have unanimously voted against Him. Therefore, when He came, He was condemned as a seducer and blasphemer. For evidence of this enmity, I will instance two things.

Proof 1: Consider the entertainment which He meets with when He comes to teach souls inwardly by His Spirit. Men do what they can to stop their ears, like the deaf adder, that they may not hear His voice. They 'always resist the Holy Ghost:' 'They desire not the knowledge of His ways;' and therefore bid Him 'depart from them.' The old calumny is often raised upon Him on that occasion (John 10.20), 'He is mad, why hear ye Him?' Soul-exercise, raised by the spirit of bondage, is accounted, by many, nothing else but distraction, and melancholy fits. Men thus blaspheme the Lord's work, because they themselves are beside themselves, and cannot judge of those matters.

Proof 2: Consider the entertainment which He meets with when He comes to teach men outwardly by His Word.

His written Word, the Bible, is slighted. Christ hath left it to us, as the book of our instruction, to show us what way we must steer our course, if we would go to Immanuel's land. It is a lamp to light us through a dark world, to eternal light. And He has enjoined us to search it with that diligence wherewith men dig into mines for silver and gold (John 5.39). But, ah! how is this sacred treasure profaned by many! They ridicule that holy Word, by which they must be judged at the last day. They will rather lose their souls than their jest, dressing up the conceits of their wanton wits in Scripture phrases, in which they act as mad a part, as one who would dig into a mine, to procure metal to melt, and pour down his own and his neighbour's throat. Many exhaust their spirits in reading romances, and their minds pursue them, as the flame doth the dry stubble; while they have no heart for, nor relish to, the holy Word, and therefore seldom take a Bible in their hands. What is agreeable to the vanity of their minds is pleasant and taking; but what recommends holiness to their unholy hearts, makes their spirits dull and flat. What pleasure they find in reading a profane ballad, or story-book, to whom the Bible is entirely tasteless! Many lay by their Bibles with their Sabbath-day's clothes; and whatever use they have for their clothes, they have none for their Bibles, till the return of the Sabbath. Alas! the dust or the finery about your Bibles is a witness now, and will, at the last day, be a witness of the enmity of your hearts against Christ as a Prophet. Besides all this, among those who usually read the Scripture, how few are there that read it as the word of the Lord to their souls, and keep up communion with Him in it! They do not make His statutes their counsellors, nor does their particular case send them to their Bibles. They are strangers to the solid comfort of the Scriptures. And when they are dejected, it is something else than the Word that revives them: as Ahab was cured of his sullen fit, by the obtaining of Naboth's vineyard for him.

Christ's Word preached is despised. The entertainment which most of the world, to whom it has come, have always given it, is that which is mentioned (Matt 22.5), 'They made light of it;' and for His sake, they are despised whom He employs to preach it; whatever other face men put upon their contempt of the ministry. (John 15.20,21), 'The servant is not greater than his lord: if they have persecuted Me, they will also persecute you: if they have kept My saying, they will keep yours also. But all these things will they do unto you for My Name's sake.' That Levi was the son of *the hated* seems not to have been without a mystery, which the world in all ages has unriddled. But though the earthen vessels, wherein God has put the treasure, be turned, with many, into vessels wherein there is no pleasure, yet why is the treasure itself slighted? But slighted it is, and that with a witness, this day. 'Lord, who hath believed our report? To whom shall we speak?' Men can, without remorse, make to themselves silent Sabbaths, one after another. And, alas! when they come to ordinances, for the most part it is but to *appear*, or as the word is, *to be seen* before the Lord; and to *tread his courts*, namely, as a company of beasts would do, if they were driven into them (Isa 1.12), so little reverence and awe of God appear on their spirits. Many stand like brazen walls before the Word, in whose corrupt conversation the preaching of the Word makes no breach. Nay, not a few are growing worse and worse, under 'precept upon precept;' and the result of all is, 'They go and fall backward, and are broken, and snared, and taken' (Isa 28.13). What tears of blood are sufficient to lament that 'the gospel of the grace of God,' is thus received in vain! Ministers are but the voice of one crying; the speaker is in heaven; and speaks to you from heaven by men: why do you 'refuse Him that speaketh?' (Heb 12.25). God has made our Master heir of all things, and we are sent to seek for a spouse for Him. There is none so worthy as He; none more unworthy than they to whom this match is proposed; but the prince of darkness is preferred before the Prince of Peace. A dismal darkness overclouded the world by Adam's fall, more terrible than if the sun, moon, and stars had been for ever wrapt up in blackness of darkness; and there we should have eternally lain, had not this grace of the gospel, as a shining sun, appeared to dispel it (Titus 2.11). But yet we fly like night-owls from it, and, like the wild beasts, lay ourselves down in our dens. When the sun arises, we are struck blind with the light thereof, and, as creatures of darkness, love darkness rather than light. Such is the enmity of the hearts of men against Christ, in His prophetical office.

Secondly, The natural man is an enemy to Christ in His priestly office. He is appointed of the Father a priest for ever, that, by His alone sacrifice and intercession, sinners may have peace with, and access to God. But Christ crucified is a stumbling-block and foolishness to the unrenewed part of mankind, to whom He is preached (1 Cor 1.23). They are not for Him as the 'new and living way;' nor is He, by the voice of the world, 'an High-priest over the house of God.' Corrupt nature goes quite another way to work.

Proof 1: None of Adam's children are naturally inclined to receive the blessing in borrowed robes; but would always, according to the spider's motto, 'owe all to themselves:' and so climb up to heaven on a thread spun themselves. For they 'desire to be under the law' (Gal 4.21), and 'go about to establish their own righteousness' (Rom 10.3). Man naturally looks on God as a great Master; and himself as His servant, that must work and win heaven as his wages. Hence, when conscience is awakened, he thinks that, to the end he may be saved, he must answer the demands of the law, serve God as well as he can, and pray for mercy wherein he comes short. And thus many come to duties, that never come out of them to Jesus Christ.

Proof 2: As men naturally think highly of their duties, that seem to them to be well done, so they look for acceptance with God, according as their work is done, not according to the share they have in the blood of Christ. 'Wherefore have we fasted, say they, and thou seest not?' They value themselves on their performances and attainments; yet, on their very opinions in religion

(Phil 3.4–7), taking to themselves what they rob from Christ the great High-priest.

Proof 3: The natural man, going to God in duties, will always be found either to go without a mediator, or with more than the one only Mediator, Jesus Christ. Nature is blind, and therefore venturesome; it sets men a-going immediately to God without Christ; to rush into His presence, and put their petitions in His hand, without being introduced by the Secretary of heaven, or putting their requests into His hand. So fixed is this disposition in the unrenewed heart, that when many hearers of the gospel are conversed with upon the point of their hopes of salvation, the name of Christ will scarcely be heard from their mouths. Ask them how they think to obtain the pardon of sin? They will tell you they beg and look for mercy, because God is a merciful God; and that is all they have to confide in. Others look for mercy for Christ's sake: but how do they know that Christ will take their plea in hand? Why, as the papists have their mediators with the Mediator, so have they. They know He cannot but do it, for they pray, confess, mourn, and have great desires and the like, and so have something of their own to commend them to Him. They were never made poor in spirit, and brought empty-handed to Christ, to lay the stress of all on His atoning blood.

Thirdly, The natural man is an enemy to Christ in his kingly office. The Father has appointed the Mediator, 'King in Zion' (Psa 2.6). All to whom the gospel comes are commanded, on their highest peril, 'to kiss the Son,' and submit themselves unto him (verse 12). But the natural voice of mankind is, 'Away with him;' as you may see (verses 2, 3), 'They will not have him to reign over them' (Luke 19.14).

Proof 1: The workings of corrupt nature would wrest the government out of His hands. No sooner was He born, but, being born a King, Herod persecuted Him (Matt 2). And when He was crucified, they 'set up over his head his accusation written, This is Jesus, the King of the Jews' (Matt 27.37). Though His kingdom be a spiritual kingdom, and not of this world, yet they cannot

[114]

allow Him a kingdom within a kingdom, which acknowledges no other head or supreme but the Royal Mediator. They make bold with His royal prerogatives, changing His laws, institutions, and ordinances, modelling His worship according to the devices of their own hearts, introducing new offices and officers into His kingdom, not to be found in 'the book of the manner of His kingdom;' disposing of the external government thereof, as may best suit their carnal designs. Such is the enmity of the hearts of men against Zion's King.

Proof 2 : How unwilling are men, naturally, to submit to, and be hedged in by, the laws and discipline of His kingdom! As a king, He is a lawgiver (Isa 33.22), and has appointed an external government, discipline, and censures, to control the unruly, and to keep His professed subjects in order, to be exercised by officers of His own appointment (Matt 18.17,18; 1 Cor 12.28; 1 Tim 5.17; Heb 13.17). But these are the great eye-sores of the carnal world, who love sinful liberty, and therefore cry out, 'Let us break their bands asunder, and cast away their cords from us' (Psa 2.3). Hence this work is found to be, in a special manner, a striving against the stream of corrupt nature, which, for the most part, puts such a face on the church, as if there were no king in Israel, every one doing that which is right in his own eyes.

Proof 3 : However natural men may be brought to feign submission to the King of saints, yet lusts always retain the throne and dominion in their hearts, and they are serving divers lusts and pleasures (Titus 3.3). None but those in whom Christ is formed, do really put the crown on His head, and receive the kingdom of Christ within them. His crown is 'the crown wherewith his mother crowned him on the day of his espousals.' Who are they, whom the power of grace has not subdued, that will allow Him to set up, and to put down, in their souls, as He will? Nay, as for others, any lord shall sooner get the rule over them, than the Lord of glory: they kindly entertain His enemies, but will never absolutely resign themselves to His government, till conquered in a day of power. Thus you may see that the natural man is an enemy to Jesus Christ in all His offices.

But O how hard it is to convince men in this point! They are very loath to believe. And, in a special manner, the enmity of the heart against Christ in His priestly office seems to be hid from the view of most of the hearers of the gospel. There appears to be a peculiar malignity in corrupt nature against this office of His. It may be observed, that the Socinians, those enemies of our blessed Lord, allow Him to be properly a Prophet and a King, but deny Him to be properly a Priest. And this is agreeable enough to the corruption of our nature: for, under the covenant of works, the Lord was known as a Prophet or Teacher, and also as a King or Ruler, but not at all as a Priest. So man knows nothing of the mystery of Christ, as the way to the Father, till it is revealed to him, and when it is revealed, the will rises up against it, for corrupt nature is opposed to the mystery of Christ, and the great contrivance of salvation, through the crucified Saviour, revealed in the gospel. For clearing of which weighty truth, let these four things be considered:

(1) The soul's falling in with the grand scheme of salvation by Jesus Christ, and setting the matters of salvation on that footing before the Lord, is declared by the Scriptures of truth to be an undoubted mark of a real saint, who is happy here, and shall be happy hereafter (Matt 11.6), 'Blessed is he whosoever shall not be offended in me.' (1 Cor 1.23,24), 'But we preach Christ crucified, unto the Jews a stumbling block, and unto the Greeks foolishness; but unto them which are called, both Jews and Greeks, Christ the power of God, and the wisdom of God.' (Phil 3.3), 'For we are the circumcision which worship God in the Spirit, and rejoice in Christ Jesus, and have no confidence in the flesh.' Now, how could this be, if nature could comply with that grand device?

(2) Corrupt nature is the very reverse of the gospel plan. In the gospel, God proposes Jesus Christ as the great means of re-uniting man to Himself; He has named Him as the Mediator, one

[116]

in whom He is well pleased, and will have none but Him (Matt 17.5); but nature will have none of Him (Psa 81.11). God appointed the place of meeting for the reconciliation, namely, the flesh of Christ. Accordingly, God was in Christ (2 Cor 5.19), as the tabernacle of meeting, to make up the peace with sinners, but natural men, although they should die for ever, will not come to Christ (John 5.40), 'Ye will not come to me that ye might have life.' In the way of the gospel, the sinner must stand before the Lord in an imputed righteousness, but corrupt nature is for an inherent righteousness; and, therefore, so far as natural men follow after righteousness, they follow after 'the law of righteousness' (Rom 9.31,32), and not after 'the Lord our righteousness.' Nature is always for building up itself, and to have some ground for boasting, but the great design of the gospel is to exalt grace, to depress nature, and exclude boasting (Rom 3.27). The sum of our natural religion is, to do good from and for ourselves (John 5.44); the sum of the gospel religion is, to deny ourselves, and to do good from and for Christ (Phil 1.21).

(3) Every thing in nature is against believing in Jesus Christ. What beauty can the blind man discern in a crucified Saviour, for which He is to be desired? How can the will, naturally impotent, yea, and averse to good, make choice of Him? Well may the soul then say to him in the day of the spiritual siege, as the Jebusites said to David in another case, 'Except thou take away the blind and the lame, thou shalt not come in hither' (2 Sam 5.6). The way of nature is to go into one's self for all, according to the fundamental maxim of unsanctified morality, 'That a man should trust in himself;' which, according to the doctrine of faith, is mere foolishness: for so it is determined (Prov 28.26), 'He that trusteth in his own heart is a fool.' Now faith is the soul's going out of itself for all: and this, nature, on the other hand, determines to be foolishness (1 Cor 1.18–23). Wherefore there is need of the working of mighty power to cause sinners to believe (Eph 1.19; Isa 53.1). We see the promises of welcome to sinners, in the gospel-covenant, are ample, large, and free, clogged with no conditions

(Isa 55.1; Rev 22.17). If they cannot believe His bare word, He has given them His oath upon it (Ezek 33.11); and, for their greater assurance, He has appended seals to His sworn covenant, namely, the holy sacraments: so that no more could be demanded of the most faithless person in the world, to make us believe Him, than the Lord hath condescended to give us, to make us believe Himself. This plainly speaks nature to be against believing, and those who flee to Christ for a refuge, to have need of strong consolation (Heb 6.18), to balance their strong doubts, and propensity to unbelief. Further, also, it may be observed, how in the Word sent to a secure, graceless generation, their objections are answered beforehand, and words of grace are heaped one upon another, as you may read (Isa 55.7–9; Joel 2.13). Why? Because the Lord knows, that when these secure sinners are thoroughly awakened, doubts, fears, and carnal reasonings against believing, will be getting into their breasts, as thick as dust in a house, raised by sweeping a dry floor.

(4) Corrupt nature is bent towards the way of the law, or covenant of works; and every natural man, so far as he sets himself to seek after salvation, is engaged in that way; and will not quit it, till beat from it by divine power. Now the way of salvation by works, and that of free grace in Jesus Christ, are inconsistent. (Rom 11.6), 'And if by grace, then is it no more of works; otherwise grace is no more grace. But if it be of works, then is it no more grace; otherwise work is no more work.' (Gal 3.12), 'And the law is not of faith; but the man that doeth them shall live in them.' Wherefore, if the will of man naturally incline to the way of salvation by the law, it lies cross to the gospel plan. And that such is the natural bent of our hearts will appear if these following things be considered:

First, The law was Adam's covenant; and he knew no other, as he was the head and representative of all mankind, that were brought into it with him, and left under it by him, though without strength to perform the condition thereof. Hence, this covenant is interwoven with our nature; and though we have lost our father's

[118]

strength, yet we still incline to the way he was set upon, as our head and representative in that covenant; that is, by doing, to live. This is our natural religion, and the principle which men naturally take for granted (Matt 19.16), 'What good thing shall I do, that I may have eternal life?'

Secondly, Consider the opposition that has always been made in the world against the doctrine of free grace in Jesus Christ by men setting up for the way of works, thereby discovering the natural tendency of the heart. It is manifest, that the great design of the gospel plan is to exalt the free grace of God in Jesus Christ (Rom 4.16), 'Therefore it is of faith, that it might be by grace.' (See Eph 1.6, and chap. 2.7–9). All Gospel truths centre in Christ: so that to learn the truth is to learn Christ (Eph 4.20), and to be truly taught it, is to be taught as 'the truth is in Jesus' (verse 21). All dispensations of grace and favour from heaven, whether to nations or particular persons, have still had something about them proclaiming the freedom of grace, as in the very first separation made by the divine favour, Cain, the elder brother is rejected, and Abel, the younger, accepted. This shines through the whole history of the Bible; but, true as it is, this has been the point principally opposed by corrupt nature. One may well say that, of all errors in religion, since Christ the seed of the woman was preached, this of works, in opposition to free grace in Him, was the first that lived, and, it is likely, will be the last that dies. There have been vast numbers of errors, which have sprung up, one after another, whereof, at length, the world became ashamed and weary, so that they died away. This has continued, from Cain, the first author of this heresy, unto this day, and never wanted some that clave to it, even in the times of greatest light. I do not, without ground, call Cain the author of it; who, when Abel brought a sacrifice of atonement, a bloody offering of the firstlings of his flock (like the publican smiting on his breast, and saying, 'God be merciful to me a sinner'), advanced with his thank-offering of the fruit of the ground (Gen 4.3,4), like the proud Pharisee with his 'God, I thank thee,' &c. For what was the cause of Cain's wrath, and of his murdering Abel? was it not that he was not accepted of God for his work? (Gen 4.4,5). 'And wherefore slew he him? Because his own works were evil and his brother's righteous' (1 John 3.12); that is, done in faith, and accepted, when his were done without faith, and rejected, as the apostle teaches (Heb 11.4). So he wrote his indignation against justification and acceptance with God through faith, in opposition to works, in the blood of his brother, to convey it down to posterity. And, since that time, the unbloody sacrifice has often swimmed in the blood of those that rejected it. The promise made to Abraham, of the seed in which all nations should be blessed, was so overclouded among his posterity in Egypt, that the generality of them saw no need of that way of obtaining the blessing, till God himself confuted their error by a fiery law from Mount Sinai, which 'was added because of transgressions, till the seed should come' (Gal 3.19). I need not insist on telling you, how Moses and the prophets had still much ado, to lead the people off from the conceit of their own righteousness. The ninth chapter of Deuteronomy is entirely spent on that purpose. They were very gross in that point in our Saviour's time. In the time of the apostles, when the doctrine of free grace was most clearly preached, that error lifted up its head in the face of the clearest light; witness the epistles to the Romans and Galatians. And since that time it has not been wanting; Popery being the common sink of former heresies, and the heart and life of that delusion. And, finally, it may be observed, that always as the church declined from her purity otherwise, the doctrine of free grace was obscured proportionably.

Thirdly, Such is the natural propensity of man's heart to the way of the law, in opposition to Christ, that, as the tainted vessel turns the taste of the purest liquor put into it, so the natural man turns the very gospel into law, and transforms the covenant of grace into a covenant of works. The ceremonial law was to the Jews a real gospel. It held blood, death, and translation of guilt before their eyes continually, as the only way of salvation; yet their very table, that is, their altar, with the several ordinances pertaining thereto (Mal 1.12), was a snare unto them (Rom 11.9), while they used it to make up the defects in their obedience to the moral law; and clave to it so, as to reject Him, whom the altar and sacrifices pointed them to, as the substance of all; even as Hagar, whose duty was only to serve, was, by their father, brought into her mistress's bed; not without a mystery in the purpose of God, 'for these are the two covenants' (Gal 4.24). Thus is the doctrine of the Gospel corrupted by papists, and other enemies to the doctrine of free grace. And indeed, however natural men's heads may be set right in this point, as surely as they are out of Christ, their faith, repentance, and obedience, such as they are, are placed by them in the room of Christ and His righteousness; and so trusted to, as if by these they fulfilled a new law.

Fourthly, Great is the difficulty, in Adam's sons, of their parting with the law as a covenant of works. None part with it, in that respect, but those whom the power of the Spirit of grace separates from it. The law is our first husband, and gets every one's virgin love. When Christ comes to the soul, He finds it married to the law, so as it neither can nor will be married to another, till it be obliged to part with the first husband, as the apostle teaches (Rom 7.1–4). Now, that you may see what sort of a parting this is, consider,

First, It is death (Rom 7.4; Gal 2.19). Entreaties will not prevail with the soul here; it says to the first husband, as Ruth to Naomi, 'The Lord do so to me, and more also, if aught but death part thee and me.' And here sinners are true to their word; they die to the law, before they are married to Christ. Death is hard to every body; but what difficulty, do you imagine, must a loving wife, on her deathbed, find in parting with her husband, the husband of her youth, and with the dear children she has brought forth to him? The law is that husband; all the duties performed by the natural man are these children. What a struggle, as for life, will be in the heart before they are parted? I may have occasion to touch upon this afterwards; in the mean time, take the apostle's short but pithy description of it (Rom 10.3), 'For they being ignorant of God's righteousness, and going about to establish their own righteousness, have not submitted themselves to the righteousness of God.' They go about to establish their own righteousness, like an eager disputant in schools, seeking to establish the point in question; or, like a tormentor, extorting a confession from one upon the rack. They go about to establish it, to make it stand. Their righteousness is like a house built on the sand, it cannot stand, but they would have it to stand; it falls, they set it up again, but still it tumbles down on them; yet they cease not to go about to make it stand. But wherefore all this pains about a tottering righteousness? Because, such as it is, it is their own. What sets them against Christ's righteousness? Why, that would make them free grace's debtors for all; and that is what the proud heart can by no means submit to. Here lies the stress of the matter (Psa 10.4), 'The wicked, through the pride of his countenance, will not seek,' (to read it without the supplement); in other terms, it means, 'He cannot dig, and to beg he is ashamed.' Such is the struggle before the soul dies to the law. But what speaks yet more of this woeful disposition of the heart, nature oft-times gets the mastery of the disease: insomuch that the soul, which was like to have died to the law while convictions were sharp and piercing, fatally recovers of the happy and promising sickness, and, what is very natural, cleaves more closely than ever to the law, even as a wife brought back from the gates of death, would cleave to her husband. This is the issue of the exercises of many about their souls' case. They are indeed brought to follow duties more closely, but they are as far from Christ as ever, if not farther.

Secondly, It is a violent death (Rom 7.4), 'Ye are become dead to the law,' being killed, slain, or put to death, as the word bears. The law itself has a great hand in this; the husband gives the wound (Gal 2.19), 'I through the law am dead to the law.' The soul that dies this death is like a loving wife matched with a rigorous husband; she does what she can to please him, yet he is never pleased, but harrasses and beats her till she breaks her heart, and death sets her free: this will afterwards more fully appear. Thus it is made evident, that men's hearts are naturally bent to the way of the law, and lie cross to the Gospel method: and the second article of the charge against you that are unregenerate is verified, namely, that you are enemies to the Son of God.

(3) You are enemies to the Spirit of God. He is the Spirit of holiness: the natural man is unholy, and loves to be so, and therefore resists the Holy Ghost (Acts 7.51). The work of the Spirit is to convince the world of 'sin, and of righteousness, and of judgment' (John 16.8). But O, how do men strive to ward off these convictions, as much as they ward off a blow threatening the loss of a right eye or a right hand! If the Spirit of the Lord dart them in, so that they cannot avoid them, the heart says, in effect, as Ahab to Elijah, whom he both hated and feared, 'Hast thou found me, O mine enemy?' And indeed they treat him as an enemy, doing their utmost to stifle convictions, and to murder these harbingers that come to prepare the Lord's way into the soul. Some fill their hands with business, to put their convictions out of their heads, as Cain, who set about building a city; some put them off with delays and fair promises, as Felix did; some will sport them away in company, and some sleep them away. The Holy Spirit is the Spirit of sanctification; whose work it is to subdue lusts, and burn up corruption. How then can the natural man, whose lusts are to him as his limbs, yea, as his life, fail of being an enemy to Him?

(4) You are enemies to the law of God. Though the natural man desires to be under the law, as a covenant of works, choosing that way of salvation, in opposition to the mystery of Christ; yet as it is a rule of life to him, requiring universal holiness, and forbidding all manner of impurity, he is an enemy to it; 'is not subject to the law of God, neither indeed can be' (Rom 8.7). For, 1. There is no unrenewed man, who is not wedded to some one lust or another, which his heart can by no means part with. Now that he cannot bring up his inclinations to the holy law, he would fain have the law brought down to his inclinations: a plain evid-

ence of the enmity of the heart against it. Therefore, 'to delight in the law of God after the inward man,' is proposed in the Word as a mark of a gracious soul (Rom 7.22; Psa 1.2). It is from this natural enmity of the heart against the law that all the pharisaical glosses upon it have arisen, whereby the commandment, which is in itself exceeding broad, had been made very narrow, to the intent that it might be the more agreeable to the natural disposition of the heart. 2. The law, laid home on the natural conscience in its spirituality, irritates corruption. The nearer it comes, nature rises the higher against it. In that case it is as oil to the fire, which instead of quenching it, makes it flame the more: 'When the commandment came, sin revived,' says the apostle (Rom 7.9). What reason can be assigned for this, but the natural enmity of the heart against the holy law? Unmortified corruption, the more it is opposed, the more it rages. Let us conclude then, that the unregenerate are heart-enemies to God, His Son, His Spirit, and His law; that there is a natural contrariety, opposition, and enmity in the will of man to God Himself, and His holy will.

(5) There is in the will of man contumacy against the Lord. Man's will is naturally wilful in an evil course. He will have his will, though it should ruin him; it is with him, as with the leviathan (Job 41.29), 'Darts are counted as stubble; he laugheth at the shaking of a spear.' The Lord calls to him by His Word; says to him, as Paul to the jailor, when he was about to kill himself, 'Do thyself no harm:' sinner, 'why will you die?' (Ezek 18.31). But they will not hearken; every one turneth to his course, 'as the horse rusheth into the battle' (Jer 8.6). We have a promise of life, in form of a command (Prov 4.4), 'Keep my commandments, and live:' it speaks impenitent sinners to be self-destroyers, wilful self-murderers. They transgress the command of living; as if one's servant should wilfully starve himself to death, or greedily drink a cup of poison, which his master commands him to forbear: even so do they; they will not live, they will die (Prov 8.36), 'All they that hate me love death.' O what a heart is this! It is a stony heart (Ezek 36.26), hard and inflexible as a

stone: mercies melt it not, judgments break it not; yet it will break ere it bow. It is an insensible heart. Though there be upon the sinner a weight of sin, which makes the earth to stagger; although there is a weight of that wrath on him, which makes the devils to tremble; yet he goes lightly under the burden; he feels not the weight any more than a stone would, till the Spirit of the Lord quickens him so far as to feel it.

(6) The unrenewed will is wholly perverse, in reference to man's chief and highest end. The natural man's chief end is not God, but himself. The being of man is merely relative, dependent, borrowed: he has neither being nor goodness originally from himself; but all he has is from his God, as the first cause and spring of all perfection, natural or moral. Dependence is woven into his very nature, so that if God were totally to withdraw from him, he would dwindle into a mere nothing. Seeing then whatever man is, he is of Him, surely in whatever he is, he should be to Him, as the waters which came from the sea do, of course, return thither again. Thus man was created, directly looking to God, as his chief end: but, falling into sin, he fell off from God, and turned into himself; and, like a traitor usurping the throne, he gathers in the rents of the crown to himself. This infers a total apostasy and universal corruption in man; for where the chief and last end is changed, there can be no goodness there. This is the case of all men in their natural state (Psa 14.2,3), 'The Lord looked down – to see if there were any that did – seek God. They are all gone aside' from God; they seek not God, but themselves. Though many fair shreds of morality are to be found amongst them, yet 'there is none that doth good, no, not one;' for though some of them in appearance run well, yet they are still off the way; they never aim at the right mark. They are 'lovers of their own selves' (2 Tim 3.2), 'more than God' (verse 4). Wherefore Jesus Christ, having come into the world to bring men back to God again, came to bring them out of themselves in the first place (Matt 16.24). The godly groan under this woeful disposition of the heart: they acknowledge it, and set themselves against it,

in its subtle and dangerous insinuations. The unregenerate, though most insensible of it, are under the power thereof, and whithersoever they turn themselves, they cannot move beyond the circle of self. They seek themselves, they act for themselves; their natural, civil, and religious actions, from whatever springs they come, all run into, and meet in the dead sea of self.

Most men are so far from making God their chief end, in their natural and civil actions, that in these matters, God is not in all their thoughts. Their eating and drinking, and such like natural actions, are for themselves; their own pleasure or necessity, without any higher end (Zech 7.6), 'Did ye not eat for yourselves?' They have no eye to the glory of God in these things, as they ought to have (1 Cor 10.31). They do not eat and drink to keep up their bodies for the Lord's service; they do them not because God has said, 'Thou shalt not kill;' neither do those drops of sweetness, which God has put into the creature, raise up their souls towards that ocean of delights that is in the Creator; though they be a sign hung out at heaven's door, to tell men of the fulness of goodness that is in God Himself (Acts 14.17). But it is self, and not God, that is sought in them, by natural men. And what are the unrenewed man's civil actions, such as buying, selling, working, &c., but fruit to himself? (Hos 10.1). So marrying, and giving in marriage, are reckoned amongst the sins of the old world (Matt 24.38): for they have no eye to God therein, to please Him; but all they had in view was to please themselves (Gen 6.3). Finally, self is natural men's highest end, in their religious actions. They perform duties for a name (Matt 6.1,2), or some other worldly interest (John 6.26). Or if they be more refined, it is their peace, and at most their salvation from hell and wrath, or their own eternal happiness, that is their chief and highest end (Matt 19.16–22). Their eyes are held, that they see not the glory of God. They seek God indeed, yet not for Himself, but for themselves. They seek Him not at all, but for their own welfare: so their whole life is woven into one web of practical blasphemy, making God the means, and self their end; yea, their chief end.

Thus I have given you a rude draught of man's will, in his natural state, drawn by Scripture, and men's own experience. Call it no more Naomi, but Marah; for bitter it is, and a root of bitterness. Call it no more free-will, but slavish lust; free to evil, but free from good, till regenerating grace loosens the bands of wickedness. Now, since all must be wrong, and nothing can be right, where the understanding and will are so corrupt, I shall briefly despatch what remains, as following of necessity, on the corruption of these prime faculties of the soul.

III: *The Corruption of the Affections*

The *affections* are corrupted. The unrenewed man's affections are wholly disordered and distempered: they are as the unruly horse, that either will not receive, or violently runs away with, the rider. So man's heart naturally is a mother of abominations (Mark 7.21,22), 'For from within, out of the heart of men, proceed evil thoughts, adulteries, fornications, murders, thefts, covetousness,' &c. The natural man's affections are wretchedly misplaced; he is a spiritual monster. His heart is where his feet should be, fixed on the earth; his heels are lifted up against heaven, which his heart should be set on (Acts 9.5). His face is towards hell, his back towards heaven; and therefore God calls to him to turn. He loves what he should hate, and hates what he should love; joys in what he ought to mourn for, and mourns for what he should rejoice in; glories in his shame, and is ashamed of his glory; abhors what he should desire, and desires what he should abhor (Prov 2.13–15). They hit the point indeed, as Caiaphas did in another case, who cried out against the apostles, as men that turned the world upside down (Acts 17.6); for that is the work which the gospel has to do in the world, where sin has put all things so out of order, that heaven lies under, and earth a-top. If the unrenewed man's affections be set on lawful objects, then they are either excessive or defective. Lawful enjoyments of the world have sometimes too little, but mostly too much of them; either they get not their due, or, if they do, it is measure pressed down, and running over. Spiritual things have always too little of them. In a word, they are never right; only evil.

Now, here is a threefold cord against heaven and holiness, not easily to be broken; a blind mind, a perverse will, and disorderly distempered affections. The mind, swelled with self-conceit, says, the man should not stoop; the will, opposite to the will of God, says, he will not; and the corrupt affections, rising against the Lord, in defence of the corrupt will, say, he shall not. Thus the poor creature stands out against God and goodness, till a day of power comes, in which he is made a new creature.

IV: *Corruption of the Conscience*

The *conscience* is corrupt and defiled (Titus 1.15). It is an evil eye, that fills one's conversation with much darkness and confusion, being naturally unable to do its office; and till the Lord, by letting in new light to the soul, awakens the conscience, it remains sleepy and inactive. Conscience can never do its work, but according to the light it has to work by. Wherefore, seeing the natural man cannot spiritually discern spiritual things (1 Cor 2.14), the conscience naturally is quite useless in that point; being cast into such a deep sleep, that nothing but saving illumination from the Lord can set it on work in that matter. The light of the natural conscience in good and evil, sin and duty, is very defective; therefore, though it may check for grosser sins, yet, as to the more subtle workings of sin, it cannot check them, because it discerns them not. Thus, conscience will fly in the face of many, if at any time they be drunk, swear, neglect prayer, or be guilty of any gross sin; who otherwise have a profound peace, though they live in the sin of unbelief, and are strangers to spiritual worship, and the life of faith. Natural light being but faint and languishing in many things which it reaches, conscience, in that case, shoots like a

[128]

stitch in one's side, which quickly goes off: its incitements to duty, and checks for, and struggles against sin, are very remiss, which the natural man easily gets over. But because there is a false light in the dark mind, the natural conscience following the same, will call evil good, and good evil (Isa 5.20). So it is often found like a blind and furious horse, which violently runs down himself, his rider, and all that comes in his way. (John 16.2), 'Whosoever killeth you will think that he doeth God service.' When the natural conscience is awakened by the Spirit of conviction, it will indeed rage and roar, and put the whole man in a dreadful consternation; awfully summon all the powers of the soul to help in a strait; make the stiff heart to tremble, and the knees to bow; set the eyes weeping, the tongue confessing; and oblige the man to cast out the goods into the sea, which he apprehends are likely to sink the ship of the soul, though the heart still goes after them. Yet it is an evil conscience which naturally leads to despair, and will do it effectually, as in Judas' case; unless either lusts prevail over it, to lull it asleep, as in the case of Felix (Acts 24.25), or the blood of Christ prevail over it, sprinkling and purging it from dead works, as in the case of all true converts (Heb 9.14, and 10.22).

v : *Corruption of the Memory*

Even the *memory* bears evident marks of this corruption. What is good and worthy to be remembered, as it makes but slender impression, so that impression easily wears off; the memory, as a leaking vessel, lets it slip (Heb 2.1). As a sieve that is full when in the water, lets all go when it is taken out, so is the memory with respect to spiritual things. But how does it retain what ought to be forgotten? Sinful things so bear in themselves upon it, that though men would fain have got them out of mind, yet they stick there like glue. However forgetful men are in other things, it is hard to forget an injury. So the memory often furnishes new fuel to old lusts; makes men in old age re-act the sins of their youth, while it presents them again to the mind with delight, which thereupon returns to its former lusts. Thus it is like a riddle, that lets through the pure grain, and keeps the refuse. Thus far of the corruption of the soul.

VI: *Corruption of the Body*

The *body* itself also is partaker of this corruption and defilement, so far as it is capable thereof. Wherefore the Scripture calls it sinful flesh (Rom 8.3). We may take this up in two things. 1. The natural temper, or rather distemper of the bodies of Adam's children, as it is an effect of original sin, so it has a natural tendency to sin, incites to sin, leads the soul into snares, yea, is itself a snare to the soul. The body is a furious beast, of such a temper, that if it be not beat down, kept under, and brought into subjection, it will cast the soul into much sin and misery (1 Cor 9.27). There is a vileness in the body (Phil 3.21), which, as to the saints, will never be removed, until it be melted down in the grave, and cast into a new form at the resurrection, to come forth a spiritual body; and will never be carried off from the bodies of those who are not partakers of the resurrection to life. 2. It serves the soul in many sins. Its members are instruments or weapons of unrighteousness, whereby men fight against God (Rom 6.13). The eyes and ears are open doors, by which impure motions and sinful desires enter the soul: the tongue is 'a world of iniquity' (James 3.6), 'an unruly evil, full of deadly poison' (verse 8): by it the impure heart vents a great deal of its filthiness. 'The throat is an open sepulchre (Rom 3.13). The feet run the devil's errands (verse 15). The belly is made a god (Phil 3.19), not only by drunkards and riotous livers, but by every natural man (Zech 7.6). So the body naturally is an agent for the devil, and a magazine of armour against the Lord.

To conclude – man by nature is wholly corrupted: 'From the sole of the foot, even unto the head, there is no soundness in him.' As in a dunghill every part contributes to the corruption of the whole, so the natural man, while in this state, grows still worse and worse; the soul is made worse by the body, and the body by the soul: and every faculty of the soul serves to corrupt another more and more. Thus much for the second general head.

III: I shall show how man's nature comes to be thus corrupted. The heathens perceived that man's nature was corrupted; but how sin had entered, they could not tell. But the Scripture is very plain on that point (Rom 5.12,19), 'By one man sin entered into the world. By one man's disobedience many were made sinners.' Adam's sin corrupted man's nature, and leavened the whole lump of mankind. We putrefied in Adam as our root. The root was poisoned, and so the branches were envenomed: the vine turned into the vine of Sodom, and so the grapes became grapes of gall. Adam, by his sin, became not only guilty, but corrupt; and so transmits guilt and corruption to his posterity (Gen 5.3; Job 14.4). By his sin he stripped himself of his original righteousness, and corrupted himself; we were in him representatively, being represented by him as our moral head in the covenant of works: we were in him seminally, as our natural head; hence we fell in him, and by his disobedience were made sinners, as Levi, in the loins of Abraham, paid tithes (Heb 7.9,10). His first sin is imputed to us; therefore we are justly left under the want of his original righteousness, which being given to him as a common person, he cast off by his sin: and this is necessarily followed, in him and us, by the corruption of the whole nature; righteousness and corruption being two contraries, one of which must needs always be in man, as a subject capable thereof. And Adam, our common father, being corrupt, we are so too; for 'who can bring a clean thing out of an unclean?'

Although it is sufficient to prove the righteousness of this dispensation, that it was from the Lord, who doeth all things well, yet, to silence the murmurings of proud nature, let these few things further be considered. 1. In the covenant wherein Adam represented us, eternal happiness was promised to him and his posterity, upon condition of his, that is, Adam's perfect obedience, as the representative of all mankind: whereas, if there had been no covenant, they could not have pleaded eternal life upon their most perfect obedience, but might have been, after all, reduced to nothing; notwithstanding, by natural justice, they would have been liable to God's eternal wrath, in case of sin. Who in that case would not have consented to that representation? 2. Adam had a power to stand given him, being made upright. He was as capable of standing for himself and all his posterity, as any after him could be for themselves. This trial of mankind in their head would soon have been over, and the crown won for them all, had he stood: whereas, had his posterity been independent of him, and every one left to act for himself, the trial would have been continually carrying on, as men came into the world. 3. He had the strongest natural affection to engage him, being our common father. 4. His own stock was in the ship, his all lay at stake, as well as ours. He had no separate interest from ours; but if he forget ours, he must necessarily forget his own. 5. If he had stood, we should have had the light of his mind, the righteousness of his will, and holiness of his affections, with entire purity, transmitted unto us; we could not have fallen; the crown of glory, by his obedience, would have been for ever secured to him and his. This is evident from the nature of a federal representation, and no reason can be given why, seeing we are lost by Adam's sin, we should not have been saved by his obedience. On the other hand, it is reasonable, that he falling, we should with him bear the loss. 6. Those who quarrel with this dispensation, must renounce their part in Christ; for we are no otherwise made sinners by Adam, than we are made righteous by Christ, from whom we have both imputed and inherent righteousness. We no more made choice of the second Adam for our head and representative in the second covenant, than we did of the first Adam in the first covenant.

Let none wonder that such a horrible change could be brought on by one sin of our first parents; for thereby they turned away from God, as their chief end, which necessarily infers a universal depravation. Their sin was a complication of evils, a total apostasy from God, a violation of the whole law: by it they broke all the ten commands at once. 1. They chose new gods. They made their belly their god, by their sensuality; self their god, by their ambition; yea, and the devil their god, by believing him, and disbelieving their Maker. 2. Though they received, yet they observed not that ordinance of God about the forbidden fruit. They contemned that ordinance so plainly enjoined them, and would needs carve out to themselves how to serve the Lord. 3. They took the name of the Lord their God in vain; despising His attributes, His justice, truth, power, &c. They grossly profaned the sacramental tree, abused His word, by not giving credit to it, abused that creature of His which they should not have touched, and violently misconstrued His providence, as if God, by forbidding them that tree, had been standing in the way of their happiness; therefore He suffered them not to escape his righteous judgment. 4. They remembered not the Sabbath to keep it holy, but put themselves out of a condition to serve God aright on His own day; neither kept they that state of holy rest wherein God had put them. 5. They cast off their relative duties; Eve forgets herself, and acts without the advice of her husband, to the ruin of both; Adam, instead of admonishing her to repent, yields to the temptation, and confirms her in her wickedness. They forgot all duty to their posterity. They honoured not their Father in heaven, and therefore their days were not long in the land which the Lord their God gave them. 6. They ruined themselves, and all their posterity. 7. Gave themselves up to luxury and sensuality. 8. Took away what was not their own, against the express will of the great Owner. 9. They bore false witness, and lied against the Lord, before angels, devils, and one another; in effect giving out that they were hardly dealt by, and that Heaven grudged their happiness. 10. They were discontented with their lot, and coveted an evil covetousness to their house; which ruined both them and theirs. Thus was the image of God on man defaced all at once.

IV: I shall now apply this Doctrine of the Corruption of Nature.

Use 1: For information. Is man's nature wholly corrupted? Then,

1: No wonder that the grave opens its devouring mouth for us, as soon as the womb has cast us forth; and that the cradle is turned into a coffin, to receive the corrupt lump: for we are all, in a spiritual sense, dead-born; yea, and filthy (Psa 14.3), noisome, rank, and stinking as a corrupt thing, as the word imports. Then let us not complain of the miseries we are exposed to at our entrance into, nor of the continuance of them while we are in the world. Here is the venom that has poisoned all the springs of earthly enjoyments we have to drink of. It is the corruption of man's nature that brings forth all the miseries of human life, in churches, states, and families, and in men's souls and bodies.

2: Behold here, as in a glass, the spring of all the wickedness, profanity, and formality, which is in the world; the source of all the disorders in thy own heart and life. Every thing acts like itself, agreeable to its own nature; and so corrupt man acts corruptly. You need not wonder at the sinfulness of your own heart and life, nor at the sinfulness and perverseness of others; if a man be crooked, he cannot but halt; and if the clock be set wrong, how can it point the hour aright?

3: See here, why sin is so pleasant, and religion such a burden to carnal spirits: sin is natural, holiness not so. Oxen cannot feed in the sea, nor fishes in the fruitful fields. A swine brought into a palace would soon get away again, to wallow in the mire; and corrupt nature tends ever to impurity.

4: Learn from this the nature and necessity of regeneration. *First*, This discovers the nature of regeneration, in these two things: 1. It is not a partial, but a total change, though imperfect in this life. Your whole nature is corrupted; therefore the cure must go through every part. Regeneration makes not only a new head, for knowledge, but a new heart, and new affections, for holiness – 'All things become new' (2 Cor. 5.17). If a man, having received many wounds, should be cured of them all, save one only, he might bleed to death by that one as well as by a thou-

[134]

sand: so, if the change go not through the whole man, it is naught. 2. It is not a change made by human industry, but by the mighty power of the Spirit of God. A man must be born of the Spirit (John 3.5). Accidental diseases may be cured by men; but those which are natural, not without a miracle (John 9.32). The change wrought upon men by good education, or forced upon them by a natural conscience, though it may pass among men for a saving change, yet it is not so; for our nature is corrupt, and none but the God of nature can change it. Though a gardener, by ingrafting a pear branch into an apple tree, may make the apple tree bear pears, yet the art of man cannot change the nature of the apple tree: so a man may fix a new life to his old heart, but he can never change the heart. *Secondly*, This also shews the necessity of regeneration. It is absolutely necessary, in order to salvation (John 3.3), 'Except a man be born again, he cannot see the kingdom of God.' No unclean thing can enter the New Jerusalem; but you are wholly unclean, while in your natural state. If every member of your body were disjointed, each joint must be loosened before the members can be set right again. This is the case of your soul, as you have heard: therefore you must be born again; otherwise you shall never see heaven, unless it be afar off, as the rich man in hell did. Deceive not yourself: no mercy of God, no blood of Christ, will bring you to heaven in your unregenerate state: for God will never open a fountain of mercy to wash away His own holiness and truth; nor did Christ shed His precious blood, to blot out the truths of God, or to overturn God's measures about the salvation of sinners. Heaven! What would you do there, you who are not born again? you who are no ways fitted for Christ the Head? That would be a strange sight! a holy Head, and members wholly corrupt! a Head full of treasures of grace, and members wherein are nothing but treasures of wickedness! a Head obedient to the death, and heels kicking against heaven! You are no better adapted for the society above, than beasts are for converse with men. You are a hater of true holiness; and at the first sight of a saint there, would cry out – 'Hast thou found me, O mine enemy!' Nay, the un-renewed man, if it were possible he could go to heaven in that state, would go to it no otherwise than now he comes to the duties of holiness; that is, leaving his heart behind him.

Use 11: For lamentation. Well may we lament your case, O natural man! for it is the saddest case one can be in out of hell. It is time to lament for you; for you are dead already, dead while you live: you carry about with you a dead soul in a living body; and because you are dead you cannot lament your own case. You are loathsome in the sight of God; for you are altogether corrupt; you have no good in you. Your soul is a mass of darkness, rebellion, and vileness, before the Lord. You think, perhaps, that you have a good heart to God, good inclinations, and good de-sires: but God knows there is nothing good in you: 'Every imagination of thine heart is only evil continually.' You can do no good; you can do nothing but sin. For,

1: You are the servant of sin (Rom 6.17), and therefore free from righteousness (verse 20). Whatever righteousness be, poor soul, you are free from it; you do not, you cannot meddle with it. You are under the dominion of sin, a dominion where righte-ousness can have no place. You are a child and servant of the devil, seeing you are yet in a state of nature (John 8.44), 'Ye are of your father the devil.' And, to prevent any mistake, consider, that sin and Satan have two sort of servants: 1. There are some employed, as it were, in coarser work; those bear the devil's mark on their foreheads, having no form of godliness; but are profane, grossly ignorant, mere moralists, not so much as performing the external duties of religion, but living in the view of the world as sons of the earth, only attending to earthly things (Phil 3.19). 2. There are some employed in a more refined sort of service to sin, who carry the devil's mark in their right hand; which they can and do hide from the eyes of the world. These are close hypo-crites, who sacrifice as much to the corrupt mind, as the others to the flesh (Eph 2.3). These are ruined by a more secret trade of sin; pride, unbelief, self-seeking, and the like, swarm in, and prey

[136]

upon their corrupted, wholly corrupted souls. Both are servants of the same house; the latter as far as the former from righteousness.

2: How is it possible that you should be able to do any good, you whose nature is wholly corrupt? – Can fruit grow where there is no root? or, Can there be an effect without a cause? 'Can the fig-tree bear olive berries? either a vine, figs?' If your nature be wholly corrupt, as indeed it is, all you do is certainly so too; for no effect can exceed the virtue of its cause. 'Can a corrupt tree bring forth good fruit?' (Matt 7.18).

Ah! what a miserable spectacle is he that can do nothing but sin! You are the man, whoever you are, that are yet in your natural state. Hear, O sinner, what is your case.

(1) Innumerable sins compass you about: mountains of guilt are lying upon you; floods of impurities overwhelm you, living lusts of all sorts roll up and down in the dead sea of your soul, where no good can breathe, because of the corruption there. Your lips are unclean; the opening of your mouth is as the opening of an unripe grave, full of stench and rottenness (Rom 3.13), 'Their throat is an open sepulchre.' Your natural actions are sin; for 'when ye did eat, and when ye did drink, did not ye eat for yourselves and drink for yourselves?' (Zech 7.6). Your civil actions are sin (Prov 21.4), 'The ploughing of the wicked is sin.' Your religious actions are sin (Prov 15.8), 'The sacrifice of the wicked is an abomination to the Lord.' The thoughts and imaginations of your heart are only evil continually. A deed may be soon done, a word soon spoken, a thought swiftly pass through the heart; but each of these is an item in your accounts. O sad reckoning! so many thoughts, words, and actions, so many sins. The longer you live, your accounts swell the more. Should a tear be dropt for every sin, your head must be waters, and your eyes a fountain of tears; for nothing but sin comes from you. Your heart frames nothing but evil imaginations: there is nothing in your life but what is framed by your heart; and, therefore, there is nothing in your heart or life but evil.

(2) All your religion, if you have any, is lost labour, as to acceptance with God, or any saving effect on yourself. Are you yet in your natural state? Truly, then, your duties are sins, as was just now hinted. Would not the best wine be loathsome in a vessel wherein there is no pleasure? So is the religion of an unregenerate man. Under the law, the garment which the flesh of the sacrifice was carried in, though it touched other things, did not make them holy: but he that was unclean who touched any thing, whether common or sacred, made it unclean. Even so your duties cannot make your corrupt soul holy, though they in themselves be good; but your corrupt heart defiles them, and makes them unclean (Hag 2.12–14). You were wont to divide your works into two sorts; some good, some evil: but you must count again, and put them all under one head: for God writes on them all 'only evil.' This is lamentable: it will be no wonder to see those beg in harvest, who fold their hands, and sleep in seed-time; but to be labouring with others in the spring, and yet have nothing to reap when the harvest comes, is a very sad case, and will be the case of all professors living and dying in their natural state.

(3) You cannot help yourself. What can you do, to take away your sin, who are wholly corrupt? Nothing, truly but sin. If a natural man begin to relent, drop a tear for his sin, and reform, presently the corrupt heart takes merit to itself; he has done much himself, he thinks, and God cannot but do more for him on that account. In the mean time, he does nothing but sin: so that the fitness of the merit is, that the leper be put out of the camp, the dead soul buried out of sight, and the corrupt lump cast into the pit. How can you think to recover yourself by any thing which you can do? Will mud and filth wash out filthiness? and will you purge out sin by sinning? 'Who can bring a clean thing out of an unclean? not one' (Job 14.4). This is the case of your corrupt soul; not to be recovered but by Jesus Christ. 'O Israel, thou hast destroyed thyself, but in me is thine help' (Hos 13.9). You are poor indeed, extremely 'miserable and poor' (Rev 3.17). You have no shelter, but a refuge of lies; no garment for your soul, but filthy

rags; nothing to nourish it, but husks that cannot satisfy. And more than this, you got such a bruise in the loins of Adam, as is not yet cured, so that you are without strength, as well as ungodly (Rom 5.6); unable to do, or work for yourself; nay, more than all this, you cannot so much as seek aright, but are lying helpless, as an infant exposed in the open field (Ezek 16.5).

Use III: I exhort you to believe this sad truth. Alas! it is evident that it is very little believed in the world. Few are concerned to get their corrupt conversation changed; but fewer, by far, to get their nature changed. Most men know not what they are, nor what spirits they are of; they are as the eye, which, seeing many things, never sees itself. But until you know every one the plague of his own heart, there is no hope of your recovery. Why will you not believe it? You have plain Scripture testimony for it; but you are loath to entertain such an ill opinion of yourselves. Alas! This is the nature of your disease (Rev. 3.17), 'Thou knowest not that thou art wretched, and miserable, and poor, and blind, and naked.' Lord, open their eyes to see it, before they die of it, and in hell lift up their eyes, and see what they will not see now.

I shall close this weighty point, of the corruption of man's nature, with a few words as to another doctrine from the text.

DOCTRINE: *God takes special notice of our natural corruption*

This He testifies two ways: 1. By His Word, as in the text – 'God saw that every imagination of the thoughts of man's heart was only evil continually' (see Psa 14.2,3). 2. By His works. God marks His particular notice of it, and displeasure with it, as in many of His works, so especially in these two.

1: In the death of the infant children of men. Many miseries they have been exposed to: they were drowned in the deluge, consumed in Sodom by fire and brimstone; they have been slain with the sword, dashed against the stones, and are still dying ordinary deaths. What is the true cause of this? On what ground does a holy God thus pursue them? Is it the sin of their parents? That may be the occasion of the Lord's raising the process against them; but it must be their own sin that is the ground of the sentence passing on them: for 'the soul that sinneth, it shall die,' saith God (Ezek 18.4). Is it their own actual sin? They have none. But as men do with serpents, which they kill at first sight, before they have done any hurt, because of their venomous nature, so it is in this case.

2 : In the birth of the elect children of God. When the Lord is about to change their nature, He makes the sin of their nature lie heavy on their spirits. When He means to let out their corruption, the lance goes deep into their souls, reaching to the root of sin (Rom 7.7–9). The flesh, or corruption of nature, is pierced, being crucified, as well as the affections and lusts (Gal 5.24).

Use: Let us then have a special eye upon the corruption and sin of our nature. God sees it: O that we saw it too, and that sin were ever before us! What avails it to notice other sins, while this mother-sin is not noticed? Turn your eyes inward to the sin of your nature. It is to be feared, that many have this work to begin yet; that they have shut the door, while the grand thief is yet in the house undiscovered. This is a weighty point; and in handling of it, I shall notice these four heads:

Men overlooking their Natural Sin

1 : I shall, for conviction, point at some evidences of men's overlooking the sin of their nature, which yet the Lord takes particular notice of. 1. Men's looking on themselves with such confidence, as if they were in no hazard of gross sins. Many would take it very unkindly to get such a caution as Christ gave his apostles (Luke 21.34), 'Take heed of surfeiting and drunkenness.' If any should suppose them to break out in gross abominations, each would be ready to say, 'Am I a dog?' It would raise the pride of their hearts, but not their fear and trembling, because they know not the corruption of their nature. 2. Want of tender-

ness towards those that fall. Many, in that case, cast off all feelings of Christian compassion, for they do not consider themselves, lest they also be tempted (Gal 6.1). Men's passions are often highest against the faults of others, when sin sleeps soundly in their own breasts. David, when he was at his worst, was most violent against the faults of others. While his conscience was asleep under his own guilt in the matter of Uriah, the Spirit of the Lord takes notice that his anger was greatly kindled against the man in the parable (2 Sam 12.5). And, on good grounds, it is thought it was at the same time that he treated the Ammonites so cruelly, as is related (verse 31), 'Putting them under saws, and under harrows of iron, and under axes of iron, and making them pass through the brick-kiln.' Grace makes men zealous against sin in others, as well as in themselves: but eyes turned inward to the corruption of nature clothe them with pity and compassion; and fill them with thankfulness to the Lord, that they themselves were not the persons left to be such spectacles of human frailty. 3. There are not a few, who, if they be kept from afflictions in worldly things, and from gross outbreakings in their conversation, know not what it is to have a sad heart. If they meet with a cross, which their proud hearts cannot stoop to bear, they are ready to say, O to be gone! but the corruption of their nature never makes them long for heaven. Lusts, scandalously breaking out at a time, will mar their peace, but the sin of their nature never makes them a heavy heart. 4. Delaying of repentance, in hopes to set about it afterwards. Many have their own appointed time for repentance and reformation, as if they were such complete masters over their lusts, that they can allow them to gather more strength, and yet overcome them. They take up resolutions to amend, without an eye to Jesus Christ, union with Him, and strength from him; a plain evidence that they are strangers to themselves; so they are left to themselves, and their flourishing resolutions wither; for, as they see not the necessity, so they get not the benefit, of the dew from heaven to water them. 5. Men's venturing freely on temptations, and promising liberally in their own strength. They cast themselves fearlessly into temptation, in confidence of their coming off fairly: but, were they sensible of the corruption of their nature, they would be cautious of entering on the devil's ground, as one girt about with bags of gunpowder would be unwilling to walk where sparks of fire are flying, lest he should be blown up. Self-jealousy well becomes Christians. 'Lord, is it I?' They that know the deceit of their bow, will not be very confident that they shall hit the mark. 6. Ignorance of heart-plagues. The knowledge of the plagues of the heart is a rare qualification. There are indeed some of them written in such great characters, that he who runs may read them: but there are others more subtle, which few discern. How few are there, to whom the bias of the heart to unbelief is a burden! Nay, they perceive it not. Many have had sharp convictions of other sins, that were never to this day convinced of their unbelief; though that is the sin especially aimed at in a thorough conviction (John 16.8,9), 'He will reprove the world of sin, because they believe not on Me.' A disposition to establish our own righteousness is a weed that naturally grows in every man's heart; but few labour at the plucking of it up, it lurks undiscovered. The bias of the heart to the way of the covenant of works is a hidden plague of the heart to many. All the difficulty they find is, in getting up their hearts to duties: they find no difficulty in getting their hearts off them, and over them to Jesus Christ. How hard it is to bring men off from their own righteousness! Yea, it is very hard to convince them of their leaning to it at all. 7. Pride and self-conceit. A view of the corruption of nature would be very humbling, and oblige him that has it to reckon himself the chief of sinners. Under the greatest attainments and enlargements, it would be ballast to his heart, and hide pride from his eyes. The want of thorough humiliation, piercing to the sin of one's nature, is the ruin of many professors: for digging deep makes great difference betwixt wise and foolish builders (Luke 6.48,49).

Original Sin to be specially noticed

11: I will lay before you a few things, in which you should have a special eye to original sin. 1. Have a special eye to it, in your application to Jesus Christ. Do you find any need of Christ, which sends you to Him as the Physician of souls? O forget not this disease when you are with the Physician. They never yet knew well their errand to Christ, who went not to Him for the sin of their nature; for His blood to take away the guilt of it, and His Spirit to break the power of it. Though, in the bitterness of your souls, you should lay before Him a catalogue of your sins of omission and commission which might reach from earth to heaven, yet, if original sin were wanting in it, assure yourselves that you have forgot the best part of the errand which a poor sinner has to the Physician of souls. What would it have availed the people of Jericho, to have set before Elisha all the vessels in their city, full of the water that was naught, if they had not led him forth to the spring, to cast in salt there? (2 Kings 2.19–21). The application is easy. 2. Have a special eye to it in your repentance, whether in its beginning or its progress; in your first repentance, and in the renewing of your repentance afterwards. Though a man be sick, there is no fear of death, if the sickness strike not to his heart: and there is as little fear of the death of sin, as long as the sin of our nature is not touched. But if you would repent indeed, let the streams lead you up to the fountain; and mourn over your corrupt nature as the cause of all sin, in heart, lip, and life (Psa 51.4,5), 'Against thee, thee only, have I sinned, and done this evil in thy sight. Behold, I was shapen in iniquity, and in sin did my mother conceive me.' 3. Have a special eye upon it in your mortification (Gal 5.24), 'They that are Christ's have crucified the flesh.' It is the root of bitterness that must be struck at; which the axe of mortification must be laid to, else we labour in vain. In vain do men go about to cleanse the stream, while they are at no pains about the muddy fountain: it is a vain religion to attempt to make the life truly good, while

[143]

the corruption of nature retains its ancient vigour, and the power of it is not broken. 4. You are to eye it in your daily walk. He that would walk aright, must have one eye upward to Jesus Christ, and another inward to the corruption of his own nature. It is not enough that we look about us, we must also look within us. There the wall is weakest; there our greatest enemy lies; and there are grounds for daily watching and mourning.

Why original Sin is to be especially noticed

III : I shall offer some reasons, why we should especially notice the sin of our nature.

1 : Because of all sins, it is the most extensive and diffusive. It goes through the whole man, and spoils all. Other sins mar particular parts of the image of God, but this at once defaces the whole. A disease affecting any particular member of the body is dangerous; but that which affects the whole, is worse. The corruption of nature is the poison of the old serpent cast into the fountain of action, which infects every action, and every breathing of the soul.

2 : It is the cause of all particular lusts, and actual sins, in our hearts and lives. It is the spawn which the great leviathan has left in the souls of men, from whence comes all the fry of actual sins and abominations (Mark 7.21), 'Out of the heart of men proceed evil thoughts, adulteries,' &c. It is the bitter fountain; particular lusts are but rivulets running from it, which bring forth into the life a part only, and not the whole of what is within. The fountain is always above the stream: and where the water is good, it is best in the fountain; where it is bad, it is worst there. The corruption of nature being that which defiles all, it must needs be the most abominable thing.

3 : It is virtually all sin, for it is the seed of all sins, which want but the occasion to set up their heads, being, in the corruption of nature as the effect in the virtue of its cause. Hence it is called 'a body of death' (Rom 7.24), as consisting of the several mem-

[144]

bers belonging to such 'a body of sins' (Col 2.11), whose life lies in spiritual death. It is the cursed ground, fit to bring forth all manner of noxious weeds. As the whole nest of venomous creatures must needs be more dreadful than any few of them that come creeping forth, so the sin of your nature, that mother of abominations, must be worse than any particular lusts that appear stirring in your heart and life. Never did every sin appear, in the conversation of the vilest wretch that ever lived; but look you into your corrupt nature, and there you may see all and every sin, in the seed and root thereof. There is a fulness of all unrighteousness there (Rom 1.29). There is atheism, idolatry, blasphemy, murder, adultery, and whatsoever is vile. Possibly none of these appear to you in your heart; but there is more in that unfathomable depth of wickedness than you know. Your corrupt heart is like an ants' nest, on which, while the stone lies, none of them appear; but take off the stone, and stir them up but with the point of a straw, you will see what a swarm is there, and how lively they be. Just such a sight would your heart afford you, did the Lord but withdraw the restraint He has upon it, and suffer Satan to stir it up by temptation.

4: The sin of our nature is, of all sins, the most fixed and abiding. Sinful actions, though the guilt and stain of them may remain, yet in themselves they pass away. The drunkard is not always at his cups, nor the unclean person always acting lewdness: but the corruption of nature is an abiding sin; it remains with men in its full power, by night and by day; at all times fixed, as with bands of iron and brass, till their nature is changed by converting grace; and it remains even with the godly, until the death of the body, though not in its reigning power. Pride, envy, covetousness, and the like, are not always stirring in you; but the proud, envious, carnal nature, is still with you, even as the clock that is wrong is not always striking wrong, but the wrong set continues with it without intermission.

5: It is the great reigning sin (Rom 6.12), 'Let not sin, therefore, reign in your mortal body, that you should obey it in the lusts thereof.' There are three things which you may observe in the corrupt heart: 1. There is the corrupt nature, the corrupt set of the heart, whereby men are unapt for all good, and fitted for all evil. This the apostle calls here 'sin which reigns.' 2. There are particular lusts, or dispositions of corrupt nature, which the apostle calls 'the lusts thereof;' such as pride, covetousness, &c. 3. There is one among these, which is, like Saul among the people, higher by far than the rest, namely, 'the sin which doth so easily beset us' (Heb 12.1). This we usually call the pre-dominant sin,' because it doth, as it were, reign over other par-ticular lusts, so that other lusts must yield to it. These three are like a river which divides itself into many streams, whereof one is greater than the rest; the corruption of nature is the river head, that has many particular lusts in which it runs, but it chiefly disburdens itself into what is commonly called one's predominant sin. Now all of these being fed by the sin of our nature, it is evi-dent that it is the reigning sin, which never loses its superiority over particular lusts, which live and die with it, and by it. But, as in some rivers, the main stream runs not always in one and the same channel, so particular ruling sins may be changed, as lust in youth may be succeeded by covetousness in old age. Now, what does it avail to reform in other things, while the reigning sin remains in its full power? What though some particular lust be broken? If sin, the sin of our nature, keep the throne, it will set up another in its stead; as when a water-course is stopped in one place, if the fountain is not closed up, it will stream forth another way. Thus some cast off their prodigality, but covetousness comes up in its stead; some cast away their profanity, and the corruption of nature sends not its main stream that way, as before, but it runs in another channel, namely, in that of a legal disposition, self-righteousness, or the like. So that people are ruined, by their not eyeing the sin of their nature.

6: It is an hereditary evil (Psa 51.5), 'In sin did my mother conceive me.' Particular lusts are not so, but in the virtue of their cause. A prodigal father may have a frugal son; but this disease is necessarily propagated in nature, and therefore hardest to cure. Surely, then, the word should be given out against this sin, as against the king of Israel (1 Kings 22.31), 'Fight neither with small nor great, save only with this;' for this sin being broken, all other sins are broken with it; and while it stands entire, there is no victory.

How to get a View of the Corruption of Nature

IV: That you may get a view of the corruption of your nature, I would recommend to you three things: 1. Study to know the spirituality and extent of the law of God, for that is the glass wherein you may see yourselves. 2. Observe your hearts at all times, but especially under temptation. Temptation is a fire that brings up the scum of the vile heart: carefully mark the first risings of corruption. 3. Go to God, through Jesus Christ, for illumination by His Spirit. Lay out your soul before the Lord, as willing to know the vileness of your nature: say unto Him, 'That which I know not, teach thou me.' And be willing to take light in from the Word. Believe, and you shall see. It is by the Word the Spirit teacheth; but without the Spirit's teaching, all other teaching will be to little purpose. Though the gospel were to shine about you like the sun at noon-day, and this great truth were ever so plainly preached, you would never see yourselves aright, until the Spirit of the Lord light His candle within your breast: the fulness and glory of Christ, and the corruption and vileness of our nature, are never rightly learned, but where the Spirit of Christ is the teacher.

To conclude this weighty point, let the consideration of what has been said commend Christ to you all. You that are brought out of your natural state of corruption unto Christ, be humble; still come to Christ, and improve your union with Him, to the further weakening of your natural corruption. Is your nature changed? It is but in part so. If you are cured, remember the cure is not yet perfected, you still go halting. Though it were better with you than it is, the remembrance of what you were by nature should keep you low. You that are yet in your natural state, take this with you: believe the corruption of your nature; and let Christ and His grace be precious in your eyes. O that you would at length be serious about the state of your souls! What do you intend to do? You must die; you must appear before the judgment-seat of God. Will you lie down and sleep another night at ease in this case? Do it not: for, before another day, you may be summoned before God's dreadful tribunal, in the grave-clothes of your corrupt state; and your vile souls be cast into the pit of destruction, as a corrupt lump, to be for ever buried out of God's sight. For I testify unto you all, there is no peace with God, no pardon, no heaven, for you, in your natural state: there is but a step between you and eternal destruction from the presence of the Lord. If the brittle thread of your life, which may break with a touch ere you are aware, be broken while you are in this state, you are ruined for ever, without remedy. But come speedily to Jesus Christ: He has cleansed souls as vile as yours; and He will yet 'cleanse the blood that he has not cleansed' (Joel 3.21). Thus far of the sinfulness of man's natural state.

THE MISERY OF MAN'S NATURAL STATE

We were by nature the children of wrath, even as
others.   EPHESIANS 2.3

Having shown you the sinfulness of man's natural state, I come
now to lay before you the misery of it. A *sinful* state cannot but
be a *miserable* state. If sin go before, wrath follows of necessity.
Corruption and destruction are so knit together, that the Holy
Ghost calls destruction, even eternal destruction, 'corruption'
(Gal 6.8). 'He that soweth to his flesh, shall of the flesh reap corruption,' that is, everlasting destruction; as is clear from its being
opposed to life everlasting, in the following clause. The apostle
having shown the Ephesians their real state by nature, namely,
that they were dead in sins and trespasses, altogether corrupt, he
tells them, in the words of the text, their relative state, namely,
that the pit was dug for them, while in that state of corruption.
Being dead in sins, they 'were by nature children of wrath, even
as others.'

In the words we have four things:

1 : The misery of a natural state; it is a state of wrath, as well
as a state of sin. 'We were,' says the apostle, 'children of wrath,'
bound over and liable to the wrath of God; under wrath in some
measure; and, in wrath, bound over to more, even the full
measure of it, in hell, where the floods of it go over the prisoners
for ever. Thus Saul, in his wrath, adjudging David to die (1 Sam
20.31); and David, in his wrath, passing sentence of death against
the man in the parable (2 Sam 12.5), say, each of them, of his
supposed criminal, 'He shall surely die;' or, as the words in the
Hebrew language are, 'He is a son of death.' So the natural man is
'a child of wrath, a son of death.' He is a malefactor, dead in law,
lying in chains of guilt, a criminal, held fast in his fetters till the

[149]

day of execution, which will not fail to come, unless a pardon be obtained from his God, who is his judge and his opponent too. By that means, indeed, children of wrath may become children of the kingdom. The phrase in the text, however common it is in the holy language, is very significant. And as it is evident that the apostle, calling natural men the 'children of disobedience' (verse 2), means more than that they were disobedient children – for such may the Lord's own children be – so, to be the children of wrath, is more than simply to be liable to, or under wrath. Jesus Christ was liable to, and under wrath; but I doubt whether we have any warrant to say He was a child of wrath. The phrase seems to intimate, that men are, whatsoever they are in their natural state, under the wrath of God; that they are wholly under wrath. Wrath is, as it were, woven into their very nature, and mixes itself with the whole of the man, who is, if I may so speak, a very lump of wrath, a child of hell, as the iron in the fire is all fire. For men naturally are children of wrath; come forth, so to speak, out of the womb of wrath; as Jonah's gourd was the 'son of a night,' which we render, 'came up in a night (Jonah 4.10); as if it had come out of the womb of the night, as we read of the 'womb of the morning' (Psa 110.3). Thus sparks of fire are called 'sons of the burning coal' (Job 5.7 marg; Isa 21.10), 'O my threshing, and the corn' or son 'of my floor,' threshed in the floor of wrath, and, as it were, brought forth by it. Thus the natural man is a 'child of wrath;' it 'comes into his bowels like water, and like oil into his bones (Psa 109.18). For, though Judas was the only son of perdition amongst the apostles; yet all men, by nature, are of the same family.

2 : Here is the rise of this misery; men have it by nature. They owe it to their nature, not to their substance or essence, for that neither is nor was sin, and therefore cannot make them children of wrath; though, for sin, it may be under wrath. Not to their nature, as qualified at man's creation by his Maker, but to their nature, as vitiated and corrupted by the fall; to the vicious quality, or corruption of their nature, as before noticed, which is their principle of action, and, ceasing from action, the only principle in

[150]

an unregenerate state. Now, by this nature, men are children of wrath; as, in time of pestilential infection, one draws in death with the disease then raging. Wherefore, seeing from our first being as children of Adam we are corrupt children, shapen in iniquity, conceived in sin, we are also from that moment children of wrath.

3: The universality of this misery. All are by nature children of wrath, 'we,' says the apostle, 'even as others;' Jews as well as Gentiles. Those that are now, by grace, the children of God were, by nature, in no better case than those that are still in their natural state.

4: Here is a glorious and happy change intimated; we *were* children of wrath, but are not so now; grace has brought us out of that state. This the apostle says of himself and other believers. And thus, it well becomes the people of God to be often standing on the shore, and looking back to the Red Sea of the state of wrath which they were once weltering in, even as others.

DOCTRINE: *The state of nature is a state of wrath*

Every one, in a natural unregenerate state, is in a state of wrath. We are born children of wrath, and continue so, until we be born again. Nay, as soon as we are children of Adam, we are children of wrath.

I shall introduce what I am to say on this point, with a few observations as to the universality of this state of wrath, which may serve to prepare the way for the word into your consciences.

Wrath has gone as wide as ever sin went. When angels sinned, the wrath of God broke in upon them like a flood. 'God spared not the angels that sinned, but cast them down to hell' (2 Pet 2.4). It was thereby demonstrated, that no natural excellence in the creature can shield it from the wrath of God, if it once becomes a sinful creature. The finest and nicest piece of the workmanship of heaven, if once the Creator's image upon it be defaced by sin, God can and will dash in pieces in His wrath, unless satisfaction be made to justice, and that image be restored; neither of which the sinner himself can do. Adam sinned; and the whole lump of mankind was leavened, and bound over to the fire of God's wrath. From the text you may learn, 1. That ignorance of this state cannot free men from it. The Gentiles, that knew not God, 'were by nature children of wrath, even as others.' A man's house may be on fire, his wife and children perishing in the flames, while he knows nothing of it; and therefore is not concerned about it. Such is your case, O ye that are ignorant of these things! Wrath is silently sinking into your souls while you are blessing yourselves, saying, 'We shall have peace.' You need not a more certain token that you are children of wrath, than that you never saw yourselves such. You cannot be the children of God, who never yet saw yourselves the children of the devil. You cannot be in the way to heaven, who never saw yourselves by nature in the high road to hell. You are grossly ignorant of your state by nature, and therefore ignorant of God and of Christ, and your need of Him. And though you look on your ignorance as a covert from wrath, yet take it out of the mouth of God Himself, that it will ruin you if it be not removed (Isa 27.11), 'It is a people of no understanding: therefore he that made them will not have mercy on them.' (See also 2 Thess 1.8; Hos 4.6.) 2. No outward privileges can exempt men from this state of wrath, for the Jews, the children of the kingdom, God's peculiar people, were 'children of wrath, even as others.' Though you be church members, partakers of all church privileges; though you be descended of godly parents, of great and honourable families; be what you will, you are by nature heirs of hell, children of wrath. 3. No profession, no attainments in a profession of religion, can exempt men from this state of wrath. Paul was one of the strictest sect of the Jewish religion (Acts 26.5), yet a child of wrath, even as others, till he was converted. The close hypocrite, and the profane, are alike as to their state, however different their conversation be; and they will be alike in their fatal end (Psa 125.5), 'As for such as turn aside unto their crooked ways, the Lord shall lead them forth with the workers of iniquity.' 4. Young ones, who are but setting out in the world, have not that to do to make themselves children of wrath, by following the graceless multitude: they are children of wrath by nature, so it is done already. They were born heirs of hell; and they will indeed make themselves more so, if they do not, while they are young, flee from that wrath to which they are born, by fleeing to Jesus Christ. 5. Whatever men are now by grace, they were even as others by nature. This may be a sad meditation to them that have been at ease from their youth, and have had no changes.

Now these things being premised, I shall, in the first place, show what this state of wrath is; secondly, confirm the doctrine; and, thirdly, apply it.

1: I am to show what the state of wrath is. But who can fully describe the wrath of an angry God? None can do it. Yet so much of it may be discovered, as may serve to convince men of the absolute necessity of fleeing to Jesus Christ, out of that state of wrath. Anger, in men, is a passion and commotion of the spirit for an injury received, with a desire to resent the same. When it comes to a height, and is fixed in one's spirit, it is called wrath. Now there are no passions in God, properly speaking: they are inconsistent with his absolute unchangeableness, and independency. Therefore Paul and Barnabas, to remove the mistake of the Lycaonians, who thought they were gods, tell them, 'they were men of like passions with themselves' (Acts 14.15). Wrath, when it is attributed to God, must not be considered in respect of the affection of wrath, but the effects thereof. Wrath is a fire in the affections of men tormenting the man himself, but there is no perturbation in God. His wrath does not in the least mar that infinite repose and happiness which He has in Himself. It is a most pure and undisturbed act of His will, producing dreadful effects against the sinner. It is little that we know of the infinite God; but, condescending to our weakness, He is pleased to speak of Himself to us after the manner of men. Let us therefore notice man's wrath, but remove every thing in our consideration of the wrath of God, that implies imperfection; and so we may attain to some view of it, however scanty. By this means we are led to consider the wrath of God against the natural man in these three particulars.

1 : There is wrath in the heart of God against him. The Lord approves him not, but is displeased with him. Every natural man lies under the displeasure of God; and that is heavier than mountains of brass. Although he be pleased with himself, and others be pleased with him too, yet God looks down on him displeased.

1. His person is under God's displeasure; 'Thou hatest all workers of iniquity (Psa 5.5). A godly man's sin is displeasing to God, yet his person is still 'accepted in the Beloved' (Eph 1.6). But 'God is angry with the wicked every day' (Psa 7.11). A fire of wrath burns continually against him in the heart of God. They are as dogs and swine, most abominable creatures in the sight of God. Though their natural state be gilded over with a shining profession, yet they are abhorred of God; and are to him as smoke in his nose (Isa 65.5), and lukewarm water, to be spewed out of his mouth (Rev 3.16); whited sepulchres (Matt 23.27); a generation of vipers (Matt 12.34); and a people of his wrath (Isa 10.6). 2. He is displeased with all they do: it is impossible for them to please Him, being unbelievers (Heb 11.6). He hates their persons, and so has no pleasure in, but is displeased with their best works (Isa 66.3), 'he that sacrificeth a lamb, is as if he cut off a dog's neck,' &c. Their duty as done by them, is 'an abomination to the Lord' (Prov 15.8). And as men turn their back on those with whom they are angry, so when the Lord refuses communion with the natural man in his duties, it is a plain indication of His wrath.

2 : There is wrath in the Word of God against him. When wrath is in the heart, it seeks a vent by the lips: so God fights against the natural man with the sword of his mouth (Rev 2.16). The Lord's Word never speaks good of him, but always curses and condemns him. Hence it is, that when he is awakened, the word read or preached often increases his horror. 1. It condemns all

[154]

his actions, together with his corrupt nature. There is nothing he does, but the law declares it to be sin. It is a rule of perfect obedience, from which he always, in all things, declines; and so it rejects every thing he does, as sinful. It pronounces his doom, and denounces God's curse against him (Gal 3.10). 'For as many as are of the works of the law are under the curse: for it is written, Cursed is every one that continueth not in all things which are written in the book of the law to do them.' Be he never so well in the world, it pronounces a woe from heaven against him (Isa 3.11). The Bible is a quiver filled with arrows of wrath against him, ready to be poured in on his soul. God's threatenings in His Word hang over his head as a black cloud, ready to shower down on him every moment. The Word is indeed the saint's security against wrath: but it binds the natural man's sin and wrath together, as a certain pledge of his ruin, if he continue in that state. So the conscience being awakened, and perceiving this tie made by the law, the man is filled with terrors in his soul.

3: There is wrath in the hand of God against the natural man. He is under heavy strokes of wrath already, and is liable to more.

(1) There is wrath on his body. It is a piece of cursed clay, which wrath is sinking into by virtue of the threatening of the first covenant (Gen 2.17), 'In the day that thou eatest thereof, thou shalt surely die.' There is not a disease or pain that affects him, but it comes on him with the sting of God's indignation in it. They are all cords of death, sent before to bind the prisoner.

(2) There is wrath upon his soul. 1. He can have no communion with God; he is 'foolish, and shall not stand in God's sight' (Psa 5.5). When Adam sinned, God turned him out of paradise: and natural men are, as Adam left them, banished from the gracious presence of the Lord and can have no access to Him in that state. There is war between heaven and them; and so all commerce is cut off. 'They are without God in the world' (Eph 2.12). The sun is gone down on them, and there is not the least glimpse of favour towards them from heaven. 2. Hence the soul is left to pine away in its iniquity: the natural darkness of their

minds, the averseness to good in their wills, the disorder of their affections, and distemper of their consciences, and all their natural plagues, are left upon them in a penal way; and, being so left increase daily. God casts a portion of this world's goods to them, more or less, as a bone is thrown to a dog: but alas! His wrath against them appears, in that they get no grace. The Physician of souls comes by them, and goes by them, and cures others on each side of them, while they are consuming away in their iniquity, and ripening daily for utter destruction. 3. They lie open to fearful additional plagues on their souls, even in this life. Sometimes they meet with deadening strokes, silent blows from the hand of an angry God; arrows of wrath, that enter into their souls without noise (Isa 6.10), 'Make the heart of this people fat, and make their ears heavy, and shut their eyes, lest they see with their eyes,' &c. God strives with them for a while, and convictions enter their consciences; but they rebel against the light and by a secret judgment, they receive a blow on the head, so that, from that time, they do as it were live and rot above ground. Their hearts are deadened, their affections withered, their consciences stupified, and their whole souls blasted; 'cast forth as a branch, and withered' (John 15.6). They are plagued with judicial blindness. They shut their eyes against the light, and they are given over to the devil, the god of this world, to be blinded more (2 Cor 4.4). Yea, 'God sends them strong delusion, that they should believe a lie (2 Thess 2.11). Even conscience, like a false light on the shore, leads them upon rocks by which they are broken in pieces. They harden themselves against God, and He leaves them to Satan and their own hearts, whereby they are hardened more and more. They are often 'given up unto vile affections' (Rom 1.26). The reins are laid on their necks, and they are left to run into all excess, as their furious lusts drive them. Sometimes they meet with sharp fiery strokes, whereby their souls become like mount Sinai, where nothing is seen but fire and smoke; nothing heard but the thunder of God's wrath, and the voice of the trumpet of a broken law, waxing louder and louder: which makes

[156]

them, like Pashur (Jer 20.4), 'a terror to themselves.' God takes the filthy garments of their sins, which they were wont to sleep in securely, overlays them with brimstone, and sets them on fire about their ears. So they have a hell within them.

(3) There is wrath on the natural man's enjoyments. Whatever be wanting in his house, there is one thing that is never wanting there (Prov 3.33), 'The curse of the Lord is in the house of the wicked.' Wrath is on all that he has, on the bread that he eats, the liquor he drinks, the clothes which he wears. 'His basket and store are cursed' (Deut 28.17). Some things fall wrong with him, and that comes to pass by virtue of this wrath; other things go according to his wish, and there is wrath in that too, for it is a snare to his soul (Prov 1.32). 'The prosperity of fools shall destroy them.' This wrath turns his blessings into curses (Mal 2.2), 'I will curse your blessings; yea, I have cursed them already.' The holy law is 'a killing letter to him' (2 Cor 3.6), the ministry of the gospel 'a savour of death unto death' (chap 2.16). In the sacrament of the Lord's Supper, 'he eateth and drinketh damnation to himself' (1 Cor 11.29). Nay, more than all that, Christ Himself is to him a stone of stumbling, and a rock of offence' (1 Pet 2.8). Thus wrath follows the natural man, as his shadow does his body.

(4) He is under the power of Satan (Acts 26.18). The devil has overcome him, so he is his by conquest, his lawful captive (Isa 49.24). The natural man is condemned already (John 3.18), and therefore under the heavy hand of 'him that hath the power of death, that is, the devil.' He keeps his prisoners in the prison of a natural state, bound hand and foot (Isa 61.1), laden with divers lusts, as chains wherewith he holds them fast. You need not, as many do, call on the devil to take you; for he has a fast hold of you already, as a child of wrath.

(5) The natural man has no security for a moment's safety, from the wrath of God coming on him to the uttermost. The curse of the law, denounced against him, has already tied him to the stake; so that the arrows of justice may pierce his soul, and in him may meet all the miseries and plagues that flow from the

avenging wrath of God. See how he is set as a mark to the arrows of wrath (Psa 7.11–13), 'God is angry with the wicked every day. If he turn not, he will whet his sword; he hath bent his bow, and made it ready; he hath also prepared for him the instruments of death.' Does he lie down to sleep? There is not a promise that he knows of, or can know, to secure him that he shall not be in hell ere he awake. Justice pursues, and cries for vengeance on the sinner; the law casts the fire-balls of its curses continually upon him; wasted and long-tired patience is that which keeps in his life. He walks amidst enemies armed against him. His name may be Magor-missabib, that is, terror round about (Jer 20.3). Angels, devils, men, beasts, stones, heaven and earth, are in readiness, on a word of command from the Lord, to ruin him.

Thus the natural man lives, but he must die too; and death is a dreadful messenger to him. It comes upon him armed with wrath, and puts three sad charges in his hand. 1. Death charges him to bid an eternal farewell to all things in this world; to leave it, and haste away to another world. Ah, what a dreadful charge must this be to a child of wrath! He can have no comfort from heaven, for God is his enemy; as for the things of the world, and the enjoyment of his lusts, which were the only springs of his comfort, these are in a moment dried up to him for ever. He is not ready for another world: he was not thinking of removing so soon: or, if he was, yet he has no portion secured to him in the other world, but that which he was born to, and was increasing all his days, namely, a treasure of wrath. But go he must; his clay god, the world, must be parted with, and what has he more? There was never a glimmering of light, or favour from heaven, to his soul: the wrath which hung in the threatening, as a cloud like a man's hand, is darkening the whole heaven above him: if he 'look unto the earth,' from whence all his light was wont to come, 'behold trouble and darkness, dimness of anguish; and he shall be driven to darkness' (Isa 8.22). 2. Death charges soul and body to part, till the great day. His soul is required of him (Luke 12.20). O what a miserable parting must this be to a child of wrath! Care

[158]

was indeed taken to provide for the body things necessary for this life; but, alas! there is nothing laid up for another life, nothing to be a seed of a glorious resurrection; as it lived, so it must die, and rise again, sinful flesh, fuel for the fire of God's wrath. As for the soul, he was never solicitous to provide for it. It lay in the body, dead to God and all things truly good; and so must be carried out into the pit, in the grave-clothes of its natural state; for now that death comes, the companions in sin must part. 3. Death charges the soul to appear before the tribunal of God, while the body lies to be carried to the grave (Eccl 12.7), 'The spirit shall return unto God who gave it.' (Heb 9.27), 'It is appointed unto men once to die, but after this the judgment.' Well were it for the sinful soul, if it might be buried together with the body. But that cannot be; it must go, and receive its sentence; and shall be shut up in the prison of hell, while the cursed body lies imprisoned in the grave, till the day of the general judgment.

When the end of the world, as appointed of God, is come, the trumpet shall sound, and the dead arise. Then shall the weary earth, at the command of the Judge, cast forth the bodies, the cursed bodies, of those that lived and died in their natural state; 'The sea, death, and hell, shall deliver up their dead' (Rev 20.13). Their miserable bodies and souls shall be reunited, and they summoned before the tribunal of Christ. Then shall they receive that fearful sentence, 'Depart from me, ye cursed, into everlasting fire, prepared for the devil and his angels' (Matt 25.41). Whereupon 'they shall go away into everlasting punishment' (verse 46). They shall be eternally shut up in hell, never to get the least drop of comfort, nor the smallest alleviation of their torment. There they will be punished with the punishment of loss, being excommunicated for ever from the presence of God, his angels, and saints. All means of grace, all hopes of a delivery, will be for ever cut off from their eyes. They shall not have a drop of water to cool their tongues (Luke 16.24,25). They shall be punished with a punishment of sense. They must not only depart from God, but depart into fire, into everlasting fire! There the worm that shall gnaw them shall never die, the fire that shall scorch them shall never be quenched. God will, through eternity, hold them up with the one hand, and pour the full vials of wrath into them with the other.

This is that state of wrath natural men live in, being under much of the wrath of God, and liable to more. But, for a further view of it, let us consider the qualities of this wrath: 1. It is irresistible, there is no standing before it; 'Who may stand in thy sight, when once thou art angry?' (Psa 76.7). Can the worm or the moth defend itself against him that designs to crush it? As little can worm man stand before an angry God? Foolish man indeed practically bids a defiance to Heaven; but the Lord often, even in this world, opens such sluices of wrath upon them, as all their might cannot stop: they are carried away thereby, as with a flood! How much more will it be so in hell! 2. It is insupportable. What a man cannot resist, he will try to endure: but, Who shall dwell in devouring fire? Who shall dwell with everlasting burnings? God's wrath is a weight that will sink men into the lowest hell. It is a burden which no man can stand under. 'A wounded spirit who can bear?' (Prov 18.14). 3. It is unavoidable to such as will go on impenitently in their sinful course. 'He that, being often reproved hardeneth his neck, shall suddenly be destroyed, and that without remedy' (Prov 29.1). We may now flee from it, indeed, by fleeing to Jesus Christ: but such as flee from Christ will never be able to avoid it. Whither can men flee from the avenging God? Where will they find a shelter? The hills will not hear them. The mountains will be deaf to their loudest supplications, when they cry to them to 'hide them from the wrath of the Lamb.' 4. It is powerful and fierce wrath (Psa 90.11), 'Who knoweth the power of thine anger? even according to thy fear, so is thy wrath.' We are apt to fear the wrath of man more than we ought; but no man can apprehend the wrath of God to be more dreadful than it really is: the power of it can never be known to the utmost; for it is infinite, and, properly speaking, has no utmost. How fierce soever it be, either on earth or in hell,

[160]

God can still carry it further. Every thing in God is most perfect in its kind; and therefore no wrath is so fierce as His. O sinner! how will you be able to endure that wrath, which will tear you in pieces (Psa 50.22), and grind you to powder! (Luke 20.18). The history of the two she-bears, that tare the children of Bethel, is an awful one (2 Kings 2.23,24). But the united force of the rage of lions, leopards, and she-bears bereaved of their whelps, is not sufficient to give us even a faint view of the power of the wrath of God (Hos 13.7,8), 'Therefore I will be unto them as a lion; as a leopard by the way will I observe them. I will meet them as a bear that is bereaved of her whelps, and will rend the caul of their heart,' &c. 5. It is penetrating and piercing wrath. It is burning wrath, and fiery indignation. There is no pain more exquisite than that which is caused by fire; and no fire so piercing as the fire of God's indignation, that burns unto the lowest hell (Deut 32.22). The arrows of men's wrath can pierce flesh, blood, and bones, but cannot reach the soul. The wrath of God will sink into the soul, and so pierce a man in the most tender part, like as, when a person is thunderstruck, oft-times there is not a wound to be seen in the skin; yet life is gone, and the bones are melted, as it were: so God's wrath can penetrate into, and melt a man's soul within him, when his earthly comforts stand about him entire and untouched; as in Belshazzar's case (Dan 5.6). 6. It is constant wrath, running parallel with the man's continuance in an unregenerate state, constantly attending him from the womb to the grave. There are few days so dark, but the sun sometimes looks out from under the clouds: but the wrath of God is an abiding cloud on the objects of it (John 3.36), 'The wrath of God abideth on him' that believeth not. 7. It is eternal. O miserable soul! if you flee not from this wrath unto Jesus Christ, though your misery had a beginning, yet it will never have an end. Should devouring death wholly swallow you up, and for ever hold you fast in the grave, it would be kind: but your body must be re-united to your immortal soul, and live again and never die; that you may be ever dying, in the hands of the living

God. Cold death will quench the flame of man's wrath against us, if nothing else do: but God's wrath, when it has come on the sinner for millions of ages, will still be the wrath to come (Matt 3.7; 1 Thess 1.10); as the water of a river is still coming, how much soever of it has passed. While God is, He will pursue the quarrel. 8. However dreadful it is, and though it be eternal, yet it is most just wrath; it is a clear fire, without the least smoke of injustice. The sea of wrath, raging with greatest fury against the sinner, is clear as crystal. The Judge of all the earth can do no wrong: He knows no transports of passion, for they are inconsistent with the perfection of His nature. 'Is God unrighteous who taketh vengeance? (I speak as a man) God forbid: for then, how shall God judge the world?' (Rom 3.5,6).

11: I shall confirm the doctrine of the state of wrath. Consider, 1. How peremptory the threatening of the first covenant is: 'In the day thou eatest thereof thou shalt surely die' (Gen 2.17). Hereby sin and punishment being connected, the veracity of God makes the execution of the threatening certain. Now, all men being by nature under this covenant, the breach of it lays them under the curse. 2. The justice of God requires that a child of sin be a child of wrath; that the law being broken, the sanction thereof should take place. God, as man's Ruler and Judge, cannot but do right (Gen 18.25). Now, it is 'a righteous thing with God to recompense sin' with wrath (2 Thess 1.6). He 'is of purer eyes than to behold evil' (Hab 1.13). And 'He hates all the workers of iniquity' (Psa 5.5). 3. The horrors of a natural conscience prove this. Conscience, in the breasts of men, tells them that they are sinners, and therefore liable to the wrath of God. Let men, at any time soberly commune with themselves, and they will find that they have the witness in themselves, 'knowing the judgment of God, that they which commit such things are worthy of death' (Rom 1.32). 4. The pangs of the new birth, the work of the Spirit on elect souls, in order to their conversion, demonstrate this. Hereby their natural sinfulness and misery, as liable to the wrath of God, are plainly taught them, filling their hearts with

[162]

fear of that wrath. As it is the Spirit's work to 'convince of sin, righteousness, and judgment' (John 16.8), this testimony must needs be true; for the Spirit of truth cannot witness an untruth. But true believers, being freed from the state of wrath, 'receive not the spirit of bondage again to fear, but receive the Spirit of adoption' (Rom 8.15). Therefore, if fears of that nature do arise after the soul's union with Christ, they come from the saint's own spirit, or from a worse. 5. The sufferings of Christ plainly prove this doctrine. Wherefore was the Son of God a son under wrath, but because the children of men were children of wrath? He suffered the wrath of God; not for Himself, but for those who were liable to it in their own persons. Nay, this not only shows us to have been liable to wrath, but also that wrath must have a vent, in the punishment of sin. If this was done in the green tree, what will become of the dry? What a miserable case must a sinner be in, that is out of Christ, that is not vitally united to Christ, and partakes not of His Spirit! God, who spared not His own Son, surely will not spare such a one.

But the unregenerate man, who has no great value for the honour of God, will be apt to rise up against his Judge, and in his own heart condemn His procedure. Nevertheless, the Judge being infinitely just, the sentence must be righteous. Therefore, to stop your mouth, O proud sinner! and to still your clamour against your righteous Judge, consider, 1. You are a sinner by nature; and it is highly reasonable that guilt and wrath be as old as sin. Why should not God begin to vindicate His honour, as soon as vile worms attempt to impair it? Why shall not a serpent bite the thief, as soon as he leaps over the hedge? Why should not the threatening take hold of the sinner, as soon as he casts away the command? The poisonous nature of the serpent affords a man sufficient ground to kill it, as soon as ever he can reach it; and by this time you may be convinced that your nature is a very compound of enmity against God. 2. You have not only enmity against God in your nature, but have revealed it by actual sins, which are, in His eye, acts of hostility. You have brought forth your lusts into the field of battle against your sovereign Lord. And because you are such a criminal, your condemnation is just: for, besides the sin of your nature, you have done that against Heaven, which if you had done against men, your life must have gone for it; and shall not wrath from Heaven overtake you? 1. You are guilty of high treason and rebellion against the King of heaven. The thought and wish of your heart, which He knows as well as the language of your mouth, has been, 'No God' (Psa 14.1). You have rejected His government, blown the trumpet, and set up the standard of rebellion against Him, being one of those that say, 'We will not have this man to reign over us' (Luke 19.14). You have striven against, and quenched His Spirit; practically disowned His laws proclaimed by His messengers; stopped your ears at their voice, and sent them away mourning for your pride. You have conspired with His grand enemy, the devil. Although you are a servant of the King of glory, daily receiving of His favours, and living on His bounty, you are holding a correspondence, and have contracted a friendship, with His greatest enemy, and are acting for him against your Lord; for 'the lusts of the devil you will do' (John 8.44). 2. You are a murderer before the Lord. You have laid the stumbling-block of your iniquity before the blind world, and have ruined the souls of others by your sinful course. Though you do not see now, the time may come when you shall see the blood of your relations, neighbours, acquaintances, and others upon your head (Matt 18.7). 'Woe unto the world because of offences – Woe to that man by whom the offence cometh.' Yea, you are a self-murderer before God (Prov 8.36), 'He that sinneth against me, wrongeth his own soul: all they that hate me love death'. (Ezek 18.31). 'Why will ye die?' The laws of men mark the self-murderer; what wonder is it, that the law of God is so severe against soul-murderers? Is it strange, that they who will needs depart from God now, cost what it will, should be forced to depart from Him at last, into everlasting fire? But, what is yet more criminal, you are guilty of the murder of the Son of God; for the

[164]

Lord will reckon you amongst those that pierced Him (Rev 1.7). You have rejected Him, as the Jews did; and by rejecting Him, you have justified their deed. They indeed did not acknowledge Him to be the Son of God, but you do. What they did against Him, was in His state of humiliation; but you have acted against Him in His state of exaltation. These things will aggravate your condemnation. What wonder then, if the voice of the Lamb change to the roaring of the Lion, against the traitor and murderer!

Objection. But some will say, 'Is there not a vast disproportion between our sin, and that wrath you talk of?' I answer, 'No; God punishes no more than the sinner deserves.' To rectify your mistake in this matter, consider, 1. The vast rewards which God has annexed to obedience. His Word is no more full of fiery wrath against sin, than it is of gracious rewards to the obedience it requires. If heaven be in the promises, it is altogether equal that hell be in the threatenings. If death were not in the balance with life, eternal misery with eternal happiness, where would be the proportion? Moreover, sin deserves the misery, but our best works do not deserve the happiness: yet both are set before us; sin and misery, holiness and happiness. What reason is there then to complain? 2. However severe the threatenings be, yet all have enough to do to reach the end of the law. 'Fear him,' says our Lord, 'which, after he hath killed, hath power to cast into hell; yea, I say unto you, Fear him' (Luke 12.5). This bespeaks our dread of divine power and majesty; yet how few fear Him indeed! The Lord knows the hearts of sinners to be exceedingly intent upon fulfilling their lusts; they cleave so fondly to their beloved sins, that a small force does not suffice to draw them away from them. They that travel through deserts, where they are in hazard from wild beasts, have need to carry fire along with them; and they have need of a hard wedge that have knotty timber to cleave: so a holy law must be fenced with dreadful wrath in a world lying in wickedness. But who are they that complain of that wrath as too great, but those to whom it is too little to draw them off from their sinful courses? It was the man who pretended to fear his

[165]

lord, because he was an austere man, that kept his pound laid up in a napkin; and so he was condemned out of his own mouth (Luke 19.20–22). You are that man, even you whose objection I am answering. How can the wrath which you are under, and liable to, be too great when as yet it is not sufficient to awaken you to flee from it? Is it time to relax the penalties of the law, when men are trampling the commands of it under foot? 3. Consider how God dealt with His own Son, whom He spared not (Rom 8.32). The wrath of God seized on His soul and body both, and brought Him into the dust of death. That His sufferings were not eternal, flowed from the quality of the Sufferer, who was infinite; and therefore able to bear at once the whole load of wrath; and, upon that account, His sufferings were infinite in value. But as the sufferings of a mere creature cannot be infinite in value, they must be protracted to an eternity. And why should a rebel subject quarrel with his punishment when punishment is executed on the King's Son? 4. The sinner does against God what he can: 'Behold, thou hast done evil things as thou couldest' (Jer 3.5). That you have not done more, and worse, thanks to Him who restrained you; to the chain by which the wolf was kept in, not to yourself. No wonder that God shows His power on the sinner, who puts forth his power against God, as far as it will reach. The unregenerate man puts no period to his sinful course; and would put no bounds to it neither, if he were not restrained by divine power, for wise ends: therefore it is just that he be for ever under wrath. 5. It is infinite majesty which sin strikes against; and so it is, in some sort, an infinite evil. Sin rises in its demerit, according to the quality of the party offended. If a man wound his neighbour, his goods must go for it; but if he wound his prince, his life must go for that. The infinity of God makes infinite wrath the just demerit of sin. God is infinitely displeased with sin; and when He acts, He must act like Himself, and show His displeasure by proportionable means. 6. Those who shall lie for ever under this wrath will be eternally sinning, and therefore must eternally suffer; not only in respect of divine judicial procedure, but because sin is its own punishment, in the same manner as holy obedience is its own reward.

III: I now proceed to apply this doctrine of the misery of man's natural state.

Use 1: Of information. Is our state by nature a state of wrath? Then,

1: Surely we are not born innocent. Those chains of wrath, which by nature are upon us, show us to be born criminals. The swaddling-bands, wherewith infants are bound hand and foot as soon as they are born, may put us in mind of the cords of wrath, with which they are held prisoners, as children of wrath.

2: What desperate madness is it, for sinners to go on in their sinful course! What is it but to heap coals of fire on your own head! to lay more and more fuel to the fire of wrath! to 'treasure up unto thyself wrath against the day of wrath!' (Rom 2.5). You may perish, 'when His wrath is kindled but a little' (Psa 2.12). Why will you increase it yet more? You are already bound with such cords of death as cannot easily be loosened; what need is there of more? Stand, careless sinner, and consider this.

3: You have no reason to complain, as long as you are out of hell. 'Wherefore doth a living man complain?' (Lam 3.39). If one, who has forfeited his life, be banished from his native country, and exposed to many hardships, he may well bear all patiently, seeing his life is spared. Do you murmur, because you are under pain and sickness? Nay, bless God, you are not there where the worm never dies. Do you grudge, that you are not in so good a condition in the world as some of your neighbours are? Be thankful, rather, that you are not in the case of the damned. Is your substance gone from you? Wonder that the fire of God's wrath has not consumed you. Kiss the rod, O sinner! and acknowledge mercy; for God 'punisheth us less than our iniquities deserve' (Ezra 9.13).

4: Here is a memorandum, both for poor and rich.

(1) The poorest, that go from door to door, and have not one penny left them by their parents, were born to an inheritance.

Their first father Adam left them 'children of wrath:' and, continuing in their natural state, they cannot escape it; for 'this is the portion of a wicked man from God, and the heritage appointed to him by God' (Job 20.29): an heritage that will furnish them with a habitation, who have not where to lay their head; they shall be 'cast into outer darkness' (Matt 25.30), for to them 'is reserved the blackness of darkness for ever' (Jude, verse 13), where their bed shall be sorrow. 'They shall lie down in sorrow (Isa 50.11); their food shall be judgment, for God will 'feed them with judgment' (Ezek 34.16), and their drink shall be the red wine of God's wrath, 'the dregs whereof all the wicked of the earth shall wring out, and drink them' (Psa 75.8). I know that those who are destitute of worldly goods, and withal void of the knowledge and grace of God, who therefore may be called the devil's poor, will be apt to say here, 'We hope God will make us suffer all our misery in this world, and that we shall be happy in the next;' as if their miserable outward condition, in time, would secure their happiness in eternity. A gross and fatal mistake! There is another inheritance which they have, namely, 'Lies, vanity, and things wherein there is no profit' (Jer 16.19). But, 'the hail shall weep away the refuge of lies' (Isa 28.17). Do you think, O sinner, that God, who commands judges on earth 'not to respect the person of the poor in judgment' (Levit 19.15), will pervert judgment for you? Nay, know for certain, that however miserable you are here, you shall be eternally miserable hereafter, if you live and die in your natural state.

(2) Many that have enough in the world, have far more than they know of. You had, it may be, O unregenerate man, an estate, a good portion, a large stock, left you by your father; you have improved it, and the sun of prosperity shines upon you; so that you can say, with Esau (Gen 33.9), 'I have enough.' But know, you have more than all that, an inheritance which you do not think of: you are a child of wrath, an heir of hell. That is an heritage which will abide with you amidst all the changes in the world, as long as you continue in an unregenerate state. When you shall

leave your substance to others, this will go along with you into another world. It is no wonder a slaughter ox is fed to the full, and is not set to work as others are (Job 21.30), 'The wicked is reserved to the day of destruction; they shall be brought forth to the day of wrath.' Well then, 'Rejoice, let thine heart cheer thee, walk in the ways of thine heart, and in the sight of thine eyes.' Live above reproofs and warnings from the Word of God; show yourself a man of a fine spirit by casting off all fear of God; mock at seriousness; live like yourself, 'a child of wrath,' 'an heir of hell': 'But know thou, that for all these things God will bring thee into judgment' (Eccl 11.9). Assure yourself, your 'breaking shall come suddenly at an instant' (Isa 30.13). 'For as the crackling of thorns under a pot, so is the laughter of a fool' (Eccl 7.6). The fair blaze, and the great noise which they make, are quickly gone: so shall your mirth be. Then that wrath, that is now silently sinking into your soul, shall make a fearful hissing.

5: Woe to him, that, like Moab, 'hath been at ease from his youth' (Jer 48.11), and never saw the black cloud of wrath hanging over his head. There are many who 'have no changes, therefore they fear not God' (Psa 55.19). They have lived in a good belief, as they call it, all their days; that is, they never had power to believe an ill report of their soul's state. Many have come by their religion too easily: and as it came lightly to them, so it will go from them, when the trial comes. Do you think men flee from wrath in a morning dream? Or will they flee from the wrath they never saw pursuing them?

6: Think it not strange, if you see one in great distress about his soul's condition, who was wont to be as jovial, and as little concerned for salvation as any of his neighbours. Can a man get a right view of himself as in a state of wrath, and not be pierced with sorrows, terrors, and anxiety? When a weight quite above a man's strength lies upon him, and he is alone, he can neither stir hand nor foot; but when one comes to lift it off him, he will struggle to get from under it. Thunder-claps of wrath from the

Word of God, conveyed to the soul by the Spirit of the Lord, will surely keep a man awake.

7: It is no wonder that wrath comes upon churches and nations, and upon us in this land, and that infants and children yet unborn smart under it. Most of the society are yet children of wrath; few are fleeing from it, or taking the way to prevent it: but people of all ranks are helping it on. The Jews rejected Christ; and their children have been smarting under wrath these eighteen hundred years. God grant that the bad entertainment given to Christ and His Gospel by this generation, be not pursued with wrath on the succeeding one.

Use 2: Of Exhortation. Here, 1. I shall drop a word to those who are yet in an unregenerate state. 2. To those who are brought out of it. 3. To all equally.

1: To you that are yet in an unregenerate state, I would sound the alarm, and warn you to see to yourselves, while there is yet hope. O you children of wrath, take no rest in this dismal state, but flee to Christ, the only refuge; haste and make your escape thither. The state of wrath is too hot a climate for you to live in (Micah 2.10), 'Arise ye, and depart, for this is not your rest.' O sinner, do you know where you are? Do you not see your danger? The curse has entered into your soul: wrath is your covering; the heavens are growing blacker and blacker above your head; the earth is weary of you, the pit is opening her mouth for you, and should the thread of your life be cut this moment, you are thenceforth past all hope for ever. Sirs, if we saw you putting a cup of poison to your mouth, we should flee to you and snatch it out of your hands. If we saw the house on fire about you, while you were fast asleep in it, we would run to you, and drag you out of it. But alas! you are in ten thousand times greater hazard: yet we can do no more than tell you your danger, invite, exhort, and beseech you to look to yourselves, and lament your stupidity and obstinacy, when we cannot prevail with you to take warning. If there were no hope of your recovery, we should be silent, and would not torment you before the time; but though you be lost and undone, there is hope in Israel concerning this thing. Wherefore, I cry unto you, in the name of the Lord, and in the words of the prophet (Zech 9.12). 'Turn ye to the stronghold, ye prisoners of hope.' Flee to Jesus Christ out of this your natural state.

Motive 1: While you are in this state, you must stand or fall according to the law, or covenant of works. If you understood this aright, it would strike through your breasts as a thousand darts. One had better be a slave to the Turks, condemned to the galleys, or under Egyptian bondage, than be under the covenant of works now. All mankind were brought under it in Adam, as we heard before; and you, in your unregenerate state, are still where Adam left you. It is true, there is another covenant brought in: but what is that to you, who are not brought into it? You must needs be under one of the two covenants; either under the law, or under grace. That you are not under grace, the dominion of sin over you manifestly proves: therefore you are under the law (Rom 6.14). Do not think God has laid aside the first covenant (Matt 5.17,18; Gal 3.10). No, He will 'magnify the law, and make it honourable.' It is broken indeed on your part; but it is absurd to think, that therefore your obligation is dissolved. Nay, you must stand and fall by it, till you can produce your discharge from God Himself, who is the party in that covenant; and this you cannot pretend to, seeing you are not in Christ.

Now, to give you a view of your misery, in this respect, consider these following things: 1. Hereby you are bound over to death, in virtue of the threatening of death in the covenant (Gen 2.17). The condition being broken, you fall under the penalty. So it concludes you under wrath. 2. There is no salvation for you under this covenant, but on a condition impossible to be performed by you. The justice of God must be satisfied for the wrong which you have done already. God has written this truth in characters of the blood of His own Son. Yea, and you must perfectly obey the law for the time to come. So says the law (Gal 3.12), 'The man that doeth them shall live in them.' Come then, O sinner! see if you can make a ladder, whereby you may reach the throne of God: stretch forth your arms, and try if you can fly on the wings of the wind, catch hold of the clouds, and pierce through these visible heavens: and then either climb over, or break through, the jasper walls of the city above. These things you may do, as well as be able to reach heaven in your natural state, under this covenant. 3. There is no pardon under this covenant. Pardon is the benefit of another covenant, with which you have nothing to do (Acts 13.39), 'By him, all that believe are justified from all things, from which ye could not be justified by the law of Moses.' As for you, you are in the hands of a merciless creditor, who will take you by the throat, saying, 'Pay what thou owest!', and cast you into prison, there to remain till you have paid the utmost farthing: unless you be so wise as to get a surety in time, who is able to answer for all your debt, and get up your discharge. This Jesus Christ alone can do. You abide under this covenant, and plead mercy; but what is your plea founded on? There is not one promise of mercy or pardon in that covenant. Do you plead mercy for mercy's sake? Justice will step in between it and you, and plead God's covenant threatening, which He cannot deny. 4. There is no place for repentance in this covenant, so as the sinner can be helped by it. For as soon as ever you sin, the law lays its curse on you, which is a dead weight you can by no means throw off; no, not though your 'head were waters, and thine eyes a fountain of tears, to weep day and night' for your sin. That is what the law cannot do, in that it is 'weak through the flesh' (Rom 8.3). You are another profane Esau, that has sold the blessing; and there is no place for repentance, though you seek it carefully with tears, while under this covenant. 5. There is no acceptance of the will for the deed under this covenant, which was not made for good will, but good works. The mistake in this point ruins many. They are not in Christ, but stand under the first covenant; and yet they will plead this privilege. This is just like a man having made a feast for those of his own family, and when they sit down at table, another man's servant, that has run away from his master, presumptuously comes forward and sits down among them: would not the master of the feast give such a stranger that check, 'Friend, how camest thou in hither' and since he is none of his family, command him to be gone quickly. Though a master accept the good-will of his own child for the deed, can a hired servant expect that privilege? 6. You have nothing to do with Christ while under that covenant. By the law of God, a woman cannot be married to two husbands at once: either death or divorce must dissolve the first marriage, ere she can marry another. So we must first be dead to the law, ere we can be married to Christ (Rom 7.4). The law is the first husband; Jesus Christ, who raises the dead, marries the widow, that was heart-broken, and slain by the first husband. But while the soul is in the house with the first husband, it cannot plead a marriage relation to Christ; nor the benefits of a marriage covenant, which is not yet entered into (Gal 5.4), 'Christ is become of no effect to you; whosoever of you are justified by the law, ye are fallen from grace.' Peace, pardon, and such like benefits, are all benefits of the covenant of grace. You must not think to stand off from Christ, and the marriage covenant with him, and yet plead these benefits, any more than one man's wife can plead the benefit of a contract of marriage past between another man and his own wife. 7. See the bill of exclusion, passed in the court of Heaven, against all under the covenant of works (Gal 4.30), 'The son of the bond-woman shall not be heir.' Compare verse 24. Heirs of wrath must not be heirs of glory. Whom the first covenant hath power to exclude from heaven, the second covenant cannot bring into it.

Objection: Then it is impossible for us to be saved. *Answer:* It is so while you are in that state; but if you would be out of that dreadful condition hasten out of that state. If a murderer be under sentence of death, so long as he lives within the kingdom the laws will seek his life; but if he can make his escape, and get over the sea, into the dominions of another prince, our laws cannot reach him there. This is what we would have you to do; flee out of the kingdom of darkness, into the kingdom of God's dear Son; out of the dominion of the law, into the dominion of grace: then all the

THE STATE OF NATURE

curses of the law, or covenant of works, shall never be able to reach you.

Motive 2: O ye children of wrath, your state is wretched, for you have lost God, and that is an unspeakable loss. You are without God in the world (Eph 2.12). Whatever you may call yours, you cannot call God yours. If we look to the earth, perhaps you can tell us, that land, that house, or that herd of cattle, is yours. But let us look upward to heaven; is that God, that grace, that glory, yours? Truly, you have neither part nor lot in this matter. When Nebuchadnezzar talks of cities and kingdoms, O how big does he speak! 'Great Babylon, that I have built – my power – my majesty;' but he tells a poor tale, when he comes to speak of God, saying, 'Your God' (Dan 2.47, and 4.30). Alas, sinner! whatever you have, God is gone from you. O the misery of a godless soul! Have you lost God? Then, 1. The sap and substance of all you have in the world is gone. The godless man, have what he will, is one that hath not (Matt 25.29). I defy the unregenerate man to attain to soul satisfaction, whatever he possesses, since God is not his God. All his days he eats in darkness: in every condition there is a secret dissatisfaction haunts his heart, like a ghost: the soul wants something though perhaps it knows not what; and so it will be always, till the soul return to God, the fountain of satisfaction. 2. You can do nothing to purpose for yourself; for God is gone, His soul is departed from you (Jer 6.8), like a leg out of joint hanging by, whereof a man has no use, as the word there used signifies. Losing God, you have lost the fountain of good; and so all grace, all goodness, all the saving influences of His Spirit. What can you do then? What fruit can you bring forth, more than a branch cut off from the stock? (John 15.5). You are become unprofitable (Rom 3.12), as a filthy rotten thing, fit only for the dunghill. 3. Death has come up into your windows, yea, and has settled on your face; for God, in whose favour life is (Psa 30.5), is gone from you, and so the life of your soul is departed. What a loathsome lump is the body when the soul is gone! Far more loathsome is your soul in this case. You are dead while you live.

Do not deny it, seeing your speech is laid, your eyes are closed, and all spiritual motion in you has ceased. Your true friends who see your case, lament, because you are gone into the land of silence. 4. You have not a steady friend amongst all the creatures of God; for now that you have lost the Master's favour, all the family is set against you. Conscience is your enemy: the Word never speaks good of you: God's people loathe you so far as they see what you are (Psa 15.4). The beasts and stones of the field are banded together against you (Job 5.23; Hos 2.18). Your meat, drink, and clothes, grudge being serviceable to the wretch that has lost God and abuses them to His dishonour. The earth groans under you: yea 'the whole creation groaneth, and travaileth in pain together,' because of you, and such as you are (Rom 8.22). Heaven will have nothing to do with you; for 'there shall in no wise enter into it, any thing that defileth' (Rev 21.27). Only 'hell from beneath is moved for thee, to meet thee at thy coming (Isa 14.9). 5. Your hell is begun already. What makes hell, but exclusion from the presence of God? 'Depart from me, ye cursed.' You are gone from God already, with the curse upon you. That which is now your choice, shall be your punishment at length, if you turn not. As a gracious state is a state of glory in the bud; so a graceless state is hell in the bud, which, if it continue, will come at length to perfection.

Motive 3 : Consider the dreadful instances of the wrath of God; and let them serve to awaken you to flee out of this state. Consider 1. How it has fallen on men. Even in this world, many have been set up as monuments of Divine vengeance, that others might fear. Wrath has swept away multitudes, who have fallen together by the hand of an angry God. Consider how the Lord 'spared not the old world – bringing in the flood upon the world of the ungodly. And turning the cities of Sodom and Gomorrah into ashes, condemned them with an overthrow, making them an example unto those that after should live ungodly' (2 Pet 2.5,6). But it is yet more dreadful to think of that weeping, wailing, and gnashing of teeth, amongst those who in hell lift up their eyes, but cannot get a drop of water to cool their tongues. Believe these things and be warned by them, lest destruction come upon you, for a warning to others. 2. Consider how wrath fell upon the fallen angels, whose case is absolutely hopeless. They were the first that ventured to break the hedge of the Divine law; and God set them up for monuments of His wrath against sin. They once 'left their own habitation,' and were never allowed to look in again at the hole of the door; but they are 'reserved in everlasting chains under darkness, unto the judgment of the great day' (Jude verse 6). 3. Behold how an angry God dealt with His own Son, standing in the room of elect sinners (Rom 8.32), 'God spared not His own Son.' Sparing mercy might have been expected, if any at all. If any person could have obtained it, surely His own Son would have got it: but He spared Him not. The Father's delight is made a Man of sorrows: He who is the wisdom of God, becomes sore amazed, ready to faint away in a fit of horror. The weight of this wrath makes Him sweat great drops of blood. By the fierceness of this fire, His heart was like wax melted in the midst of his bowels. Behold, here, how severe God is against sin! The sun was struck blind with this terrible sight, rocks were rent, graves opened; death, as it were, in the excess of astonishment, letting its prisoners slip away. What is a deluge, a shower of fire and brimstone on the people of Sodom, the terrible noise of a dissolving world, the whole fabric of heaven and earth disuniting at once, and angels cast down from heaven into the bottomless pit! What are all these, I say, in comparison with this, God in human nature suffering! groaning! dying upon a cross! Infinite holiness did it, to make sin look like itself, that is, infinitely odious. And will men live at ease, while exposed to this wrath?

Motive 4: Consider what a God He is with whom you have to do, and whose wrath you are liable unto. He is the God of infinite knowledge and wisdom; so that none of your sins, however secret, can be hid from Him. He infallibly finds out all means, whereby wrath may be executed, toward the satisfying of justice. He is of infinite power, and so can do what He will against the sinner. How

[176]

heavy must the strokes of wrath be, which are laid on by an omnipotent hand! Infinite power can make the sinner prisoner, even when he is in his greatest rage against Heaven. It can bring again the several parcels of dust out of the grave, put them together again, re-unite the soul and body, summon them before the tribunal, hurry them away to the pit, and hold them up with the one hand, through eternity, while they are lashed with the other. He is infinitely just, and therefore must punish; it were acting contrary to His nature to suffer the sinner to escape wrath. Hence the executing of this wrath is pleasing to Him: for though the Lord hath no delight in the death of a sinner, as it is the destruction of His own creature, yet He delights in it, as it is the execution of justice. 'Upon the wicked He shall rain snares, fire and brimstone, and an horrible tempest.' Mark the reason; 'For the righteous Lord loveth righteousness (Psa 11.6,7), 'I will cause my fury to rest upon them, and I will be comforted' (Ezek 5.13). 'I also will laugh at your calamity' (Prov 1.26). Finally, He lives for ever, to pursue the quarrel. Let us therefore conclude, 'It is a fearful thing to fall into the hands of the living God.'

Be awakened then, O young sinner! be awakened, O old sinner! who are yet in the state you were born in! Your security is none of God's allowance; it is the sleep of death; rise out of it, ere the pit close its mouth upon you. It is true, you may put on a breastplate of iron, make your brow brass, and your heart as an adamant. Who can help it? But God will break that brazen brow, and make that adamantine heart at last to fly into a thousand pieces. You may, if you will, labour to put these things out of your heads, that you may sleep in fancied safety, though in a state of wrath. You may run away, with the arrows sticking in your consciences, to your labour, to work them away; or to your beds, to sleep them out; or to company, to sport and laugh them away. But convictions, so stifled, will have a fearful resurrection and the day is coming, unless you take warning in time, when the arrows of wrath shall so stick in your soul, as you shall never be able to pluck them out through the ages of eternity.

But if any desire to flee from the wrath to come, and, for that end to know what course to take, I offer them these few advices; and implore and beseech them, as they love their own souls, to fall in with them. 1. Retire to some secret place and there meditate on this your misery. Believe it, and fix your thoughts on it. Let each put the question to himself, How can I live in this state? How can I die in it? How shall I rise again, and stand before the tribunal of God in it? 2. Consider seriously the sin of your nature, heart, and life. A proper sight of wrath flows from a deep sense of sin. They who see themselves exceedingly sinful, will find no great difficulty to perceive themselves to be heirs of wrath. 3. Labour to justify God in this matter. To quarrel with God about it, and to rage like a wild bull in a net, will but fix you the more in it. Humiliation of soul before the Lord is necessary for an escape. God will not sell deliverance, but freely gives it to those who see themselves altogether unworthy of His favour. 4. Turn your eyes, O prisoners of hope, towards the Lord Jesus Christ; and embrace Him, as He offers Himself in the Gospel. 'There is no salvation in any other' (Acts 4.12). God is a consuming fire; you are children of wrath: if the Mediator interpose not between Him and you, you are undone for ever. If you would be safe, come under His shadow: one drop of that wrath cannot fall there, for He 'delivereth us from the wrath to come' (1 Thess 1.10). Accept of Him in this covenant, wherein He offers Himself to you; so you shall, as the captive woman, redeem your life by marrying the Conqueror. His blood will quench that fire of wrath which burns against you: in the white raiment of His righteousness you will be safe; for no storm of wrath can pierce it.

2: I shall drop a few words to the saints.

(1) 'Remember – that at that time,' namely, when you were in your natural state, 'ye were without Christ – having no hope, and without God in the world.' Call to mind the state you were in formerly; and review the misery of it. There are five memorials which I may thence give in to the whole assembly of the saints, who are no more children of wrath, but 'heirs of God, and joint

heirs with Christ,' though as yet in their minority. 1. Remember, that in the day our Lord first took you by the hand, you were in no better condition than others. O! what moved Him to take you when He passed by your neighbours? He found you children of wrath, even as others; but He did not leave you so. He came into the common prison, where you lay in your fetters, even as others: from among the multitude of condemned malefactors, He picked you out, commanded your fetters to be taken off, put a pardon in your hand and brought you into the glorious liberty of the children of God, while He left others in the devil's fetters. 2. Remember there was nothing in you to engage Him to love you, in the day He appeared for your deliverance. You were children of wrath, even as others, fit for hell, and altogether unfit for Heaven; yet the King brought you into the palace, the King's son made love to you, a condemned criminal, and espoused you to Himself, on the day in which you might have been led forth to execution. 'Even so, Father, for so it seemed good in thy sight' (Matt 11.26). 3. Remember, you were fitter to be loathed than loved in that day. Wonder, that when He saw you in your blood, He looked not at you with abhorrence, and passed by. Wonder, that ever such a time could be a time of love (Ezek 16.8). 4. Remember, you are decked with borrowed feathers. It is His comeliness which is upon you (verse 14). It was He that took off your prison garments, and clothed you with robes of righteousness, garments of salvation, garments wherewith you are arrayed as the lilies, which toil not, neither do they spin. He took the chains from off your arms, the rope from about your neck, and put you in such a dress, as you might be fit for the court of heaven, even to eat at the King's table. 5. Remember your faults this day, as Pharaoh's butler, who had forgotten Joseph. Mind how you have forgotten, and how unkindly you have treated Him who remembered you in your low estate. Is this your kindness to your friend? In the day of your deliverance, did you think you could have thus requited Him, your Lord?

(2) Pity the children of wrath, the world that lies in wickedness. Can you be unconcerned for them, you who were once in the same condition? You have got ashore, indeed, but your companions are yet in hazard of perishing; and will not you afford them all possible help for their deliverance? What they are, you formerly were. This may draw pity from you, and engage you to use all means for their recovery. (See Titus 3.1–3.)

(3) Admire that matchless love which brought you out of the state of wrath. Christ's love was active love; He brought your soul from the pit of corruption! It was no easy work to purchase the life of the condemned sinner; but He gave His life for your life. He gave his precious blood to quench the flame of wrath, which otherwise would have consumed you. Men get the best view of the stars from the bottom of a deep pit; from this pit of misery, into which you were cast by the fall of the first Adam, you may get the best view of the Sun of Righteousness, in all His dimensions. He is the second Adam, who took you out of the horrible pit, and out of the miry clay. How broad was that love, which covered such a multitude of sins! Behold the length of it, reaching from everlasting to everlasting (Psa 103.17). The depth of it, going so low as to deliver you from the lowest hell (Psa 86.13). The height of it, raising you up to sit in heavenly places (Eph 2.6).

(4) Be humble, carry low sails, walk softly all your years. Be not proud of your gifts, graces, privileges, or attainments; but remember you were children of wrath, even as others. The peacock walks slowly, and hangs down his starry feathers, while he looks to his black feet. 'Look ye to the hole of the pit whence ye are digged;' and walk humbly, as it becomes free grace's debtors.

(5) Be wholly for your Lord. Every wife is obliged to be dutiful to her husband; but double ties lie upon her who was taken from a prison, or a dunghill. If your Lord has delivered you from wrath, you ought, on that very account, to be wholly His; to act for Him, to suffer for Him, and to do whatever He calls you to. The saints have no reason to complain of their lot in the world,

whatever it be. Well may they bear the cross for Him, by whom the curse was borne away from them. Well may they bear the wrath of men in His cause, who has freed them from the wrath of God; and cheerfully go to a fire for Him, by whom hell-fire is quenched as to them. Soul and body, and all you had in the world, were formerly under wrath: He has removed that wrath, shall not all these be at His service? That your soul is not overwhelmed with the wrath of God, is owing purely to Jesus Christ; and shall it not then be a temple for His Spirit? That your heart is not filled with horror and despair is owing to Him only; to whom then should it be devoted, but to Him alone? That your eyes are not blinded with the smoke of the pit, your hands are not fettered with chains of darkness, your tongue is not broiling in the fire of hell, and your feet are not standing in the lake that burns with fire and brimstone – is owing purely to Jesus Christ! And shall not these eyes be employed for Him, these hands act for Him, this tongue speak for Him, and these feet speedily run His errands? To him who believes that he was a child of wrath, even as others, but is now delivered by the blessed Jesus, nothing will appear too much to do or suffer for his Deliverer, when he has a fair call to it.

3: To conclude with a word to all. Let no man think lightly of sin, which lays the sinner open to the wrath of God. Let not the sin of our nature, which wreathes the yoke of God's wrath so early about our necks, seem a small thing in our eyes. Fear the Lord because of His dreadful wrath. Tremble at the thought of sin, against which God has such fiery indignation. Look on His wrath, and stand in awe, and sin not. Do you think this is to press you to slavish fear? If it were so, one had better be a slave to God with a trembling heart, than a free man to the devil, with a seared conscience and a heart of adamant. But it is not so; you may love Him and thus fear Him too, yea, you ought to do it, though you were saints of the first magnitude. (See Psa 119.120; Matt 10.28; Luke 12.5; Heb 12.28,29.) Although you have passed the gulf of wrath, being in Jesus Christ, yet it is but reasonable that your hearts should shiver when you look back to it. Your sin still deserves wrath, even as the sins of others; and it would be terrible to be in a fiery furnace, although by a miracle we were so protected against it, as that it could not harm us.

3

MAN'S UTTER INABILITY
TO RECOVER HIMSELF

For when we were yet without strength, in due time
Christ died for the ungodly.   ROMANS 5.6

No man can come to me, except the Father which
hath sent me draw him.   JOHN 6.44

We have now had a view of the total corruption of man's nature,
and that load of wrath which lies on him, that gulf of misery into
which he is plunged in his natural state. But there is one part of
his misery that deserves particular consideration; namely, his
utter inability to recover himself, the knowledge of which is necessary for the due humiliation of a sinner. What I design here, is
only to propose a few things, whereby to convince the unregenerate man of this his inability, that he may see an absolute
need of Christ and of the power of His grace.

A man that is fallen into a pit cannot be supposed to help himself out of it, but by one of two ways; either by doing all himself
alone, or taking hold of, and improving, the help offered him by
others. Likewise an unconverted man cannot be supposed to help
himself out of his natural state, but either in the way of the law,
or covenant of works, by doing all himself without Christ; or else
in the way of the Gospel, or covenant of grace, by exerting his
own strength to lay hold upon, and to make use of the help
offered him by a Saviour. But, alas! the unconverted man is dead
in the pit, and cannot help himself either of these ways; not the
first way, for the first text tells us, that when our Lord came to
help us, 'we were without strength,' unable to recover ourselves.
We were ungodly, therefore under a burden of guilt and wrath,
yet 'without strength,' unable to stand under it; and unable to
throw it off, or get from under it: so that all mankind would

have undoubtedly perished, had not 'Christ died for the ungodly,' and brought help to those who could never have recovered themselves. But when Christ comes and offers help to sinners, cannot they take it? Cannot they improve help when it comes to their hands? No, the second text tells, they cannot; 'No man can come unto me,' that is, believe in me (John 6.44), 'except the Father draw him.' This is a drawing which enables them to come, who till then could not come; and therefore could not help themselves by improving the help offered. It is a drawing which is always effectual; for it can be no less than 'hearing and learning of the Father,' which, whoever partakes of, come to Christ (verse 45). Therefore it is not drawing in the way of mere moral suasion, which may be, yea, and always is ineffectual. But it is drawing by mighty power (Eph 1.9), absolutely necessary for those who have no power in themselves to come and take hold of the offered help.

Hearken then, O unregenerate man, and be convinced that as you are in a most miserable state by nature, so you are utterly unable to recover yourself any way. You are ruined; and what way will you go to work to recover yourself? Which of the two ways will you choose? Will you try it alone, or will you make use of help? Will you fall on the way of works, or on the way of the Gospel? I know very well that you will not so much as try the way of the Gospel, till once you have found the recovery impracticable in the way of the law. Therefore, we shall begin where corrupt nature teaches men to begin, namely, at the way of the law of works.

1: Sinner, I would have you believe that your working will never effect it. Work, and do your best; you will never be able to work yourself out of this state of corruption and wrath. You must have Christ, else you will perish eternally. It is only 'Christ in you' that can be the hope of glory. But if you will needs try it, then I must lay before you, from the unalterable Word of the living God, two things which you must do for yourself. If you can do them, it must be yielded that you are able to recover yourself; but if not, then you can do nothing this way for your recovery.

1 : 'If thou wilt enter into life keep the commandments' (Matt 19.17). That is, if you will by doing enter into life, then perfectly keep the ten commandments; for the object of these words is to beat down the pride of the man's heart, and to let him see an absolute need of a Saviour, from the impossibility of keeping the law. The answer is given suitably to the address. Our Lord checks him for his compliment, 'Good Master' (verse 16), telling him, 'There is none good but one, that is God' (verse 17). As if he had said, You think yourself a good man, and me another; but where goodness is spoken of, men and angels may veil their faces before the good God. As to his question, wherein he revealed his legal disposition, Christ does not answer him, saying, 'Believe and thou shalt be saved;' that would not have been so seasonable in the case of one who thought he could do well enough for himself, if he but knew 'what good he should do;' but, suitable to the humour the man was in, He bids him 'keep the commandments;' keep them nicely and accurately, as those that watch malefactors in prison, lest any of them escape, and their life be taken for those which escape. See then, O unregenerate man, what you can do in this matter; for if you will recover yourself in this way, you must perfectly keep the commandments of God.

(1) Your obedience must be perfect, in respect of the principle of it; that is, your soul, the principle of action, must be perfectly pure, and altogether without sin. For the law requires all moral perfection; not only actual, but habitual : and so condemns original sin; impurity of nature, as well as of actions. Now, if you can bring this to pass you will be able to answer that question of Solomon, so as never one of Adam's posterity could yet answer it, 'Who can say, I have made my heart clean?' (Prov 20.9). But if you cannot, the very want of this perfection is sin, and so lays you open to the curse and cuts you off from life. Yea, it makes all your actions, even your best actions, sinful: 'For who can

bring a clean thing out of an unclean?' (Job 14.4). And do you think by sin to help yourself out of sin and misery?

(2) Your obedience must also be perfect in parts. It must be as broad as the whole law of God: if you lack one thing, you are undone; for the law denounces the curse on him that continues not in every thing written therein (Gal 3.10). You must give internal and external obedience to the whole law, keep all the commands in heart and life. If you break any one of them, that will ensure your ruin. A vain thought, or idle word, will still shut you up under the curse.

(3) It must be perfect in respect of degrees, as was the obedience of Adam, while he stood in his innocence. This the law requires, and will accept of no less (Matt 22.37), 'Thou shalt love the Lord thy God with all thy heart, and with all thy soul, and with all thy mind.' If one degree of that love, required by the law, be wanting, if each part of your obedience be not brought up to the greatest height commanded, that want is a breach of the law, and so leaves you still under the curse. A man may bring as many buckets of water to a house that is on fire, as he is able to carry, and yet it may be consumed, and will be so, if he bring not as many as will quench the fire. Even so, although you should do what you are able, in keeping the commandments, if you fail in the least degree of obedience which the law enjoins, you are certainly ruined for ever, unless you take hold of Christ, renouncing all your righteousness as filthy rags. (See Rom 10.5; Gal. 3.10.)

(4) It must be perpetual, as the man Christ's obedience was, who always did the things which pleased the Father, for the tenor of the law is, 'Cursed is he that continueth not in all things written in the law to do them.' Hence, though Adam's obedience was, for a while, absolutely perfect; yet because at length he failed in one point, namely, in eating the forbidden fruit, he fell under the curse of the law. If a man were to live a dutiful subject to his prince till the close of his days, and then conspire against him, he must die for his treason. Even so, though you should, all the

[186]

time of your life, live in perfect obedience to the law of God, and yet at the hour of death only entertain a vain thought, or pronounce an idle word, that idle word, or vain thought, would blot out all your former righteousness, and ruin you; namely, in this way in which you are seeking to recover yourself.

Now, such is the obedience which you must perform, if you would recover yourself in the way of the law. But though you would thus obey, the law stakes you down in the state of wrath, till another demand of it be satisfied.

2: You must pay what you owe. It is undeniable that you are a sinner; and whatever you may be in time to come, justice must be satisfied for your sins already committed. The honour of the law must be maintained, by your suffering the denounced wrath. It may be you have changed your course of life, or are now resolved to do it, and to set about keeping the commands of God: but what have you done, or what will you do, with the old debt? Your obedience to God, though it were perfect, is a debt due to him for the time wherein it is performed, and can no more satisfy for former sins, than a tenant's paying the current year's rent can satisfy the landlord for all arrears. Can the paying of new debts acquit a man from old accounts? Nay, deceive not yourselves; you will find these laid up in store with God, and sealed up among his treasures (Deut 32.34). It remains then, that either you must bear that wrath, to which for your sin you are liable, according to the law; or else you must acknowledge that you cannot bear it, and thereupon have recourse to the Surety, the Lord Jesus Christ. Let me now ask you, Are you able to satisfy the justice of God? Can you pay your own debt? Surely not: for, as He is the infinite God, whom you have offended, the punishment, being suited to the quality of the offence, must be infinite. But your punishment, or sufferings for sin, cannot be infinite in value, for you are a finite creature: therefore, they must be infinite in duration or continuance; that is, they must be eternal. And so all your sufferings in this world are but an earnest of what you must suffer in the world to come.

Now, sinner, if you can answer these demands, you may recover yourself in the way of the law. But are you not conscious of your inability to do any of these things, much more to do them all? yet if you do not all, you do nothing. Turn then to what course of life you will, you are still in a state of wrath. Screw up your obedience to the greatest height you can; suffer what God lays upon you; yea, add, if you will, to the burden, and walk under all without the least impatience: yet all this will not satisfy the demands of the law; therefore you are still a ruined creature. Alas, sinner! what are you doing, while you strive to help yourself, but do not receive, and unite with, Jesus Christ? You are labouring in the fire, wearying yourself for very vanity; labouring to enter into heaven by the door which Adam's sin so bolted, that neither he, nor any of his lost posterity, can ever enter by it. Do you not see the flaming sword of justice, keeping you off from the tree of life? Do you not hear the law denouncing a curse on you for all you are doing, even for your obedience, your prayers, your tears, your reformation of life, and so on; because, being under the law's dominion, your best works are not so good as it requires them to be under the pain of the curse? Believe it, sirs, if you live and die out of Christ, without being actually united to Him as the second Adam, the life-giving Spirit, and without coming under the covert of His atoning blood, though you should do the utmost that any man can do, in keeping the commands of God, you will never see the face of God in peace. If you should, from this moment, bid an eternal farewell to this world's joys, and all the affairs thereof, and henceforth busy yourselves with nothing but the salvation of your souls; if you should go into some wilderness, live upon the grass of the field, and be companions to dragons and owls; if you should retire to some dark cavern of the earth, and weep there for your sins, until you had wept yourselves blind; if you should confess with your tongue, until it cleave to the roof of your mouth; pray, till your knees grow hard as horns; fast, till your body become like a skeleton, and, after all this, give it to be burnt; the word is gone out of the Lord's mouth in righteousness and cannot return, that you shall perish for ever, notwithstanding all this, as not being in Christ (John 14.6), 'No man cometh unto the Father, but by me (Acts 4.12), 'Neither is there salvation in any other.' (Mark 16.16), 'He that believeth not shall be damned.'

Objection: But God is a merciful God, and He knows that we are not able to answer these demands; we hope therefore to be saved, if we do as well as we can, and keep the commands as well as we are able. *Answer* 1: Though you are able to do many things, you are not able to do one thing right: you can do nothing acceptable to God, being out of Christ (John 15.5), 'Without me ye can do nothing.' An unrenewed man, as you are, can do nothing but sin, as we have already proved. Your best actions are sin, and so they increase your debt to justice: how then can it be expected they should lessen it? 2: Though God should offer to save men, upon condition that they did all they could do, in obedience to His commands, yet we have reason to think that those who should attempt it would never be saved: for where is the man that does as well as he can? Who sees not many false steps he has made, which he might have avoided? There are so many things to be done, so many temptations to carry us out of the road of duty, and our nature is so very apt to be set on fire of hell, that we surely must fail, even in some point that is within the compass of our natural abilities. But, 3: Though you should do all you are able to do, in vain do you hope to be saved in that way. What word of God is this hope of yours founded on? It is founded on neither law nor Gospel; therefore it is but a delusion. It is not founded on the Gospel; for the Gospel leads the soul out of itself to Jesus Christ for all; and it establishes the law (Rom 3.31). Whereas this hope of yours cannot be established but on the ruins of the law, which God will magnify and make honourable. Hence it appears, that it is not founded on the law neither. When God set Adam working for happiness to himself and his posterity, perfect obedience was the condition required of him; and the curse was denounced in case of disobedience. The law being broken by him, he and his posterity were subjected to the penalty for sin committed; and withal were still bound to perfect obedience. For it is absurd to think, that man's sinning, and suffering for his sin, should free him from his duty of obedience to his Creator. When Christ came in the room of the elect, to purchase their salvation, the terms were the same. Justice had the elect under arrest: if He is desirous to deliver them, the terms are known. He must satisfy for their sin, by suffering the punishment due to it; He must do what they cannot do, namely, obey the law perfectly, and so fulfil all righteousness. Accordingly, all this He did, and so became 'the end of the law for righteousness, to every one that believeth' (Rom 10.4). And do you think that God will abate these terms as to you, when His own Son got no abatement of them? Expect it not, though you should beg it with tears of blood; for if they prevailed, they must prevail against the truth, justice, and honour of God (Gal 3.10), 'Cursed is every one that continueth not in all things which are written in the book of the law to do them. (Verse 12), 'And the law is not of faith: but the man that doeth them shall live in them.' It is true, that God is merciful: but cannot He be merciful unless He save you in a way that is neither consistent with His law nor His Gospel? Have not His goodness and mercy sufficiently appeared, in sending the Son of His love, to do 'what the law could not do, in that it was weak through the flesh?' He has provided help for those who cannot help themselves: but you, insensible of your own weakness, must needs think to recover yourself by your own works, while you are no more able to do it than to remove mountains of brass out of their place.

Wherefore I conclude, that you are utterly unable to recover yourself, in the way of works, or by the law. O that you would conclude the same concerning yourself!

11: Let us try next what the sinner can do to recover himself, in the way of the Gospel. It may be you think that you cannot do all by yourself alone, yet Jesus Christ offering you help, you can of yourself embrace it, and use it for your recovery. But, O sinner, be convinced of your absolute need of the grace of Christ: for truly, there is help offered, but you cannot accept it: there is a rope cast out to draw shipwrecked sinners to land, but, alas! they have no hands to lay hold of it. They are like infants exposed in the open field, who must starve, though their food be lying by them, unless some one put it in their mouths. To convince natural men of this, let it be considered,

1 : That although Christ is offered in the Gospel, yet they cannot believe in Him. Saving faith is the faith of God's elect, the special gift of God to them, wrought in them by His Spirit. Salvation is offered to them that will believe in Christ, but how can you believe? (John 5.44). It is offered to those that will come to Christ; but 'no man can come unto Him, except the Father draw him.' It is offered to those that will look to Him, as lifted on the pole of the Gospel (Isa 45.22); but the natural man is spiritually blind (Rev 3.17); and as to the things of the Spirit of God, he cannot know them, for they are spiritually discerned (1 Cor 2.14). Nay, whosoever will, he is welcome; let him come (Rev 22.17); but there must be a day of power on the sinner, before he can be willing (Psa 110.3).

2 : Man naturally has nothing wherewithal to improve, for his recovery, the help brought in by the Gospel. He is cast away in a state of wrath, and is bound hand and foot, so that he cannot lay hold of the cords of love thrown out to him in the Gospel. The most cunning artificer cannot work without tools; neither can the most skilful musician play well on an instrument that is out of tune. How can anyone believe, or repent, whose understanding is darkness (Eph 5.8), whose heart is a stony heart, inflexible, insensible (Ezek 36.26), whose affections are wholly disordered and distempered, who is averse to good, and bent to evil? The arms of natural abilities are too short to reach supernatural help; hence those who most excel in them are often most estranged from spiritual things (Matt 11.25), 'Thou hast hid these things from the wise and prudent.'

3: Man cannot work a saving change on himself; but so changed he must be, else he can neither believe nor repent, nor ever see heaven. No action can be without a suitable principle. Believing, repenting, and the like, are the product of the new nature and can never be produced by the old corrupt nature. Now, what can the natural man do in this matter? He must be regenerate, begotten again unto a lively hope; but as the child cannot be active in his own generation, so a man cannot be active but passive only, in his own regeneration. The heart is shut against Christ: man cannot open it, only God can do it by His grace (Acts 16.14). He is dead in sin; he must be quickened, raised out of his grave; who can do this but God Himself? (Eph 2.1-5). Nay, he must be 'created in Christ Jesus, unto good works' (Eph 2.10). These are works of omnipotence, and can be done by no less a power.

4: Man, in his depraved state, is under an utter inability to do any thing truly good, as was proved before at large: how then can he obey the Gospel? His nature is the very reverse of the Gospel: how can he, of himself, fall in with that plan of salvation, and accept the offered remedy? The corruption of man's nature infallibly includes his utter inability to recover himself in any way, and whoso is convinced of the one, must needs admit the other; for they stand and fall together. Were all the purchase of Christ offered to the unregenerate man for one good thought, he cannot command it (2 Cor. 3.5), 'Not that we are sufficient of ourselves, to think any thing as of ourselves.' Were it offered on condition of a good word, yet 'how can ye, being evil, speak good things?' (Matt 12.35). Nay, were it left to yourselves to choose what is easiest, Christ Himself tells you (John 15.5), 'Without me, ye can do nothing.'

5: The natural man cannot but resist the Lord's offering to help him; yet that resistance is infallibly overcome in the elect, by converting grace. Can the stony heart choose but to resist the stroke? There is not only an inability, but an enmity and obstinacy in man's will by nature. God knows, O natural man, whether you know it or not, that 'thou art obstinate, and thy neck is an iron sinew, and thy brow brass' (Isa 48.4), and cannot be overcome, but by Him who hath 'broken the gates of brass, and cut the bars of iron in sunder.' Hence, humanly speaking, there is such hard work in converting a sinner. Sometimes he seems to be caught in the net of the Gospel; yet quickly he slips away again. The hook catches hold of him; but he struggles, till, getting free of it, he goes away with a bleeding wound. When good hopes are conceived of him, by those that travail in birth for the forming of Christ in him, there is oft-times nothing brought forth but wind. The deceitful heart makes many contrivances to avoid a Saviour, and cheat the man of his eternal happiness. Thus the natural man lies sunk in a state of sin and wrath, utterly unable to recover himself.

Objection 1 : If we be under an utter inability to do any good, how can God require us to do it? *Answer:* God making man upright (Eccl 7.29), gave him a power to do everything that He should require of him; this power man lost by his own fault. We were bound to serve God, and do whatever He commanded us, as being His creatures; and also, we were under the superadded tie of a covenant, for that purpose. Now, we having, by our own fault, disabled ourselves, shall God lose His right of requiring our task, because we have thrown away the strength He gave us whereby to perform it? Has the creditor no right to require payment of his money because the debtor had squandered it away, and is not able to pay him? Truly, if God can require no more of us than we are able to do, we need no more to save us from wrath, but to make ourselves unable for every duty, and to incapacitate ourselves for serving God any manner of way, as profane men frequently do. So the deeper a man is plunged in sin, he will be the more secure from wrath, for where God can require no duty of us, we do not sin in omitting it; and where there is no sin, there can be no wrath. As to what may be urged by the unhumbled soul, against the putting our stock in Adam's hand, the righteousness of that dispensation was explained before. But moreover, the unrenewed man is daily throwing away the very remains of natural abilities, that rational light and strength which are to be found amongst the ruins of mankind. Nay, further, he will not believe his own utter inability to help himself; so that out of his own mouth, he must be condemned. Even those who make their natural impotency to good a covert to their sloth, do, with others, delay the work of turning to God from time to time, and, under convictions, make large promises of reformation, which afterwards they never regard, and delay their repentance to a death-bed, as if they could help themselves in a moment; which shows them to be far from a due sense of their natural inability, whatever they pretend.

Now, if God can require of men the duty they are not able to do, He can in justice punish them for their not doing it, notwithstanding their inability. If He has power to exact the debt of obedience, He has also power to cast the insolvent debtor into prison, for his not paying it. Further, though unregenerate men have no gracious abilities, yet they want not natural abilities which nevertheless they will not improve. There are many things they can do, which they do not; they will not do them, and therefore their damnation will be just. Nay, all their inability to do good is voluntary; they will not come to Christ (John 5.40). They will not repent, they will die (Ezek 18.31). So they will be justly condemned, because they will neither turn to God, nor come to Christ, but love their chains better than their liberty, and darkness rather than light (John 3.19).

Objection 2: Why do you then preach Christ to us, call us to come to Him, to believe, repent, and use the means of salvation? *Answer:* Because it is your duty so to do. It is your duty to accept of Christ, as He is offered in the Gospel, to repent of your sins, and to be holy in all manner of conversation; these things are commanded you of God; and His command, not your ability, is the measure of your duty. Moreover, these calls and exhortations are the means that God is pleased to make use of, for converting His elect, and working grace in their hearts: to them, 'faith

[194]

cometh by hearing' (Rom 10.17), while they are as unable to help themselves as the rest of mankind are. Upon very good grounds may we, at the command of God, who raises the dead, go to their graves, and cry in His name, 'Awake, thou that sleepest, and arise from the dead, and Christ shall give thee light' (Eph 5.14). And seeing the elect are not to be known and distinguished from others before conversion, as the sun shines on the blind man's face, and the rain falls on the rocks as well as on the fruitful plains, so we preach Christ to all, and shoot the arrow at a venture, which God Himself directs as He sees fit. Moreover, these calls and exhortations are not altogether in vain, even to those who are not converted by them. Such persons may be convinced, though they be not converted: although they be not sanctified by these means, yet they may be restrained by them from running into that excess of wickedness, which otherwise they would arrive at. The means of grace serve, as it were, to embalm many dead souls, which are never quickened by them; though they do not restore them to life, yet they keep them from putrefying, as otherwise they would do. Finally, though you cannot recover yourselves, nor take hold of the saving help offered to you in the Gospel, yet even by the power of nature you may use the outward and ordinary means, whereby Christ communicates the benefit of redemption to ruined sinners, who are utterly unable to recover themselves out of the state of sin and wrath. You may and can, if you please, do many things that would set you in a fair way for help from the Lord Jesus Christ. You may go so far on, as not to be far from the kingdom of God, as the discreet scribe had done (Mark 12.34), though, it should seem, he was destitute of supernatural abilities. Though you cannot cure yourselves, yet you may come to the pool, where many such diseased persons as you are have been cured; though you have none to put you into it, yet you may lie at the side of it: 'Who knows but the Lord may return, and leave a blessing behind Him?' as in the case of the impotent man (recorded in John 5.5–8). I hope Satan does not chain you to your houses, nor stake you down in your fields on the Lord's day; but you are at liberty and can wait at the posts of wisdom's doors if you will. When you come thither he does not beat drums at your ears, that you cannot hear what is said; there is no force upon you, obliging you to apply all you hear to others; you may apply to yourselves what belongs to your state and condition. When you go home, you are not fettered in your houses, where perhaps no religious discourse is to be heard, but you may retire to some separate place, where you can meditate, and exercise your consciences with suitable questions upon what you have heard. You are not possessed with a dumb devil, that you cannot get your mouths opened in prayer to God. You are not so driven out of your beds to your worldly business, and from your worldly business to your beds again, but you might, if you would, make some prayers to God upon the case of your perishing souls. You may examine yourselves as to the state of your souls, in a solemn manner, as in the presence of God; you may discern that you have no grace, and that you are lost and undone without it, and you may cry to God for it. These things are within the compass of natural abilities, and may be practised where there is no grace. It must aggravate your guilt, that you will not be at so much pains about the state and case of your precious souls. If you do not what you can, you will be condemned, not only for your want of grace, but for your despising it.

Objection 3: But all this is needless, seeing we are utterly unable to help ourselves out of the state of sin and wrath. *Answer:* Give not place to that delusion, which puts asunder what God has joined, namely, the use of means and a sense of our own impotency. If ever the Spirit of God graciously influence your souls, you will become thoroughly sensible of your absolute inability, and yet enter upon a vigorous use of means. You will do for yourselves, as if you were to do all, and yet overlook all you do, as if you had done nothing. Will you do nothing for yourselves because you cannot do all? Lay down no such impious conclusion against your own souls. Do what you can; and, it may be, while you are doing what you can for yourselves, God will do for you what you cannot. 'Understandest thou what thou readest?' said Philip to the eunuch; 'How can I,' said he, 'except some man should guide me?' (Acts 8.30,31). He could not understand the Scripture he read, yet he could read it: he did what he could, he read; and while he was reading, God sent him an interpreter. The Israelites were in a great strait at the Red Sea; and how could they help themselves, when on the one hand were mountains, and on the other the enemy in pursuit; when Pharaoh and his host were behind them, and the Red Sea before them? What could they do? 'Speak unto the children of Israel,' said the Lord to Moses, 'that they go forward' (Exod 14.15). For what end should they go forward? Can they make a passage to themselves through the sea? No; but let them go forward, saith the Lord: though they cannot turn the sea to dry land, yet they can go forward to the shore. So they did; and when they did what they could, God did for them what they could not do.

Question: Has God promised to convert and save those who, in the use of means, do what they can towards their own relief? *Answer:* We may not speak wickedly for God; natural men, being strangers to the covenants of promise (Eph 2.12), have no such promise made to them. Nevertheless they do not act rationally unless they exert the powers they have, and do what they can. For, 1. It is possible this course may succeed with them. If you do what you can, it may be, God will do for you what you cannot do for yourselves. This is sufficient to determine a man in a matter of the utmost importance, such as this is (Acts 8.22), 'Pray God, if perhaps the thought of thy heart may be forgiven thee.' (Joel 2.14), 'Who knoweth if he will return?' If success may be, the trial should be. If, in a wreck at sea, all the sailors and passengers betake themselves each to a broken board for safety, and one of them should see all the rest perish, notwithstanding their utmost endeavour to save themselves, yet the very possibility of escaping by that means would determine that one still to do his best with his board. Why then do not you reason with yourselves, as the four lepers did who sat at the gate of Samaria?

(2 Kings 7.3,4). Why do you not say, 'If we sit still,' not doing what we can, 'we die;' let us put it to a trial; if we be saved, 'we shall live;' if not, 'we shall but die?' 2. It is probable this course may succeed; God is good and merciful; He loves to surprise men with His grace, and is often 'found of them that sought him not' (Isa 65.1). If you do this, you are so far in the road of your duty, and you are using the means, which the Lord is wont to bless for men's spiritual recovery: you lay yourselves in the way of the great Physician, and so it is probable you may be healed. Lydia went, with others, to the place 'where prayer was wont to be made;' and 'the Lord opened her heart' (Acts 16.13,14). You plough and sow, though nobody can tell you for certain that you will get so much as your seed again: you use means for the recovery of your health, though you are not sure they will succeed. In these cases probability determines you; and why not in this also? Importunity, we see, does very much with men. Therefore pray, meditate, desire help of God, be much at the throne of grace, supplicating for grace, and do not faint. Though God regard you not, who in your present state are but one mass of sin, universally depraved, and vitiated in all the powers of your soul, yet He may regard prayer, meditation, and the like means of His own appointment, and He may bless them to you. Wherefore, if you will not do what you can, you are not only dead, but you declare yourselves unworthy of eternal life.

To conclude. – Let the saints admire the freedom and power of grace, which came to them in their helpless condition, made their chains fall off, the iron gate to open to them, raised the fallen creatures, and brought them out of the state of sin and wrath, wherein they would have lain and perished, had not they been mercifully visited. Let the natural man be sensible of his utter inability to recover himself. Know, that you are without strength: and cannot come to Christ, till you be drawn. You are lost, and cannot help yourself. This may shake the foundation of your hopes, if you never saw your absolute need of Christ and his grace, but think to contrive for yourself by your civility, morality, drowsy wishes, and duties, and by a faith and repentance which have sprung out of your natural powers, without the power and efficacy of the grace of Christ. O be convinced of your absolute need of Christ, and His overcoming grace, believe your utter inability to recover yourself, that so you may be humbled, shaken out of your self-confidence, and lie down in dust and ashes, groaning out your miserable case before the Lord. A proper sense of your natural impotence, the impotence of depraved human nature, would be a step towards a delivery.

Thus far of man's natural state, the state of entire depravity.

III
THE STATE OF GRACE

REGENERATION

Being born again, not of corruptible seed, but of
incorruptible, by the word of God, which liveth and
abideth for ever.   I PETER 1.23

We proceed now to the state of grace, the state of begun recovery
of human nature, into which all that shall partake of eternal happiness are translated, sooner or later, while in this world. It is the
result of a gracious change made upon those who shall inherit
eternal life, which change may be taken up in these two particulars: 1. In opposition to their natural relative state, the state of
corruption, there is a change made upon them in regeneration
whereby their nature is changed. 2. In opposition to their natural
relative state, the state of wrath, there is a change made upon
them in their union with the Lord Jesus Christ, by which they
are placed beyond the reach of condemnation. These, therefore,
regeneration and union with Christ, I desire to treat of as the
great and comprehensive changes on a sinner, bringing him into
the state of grace.

The first of these we have in the text, together with the outward and ordinary means by which it is brought about. The
apostle here, to excite the saints to the study of holiness, and
particularly of brotherly love, puts them in mind of their spiritual
original. He tells them that they were born again, and that of
incorruptible seed, the Word of God. This shows them to be
brethren, partakers of the same new nature: which is the root
from which holiness, and particularly brotherly love, springs. We
have been once born sinners: we must be born again, that we
may be saints. The simple word signifies 'to be begotten;' and
so it may be read (Matt 11.11); 'to be conceived' (Matt 1.20);
and 'to be born' (Matt 2.1). Accordingly, the compound word,

[203]

used in the text, may be taken in its full latitude, the last idea presupposing the two former. So regeneration is a supernatural real change on the whole man, fitly compared to the natural generation, as will afterwards appear. The ordinary means of regeneration, called the 'seed,' whereof the new creature is formed, is not corruptible seed. Of such, indeed, our bodies are generated: but the spiritual seed of which the new creature is generated, is incorruptible, namely, 'the Word of God, which liveth and abideth for ever.' The sound of the Word of God passes even as other sounds do; but the Word lasts, lives, and abides, in respect of its everlasting effects, on all upon whom it operates. This 'Word, which by the Gospel is preached unto you' (verse 25), impregnated by the Spirit of God, is the means of regeneration: and by it dead sinners are raised to life.

DOCTRINE: *All men in the state of grace are born again*

All gracious persons, namely, such as are in a state of favour with God, and endowed with gracious qualities and dispositions, are regenerate persons. In discoursing on this subject, I shall show, What regeneration is; next, Why it is so called; and then apply the doctrine.

1 : The Nature of Regeneration

For the better understanding of the nature of regeneration, take this along with you, that as there are false conceptions in nature, so there are also in grace: by these many are deluded, mistaking some partial changes made upon them for this great and thorough change. To remove such mistakes, let these few things be considered: (1) Many call the church their mother, whom God will not own to be His children (Cant 1.6). 'My mother's children,' that is, false brethren, 'were angry with me.' All that are baptized are not born again. Simon was baptized, yet still 'in the gall of bitterness, and in the bond of iniquity' (Acts 8.13,23). Where Christianity is the religion of the country, many are called by the name of Christ, who have no more of Him than the name; and no wonder, for the devil had his goats among Christ's sheep, in those places where but few professed the Christian religion (1 John 2.19), 'They went out from us, but they were not of us.' (2) Good education is not regeneration. Education may chain up men's lusts, but cannot change their hearts. A wolf is still a ravenous beast, though it be in chains. Joash was very devout during the life of his good tutor Jehoiada; but afterwards he quickly shewed what spirit he was of, by his sudden apostasy (2 Chron 24.2–18). Good example is of mighty influence to change the outward man, but the change often goes off when a man changes his company, of which the world affords many sad instances. (3) A turning from open profanity, to civility and sobriety, falls short of this saving change. Some are, for a while, very loose, especially in their younger years, but at length they reform, and leave their profane courses. Here is a change, yet only such as may be found in men utterly void of the grace of God, and whose righteousness is so far from exceeding, that it does not come up to the righteousness of the scribes and Pharisees. (4) One may engage in all the outward duties of religion, and yet not be born again. Though lead be cast into various shapes, it remains still but a base metal. Men may escape the pollutions of the world, and yet be but dogs and swine (2 Pet 2.20–22). All the external acts of religion are within the compass of natural abilities. Yea, hypocrites may have the counterfeit of all the graces of the Spirit; for we read of 'true holiness' (Eph 4.24); and 'faith unfeigned' (1 Tim 1.5), which shows us that there is counterfeit holiness, and a feigned faith. (5) Men may advance to a great deal of strictness in their own way of religion, and yet be strangers to the new birth (Acts 26.5), 'After the most straitest sect of our religion, I lived a Pharisee.' Nature has its own unsanctified strictness in religion. The Pharisees had so much of it, that they looked on Christ as little better than a mere libertine. A man whose conscience has been awakened, and who lives under the felt influence of the covenant of works, what will he not do that is within the compass of natural abilities? It is a truth, though it came out of a hellish mouth, that 'skin for skin, yea, all that a man hath will he give for his life' (Job 2.4). (6) A person may have sharp soul-exercises and pangs, and yet die in the birth. Many 'have been in pain,' that have but, 'as it were, brought forth wind.' There may be sore pangs of conscience, which turn to nothing at last. Pharaoh and Simon Magus had such convictions as made them to desire the prayers of others for them. Judas repented himself, and, under terrors of conscience, gave back his ill-gotten pieces of silver. All is not gold that glitters. Trees may blossom fairly in the spring, on which no fruit is to be found in the harvest: and some have sharp soul-exercises, which are nothing but foretastes of hell.

The new birth, however in appearance hopefully begun, may be marred two ways. Some have sharp convictions for a while, but these go off, and they become as careless about their salvation, and as profane as ever, and usually worse than ever; 'their last state is worse than their first' (Matt 12.45). They get awakening grace, but not converting grace; and that goes off by degrees, as the light of the declining day, till it issues in midnight darkness. Others come forth too soon; they are born, like Ishmael, before the time of the promise (Gen 16.2; compare Gal 4.22–31). They take up with a mere law work, and stay not till the time of the promise of the Gospel. They snatch at consolation, not waiting till it be given them; and foolishly draw their comfort from the law that wounded them. They apply the healing plaster to themselves before their wound is sufficiently searched. The law, that rigorous husband, severely beats them, and throws in curses and vengeance upon their souls; then they fall to reforming, praying, mourning, promising and vowing till this ghost be laid; which done, they fall asleep again in the arms of the law. But they are never shaken out of themselves and their own righteousness, nor brought forward to Jesus Christ. There may be a wonderful moving of the affections in souls that are not at all touched with regenerating grace. When there is no grace, there may, notwithstanding, be a flood of tears, as in Esau, who 'found no place of repentance, though he sought it carefully with tears' (Heb 12.17). There may be great flashes of joy, as in the hearers of the word represented in the parable of the stony ground, who 'anon with joy receive it' (Matt 13.20). There may be also great desires after good things, and great delight in them too; as in those hypocrites described in Isa 58.2, 'Yet they seek me daily, and delight to know my ways: they take delight in approaching to God.' See how high they may sometimes stand, who yet fall away (Heb 6.4–6). They may be 'enlightened, taste of the heavenly gift, be partakers of the Holy Ghost, taste the good word of God, and the powers of the world to come.' Common operations of the divine Spirit, like a land-flood, make a strange turning of things upside down: but when they are over, all runs again in the ordinary channel. All these things may be, where the sanctifying Spirit of Christ never rests upon the soul, but the stony heart still remains; and in that case these affections cannot but wither, because they have no root.

But regeneration is a real, thorough change, whereby the man is made a new creature (2 Cor 5.17). The Lord God makes the creature a new creature, as the goldsmith melts down a vessel of dishonour, and makes it a vessel of honour. Man is, in respect of his spiritual state, altogether disjointed by the fall; every faculty of the soul is, as it were, dislocated: in regeneration, the Lord loosens every joint, and sets it right again. Now this change made in regeneration is,

1: A change of qualities or dispositions: it is not a change of the substance, but of the qualities of the soul. Vicious qualities are removed, and the contrary dispositions are brought in, in their stead. 'The old man is put off' (Eph 4.22); 'the new man is put on' (verse 24). Man lost none of the rational faculties of his soul by sin: he had an understanding still, but it was darkened; he had still a will, but it was contrary to the will of God. So in regeneration, there is not a new substance created, but new qualities are infused; light instead of darkness, righteousness instead of unrighteousness.

2: It is a supernatural change; he that is born again, is born of the Spirit (John 3.5). Great changes may be made by the power of nature, especially when assisted by external revelation. Nature may be so elevated by the common influences of the Spirit, that a person may thereby be turned into another man, as Saul was (1 Sam 10.6), who yet never becomes a new man. But in regeneration, nature itself is changed, and we become partakers of the divine nature, and this must needs be a supernatural change. How can we, who are dead in trespasses and sins, renew ourselves, any more than a dead man can raise himself out of his grave? Who but the sanctifying Spirit of Christ can form Christ in a soul, changing it into the same image? Who but the Spirit of sanctification can give the new heart? Well may we say, when we see a man thus changed, 'This is the finger of God!'

3: It is a change into the likeness of God (2 Cor 3.18), 'We, beholding, as in a glass, the glory of the Lord, are changed into the same image.' Every thing generates its like; the child bears the image of the parent, and they who are born of God bear God's image. Man aspiring to be as God, made himself like the devil. In his natural state he resembles the devil, as a child doth his father (John 8.44), 'Ye are of your father the devil.' But when this happy change comes, that image of Satan is defaced, and the image of God is restored. Christ Himself, who is the brightness of His Father's glory, is the pattern after which the new creature is made (Rom 8.29), 'For whom he did foreknow, he also did predestinate to be conformed to the image of his son.' Hence He is said to be formed in the regenerate (Gal 4.19).

4: It is a universal change; 'all things become new' (2 Cor 5.17). It is a blessed leaven, that leavens the whole lump, the whole spirit, and soul, and body. Original sin infects the whole man; and regenerating grace, which is the cure, goes as far as the disease. This fruit of the Spirit is in all goodness; goodness of the mind, goodness of the will, goodness of the affections, goodness of the whole man. He gets not only a new head, to know religion, or a new tongue, to talk of it, but a new heart to love

[208]

and embrace it, in the whole of his conversation. When the Lord opens the sluice of grace on the soul's new-birthday, the waters run through the whole man, to purify and make him fruitful. In those natural changes spoken of before, there are, as it were, pieces of new cloth put into an old garment; new life sewed to an old heart: but the gracious change is a thorough change, a change both of heart and life.

5. Yet it is but an imperfect change. Though every part of the man is renewed, there is no part of him perfectly renewed. As an infant has all the parts of a man but none of them come to a perfect growth, so regeneration brings a perfection of parts, to be brought forward in the gradual advances of sanctification (1 Pet 2.2), 'As new-born babes, desire the sincere milk of the word, that ye may grow thereby.' Although, in regeneration, there is heavenly light let into the mind, yet there is still some darkness there. Though the will is renewed, it is not perfectly renewed, there is still some of the old inclination to sin remaining. Thus it will be, till that which is in part is done away, and the light of glory come. Adam was created at his full stature, but as those who are born must have their time to grow up, so those who are born again come forth into the new world of grace but imperfectly holy: though Adam being created upright, was at the same time perfectly righteous, without the least mixture of sinful imperfection.

6: Nevertheless, it is a lasting change, which never goes off. The seed is incorruptible, says the text; and so is the creature that is formed of it. The life given in regeneration, whatever decays it may fall under, can never be utterly lost. 'His seed remaineth in him' who 'is born of God' (1 John 3.9). Though the branches should be cut down, the root abides in the earth; and being watered with the dew of heaven, shall sprout again: for 'the root of the righteous shall not be moved' (Prov 12.3). But to come to particulars.

1: In regeneration the mind is savingly enlightened. There is a new light let into the understanding; so that they who were 'sometimes darkness, are now light in the Lord' (Eph 5.8). The beams of the light of life make their way into the dark dungeon of the heart: then the night is over, and morning light is come, which will shine more and more unto the perfect day. Now the man is illuminated,

(1) In the knowledge of God. He has far other thoughts of God, than ever he had before (Hos 2.20), 'I will even betroth thee unto me in faithfulness, and thou shalt know the Lord.' The Spirit of the Lord brings him back to this question, 'What is God?' and catechises him anew upon that grand point, so that he is made to say, 'I have heard of thee by the hearing of the ear; but now mine eye seeth thee' (Job 42.5). The spotless purity of God, His exact justice, His all-sufficiency, and other glorious perfections revealed in His word, are by this new light discovered to the soul, with a plainness and certainty which as far exceed the knowledge it had of these things before, as ocular demonstration exceeds common report. For now he sees what he only heard of before.

(2) He is enlightened in the knowledge of sin. He has different thoughts of it than he used to have. Formerly his sight could not pierce through the cover Satan laid over it: but now the Spirit of God removes it, wipes off the paint and varnish, and so he sees it in its natural colours as the worst of evils, exceedingly sinful (Rom 7.13). O what deformed monsters do formerly beloved lusts appear! Were they right eyes, he would pluck them out; were they right hands, he would consent to their being cut off. He sees how offensive sin is to God, how destructive it is to the soul, and calls himself a fool for fighting so long against the Lord, and harbouring that destroyer as a bosom friend.

(3) He is instructed in the knowledge of himself. Regenerating grace brings the prodigal to himself (Luke 15.17), and makes men full of eyes within, knowing every one the plague of his own heart. The mind being savingly enlightened, the man sees how desperately corrupt his nature is; what enmity against God, and His holy law, has long lodged there, so that his soul loathes itself. No open sepulchre so vile and loathsome, in his eyes, as himself (Ezek

36.31), 'Then shall ye remember your own evil ways, and your doings that were not good, and shall loathe yourselves in your own sight.' He is no worse than he was before: but the sun is shining, and so those pollutions are seen, which he could not discern when there was no dawning in him, as the word is (Isa 8.20), while as yet there was no breaking of the day of grace upon him.

(4) He is enlightened in the knowledge of Jesus Christ. (1 Cor 1.23,24), 'But we preach Christ crucified, unto the Jews a stumbling-block, and unto the Greeks foolishness: but unto them which are called, both Jews and Greeks, Christ the power of God, and the wisdom of God.' The truth is, unregenerate men, though capable of preaching Christ, have not, properly speaking, the knowledge of Him, but only an opinion, a good opinion, of Him; as one has of many controverted points of doctrine, wherein he is far from certainty. As when you meet with a stranger on the road, if he behaves himself discreetly, you conceive a good opinion of him, and therefore willingly converse with him: but yet you will not commit your money to him, because, though you have a good opinion of the man, he is a stranger to you, you do not know him. So may they think well of Christ, but they will never commit themselves to Him, seeing they know Him not. But saving illumination carries the soul beyond opinion, to the certain knowledge of Christ and His excellency (1 Thess 1.5), 'For our Gospel came not unto you in word only, but also in power, and in the Holy Ghost, and in much assurance.' The light of grace thus discovers the suitableness of the mystery of Christ to the divine perfections, and to the sinner's case. Hence the regenerate admire the glorious plan of salvation through Christ crucified, rest their whole dependence upon it, heartily acquiesce therein; for whatever He be to others, He is to them 'Christ the power of God, and the wisdom of God.' But unrenewed men, not seeing this, are offended in Him; they will not venture their souls in that vessel, but betake themselves to the broken boards of their own righteousness. The same light convincingly discovers a superlative worth, a transcendent glory and excellency in Christ, which darken all

created excellencies as the rising sun makes the stars hide their heads: it engages the 'merchantman to sell all that he hath, to buy the one pearl of great price' (Matt 13.45,46), and makes the soul heartily content to take Christ for all, and instead of all. Even as an unskilful merchant, to whom one offers a pearl of great price for all his petty wares, dares not venture on the bargain, for though he thinks that one pearl may be worth more than all he has, yet he is not sure of it; but when a jeweller comes to him and assures him it is worth double all his wares, he then eagerly makes the bargain, and cheerfully parts with all he has for that pearl. Finally, this illumination in the knowledge of Christ convincingly discovers to men a fulness in Him, sufficient for the supply of all their wants, enough to satisfy the boundless desires of an immortal soul. And they are persuaded that such fulness is in Him, and that, in order to be communicated: they depend upon it as a certain truth, and therefore their souls take up their eternal rest in Him.

(5) The man is instructed in the knowledge of the vanity of the world (Psa 119.96), 'I have seen an end of all perfection.' Regenerating grace elevates the soul, translates it into the spiritual world, from whence this earth cannot but appear a little, yea, a very little thing; even as heaven appeared before, while the soul was grovelling in the earth. Grace brings a man into a new world where this world is reputed but a stage of vanity, a howling wilderness, a valley of tears. God has hung the sign of vanity at the door of all created enjoyments, yet how do men throng into the house, calling and looking for somewhat that is satisfying; even after it has been a thousand times told them that there is no such thing in it, it is not to be got there (Isa 57.10), 'Thou art wearied in the greatness of thy way: yet saidst thou not, There is no hope.' Why are men so foolish? The truth of the matter lies here, they do not see by the light of grace, they do not spiritually discern that sign of vanity. They have often indeed made a rational discovery of it: but can that truly wean the heart from the world? Nay, no more than painted fire can burn off the

prisoner's bands. But the light of grace is the light of life, powerful and efficacious.

(6) To sum up all. In regeneration, the mind is enlightened in the knowledge of spiritual things (1 John 2.20), 'Ye have an unction from the Holy One,' that is, from Jesus Christ (Rev 3.18). It is an allusion to the sanctuary, whence the holy oil was brought to anoint the priests, 'and ye know all things' necessary to salvation. Though men be not book-learned, if they are born again they are Spirit-learned; for all such are taught of God (John 6.45). The Spirit of regeneration teaches them what they knew not before; and what they knew by the ear only, he teaches them over again as by the eye. The light of grace is an overcoming light, determining men to assent to divine truths on the mere testimony of God. It is no easy thing for the mind of man to acquiesce in divine revelation. Many pretend great respect to the Scriptures, whom, nevertheless, the clear Scripture testimony will not divorce from their preconceived opinions. But this illumination will make men's minds run, as willing captives, after Christ's chariot wheels, which they are ready to allow to drive over, and 'cast down' their 'imaginations, and every high thing that exalteth itself against the knowledge of God' (2 Cor 10.5). It will bring them to 'receive the kingdom of God as a little child' (Mark 10.15), who thinks he has sufficient ground to believe any thing, if his father do but say it is so.

2 : The will is renewed. The Lord takes away the stony heart, and gives a heart of flesh (Ezek 36.26) and so, of stones, raiseth up children to Abraham. Regenerating grace is powerful and efficacious, and gives the will a new turn. It does not indeed force it, but sweetly, yet powerfully draws it, so that His people are willing in the day of His power (Psa 110.3). There is heavenly oratory in the Mediator's lips to persuade sinners (Psa 45.2). 'Grace is poured into thy lips.' There are cords of a man, and bands of love in His hands, to draw them after Him (Hos 11.4) Love makes a net for elect souls, which will infallibly catch them, and haul them to land. The cords of Christ's love are strong

cords: and they need to be so, for every sinner is heavier than a mountain of brass; and Satan, together with the heart itself, draws the contrary way. But love is strong as death; and the Lord's love to the soul He died for, is the strongest love. It acts so powerfully that it must come off victorious.

(1) The will is cured of its utter inability to will what is good. While the opening of the prison to them that are bound, is proclaimed in the Gospel, the Spirit of God comes and opens the prison door, goes to the prisoner, and, by the power of His grace, makes his chains fall off, breaks the bonds of iniquity, wherewith he was held in sin, so as he could neither will nor do any thing truly good, and brings him forth into a large place, 'working in him both to will and to do of his good pleasure' (Phil 2.13). Then it is that the soul, that was fixed to the earth, can move heavenward; the withered hand is restored, and can be stretched out.

(2) There is wrought in the will a fixed aversion to evil. In regeneration, a man gets a new spirit put within him (Ezek 36.26); and that spirit striveth against the flesh (Gal 5.17). The sweet morsel of sin, so greedily swallowed down, he now loathes, and would fain be rid of it, even as willingly as one who had drunk a cup of poison would throw it up again. When the spring is stopped, the mud lies in the well unmoved; but when once the spring is cleared, the waters, springing up, will work the mud away by degrees. Even so, while a man continues in an unregenerate state, sin lies at ease in the heart, but as soon as the Lord strikes the rocky heart with the rod of His strength, in the day of conversion, grace is 'in him a well of water, springing up into everlasting life' (John 4.14), working away natural corruption, and gradually purifying the heart (Acts 15.9). The renewed will rises up against sin, strikes at the root thereof, and the branches too. Lusts are now grievous, and the soul endeavours to starve them. The corrupt nature is the source of all evil, and therefore the soul will be often laying it before the great Physician. O what sorrow, shame, and self-loathing fill the heart, in the day that grace makes its triumphant entrance into it! For now the mad-

man is come to himself, and the remembrance of his follies cannot but cut him to the heart.

(3) The will is endowed with an inclination, bent, and propensity to good. In its depraved state, it lay quite another way, being prone and bent to evil only: but now, by the operation of the omnipotent, all-conquering arm, it is drawn from evil to good, and gets another disposition. As the former was natural, so this is natural too, in regard to the new nature given in regeneration, which has its own holy strivings, as well as the old corrupt nature has its sinful lustings (Gal 5.17). The will, as renewed, points towards God and godliness. When God made man, his will, in respect of its intention, was directed towards God as his chief end; in respect of its choice, it pointed towards that which God willed. When man unmade himself, his will was framed to the very reverse hereof. he made himself his chief end and his own will his law. But when man is new made in regeneration, grace rectifies this disorder in some measure, though not perfectly: because we are but renewed in part, while in this world. It brings back the sinner out of himself to God, as his chief end (Psa 73.25), 'Whom have I in heaven but thee? and there is none upon earth that I desire beside thee.' (Phil 1.21), 'For me to live is Christ.' It makes him to deny himself, and whatever way he turns, to point habitually towards God, who is the centre of the gracious soul, its home, its 'dwelling place in all generations' (Psa 90.1). By regenerating grace, the will is brought into conformity to the will of God. It is conformed to His preceptive will, being endowed with holy inclinations, agreeable to every one of His commands. The whole law is impressed on the gracious soul: every part of it is written on the renewed heart. Although remaining corruption makes such blots in the writing that oft-times the man himself cannot read it, yet He that wrote it can read it at all times; it is never quite blotted out, nor can be. What He has written, He has written; and it shall stand: 'For this is the covenant – I will put my laws into their mind, and write them in their hearts' (Heb 8.10). It is a covenant of salt, a perpetual covenant. It is also

conformed to His providential will; so that the man would no more be master of his own process, nor carve out his lot for himself. He learns to say, from his heart, 'The will of the Lord be done.' 'He shall choose our inheritance for us' (Psa 47.4). Thus the will is disposed to fall in with those things which, in its depraved state, it could never be reconciled to.

Particularly, 1. The soul is reconciled to the covenant of peace. The Lord God proposes a covenant of peace to sinners, a covenant which He Himself has framed, and registered in the Bible: but they are not pleased with it. Nay, unregenerate hearts cannot be pleased with it. Were it put into their hands to frame it according to their minds, they would blot many things out of it which God has put in, and put in many things which God has kept out. But the renewed heart is entirely satisfied with the covenant (2 Sam 23.5), 'He hath made with me an everlasting covenant, ordered in all things and sure; this is all my salvation, and all my desire.' Though the covenant could not be brought down to their depraved will, their will is, by grace, brought up to the covenant: they are well pleased with it; there is nothing in it which they would have out; nor is any thing left out of it, which they would have in. 2. The will is disposed to receive Christ Jesus the Lord. The soul is content to submit to Him. Regenerating grace undermines, and brings down the towering imaginations of the heart, raised up against its rightful Lord; it breaks the iron sinew, which kept the sinner from bowing to Him; and disposes him to be no more stiff-necked, but to yield. He is willing to take on the yoke of Christ's commands, to take up the cross, and to follow Him. He is content to take Christ on any terms (Psa 110.3), 'Thy people shall be willing in the day of thy power.'

The mind being savingly enlightened, and the will renewed, the sinner is thereby determined and enabled to answer the gospel call. So the chief work in regeneration is done; the fort of the heart is taken; there is room made for the Lord Jesus Christ in the inmost parts of the soul, the inner door of the will being now opened to Him as well as the outer door of the understanding. In one word, Christ is passively received into the heart; He is come into the soul, by His quickening Spirit, whereby spiritual life is given to the man, who in himself was dead in sin. His first vital act we may conceive to be an active receiving of Jesus Christ, discerned in His glorious excellencies, that is, a believing on Him, a closing with Him, as discerned, offered and exhibited in the word of His grace, the glorious Gospel. The immediate effect is union with Him (John 1.12,13), 'To as many as received him to them gave he power,' or privilege, 'to become the sons of God, even to them that believe on his name: which were born not of blood, nor of the will of the flesh, nor of the will of man, but of God.' (Eph 3.17), 'That Christ may dwell in your hearts by faith.' Christ having taken the heart by storm, and triumphantly entered into it, in regeneration, the soul by faith yields itself to Him, as it is expressed (2 Chron 30.8). Thus, this glorious King who came into the heart by His Spirit, dwells in it by faith. The soul being drawn, runs; and being effectually called, comes.

3: In regeneration there is a happy change made on the affections; they are both rectified and regulated.

(1) This change rectifies the affections, placing them on suitable objects. (2 Thess 3.5), 'The Lord direct your hearts into the love of God.' The regenerate man's desires are rectified; they are set on God Himself, and the things above. He, who before cried with the world, 'Who will shew us any good?' has changed his note, and says, 'Lord, lift up the light of thy countenance upon us' (Psa 4.6). Before, he saw no beauty in Christ, for which He was to be desired; but now He is all he desires, He is altogether lovely (Cant 5.16). The main stream of his desires is turned to run towards God; for there is the one thing he desires (Psa 27.4). He desires to be holy as well as happy; and rather to be gracious than great. His hopes, which before were low, and fastened down to things on earth, are now raised, and set on the glory which is to be revealed. He entertains the hope of eternal life, founded on the word of promise (Tit 1.2). Which hope he has, as an anchor of the soul, fixing the heart under trials (Heb 6.19).

It puts him upon purifying himself, even as God is pure (1 John 3.3). For he is begotten again unto a lively hope (1 Pet 1.3). His love is raised, and set on God himself (Psa 18.1), and on His holy law (Psa 119.97). Though it strike against his most beloved lust, he says, 'The law is holy, and the commandment holy, and just, and good' (Rom 7.12). 'He loves the ordinances of God' (Psa 84.1), 'How amiable are thy tabernacles, O Lord of hosts!' Being passed from death unto life, he loves the brethren (1 John 3.14); the people of God, as they are called (1 Pet 2.10). He loves God for Himself; and what is God's, for His sake. Yea, as being a child of God, he loves his own enemies. His heavenly Father is compassionate and benevolent: 'He maketh his sun to rise on the evil and on the good; and sendeth rain on the just and on the unjust:' therefore he is in like manner disposed (Matt 5.44,45). His hatred is turned against sin, in himself and others (Psa 101.3), 'I hate the work of them that turn aside, it shall not cleave to me.' He groans under the remains of it, and longs for deliverance (Rom 7.24), 'O wretched man that I am! who shall deliver me from the body of this death?' His joys and delights are in God the Lord, in the light of His countenance, in His law, and in His people, because they are like Him. Sin is what he chiefly fears: it is a fountain of sorrow to him now, though formerly a spring of pleasure.

(2) It regulates the affections placed on suitable objects. Our affections, when placed on the creature, are naturally exorbitant; when we joy in it, we are apt to overjoy, and when we sorrow, we are ready to sorrow overmuch: but grace bridles these affections, clips their wings, and keeps them within bounds, that they overflow not all their banks. It makes a man 'hate his father, and mother, and wife, and children; yea, and his own life also,' comparatively; that is, to love them less than he loves God (Luke 14.26). It also sanctifies lawful affections, bringing them forth from right principles, and directing them to right ends. There may be unholy desires after Christ and His grace, as when men desire Christ, not from any love to Him, but merely out of love to themselves.

[218]

'Give us of your oil,' said the foolish virgins, 'for our lamps are gone out' (Matt 25.8). There may be an unsanctified sorrow for sin; as when one sorrows for it, not because it is displeasing to God, but only because of the wrath annexed to it, as did Pharaoh, Judas, and others. So a man may love his father and mother from mere natural principles, without any respect to the command of God binding him thereto. But grace sanctifies the affections in such cases, making them to run in a new channel of love to God, respect to His commands, and regard to His glory. Again, grace raises the affections where they are too low. It gives the chief seat in them to God, and pulls down all other rivals, whether persons or things, making them lie at His feet. (Psa. 73.25), 'Whom have I in heaven but thee? and there is none upon earth that I desire beside thee.' He is loved for Himself, and other persons or things for His sake. What is lovely in them, to the renewed heart, is some ray of the divine goodness appearing in them: for unto gracious souls they shine only by borrowed light. This accounts for the saints loving all men; and yet hating those that hate God, and contemning the wicked as vile persons. They hate and contemn them for their wickedness; there is nothing of God in that, and therefore nothing lovely nor honourable in it: but they love them for their commendable qualities or perfections, whether natural or moral; because, in whomsoever these are, they are from God, and can be traced to Him as their fountain.

(3) Regenerating grace sets the affections so firmly on God, that the man is disposed, at God's command, to quit his hold of every thing else, in order to keep his hold of Christ; to hate father and mother, in comparison with Christ (Luke 14.26). It makes even lawful enjoyments, like Joseph's mantle, to hang loose about a man, that he may quit them, when he is in danger of being ensnared by holding them.

If the stream of our affections was never thus turned, we are, doubtless, going down the stream into the pit. If 'the lust of the eyes, the lust of the flesh, and the pride of life,' have the throne in our hearts, which should be possessed by the Father, Son, and

Holy Ghost; if we never had so much love to God as to ourselves; if sin has been somewhat bitter to us,, but never so bitter as suffering, never so bitter as the pain of being weaned from it; truly we are strangers to this saving change. For grace turns the affections upside down, whenever it comes into the heart.

4: The conscience is renewed. As a new light is set up in the soul in regeneration, conscience is enlightened, instructed and informed. That candle of the Lord (Prov 20.27), is now snuffed and brightened; so that it shines, and sends forth its light into the most retired corners of the heart, discovering sins which the soul was not aware of before: and, in a special manner, discovering the corruption or depravity of nature, that seed and spawn whence all actual sins proceed. This produces the new complaint (Rom 7.24), 'O wretched man that I am! who shall deliver me from the body of this death?' Conscience, which lay sleeping in the man's bosom before, is now awakened, and makes its voice to be heard through the whole soul; therefore there is no more rest for him in the sluggard's bed; he must get up and be doing, arise, 'haste, and escape for his life.' It powerfully incites to obedience, even in the most spiritual acts, which lie not within the view of the natural conscience; and powerfully restrains from sin, even from those sins which do not lie open to the observation of the world. It urges the sovereign authority of God, to which the heart is now reconciled, and which it willingly acknowledges; and so it engages the man to his duty, whatever be the hazard from the world; for it fills the heart so with the fear of God, that the force of the fear of man is broken. This has engaged many to put their life in their hand, and follow the cause of religion, which they once contemned, and resolutely walk in the path they formerly abhorred (Gal 1.23), 'He which persecuted us in times past, now preacheth the faith which once he destroyed.' Guilt now makes the conscience smart. It has bitter remorse for sins past, which fills the soul with anxiety, sorrow, and self-loathing. And every new reflection on these sins is apt to affect, and make its wounds bleed afresh with regret. It is made tender, in point of sin and

[220]

duty, for the time to come: being once burnt, it dreads the fire, and fears to break the hedge where it was formerly bit by the serpent. Finally, the renewed conscience drives the sinner to Jesus Christ, as the only Physician who can draw out the sting of guilt and whose blood alone can purge the conscience from dead works (Heb 9.14), refusing all ease offered to it from any other hand. This is an evidence that the conscience is not only fired, as it may be in an unregenerate state, but oiled also, with regenerating grace.

5: As the memory wanted not its share of depravity, it also is bettered by regenerating grace. The memory s weakened with respect to those things that are not worth their room therein; and men are taught to forget injuries, and drop their resentments (Matt 5.44,45), 'Do good to them that hate you, and pray for them which despitefully use you – that ye may be,' that is, appear to be, 'the children of your Father which is in heaven.' It is strengthened for spiritual things. We have Solomon's recipe for an ill memory (Prov 3.1), 'My son,' saith he, 'forget not my law.' But how shall it be kept in mind? 'Let thine heart keep my commandments.' Grace makes a heart-memory, even where there is no good head-memory (Psa 119.11), 'Thy word have I hid in mine heart.' The heart, truly touched with the powerful sweetness of truth, will help the memory to retain what is so relished. If divine truths made deeper impressions on our hearts, they would impress themselves with more force on our memories (Psa 119.93), 'I will never forget thy precepts, for with them thou hast quickened me.' Grace sanctifies the memory. Many have large, but unsanctified, memories, which serve only to gather knowledge, whereby to aggravate their condemnation; but the renewed memory serves to 'remember his commandments to do them' (Psa 103.18). It is a sacred storehouse, from whence a Christian is furnished in his way to Zion, for faith and hope are often supplied out of it, in a dark hour. It is the storehouse of former experiences, and these are the believer's way-marks, by noticing of which he comes to know where he is, even in a dark time.

(Psa 42.6), 'O my God, my soul is cast down within me: therefore will I remember thee from the land of Jordan,' &c. It also helps the soul to godly sorrow and self-loathing, presenting old guilt anew before the conscience, and making it bleed afresh, though the sin be already pardoned; (Psa 25.7), 'Remember not the sins of my youth.' Where unpardoned guilt is lying on the sleeping conscience, it is often employed to bring in a word, which in a moment sets the whole soul astir; as when 'Peter remembered the words of Jesus – he went out and wept bitterly' (Matt 26.75). The Word of God laid up in a sanctified memory, serves a man to resist temptations, puts the sword in his hand against his spiritual enemies, and is a light to direct his steps in the way of religion and righteousness.

6: There is a change made on the body, and the members thereof, in respect of their use; they are consecrated to the Lord. Even 'the body is – for the Lord' (1 Cor 6.13). It is 'the temple of the Holy Ghost' (verse 19). The members thereof, that were formerly 'instruments of unrighteousness unto sin,' become 'instruments of righteousness unto God' (Rom 6.13), 'servants to righteousness unto holiness' (verse 19). The eye, that conveyed sinful imaginations into the heart, is under a covenant (Job 31.1) to do so no more, but to serve the soul , in viewing the works, and reading the Word, of God. The ear, that had often been death's porter, to let in sin, is turned to be the gate of life, by which the Word of life enters the soul. The tongue, that set on fire the whole course of nature, is restored to the office it was designed for by the Creator, namely, to be an instrument of glorifying Him, and setting forth His praise. In a word, the whole man is for God, in soul and body, which by this blessed change are made His.

7: This gracious change shines forth in the conversation. Even the outward man is renewed. A new heart makes newness of life. When 'the king's daughter is all glorious within, her clothing is of wrought gold' (Psa 45.13). 'The single eye' makes 'the whole body full of light' (Matt 6.22). This change will appear in

[222]

every part of a man's conversation, particularly in the following things.

(1) In the change of his company. Formerly, he despised the company of the saints, but now they are 'the excellent, in whom is all his delight' (Psa 16.3). 'I am a companion of all that fear thee,' said the royal psalmist (Psa 119.63). A renewed man joins himself with the saints, for he and they are like-minded in that which is their main work and business; they have all one new nature: they are travelling to Immanuel's land, and converse together in the language of Canaan. In vain do men pretend to religion, while ungodly company is their choice; for 'a companion of fools shall be destroyed' (Prov 13.20). Religion will make a man shy of throwing himself into an ungodly family, or any unnecessary familiarity with wicked men; as one who is healthy will beware of going into an infected house.

(2) In his relative capacity, he will be a new man. Grace makes men gracious in their several relations, and naturally leads them to the conscientious performance of relative duties. It does not only make good men and good women, but makes good subjects, good husbands, good wives, children, servants, and, in a word, good relatives in the church, commonwealth, and family. It is a just exception made against the religion of many, namely, that they are bad relatives, they are ill husbands, wives, masters, servants, &c. How can we prove ourselves to be new creatures, if we be just such as we were before, in our several relations? (2 Cor 5.17), 'Therefore, if any man be in Christ, he is a new creature: old things are passed away; behold, all things are become new.' Real godliness will gain a testimony to a man from the consciences of his nearest relations, though they know more of his sinful infirmities than others do, as we see in the case (2 Kings 4.1), 'Thy servant my husband is dead, and thou knowest that thy servant did fear the Lord.'

(3) In the way of his following his worldly business there is a great change. It appears to be no more his all, as it was before. Though saints apply themselves to worldly business, as well as

others, yet their hearts are not swallowed up in it. It is evident that they are carrying on a trade with heaven, as well as a trade with earth (Phil 3.20), 'For our conversation is in heaven.' They go about their employment in the world, as a duty laid upon them by the Lord of all, doing their lawful business as the will of God (Eph 6.7), working because He has said, 'Thou shalt not steal.'

(4) Such have a special concern for the advancement of the kingdom of Christ in the world; they espouse the interests of religion, and 'prefer Jerusalem above their chief joy' (Psa 137.6). However privately they live, grace gives them a public spirit, which will concern itself in the ark and work of God, in the Gospel of God, and in the people of God, even in those of them whom they never saw. As children of God, they naturally care for these things. They have a new concern for the spiritual good of others: no sooner do they taste of the power of grace themselves, but they are inclined to set up to be agents for Christ and holiness in the world, as appears in the case of the woman of Samaria, who, when Christ had manifested Himself to her, 'went her way into the city, and said unto the men, Come, see a man which told me all things that ever I did: is not this the Christ?' (John 4.28,29). They have seen and felt the evil of sin, and therefore pity the world lying in wickedness. They would fain pluck the brands out of the fire, remembering that they themselves were plucked out of it. They labour to commend religion to others, both by word and example; and rather deny themselves their liberty in indifferent things, than, by the uncharitable use of it, destroy others; (1 Cor 8.13), 'Wherefore, if meat make my brother to offend, I will eat no flesh while the world standeth, lest I make my brother to offend.'

(5) In their use of lawful comforts there is a great change. They rest not in them as their end, but use them as means to help them in their way. They draw their satisfaction from the higher springs even while the lower springs are running. Thus Hannah, having obtained a son, rejoiced not so much in the gift, as in the

Giver (1 Sam 2.1), 'And Hannah prayed and said, My heart rejoiceth in the Lord.' Yea, when the comforts of life are gone, they can subsist without them, and 'rejoice in the Lord although the fig-tree do not blossom' (Hab 3.17,18). Grace teaches to use the conveniences of the present life as pilgrims and to shew a holy moderation in all things. The heart, which formerly revelled in these things without fear, is now shy of being overmuch pleased with them. Being apprehensive of danger, it uses them warily; as the dogs of Egypt run, while they lap their water out of the river Nile, for fear of the crocodiles that are in it.

(6) This change shines forth in the man's performance of religious duties. He who lived in the neglect of them will do so no more, if once the grace of God enter into his heart. If a man be new-born, he will desire the sincere milk of the word (1 Pet 2.2,3). Whenever the prayerless person gets the Spirit of grace, He will be in him a Spirit of supplication (Zech 12.10). It is as natural for one that is born again to pray, as for the new-born babe to cry. (Acts 9.11), 'Behold, he prayeth!' His heart will be a temple for God, and his house a church. His devotion, which before was superficial and formal, is now spiritual and lively, forasmuch as heart and tongue are touched with a live coal from heaven. He rests not in the mere performance of duties, as careful only to get his task done, but in every duty seeks communion with God in Christ, justly considering them as means appointed of God for that end, and reckoning himself disappointed if he miss of it. Thus far of the nature of regeneration.

II: I come to show why this change is called regeneration or being born again. It is so called, because of the resemblance between natural and spiritual generation, which lies in the following particulars.

1: Natural generation is a mysterious thing: and so is spiritual generation (John 3.8), 'The wind bloweth where it listeth, and thou hearest the sound thereof, but canst not tell whence it cometh and whither it goeth: so is every one that is born of the Spirit.' The work of the Spirit is felt; but His way of working is a mystery we cannot comprehend. A new light is let into the mind, and the will is renewed; but how that light is conveyed thither, how the will is fettered with cords of love, and how the rebel is made a willing captive, we can no more tell, than we can tell 'how the bones do grow in the womb of her that is with child' (Eccl 11.5). As a man hears the sound of the wind, and finds it stirring, but knows not where it begins, and where it ends; 'so is every one that is born of the Spirit:' he finds the change that is made upon him; but how it is produced he knows not. One thing he may know, that whereas he was blind, now he sees: but 'the seed (of grace) springs and grows up, he knoweth not how' (Mark 4.26,27).

2 : In both, the creature comes to a being it had not before. The child is not, till it be generate; and a man has no gracious being, no being in grace, till he is regenerate. Regeneration is not so much the curing of a sick man, as 'the quickening of a dead man' (Eph 2.1–5). Man in his depraved state, is a mere nonentity in grace, and is brought into a new being by the power of Him 'who calleth things that be not as though they were;' being 'created in Jesus Christ unto good works' (Eph 2.10). Therefore our Lord Jesus, to give ground of hope to the Laodiceans in their wretched and miserable state, proposes himself as 'the beginning of the creation of God' (Rev 3.14), namely, the active beginning of it; 'for all things were made by him' at first (John 1.3). From whence they might gather, that as He made them when they were nothing, He could make them over again, when worse than nothing; the same hand that made them His creatures, could make them new creatures.

3 : As the child is passive in generation, so is the child of God in regeneration. The one contributes nothing to its own generation; neither does the other contribute any thing, by way of efficiency, to its own regeneration: for though a man may lay himself down at the pool, yet he has no hand in moving the water, no power in performing the cure. One is born the child of a king, another the child of a beggar: the child has no hand at all in this difference.

God leaves some in their depraved state; others he brings into a state of grace, or regeneracy. If you be thus honoured, no thanks to you; for 'who maketh thee to differ from another? and what hast thou that thou didst not receive?' (1 Cor 4.7).

4: There is a wonderful contexture of parts in both births. Admirable is the structure of man's body, in which there is such a variety of organs; nothing wanting, nothing superfluous. The psalmist, considering his own body, looks on it as a piece of marvellous work; 'I am fearfully and wonderfully made,' says he (Psa 139.14), 'and curiously wrought in the lowest parts of the earth' (verse 15); that is, in the womb, where I know not how the bones grow, any more than I know what is a-doing in the lowest parts of the earth. In natural generation we are curiously wrought, like a piece of needle-work, as the word imports: even so it is in regeneration: (Psa 45.14), 'She shall be brought unto the king in raiment of needle-work,' raiment curiously wrought. It is the same word in both texts. What that raiment is, the apostle tells us (Eph 4.24). It is 'the new man, which after God is created in righteousness and true holiness.' This is the raiment which he says, in the same place, we must put on; not excluding the imputed righteousness of Christ. Both are curiously wrought, as masterpieces of the manifold wisdom of God. O the wonderful contexture of graces in the new creature! O glorious creature, new-made after the image of God! It is grace for grace in Christ, which makes up this new man (John 1.16); even as in bodily generation, the child has member for member in the parent, has every member which the parent has in a certain proportion.

5: All this, in both cases, has its rise from that which is in itself very small and inconsiderable. O the power of God, in making such a creature of the corruptible seed, and much more in bringing forth the new creature from such small beginnings! It is as 'the little cloud, like a man's hand,' which spread, till 'heaven was black with clouds and wind, and there was a great rain' (1 Kings 18.44,45). A man gets a word at a sermon, which hundreds besides him hear, and let slip: but it remains with him, works in

[227]

him, and never leaves him, till the little world is turned upside down by it; that is, till he becomes a new man. It is like the vapour that got up into Ahasuerus's head, and cut off sleep from his eyes (Esther 6.1), which proved a spring of such motions as never ceased, until Mordecai, in royal pomp, was brought on horseback through the streets, proud Haman trudging at his foot; the same Haman afterwards hanged, Mordecai advanced, and the church delivered from Haman's hellish plot. 'The grain of mustard seed becometh a tree' (Matt 13.31,32). God loves to bring great things out of small beginnings.

6: Natural generation is carried on by degrees. (Job 10.10), 'Hast thou not poured me out as milk, and curdled me like cheese?' So is regeneration. It is with the soul, ordinarily, in regeneration, as with the blind man cured by our Lord, who first 'saw men as trees walking,' and afterwards 'saw every man clearly' (Mark 8.23–25). It is true, regeneration being, strictly speaking, a passing from death to life, the soul is quickened in a moment; like as when the embryo is brought to perfection in the womb, the soul is infused into the lifeless lump. Nevertheless, we may imagine somewhat similar conception in spiritual regeneration, whereby the soul is prepared for quickening, and the new creature is capable of growth (1 Pet 2.2), and of having life more abundantly (John 10.10).

7: In both there are new relations. The regenerate may call God, Father; for they are His children (John 1.12,13), 'begotten of him' (1 Pet 1.3). The bride, the Lamb's wife, that is, the church, is their mother (Gal 4.26). They are related, as brethren and sisters, to angels and glorified saints; 'the family of heaven.' They are of the heavenly stock: the meanest of them, 'the base things of the world' (1 Cor 1.28), the kinless things, as the word imports, who cannot boast of the blood that runs in their veins, are yet, by their new birth, near of kin with the excellent in the earth.

8: There is a likeness between the parent and the child. Every thing that generates, generates its like; and the regenerate are 'partakers of the divine nature' (2 Pet 1.4). The moral perfections of the divine nature are, in measure and degree, communicated to the renewed soul: thus the divine image is restored; so that, as the child resembles the father, the new creature resembles God Himself, being holy as He is holy.

9: As there is no birth without pain, both to the mother and to the child, so there is great pain in bringing forth the new creature. The children have more or less of these birth-pains, whereby they are 'pricked in their heart' (Acts 2.37). The soul has sore pains when under conviction and humiliation. 'A wounded spirit who can bear?' The mother is pained; 'Zion travails' (Isa 66.8). She sighs, groans, cries, and has hard labour, in her ministers and members, to bring forth children to her Lord (Gal 4.19), 'My little children, of whom I travail in birth again, until Christ be formed in you.' Never was a mother more feelingly touched with 'joy, that a man child is born into the world,' than she is upon the new birth of her children. But, what is more remarkable than all this, we read not only of our Lord Jesus Christ's 'travail,' or toil 'of soul' (Isa 53.11), but, what is more directly to our purpose, of His 'pains,' or pangs, as of one travailing in childbirth; so the word used (Acts 2.24), properly signifies. Well might he call the new creature, as Rachel called her dear-bought son, Benoni, that is, the son of my sorrow, and as she called another, Naphtali, that is, my wrestling, for the pangs of that travail put him to 'strong crying and tears' (Heb 5.7), yea, into an 'agony and bloody sweat' (Luke 22.44). And in the end he died of these pangs; they became to him 'the pains of death' (Acts 2.24).

III: I shall now apply this doctrine.

Use 1: By what is said, you may try whether you are in the state of grace or not. If you are brought out of the state of wrath or ruin, into the state of grace or salvation, you are new creatures, you are born again. But you will say, How shall we know whether we are born again, or not? *Answer:* Were you to ask me if the sun were risen, and how you should know whether it were risen or not, I would bid you look up to the heavens, and see it with your eyes. And would you know if the light be risen in your heart? Look in, and see. Grace is light, and discovers itself. Look into your mind, see if it has been illuminated in the knowledge of God. Have you been inwardly taught what God is? Were your eyes ever turned inward to see yourself, the sinfulness of your depraved state, the corruption of your nature, the sins of your heart and life? Were you ever led into a view of the exceeding sinfulness of sin? Have your eyes seen King Jesus in His beauty, the manifold wisdom of God in Him, His transcendent excellency, and absolute fulness and sufficiency, with the vanity and emptiness of all things else? Next, What change is there on your will? Are the fetters taken off, wherewith it was formerly bound up from moving heavenward? Has your will got a new disposition? Do you find an aversion to sin, and an inclination to good, wrought in your heart? Is your soul turned towards God as your chief end? Is your will new-moulded into some measure of conformity to the preceptive and providential will of God? Are you heartily reconciled to the covenant of peace, and fixedly disposed to the receiving of Christ, as He is offered in the gospel? And as to a change on your affections, are they rectified, and placed on right objects? Are your desires going out after God? Are they to His name, and the remembrance of Him? (Isa 26.8). Are your hopes in Him? Is your love set upon Him, and your hatred set against sin? Does your offending a good God affect your heart with sorrow, and do you fear sin more than suffering? Are your affections regulated? Are they, with respect to created comforts, brought down, as being too high; and with respect to God in Christ, raised up, as being too low? Has He the chief seat in your heart? And are all your lawful worldly comforts and enjoyments laid at His feet? Has your conscience been enlightened and awakened, refusing all ease, but from the application of the blood of a Redeemer? Is your memory sanctified, your body consecrated to the service of God? And are you now walking in newness of life? Thus you may discover whether you are born again or not.

But, for your further help in this matter, I will discourse a little of another sign of regeneration, namely, the love of the brethren; an evidence whereby the weakest and most timorous saints have often had comfort, when they could have little or no consolation from other marks proposed to them. This the apostle lays down (1 John 3.14), 'We know that we have passed from death unto life, because we love the brethren.' It is not to be thought that the apostle, by the brethren in this place means brethren by a common relation to the first Adam, but to the second Adam, Christ Jesus; because, however true it is that universal benevolence, a good will to the whole race of mankind, takes place in the renewed soul, as being a lively lineament of the divine image, yet the whole context speaks of those that are 'the sons of God' (verses 1, 2); 'children of God' (verse 10); 'born of God' (verse 9); distinguishing between 'the children of God,' and 'the children of the devil' (verse 10); between those that are 'of the devil' (verses 8, 12), and those that are 'of God' (verse 10). The text itself comes in as a reason why we should not marvel that the world hates the brethren, the children of God (verse 13). How can we marvel at it, seeing the love of the brethren is an evidence of one's having passed from death to life? Therefore it were absurd to look for that love amongst the men of the world, who are dead in trespasses and sins. They cannot love the brethren; no wonder, then, that they hate them. Wherefore it is plain, that by brethren here, are meant brethren by regeneration.

Now, in order to set this mark of regeneration in a true light, consider these three things. 1. This love to the brethren, is a love to them as such. Then do we love them in the sense of the text, when the grace, or image of God in them, is the chief motive of our love to them. When we love the godly for their godliness, the saints for their sanctity or holiness, then we love God in them, and so may conclude are born of God; for 'every one that loveth him that begat, loveth him also that is begotten of him' (1 John 5.1). Hypocrites may love saints on account of civil relations to them, because of their obliging conversation, for their being of the same opinion as to outward religious matters, and on many other such like accounts, whereby wicked men may be induced to love the godly. But happy they who love them merely for grace in them, for their heaven-born temper and disposition, who can pick this pearl even out of infirmities in and about them, lay hold of it, and love them for it. 2. It is a love that will be given to all in whom the grace of God appears. They that love one saint, because he is a saint, will have 'love to all the saints' (Eph 1.15). They will love all, who, in their view, bear the image of God. Those that cannot love a gracious person in rags, but confine their love to those of them who wear gay clothing, have not this love to the brethren in them. Those who confine their love to a party to whom God has not confined his grace, are souls too narrow to be put among the children. In what points soever men differ from us in their judgment or way, yet if they appear to agree with us, in love to God, and our Saviour Jesus Christ, and in bearing His image, we shall love them as brethren, if we are of the heavenly family. 3. If this love be in us, the more grace any person appears to be possessed of, he will be the more beloved by us. The more vehemently the holy fire of grace does flame in any, the hearts of true Christians will be the more warmed in love to them. It is not with the saints as with many other men, who make themselves the standards for others, and love them so far as they think they are like themselves; but, if they seem to outshine and darken them, their love is turned to hatred and envy, and they endeavour to detract from the due praise of their exemplary piety because nothing relishes with them, in the practice of religion, that goes beyond their own measure. What of the life and power of religion appears in others, serves only to raise the serpentine grudge in their pharisaical hearts. But as for those who are born again, their love and affection to the brethren bears proportion to the degrees of the divine image they discern in them.

Now, if you would improve these things to the knowledge of your state, I would advise you, 1. To set apart some time, when you are at home, for a review of your case, to try your state by what has been said. Many have comfort and clearness as to their state, at a sermon, who in a little time lose it again, because while they hear the Word preached, they make application of it, but do not consider these things more deliberately and leisurely when alone. The impression is too sudden and short to give lasting comfort; and it is often so indeliberate, that it has bad consequences. Therefore set about this work at home, after earnest and serious prayer to God for His help in it. Complain not of your want of time while the night follows the busy day, nor of place, while fields and outhouses are to be got. 2. Renew your repentance before the Lord. Guilt lying on the conscience, unrepented of, may darken all your evidences and marks of grace. It provokes the Spirit of grace to withdraw; and when He goes, our light ceases. It is not a fit time for a saint to read his evidences, when the candle is blown out by some conscience-wounding guilt. 3. Exert the powers of the new nature; let the graces of the divine Spirit discover themselves in you by action. If you would know whether there is sacred fire in your breast, or not, you must blow the coal; for although it exist, and be a live coal, yet if it be under the ashes, it will give you no light. Settle in your hearts a firm purpose, through the grace that is in Christ Jesus, to comply with every known duty, and watch against every known sin, having readiness of mind to be instructed in what you know not. If gracious souls would thus manage their inquiries into their state, it is likely that they would have a comfortable issue. And if others would take such a solemn review, and make trial of their state, impartially examining themselves before the tribunal of their consciences, they might have a timely discovery of their own sinfulness; but the neglect of self-examination leaves most men under sad delusions as to their state, and deprives many saints of the comfortable sight of the grace of God in them.

But that I may afford some further help to true Christians in their inquiries into their state, I shall propose and briefly answer some cases or doubts, which may possibly hinder some persons from the comfortable view of their happy state. The children's bread must not be withheld, though, while it is held forth to them, the dogs should snatch at it.

Case 1: 'I doubt if I be regenerate, because I know not the precise time of my conversion; nor can I trace the particular steps of the way in which it was brought to pass.' *Answer:* Though it is very desirable to be able to give an account of the beginning, and the gradual advances, of the Lord's work upon our souls, as some saints can distinctly do, the manner of the Spirit's working being still a mystery, yet this is not necessary to prove the truth of grace. Happy he that can say, in this case, as the blind man in the Gospel, 'One thing I know, that whereas I was blind, now I see.' As, when we see flame, we know there is fire, though we know not how or when it began; so the truth of grace may be discerned in us, though we know not how or when it was dropped into our hearts. If you can perceive the happy change which is wrought on your soul; if you find your mind is enlightened, your will inclined to comply with the will of God in all things, especially to fall in with the divine plan of salvation through a crucified Redeemer; in vain do you trouble yourself, and refuse comfort, because you know not how and what way it was brought about.

Case 2: 'If I were a new creature, sin could not prevail against me as it does.' Answer: Though we must not lay pillows for hypocrites to rest their heads upon, who indulge themselves in their sins, and make the doctrine of God's grace subservient to their lusts, lying down contentedly in the bond of iniquity like men that are fond of golden chains, yet it must be owned, 'the just man falleth seven times a day'; and iniquity may prevail against the children of God. But if you are groaning under the weight of the body of death, the corruption of your nature; loathing yourself for the sins of your heart and life; striving to mortify your lusts; fleeing daily to the blood of Christ for pardon, and looking to His Spirit for sanctification: though you may be obliged to say with the Psalmist, 'Iniquities prevail against me;' yet you may add with him, 'As for our transgressions, thou shalt purge them away' (Psa 65.3). The new creature does not yet possess the house alone: it dwells by the side of an ill neighbour, namely, remaining corruption, the relics of depraved nature. They struggle together for the mastery: 'The flesh lusteth against the spirit, and the spirit against the flesh' (Gal 5.17). And sometimes corruption prevails, bringing the child of God into captivity to the law of sin (Rom 7.23). Let not therefore the prevailing of corruption make you, in this case, conclude you are none of God's children: but let it humble you, to be the more watchful, and to thirst the more intensely after Jesus Christ, His blood and Spirit; and that very disposition will evidence a principle of grace in you which seeks the destruction of sin that prevails so often against you.

Case 3: 'I find the motions of sin in my heart more violent since the Lord began His work on my soul, than they were before that time. Can this consist with a change of my nature?' *Answer:* Dreadful is the case of many, who, after God has had a remarkable dealing with their souls, tending to their reformation, have thrown off all bonds, and have become grossly and openly immoral and profane; as if the devil had returned into their hearts with seven spirits worse than himself. All I shall say to such persons is, that their state is exceedingly dangerous; they are in danger of sinning against the Holy Ghost; therefore let them repent, before it be too late. But if it be not thus with you; though corruption is stirring itself more violently than formerly, as if all the forces of hell were raised, to hold fast, or bring back, a fugitive; yet these stirrings may consist with a change of your nature. When the restraint of grace is newly laid upon corruption, it is no wonder if it acts more vigorously than before, 'warring against the law of the mind' (Rom 7.23). The motions of sin may really be most violent when the new principle is brought in to cast it out. The sun, sending its beams through the window, discovers the motes in the house, and their motions, which were not seen before; so the light of grace may discover the risings and actings of corruption, in another manner than ever the man saw them before, though they really do not rise nor act more vigorously. Sin is not quite dead in the regenerate soul; it is but dying, and dying

[235]

a lingering death, being crucified; no wonder there are great fightings, when it is sick at the heart, and death is at the door. Besides, temptations may be more in number, and stronger, while Satan is striving to bring you back, who are escaped, than while he only endeavoured to retain you: 'After ye were illuminated, ye endured a great fight of afflictions,' says the apostle to the Hebrews (chap 10.32). But 'cast not away your confidence' (verse 35). Remember His 'grace is sufficient for you, and the God of peace shall bruise Satan under your feet shortly.' Pharaoh and his Egyptians never made such a formidable appearance against the Israelites, as at the Red Sea, after they were brought out of Egypt: but then were the pursuers nearest to a total overthrow (Exod chap 14). Let not this case, therefore, make you raze the foundations of your trust, but be ye emptied of self, and strong in the Lord, and in the power of His might, and you shall come off victorious.

Case 4: 'But when I compare my love to God with my love to some created enjoyments, I find the pulse of my affections beats stronger to the creature than to the Creator. How then can I call Him Father? Nay, alas! those turnings of heart within me, and glowings of affection to Him, which I had, are gone; so that I fear all the love which I ever had to the Lord has been but a fit and flash of affection, such as hypocrites often have.' *Answer:* It cannot be denied, that the predominant love of the world is a certain mark of an unregenerate state (1 John 2.15), 'If any man love the world, the love of the Father is not in him.' Nevertheless, those are not always the strongest affections which are most violent. A man's affections may be more moved, on some occasions, by an object that is little regarded, than by another that is exceedingly beloved; even as a little brook sometimes makes more noise than a great river. The strength of our affections is to be measured by the firmness and fixedness of the root, not by the violence of their actings. Suppose a person meeting with a friend, who has been long abroad, finds his affections more vehemently acting towards his friend on that occasion, than towards his own wife and

[236]

children; will he therefore say, that he loves his friend more than them? Surely not. Even so, although the Christian may find himself more moved in his love to the creature, than in his love to God; yet it is not therefore to be said, that he loves the creature more than God, seeing love to God is always more firmly rooted in a gracious heart, than love to any created enjoyment whatever; as appears when competition arises in such a manner, that the one or other is to be foregone. Would you then know your case? Retire into your own hearts, and there lay the two in the balance, and try which of them weighs down the other. Ask yourself, as in the sight of God, whether you would part with Christ for the creature, or part with the creature for Christ, if you were left to your choice in the matter? If you find your heart disposed to part with what is dearest to you in the world for Christ at His call, you have no reason to conclude you love the creature more than God; but, on the contrary, that you love God more than the creature, although you do not feel such violent motions in the love of God, as in the love of some created thing (Matt 10.37), 'He that loveth father or mother more than me, is not worthy of me.' (Luke 14.26), 'If any man come to me, and hate not his father and mother – he cannot be my disciple.' From which texts compared we may infer, that he who hates, that is, is ready to part with father and mother for Christ, is, in our Lord's account, one that loves them less than Him, and not one who loves father and mother more than Him. Moreover, you are to consider that there is a twofold love to Christ. 1. There is a sensible love to Him, which is felt as a dart in the heart, and makes a holy love-sickness in the soul, arising from want of enjoyment, as in that case of the spouse (Cant 5.8), 'I charge you, O daughters of Jerusalem, if ye find my beloved, that ye tell him that I am sick of love:' or else from the fulness of it, as in Cant 2.5, 'Stay me with flagons, comfort me with apples; for I am sick of love.' These glowings of affection are usually wrought in young converts, who are ordinarily made 'to sing in the days of their youth' (Hos 2.15). While the fire-edge is upon the young convert, he looks upon others, reputed to be godly, and not finding them in such a temper or disposition as himself, he is ready to censure them, and to think there is far less religion in the world than indeed there is. But when his own cup comes to settle below the brim, and he finds that in himself which made him question the state of others, he is more humbled, and feels more and more the necessity of daily recourse to the blood of Christ for pardon, and to the Spirit of Christ for sanctification; and thus grows downwards in humiliation, self-loathing, and self-denial. 2. There is a rational love to Christ, which, without these sensible emotions felt in the former case, evidences itself by a dutiful regard to the divine authority and command. When one bears such a love to Christ, though the vehement stirrings of affection be wanting, yet he is truly tender of offending a gracious God, endeavours to walk before Him unto all well pleasing, and is grieved at the heart for what is displeasing unto Him (1 John 5.3), 'For this is the love of God, that we keep his commandments.' Now, although that sensible love does not always continue with you, you have no reason to deem it a hypocritical fit, while the rational love remains with you; any more than a loving and faithful wife needs question her love to her husband, when her fondness is abated.

Case 5: 'The attainments of hypocrites and apostates are a terror to me, and come like a shaking storm on me, when I am about to conclude, from the marks of grace which I seem to find in myself, that I am in the state of grace.' *Answer:* These things should indeed stir us up to a most serious and impartial examination of ourselves, but ought not to keep us in a continued suspense as to our state. Sirs, you see the outside of hypocrites, their duties, their gifts, their tears, and so on, but you see not their inside; you do not discern their hearts, the bias of their spirits. Upon what you see of them, you found a judgment of charity as to their state; and you do well to judge charitably in such a case, because you cannot know the secret springs of their actions: but you are seeking, and ought to have, a judgment of certainty as to your own state, and therefore are to look into that part of religion which none in the world but yourselves can discern in you and which you can as little see in others. A hypocrite's religion may appear far greater than that of a sincere soul: but that which makes the greatest figure in the eyes of men, is often of least worth before God. I would rather utter one of those groans which the apostle speaks of (Rom 8.26), than shed Esau's tears, have Balaam's prophetic spirit, or the joy of the stony-ground hearer. 'The fire that shall try every man's work,' will try, not of what bulk it is, but 'of what sort it is' (1 Cor 3.13). Though you may know what bulk of religion another has, and that it be more bulky than your own, yet God doth not regard that; why then do you make such a matter of it? It is impossible for you, without divine revelation, certainly to know of what sort another man's religion is: but you may certainly know what sort your own is of, without extraordinary revelation; otherwise the apostle would not exhort the saints to 'give diligence to make their calling and election sure' (2 Pet 1.10). Therefore the attainments of hypocrites and apostates should not disturb you, in your serious inquiry into your own state. I will tell you two things, wherein the meanest saints go beyond the most refined hypocrites: 1. In denying themselves, renouncing all confidence in themselves, and their own works, acquiescing in, being well pleased with, and venturing their souls upon God's plan of salvation through Jesus Christ (Matt 5.3), 'Blessed are the poor in spirit, for theirs is the kingdom of heaven.' And (chap 11.6), 'Blessed is he, whosoever shall not be offended in me.' (Phil 3.3), 'We are the circumcision, which worship God in the spirit, and rejoice in Christ Jesus, and have no confidence in the flesh.' 2. In a real hatred of all sin, being willing to part with every lust, without exception, and to comply with every duty which the Lord makes, or shall make known to them (Psa 119.6), 'Then shall I not be ashamed, when I have respect unto all thy commandments.' Try yourselves by these.

Case 6: 'I see myself fall so far short of the saints mentioned in the Scriptures, and of several excellent persons of my own acquaintance, that, when I look on them, I can hardly look on myself as one of the same family with them.' *Answer:* It is indeed matter of humiliation, that we do not get forward to that measure of grace and holiness which we see is attainable in this life. This should make us more vigorously press towards the mark: but surely it is from the devil, that weak Christians make a rack for themselves of the attainments of the strong. To yield to the temptation is as unreasonable as for a child to dispute away his relation to his father, because he is not of the same stature with his elder brethren. There are saints of several sizes in Christ's family; some fathers, some young men, and some little children (1 John 2.13,14).

Case 7: 'I never read in the word of God, nor did I ever know of a child of God, so tempted, and so left of God, as I am; and therefore, no saint's case being like mine, I cannot but conclude that I am none of their number.' *Answer:* This objection arises to some from their ignorance of the Scriptures and the experience of Christians. It is profitable, in this case, to impart the matter to some experienced Christian friend, or to some godly minister. This has been a blessed means of peace to some persons, while their case, which appeared to them to be singular, has been proved to have been the case of other saints. The Scriptures give instances of very horrid temptations, wherewith the saints have been assaulted. Job was tempted to blaspheme; this was the great thing the devil aimed at in the case of that great saint (Job 1.11), 'He will curse thee to thy face.' (Chap 2.9), 'Curse God and die.' Asaph was tempted to think it was in vain to be religious, which was in effect to throw off all religion (Psa 73.13), 'Verily I have cleansed my heart in vain.' Yea, Christ Himself was tempted to 'cast himself down from a pinnacle of the temple,' and to 'worship the devil' (Matt 4.6-9). And many of the children of God have not only been attacked with, but have actually yielded to very gross temptations for a time. Peter denied Christ, and cursed and swore that he knew Him not (Mark 14.71). Paul, when a persecutor, compelled even saints to blaspheme (Acts 26. 10,11). Many of the saints can, from their sad experience, bear witness to very gross temptations, which have astonished their spirits, made their very flesh to tremble, and sickened their bodies. Satan's fiery darts make terrible work, and will cost some pains to quench them, by a vigorous managing of the shield of faith (Eph 6.16). Sometimes he makes such desperate attacks, that never was one more put to it, in running to and fro, without intermission, to quench the fire-balls incessantly thrown into his house by an enemy, designing to burn the house about him, than the poor tempted saint is, to repel Satanical injections. But these injections, these horrid temptations, though they are a dreadful affliction, they are not the sins of the tempted, unless they make them theirs by consenting to them. They will be charged upon the tempter alone, if they be not consented to; and will no more be laid to the charge of the tempted party, than a bastard's being laid down at a chaste man's door will fix guilt upon him.

But suppose neither minister nor private Christian, to whom you go, can tell you of any who has been in your case; yet you ought not thence to infer that your case is singular, far less to give up hope: for it is not to be thought that every godly minister, or private Christian, has had experience of all the cases which a child of God may be in. We need not doubt that some have had distresses known only to God and their own consciences; and so to others these distresses are as if they had never been. Yea, and though the Scripture contain suitable directions for every case which a child of God can be in, and these illustrated with a sufficient number of examples, yet it is not to be imagined that there are in the Scriptures perfect instances of every particular case incident to the saints. Therefore, though you cannot find an instance of your case in the Scripture, yet bring your case to it, and you shall find suitable remedies prescribed there for it. Study rather to make use of Christ for your case, who has a remedy for all diseases, than to know if ever any was in your case. Though one should show you an instance of your case in an undoubted saint, yet none could promise that it would certainly give you ease, for a scrupulous conscience would readily find out some difference. And if nothing but a perfect conformity of another's case to yours will satisfy, it will be hard, if not impossible, to satisfy you; for it is with people's cases, as with their natural faces: though the faces of all men are of one make, and some are so very like others, that, at first view, we are ready to take them for the same, yet if you view them more accurately, you will see something in every face, distinguishing it from all others, though possibly you cannot tell what it is. Wherefore I conclude, that if you can find in yourselves the marks of regeneration, proposed to you from the Word, you ought to conclude you are in the state of grace, though your case were singular, which is indeed unlikely.

Case 8: 'The afflictions I meet with are strange and unusual. I doubt if ever a child of God was tried with such dispensations of providence as I am.' *Answer:* Much of what was said on the preceding case, may be helpful in this. Holy Job was assaulted with this temptation (Job 5.1), 'To which of the saints wilt thou turn?' But he rejected it, and held fast his integrity. The apostle supposes that Christians may be tempted to 'think it strange concerning the fiery trial' (1 Pet 4.12). But they have need of larger experience than Solomon's, who will venture to say, 'See, this is new' (Eccl 1.10). What though, in respect of the outward dispensations of providence, 'it happen to you according to the work of the wicked?' Yet you may be just, notwithstanding, according to Solomon's observation (Eccl 8.14). Sometimes we travel in ways where we can neither perceive the prints of the foot of man nor beast, yet we cannot from thence conclude that there was never any there before us: so though you cannot perceive the footsteps of the flock, in the way of your affliction, you must not therefore conclude that you are the first that ever travelled that road. But what if it were so? Some one saint or other must be first, in drinking of each bitter cup the rest have drunk of. What warrant have you or I to limit the Holy One of Israel to a trodden path, in His dispensations towards us? 'Thy way is in the sea, and thy path in the great waters; and thy footsteps are not known' (Psa 77.19). If the Lord should carry you to heaven by some retired road, so to speak, you would have no ground of complaint. Learn to allow sovereignty a latitude; be at your duty and let no affliction cast a veil over any evidences you otherwise have for your being in the state of grace: for 'no man knoweth either love or hatred by all that is before them' (Eccl 9.1).

Use 11: You that are strangers to this new birth, be convinced of the absolute necessity of it. Are all who are in the state of grace born again? then you have neither part nor lot in it, who are not born again. I must tell you in the words of our Lord and Saviour – and O that He would speak them to your hearts! – 'Ye *must* be born again' (John 3.7). For your conviction, consider these few things.

1: Regeneration is absolutely necessary to qualify you to do any thing really good and acceptable to God. While you are not born again, your best works are but glittering sins; for though the matter of them is good, they are quite marred in the performance. Consider, 1. That without regeneration there is no faith, and 'without faith it is impossible to please God' (Heb 11.6). Faith is a vital act of the new-born soul. The evangelist, showing the different entertainment which our Lord Jesus had from different persons, some receiving Him, some rejecting Him, points at regenerating grace as the true cause of that difference, without which never any one would have received Him. He tells us, that 'as many as received him,' were those 'which were born – of God' (John 1.11–13). Unregenerate men may presume; but true faith they cannot have. Faith is a flower that grows not in the field of nature. As the tree cannot grow without a root, neither can a man believe without the new nature, whereof the principle of believing is a part. 2. Without regeneration a man's works are dead works. As is the principle, so must the effects be: if the lungs are rotten, the breath will be unsavoury; and he who at best is dead in sin, his works at best will be but dead works. 'Unto them that are defiled and unbelieving, is nothing pure – being abominable, and disobedient, and unto every good work reprobate' (Titus 1.15,16). If we could say of a man, that he is more blameless in his life than any other in the world, that he reduces his body with fasting and has made his knees as horns with continual praying, if he is not born again, that exception would mar all. As if one should say, There is a well-proportioned body, but the soul is gone; it is but a dead lump. This is a melting consideration. You do many things materially good; but God says, All these things avail not, as long as I see the old nature reigning in the man. (Gal 6.15), 'For in Jesus Christ neither circumcision availeth any thing, nor uncircumcision, but a new creature.'

If you are not born again (1) All your reformation is naught in the sight of God. You have shut the door, but the thief is still in the house. It may be you are not what once you were; yet you are not what you must be, if ever you see heaven; for 'except a man be born again, he cannot see the kingdom of God' (John 3.3). (2) Your prayers are an 'abomination to the Lord (Prov 15.8). It may be, others admire your seriousness; you cry as for your life; but God accounts of the opening of your mouth as one would account of the opening of a grave full of rottenness (Rom 3.13), 'Their throat is an open sepulchre.' Others are affected with your prayers, which seem to them as if they would rend the heavens; but God accounts them but as the howling of a dog: 'They have not cried unto me with their hearts, when they howled upon their beds' (Hos 7.14). Others take you for a wrestler and prevailer with God; but He can take no delight in you nor your prayers (Isa 66.3), 'He that killeth an ox is as if he slew a man: he that sacrificeth a lamb, as if he cut off a dog's neck; – he that burneth incense, as if he blessed an idol.' Why, because you are yet 'in the gall of bitterness, and bond of iniquity!' (3) All you have done for God, and His cause in the world, though it may be followed with temporal rewards, yet it is lost as to divine acceptance. This is clear from the case of Jehu, who was indeed rewarded with a kingdom, for his executing due vengeance upon the house of Ahab, as being a work good for the matter of it because it was commanded of God, as you may see (2 Kings 9.7); yet was he punished for it in his posterity, because he did it not in a right manner (Hos 1.4), 'I will avenge the blood of Jezreel upon the house of Jehu.' God looks chiefly to the heart: and if so, truly, though the outward appearance be fairer than that of many others, yet the hidden man of thy heart is loathsome; you look well before men, but are not, as Moses was, fair to God, as the margin has it (Acts 7.20). O what a difference is there between the characters of Asa and Amaziah! 'The high places were not removed; nevertheless, Asa's heart was perfect with the Lord all his days' (1 Kings 15.14). 'Amaziah did that which was right in the sight of the Lord, but not with a perfect heart' (2 Chron 25.2). It may be you are zealous against sin in others, and admonish them of their duty, and reprove them for their sin; and they hate you, because you do your duty; but I must tell you, God hates you too, because you do it not in a right manner; and that you can never do, whilst you are not born again. (4) All your struggles against sin in your own heart and life, are naught. The proud Pharisee afflicted his body with fasting, and God struck his soul, in the mean time, with a sentence of condemnation (Luke 18). Balaam struggled with his covetous temper, to that degree, that though he loved the wages of unrighteousness, yet he would not win them by cursing Israel: but he died the death of the wicked (Numb 31.8). All you do, while in an unregenerate state, is for yourself: therefore it will fare with you as with a subject, who having reduced the rebels, puts the crown on his own head, and loses all his good service and his head too.

Objection: 'If it be thus with us, then we need never perform any religious duty at all.' *Answer:* The conclusion is not just. No inability of yours can excuse from the duty which God's law lays on you: and there is less evil in doing your duty than there is in the omission of it. But there is a difference between omitting a duty, and doing it as you do it. A man orders the masons to build him a house. If they quite neglect the work, that will not be accepted; if they build on the old rotten foundation, neither will that please: but they must raze the foundation, and build on firm ground. 'Go thou and do likewise.' In the mean time, it is not in vain even for you to seek the Lord: for though He regards you not, yet He may have respect to His own ordinances, and do you good thereby, as was said before.

2: Without regeneration there is no communion with God. There is a society on earth, whose 'fellowship is with the Father, and with his Son Jesus Christ' (1 John 1.3). But out of that society, all the unregenerate are excluded; for they are all enemies to God, as you heard before at large. Now, 'can two walk together, except they be agreed?' (Amos 3.3.). They are all unholy: and 'what communion hath light with darkness – Christ with Belial?' (2 Cor 6.14,15). They may have a show and semblance of holiness; but they are strangers to true holiness, and therefore 'without God in the world.' How sad it is, to be employed in religious duties, yet to have no fellowship with God in them! You would not be content with your meat, unless it nourished you; nor with your clothes, unless they kept you warm: and how can you satisfy yourselves with your duties, while you have no communion with God in them?

3: Regeneration is absolutely necessary to qualify you for heaven. None go to heaven but those who are made meet for it (Col 1.12). As it was with Solomon's temple (1 Kings 6.7), so is it with the temple above. It is 'built of stone made ready before it is brought thither;' namely, of 'lively stones' (1 Pet 2.5), 'wrought for the selfsame thing' (2 Cor 5.5); for they cannot be laid in that glorious building just as they come out of the quarry of depraved nature. Jewels of gold are not meet for swine, and far less jewels of glory for unrenewed sinners. Beggars, in their rags, are not fit for kings' houses, nor sinners to enter into the King's palace, without the raiment of needlework (Psa 45.14,15). What wise man would bring fish out of the water to feed in his meadows? or send his oxen to feed in the sea? Even as little are the unregenerate fit for heaven, or heaven fit for them. It would never be relished by them.

The unregenerate would find fault with heaven on several accounts. As (1) That it is a strange country. Heaven is the renewed man's native country: his Father is in heaven; his mother is Jerusalem, which is above (Gal 4.26). He is born from above (John 3.3.). Heaven is his home (2 Cor 5.1); therefore he looks on himself as a stranger on this earth, and his heart is homeward (Heb 11.16), 'They desire a better country, that is, a heavenly country.' But the unregenerate man is the man of the earth (Psa 10.18); written in the earth (Jer 17.13). Now, 'Home is home, be it never so homely:' therefore he minds earthly things (Phil 3.19). There is a peculiar sweetness in our native soil; and with difficulty are men drawn to leave it, and dwell in a strange country. In no case does that prevail more than in this; for unrenewed men would quit their pretensions to heaven, were it not that they see they cannot make a better bargain. (2) There is nothing in heaven that they delight in, as agreeable to the carnal heart (Rev 21.27), 'For there shall in no wise enter into it any thing that defileth.' When Mahomet pronounced paradise to be a place of sensual delights, his religion was greedily embraced; for that is the heaven men naturally choose. If the covetous man could get bags full of gold there, and the voluptuous man could promise himself his sensual delights, they might be reconciled to heaven, and made meet for it too; but since it is not so, though they may utter fair words about it, truly it has little of their hearts. (3) Every corner there is filled with that which of all things they have the least liking for; and that is holiness, true holiness, perfect holiness. Where one that abhors swine's flesh bidden to a feast where all the dishes were of that sort of meat, but variously prepared, he would find fault with every dish at the table, notwithstanding all the art used to make them palatable. It is true, there is joy in heaven, but it is holy joy; there are pleasures in heaven, but they are holy pleasures; there are places in heaven, but it is holy ground. That holiness which is in every place, and in every thing there, would mar all to the unregenerate. (4) Were they carried thither, they would not only change their place, which would be a great heart-break, but they would change their company too. Truly, they would never like the company there, who care not for communion with God here, nor value the fellowship of His people, at least in the vitals of practical godliness. Many, indeed, mix themselves with the godly on earth, to procure a name to themselves, and to cover the sinfulness of their hearts, but that trade cannot be managed there. (5) They would never like the employment of heaven, they care so little for it now. The business of the saints there would be an intolerable burden to them, seeing it is not agreeable to their nature. To be taken up in beholding, admiring, and praising Him that sits on the throne, and the Lamb, would be work unsuitable, and therefore unsavoury to an unrenewed soul. (6) They would find this fault with it, that the whole is of everlasting continuance. This would be a killing ingredient in it to them. How would such as now account the Sabbath day a burden, brook the celebration of an everlasting Sabbath in the heavens!

4 : Regeneration is absolutely necessary to your being admitted into heaven (John 3.3). No heaven without it. Though carnal men could digest all those things which make heaven so unsuitable for them, yet God will never bring them thither. Therefore born again you must be, else you shall never see heaven; you shall perish eternally. For (1) There is a bill of exclusion against you in the court of heaven, and against all of your sort; 'Except a man be born again, he cannot see the kingdom of God (John 3.3). Here is a bar before you, that men and angels cannot remove. To hope for heaven, in the face of this peremptory sentence, is to hope that God will recall His Word, and sacrifice His truth and faithfulness to your safety; which is infinitely more than to hope that 'the earth shall be forsaken for you, and the rock removed out of its place.' (2) There is no holiness without regeneration. It is 'the new man which is created in true holiness' (Eph 4.24). And no heaven without holiness; for 'without holiness no man shall see the Lord' (Heb 12.14). Will the gates of pearl be opened to let in dogs and swine? No; their place is without (Rev 22.15). God will not admit such into the holy place of communion with Him here; and will he admit them into the holiest of all hereafter? Will He

take the children of the devil, and permit them to sit with Him in His throne? Or, will He bring the unclean into the city whose street is pure gold? Be not deceived; grace and glory are but two links of one chain, which God has joined, and no man shall put asunder. None are transplanted into the paradise above, but out of the nursery of grace below. If you be unholy while in this world, you will be for ever miserable in the world to come. (3) All the unregenerate are without Christ, and therefore have no hope while in that case (Eph 2.12). Will Christ prepare mansions of glory for those who refuse to receive Him into their hearts? Nay, rather, will He not 'laugh at their calamity,' who now 'set at nought all his counsel?' (Prov 1.25,26). (4) There is an infallible connexion between a finally unregenerate state and damnation, arising from the nature of the things themselves, and from the decree of heaven which is fixed and immovable as mountains of brass (John 3.3; Rom 8.6). 'To be carnally minded is death.' An unregenerate state is hell in the bud. It is eternal destruction in embryo, growing daily, though you do not discern it. Death is painted on many a fair face, in this life. Depraved nature makes men meet to be partakers of the inheritance of the damned, in utter darkness. 1. The heart of stone within you is a sinking weight. As a stone naturally goes downward, so the hard stony heart tends downward to the bottomless pit. You are hardened against reproof; though you are told your danger, yet you will not see it, you will not believe it. But remember that the conscience being now seared with a hot iron, is a sad presage of everlasting burnings. 2. Your unfruitfulness under the means of grace, fits you for the axe of God's judgments (Matt 3.10), 'Every tree that bringeth not forth good fruit is hewn down, and cast into the fire.' The withered branch is fuel for the fire (John 15.6). Tremble at this, you despisers of the Gospel: if you be not thereby made meet for heaven, you will be like the barren ground, bearing briers and thorns, 'nigh unto cursing, whose end is to be burned' (Heb 6.8). 3. The hellish dispositions of mind, which discover themselves in profanity of life, fit the guilty for the regions of horror. A profane life will have a miserable end. 'They which do such things shall not inherit the kingdom of God' (Gal 5.19–21). Think on this, you prayerless persons, you mockers of religion, you cursers and swearers, you unclean and unjust persons, who have not so much as moral honesty to keep you from lying, cheating, and stealing. What sort of a tree do you think it is, upon which these fruits grow? Is it a tree of righteousness, which the Lord has planted? Or is it not such a one as cumbers the ground, which God will pluck up for fuel to the fire of His wrath? 4. Your being dead in sin makes you meet to be wrapped in flames of brimstone as a winding-sheet; and to be buried in the bottomless pit, as in a grave. Great was the cry in Egypt, when the first-born in each family was dead; but are there not many families, where all are dead together? Nay, many there are who are twice dead, plucked up by the root. Sometimes in their life they have been roused by apprehensions of death and its consequences; but now they are so far on in their way to the land of darkness, that they hardly ever have the least glimmering of light from heaven. 5. The darkness of your minds presages eternal darkness. O the horrid ignorance with which some are plagued; while others, who have got some rays of the light of reason in their heads, are utterly void of spiritual light in their hearts! If you knew your case, you would cry out, Oh! darkness! darkness! darkness! making way for the blackness of darkness for ever! The face-covering is upon you already, as condemned persons, so near are you to everlasting darkness. It is only Jesus Christ who can stop the execution, pull the napkin off the face of the condemned malefactor, and put a pardon in his hand (Isa 25.7). 'He will destroy, in this mountain, the face of the covering cast over all people,' that is, the face-covering cast over the condemned, as in Haman's case (Esth 7.8). 'As the word went out of the king's mouth, they covered Haman's face.' 6. The chains of darkness you are bound with in the prison of your depraved state (Isa 61.1), fits you to be cast into the burning fiery furnace. Ah, miserable men! Sometimes their consciences stir within them, and they begin to think of amending their ways. But alas! they are in chains, they cannot do it. They are chained by the heart; their lusts cleave so fast to them, that they cannot, nay, they will not shake them off. Thus you see what affinity there is between an unregenerate state, and the state of the damned, the state of absolute and irretrievable misery. Be convinced, then, that you must be born again; put a high value on the new birth, and eagerly desire it.

The text tells you, that the Word is the seed, whereof the new creature is formed: therefore take heed to it, and entertain it, as it is your life. Apply yourself to the reading of the Scripture. You that cannot read, get others to read it to you. Wait diligently on the preaching of the Word, as by divine appointment the special means of conversion; for – it pleased God, by the foolishness of preaching, to save them that believe' (1 Cor 1.21). Wherefore cast not yourselves out of Christ's way; reject not the means of grace, lest you be found to judge yourselves unworthy of eternal life. Attend carefully to the Word preached. Hear every sermon, as if you were hearing for eternity; take heed that the fowls of the air pick not up this seed from you, as it is sown. 'Give thyself wholly to it' (1 Tim 4.15). 'Receive it not as the word of men, but, as it is in truth, the word of God' (1 Thess 2.13). Hear it with application, looking on it as a message sent from heaven to you in particular; though not to you only (Rev 3.22). 'He that hath an ear, let him hear what the Spirit saith unto the churches.' Lay it up in your hearts; meditate upon it; and be not as the unclean beasts, that chew not the cud. But by earnest prayer, beg that the dew of Heaven may fall on your heart, that the seed may spring up there.

More particularly, 1. Receive the testimony of the Word of God concerning the misery of an unregenerate state, the sinfulness thereof, and the absolute necessity of regeneration. 2. Receive its testimony concerning God, what a holy and just One He is. 3. Examine your ways by it; namely, the thoughts of your heart, the expressions of your lips, and the tenor of your life. Look back through the several periods of your life; see your sins from the precepts of the Word, and learn, from its threatening, what you are liable to on account of these sins. 4. By the help of the same Word of God, view the corruption of your nature, as in a glass which manifests our ugly face in a clear manner. Were these things deeply rooted in the heart, they might be the seed of that fear and sorrow, on account of your soul's state, which are necessary to prepare and stir you up to look after a Saviour. Fix your thoughts upon Him offered to you in the Gospel, as fully suited to your case; having, by His obedience unto death, perfectly satisfied the justice of God, and brought in everlasting righteousness. This may prove the seed of humiliation, desire, hope and faith; and move you to stretch out the withered hand unto Him, at His own command.

Let these things sink deeply into your hearts, and improve them diligently. Remember, whatever you are, you *must* be born again; else it had been better for you that you had never been born. Wherefore, if any of you shall live and die in an unregenerate state, you will be inexcusable, having been fairly warned of your danger.

2

MYSTICAL UNION BETWEEN CHRIST AND BELIEVERS

I am the vine, ye are the branches. JOHN 15.5

Having spoken of the change made by regeneration on all those who will inherit eternal life, in opposition to their natural real state, the state of degeneracy, I proceed to speak of the change made on them, in their union with the Lord Jesus Christ, in opposition to their natural relative state, the state of misery. The doctrine of the saints' union with Christ is very plainly and fully insisted on, from the beginning to the twelfth verse of this chapter; which is a part of our Lord's farewell sermon to His disciples. Sorrow had now filled their hearts; they were apt to say, Alas! what will become of us, when our Master is taken from our head? Who will then instruct us? Who will solve our doubts? How shall we be supported under our difficulties and discouragements? How shall we be able to live without our wonted communication with Him? Therefore our Lord Jesus Christ seasonably teaches them the mystery of their union with Him, comparing Himself to the vine, and them to the branches.

He compares, 1. Himself to a vine stock. 'I am the vine.' He had been celebrating, with his disciples, the sacrament of His supper, that sign and seal of His people's union with Him; and had told them, 'That he would drink no more of the fruit of the vine, till He should drink it new with them in His Father's kingdom:' and now He shows Himself to be the vine, from whence the wine of their consolation should come. The vine has less beauty than many other trees, but it is exceedingly fruitful; fitly representing the low condition in which our Lord was in, yet bringing many sons to glory. But that which is chiefly aimed at, in His comparing Himself to a vine, is to represent Himself as the supporter and

[253]

nourisher of His people, in whom they live and bring forth fruit.
2. He compares them to branches; you are the branches of that
vine. You are the branches knit to, and growing on this stock,
drawing all your life and sap from it. It is a beautiful comparison;
as if He had said, I am as a vine; you are as the branches of that
vine. Now there are two sorts of branches: 1. Natural branches,
which at first spring out of the stock. These are the branches that
are in the tree, and were never out of it. 2. There are ingrafted
branches, which are branches cut off from the tree that first gave
them life, and put into another, to grow upon it. Thus branches
come to be on a tree, which originally were not on it. The
branches mentioned in the text are of the latter sort; branches
broken off, as the word in the original language denotes, namely,
from the tree that first gave them life. None of the children of
men are natural branches of the second Adam, that is, Jesus
Christ, the true vine; they are the natural branches of the first
Adam, that degenerate vine: but the elect are, all of them, sooner
or later, broken off from their natural stock, and ingrafted into
Christ, the true Vine.

DOCTRINE: *They who are in the state of grace are ingrafted
in, and united to, the Lord Jesus Christ. They are taken out of
their natural stock, cut off from it; and are now ingrafted into
Christ, as the new stock*

In general, for understanding the union between the Lord
Jesus Christ and His elect, who believe in Him, and on Him, I
observe,

1: It is a spiritual union. Man and wife, by their marriage-
union, become one flesh; Christ and true believers, by this union,
become one spirit (1 Cor 6.17). As one soul or spirit actuates both
the head and the members in the natural body, so the one Spirit
of God dwells in Christ and the Christian; for, 'if any man have
not the Spirit of Christ, he is none of his' (Rom 8.9). Corporal
union is made by contact; so the stones in a building are united.
But this is a union of another nature. Were it possible that we

could eat the flesh and drink the blood of Christ, in a corporal and carnal manner, it would profit nothing (John 6.63). It was not Mary's bearing Him in her womb, but her believing on Him, that made her a saint (Luke 11.27,28), 'A certain woman – said unto him, Blessed is the womb that bare thee, and the paps which thou hast sucked. But he said, Yea, rather, blessed are they that hear the word of God, and keep it.'

2: It is a real union. Such is our weakness in our present state, so much are we sunk in sin, that in our fancy we are prone to form an image of every thing proposed to us: and as to whatever is denied us, we are apt to suspect it to be only a fiction. But nothing is more real than what is spiritual, as approaching nearest to the nature of Him who is the fountain of all reality, namely, God Himself. We do not see with our eyes the union between our own soul and body; neither can we represent it to ourselves truly, by imagination, as we do sensible things; yet the reality of it is not to be doubted. Faith is no fancy, but 'the substance of things hoped for' (Heb 11.1). Neither is the union thereby made between Christ and believers imaginary, but most real: 'For we are members of his body, of his flesh, and of his bones' (Eph 5.30).

3: It is a most close and intimate union. Believers, regenerate persons, who believe in Him, and rely on Him, have put on Christ (Gal 3.27). If that be not enough, He is in them (John 17.23), formed in them as the child in the womb (Gal 4.19). He is the foundation (1 Cor 3.11); they are the lively stones built upon Him (1 Pet 2.5). He is the head and they the body (Eph 1.22,23). Nay, He liveth in them, as their very souls live in their bodies (Gal 2.20). And what is more than all this, they are one in the Father and the Son, as the Father is in Christ, and Christ in the Father (John 17.21), 'That they all may be one; as thou, Father, art in me, and I in thee, that they also may be one in us.'

4: Though it is not a mere legal union, yet it is a union sustained in law. Christ, as the surety, and Christians as the debtors, are one in the eye of the law. When the elect had run themselves, with the rest of mankind, in debt to the justice of God, Christ became surety for them, and paid the debt. When they believe on Him, they are united to Him in a spiritual marriage union; which takes effect so far, that what He did and suffered for them is reckoned in law, as if they had done and suffered it themselves. Hence, they are said to be crucified with Christ (Gal 2.20); buried with him (Col 2.12); yea, raised up together, namely, with Christ, 'and made to sit together in heavenly places in Christ Jesus' (Eph 2.6). In which places, saints on earth, of whom the apostle there speaks, cannot be said to be sitting, but in the way of law reckoning.

5: It is an indissoluble union. Once in Christ, ever in Him. Having taken up His habitation in the heart, He never removes. None can untie this happy knot. Who will dissolve this union? Will He Himself? No, He will not; we have His word for it, 'I will not turn away from them' (Jer 32.40). But perhaps the sinner will do this mischief to himself? No, he shall not; 'they shall not depart from me,' says their God. Can devils do it? No, unless they be stronger than Christ and His Father too; 'Neither shall any man pluck them out of my hand,' says our Lord (John 10.28). 'And none is able to pluck them out of my Father's hand' (verse 29). But what say you of death, which parts husband and wife; yea, separates the soul from the body? Will not death do it? No: the apostle (Rom 8.38,39) is 'persuaded that neither death,' terrible as it is, 'nor life,' desirable as it is; 'nor' devils, those evil 'angels, nor' the devil's persecuting agents, though they be 'principalities, or powers' on earth; 'nor' evil 'things present,' already lying on us; 'nor' evil 'things to come' on us; 'nor' the 'height' of worldly felicity; 'nor depth' of worldly misery; 'nor any other creature,' good or evil, 'shall be able to separate us from the love of God, which is in Christ Jesus our Lord.' As death separated Christ's soul from His body, but could not separate either His soul or body from His divine nature; so, though the saints should be separated from their nearest relations in the world, and from all their earthly enjoyments; yea, though their souls should be

[256]

separated from their bodies, and their bodies separated in a thousand pieces, their bones scattered, as one cutteth or cleaveth wood;' yet soul and body shall remain united to the Lord Christ, for even in death, 'they sleep in Jesus' (1 Thess 4.14); and 'He keepeth all their bones' (Psa 34.20). Union with Christ is 'the grace wherein we stand,' firm and stable, 'as Mount Zion, which cannot be removed.'

6: It is a mysterious union. The Gospel is a doctrine of mysteries. It discovers to us the substantial union of the three persons in one Godhead (1 John 5.7), 'These three are one;' the hypostatical union, of the divine and human natures, in the person of the Lord Jesus Christ (1 Tim 3.16), 'God was manifest in the flesh.' And the mystical union between Christ and believers, 'This is a great mystery' also (Eph 5.32). O what mysteries are here! The Head in heaven, the members on earth, yet really united! Christ in the believer, living in Him, walking in Him: and the believer dwelling in God, putting on the Lord Jesus, eating His flesh and drinking His blood! This makes the saints a mystery to the world, yea, a mystery to themselves.

I come now more particularly to speak of this union with, and ingrafting into, Jesus Christ.

I: I shall consider the natural stock, which the branches are taken out of.

II: The supernatural stock they are ingrafted into.

III: What branches are cut off the old stock, and put into the new.

IV: How it is done. And,

V: The benefits flowing from this union and ingrafting.

I: Let us take a view of the stock, which the branches are taken out of. The two Adams, that is, Adam and Christ, are the two stocks: for the Scripture speaks of these two, as if there had been no more men in the world than they (1 Cor 15.45), 'The first man Adam was made a living soul, the last Adam was made a quickening spirit;' (verse 47), 'The first man is of the earth, earthy: the second man is the Lord from heaven.' And the reason is, there never were any that were not branches of one of these two, all men being either in the one stock or in the other; for in these two sorts all mankind stands divided (verse 48), As is the earthy, such are they also which are earthy; and as is the heavenly, such are they also that are heavenly.' The first Adam, then, is the natural stock: on this stock are the branches found growing at first, which are afterwards cut off, and ingrafted into Christ. As for the fallen angels, as they had no relation to the first Adam, so they have none to the second.

There are four things to be remembered here. (1) That all mankind, the man Christ excepted, are naturally branches of the first Adam (Rom 5.12), 'By one man sin entered into the world, and death by sin: and so death passed upon all men.' (2) The bond which knits us unto the natural stock was the covenant of works. Adam, being our natural root, was made the moral root also, bearing all his posterity, as representing them in the covenant of works. For 'by one man's disobedience many were made sinners' (Rom 5.19). It was necessary that there should be a peculiar relation between that one man and the many, as a foundation for imparting his sin to them. This relation did not arise from the mere natural bond between him and us, as a father to his children; for so we are related to our immediate parents, whose sins are not thereupon imputed to us, as Adam's sin is, but it arose from a moral bond between Adam and us, the bond of a covenant, which could be no other than the covenant of works, wherein we are united to him, as branches to a stock. Hence Jesus Christ, though a son of Adam (Luke 3.23–38), was none of these branches, for as He came not of Adam in virtue of the blessing of marriage, which was given before the fall (Gen 1.28), 'Be fruitful, and multiply,' &c. but in virtue of a special promise made after the fall (Gen 3.15), 'The seed of the woman shall bruise the serpent's head,' He could not be represented by Adam in a covenant made before his fall. (3) As it is impossible for a branch to be in two stocks at once, so no man can be at one and the same time both in the first and second Adam. (4) Hence it evidently follows, that all who are not ingrafted in Jesus Christ, are yet branches of the old stock, and so partake of the nature of the same. Now, as to the first Adam, our natural stock, consider,

First, What a stock he was originally. He was a vine of the Lord's planting, a choice vine, a noble vine, wholly good. There was a consultation of the Trinity at the planting of this vine (Gen 1.26), 'Let us make man in our image, after our own likeness.' There was no rottenness at the heart of it. There was sap and juice enough in it to have nourished all the branches, to bring forth fruit unto God. By meaning is, Adam was made able perfectly to keep the commandments of God, which would have procured eternal life to himself and to all his posterity; for as all die by Adam's disobedience, all would have had life by his obedience, if he had stood. Consider,

Secondly, What that stock now is. Ah! most unlike to what it was when planted by the Author of all good. A blast from hell, and a bite with the venomous teeth of the old serpent, have made it a degenerate stock, a dead stock, nay, a killing stock.

1 : It is a degenerate evil stock. Therefore the Lord God said to Adam in that dismal day, 'Where art thou?' (Gen 3.9). In what condition art thou now? 'How art thou turned into the degenerate plant of a strange vine unto me!' Or, 'Where wast thou?' Why not in the place of meeting with Me? Why so long in coming? What means this fearful change, this hiding of thyself from me? Alas! the stock is degenerate, quite spoiled, is become altogether naught, and brings forth wild grapes. Converse with the devil is preferred to communion with God. Satan is believed; and God, who is truth itself, disbelieved. He who was the friend of God is now in conspiracy against Him. Darkness is come in the place of light; ignorance prevails in the mind, where divine knowledge shone; the will, which was righteous and regular, is now turned rebel against its Lord and the whole man is in dreadful disorder.

Before I go further, let me stop and observe, Here is a mirror both for saints and sinners. Sinners, stand here and consider what you are, and saints, learn what you once were. You, sinners, are branches of a degenerate stock. Fruit you may bear indeed; but now that your vine is the vine of Sodom, your grapes must of necessity be grapes of gall (Deut 32.32). The Scripture speaks of two sorts of fruit which grow on the branches of the natural stock; and it is plain that they are of the nature of their degenerate stock. (1) The wild grapes of wickedness (Isa 5.2). These grow in abundance, by influence from hell. (See Gal 5.19–21.) At their gates are all manner of these fruits, both new and old. Storms come from heaven to check them; but still they grow. They are struck at with the sword of the Spirit, the Word of God; conscience gives them many a secret blow; yet they thrive. (2) Fruit to themselves (Hos 10.1). What else are all the unrenewed man's acts of obedience, his reformation, sober deportment, his prayers, and good works? They are all done chiefly for himself, not for the glory of God. These fruits are like the apples of Sodom, fair to look at, but fall to ashes when handled and tried. You think you have not only the leaves of a profession, but the fruits of a holy practice too; but if you be not broken off from the old stock, and ingrafted in Christ Jesus, God accepts not, and regards not your fruits.

Here I must take occasion to tell you, there are five faults will be found in heaven with your best fruits: 1. Their bitterness; your 'clusters are bitter' (Deut 32.32). There is a spirit of bitterness, wherewith some come before the Lord, in religious duties, living in malice and envy, and which some professors entertain against others, because they outshine them in holiness of life, or because they are not of their opinion. This, wherever it reigns, is a fearful symptom of an unregenerate state. But I do not so much mean this, as that which is common to all the branches of the old stock, namely, the leaves of hypocrisy (Luke 12.1), which sours and embitters every duty they perform. The wisdom that is full of good fruits, is without hypocrisy (James 3.17). 2. Their ill savour. Their works are abominable, for they themselves are corrupt (Psa 14.1). They all savour of the old stock, not of the new. It is the peculiar privilege of the saints, that they are unto God a sweet savour of Christ (2 Cor 2.15). The unregenerate man's fruits savour not of love to Christ, nor of the blood of Christ, nor of the incense of His intercession, and therefore will never be accepted in heaven. 3. Their unripeness. Their grape is an unripe grape (Job 15.33). There is no influence on them from the Sun of Righteousness to bring them to perfection. They have the shape of fruit, but no more. The matter of duty is in them, but they want right principles and ends: their works are not wrought in God (John 3.21). Their prayers drop from their lips before their hearts are impregnated with the vital sap of the Spirit of supplication; their tears fall from their eyes before their hearts are truly softened; their feet turn to new paths, and their way is altered, while their nature still is unchanged. 4. Their lightness. Being weighed in the balances, they are found wanting (Dan 5.27). For evidence whereof you may observe that they do not humble the soul, but lift it up in pride. The good fruits of holiness bear down the branches they grow upon, making them to salute the ground (1 Cor 15.10), 'I laboured more abundantly than they all: yet not I, but the grace of God which was with me.' But the blasted fruits of unrenewed men's performances hang lightly on branches towering up to heaven (Judges 17.13), 'Now know I that the Lord will do me good, seeing I have a Levite to my priest.' They look indeed too high for God to behold them: 'Wherefore have we fasted, say they, and thou seest not?' (Isa 58.3). The more duties they do, and the better they seem to perform them, the less are they humbled, and the more are they lifted up. This disposition of the sinner is the exact reverse of what is to be found in the saint. To men who neither are in Christ, nor are solicitous to be found in Him, their duties are like windy bladders, wherewith they think to swim ashore to Immanuel's land; but these must needs break, and they consequently sink, because they take not Christ for the lifter up of their heads (Psa 3.3). 5. They are not all manner of pleasant fruits (Cant 7.13). Christ, as a king, must be served with variety. Where God makes the heart His garden, He plants it as Solomon did his, with trees of all kinds of fruits (Eccl 2.5). Accordingly it brings forth the fruit of the Spirit in all goodness (Eph 5.9). But the ungodly are not so, their obedience is never universal; there is always some one thing or other excepted. In one word, their fruits are fruits of an ill tree, that cannot be accepted in heaven.

2: Our natural stock is a dead stock, according to the threatening (Gen 2.17), 'In the day thou eatest thereof, thou shalt surely die.' Our root now is rottenness, no wonder the blossom goes up as dust. The stroke has gone to the heart, the sap is let out, and the tree is withered. The curse of the first covenant, like a hot thunderbolt from heaven, has lighted on it, and ruined it. It is cursed now as that fig-tree (Matt 21.19), 'Let no fruit grow on thee henceforward for ever.' Now it is good for nothing, but to cumber the ground, and furnish fuel for Tophet.

Let me enlarge a little here also. Every unrenewed man is a branch of a dead stock. When you see, O sinner, a dead stock of a tree, exhausted of all its sap, having branches on it in the same condition, look on it as a lively representation of your soul's state. 1. Where the stock is dead, the branches must needs be barren. Alas! the barrenness of many professors plainly discovers on what stock they are growing. It is easy to pretend to faith, but 'show me thy faith without thy works!' if you can (James 2.18). 2. A dead stock can convey no sap to the branches, to make them bring forth fruit. The covenant of works was the bond of our union with the natural stock; but now it is become weak through the flesh, that is, through the degeneracy and depravity of human nature (Rom 8.3). It is strong enough to command, and to bind heavy burdens on the shoulders of those who are not in Christ, but it affords no strength to bear them. The sap that was once in the root, is now gone; the law, like a merciless creditor, apprehends Adam's heirs, saying to each, 'Pay what thou owest;' when, alas! his effects are riotously spent. 3. All pains and cost are lost on the tree, whose life is gone. In vain do men labour to get fruit on the branches, when there is no sap in the root. The gardener's pains are lost; ministers lose their labour on the branches of the old stock, while they continue on it. Many sermons are preached to no purpose, because there is no life to give sensation. Sleeping men may be awakened, but the dead cannot be raised without a miracle; even so the dead sinner must remain, if he be not restored to life by a miracle of grace. The influences of heaven are lost on such a tree: in vain doth the rain fall upon it; in vain is it laid open to the winter cold and frosts. The Lord of the vine-yard digs about many a dead soul, but it is not bettered. 'Bruise the fool in a mortar, his folly will not depart.' Though he meets with many crosses, yet he retains his lusts: let him be laid on a sick bed, he will lie there like a sick beast, groaning under his pain, but not mourning for, nor turning from, his sin. Let death itself stare him in the face, he will presumptuously maintain his hope, as if he would look the grim messenger out of countenance. Sometimes there are common operations of the divine Spirit performed on him, he is sent home with a trembling heart, and with arrows of conviction sticking in his soul, but at length he prevails against these things, and becomes as secure as ever. Summer and winter are alike to the branches on the dead stock. When others about them are budding, blossoming, and bringing forth fruit, there is no change on them; the dead stock has no growing time at all. Perhaps it may be difficult to know, in the winter, what trees are dead, and what are alive; but the spring plainly discovers it. There are some seasons wherein there is little life to be perceived, even among saints; yet times of reviving come at length. But even when 'the vine flourisheth, and the pomegranates bud forth,' when saving grace is discovering itself by its lively actings wherever it is, the branches on the old stock are still withered. When the dry bones are coming together, bone to bone amongst saints, the sinner's bones are still lying about the grave's mouth. They are trees that cumber the ground, ready to be cut down; and will be cut down for the fire, if God in mercy prevent it not by cutting them off from that stock, and ingrafting them into another.

3: Our natural stock is a killing stock. If the stock die, how can the branches live? If the sap be gone from the root and heart, the branches must needs wither. 'In Adam all die' (1 Cor 15.22). The root died in Paradise, and all the branches in it, and with it. The root is poisoned, and from thence the branches are infected; 'death is in the pot;' and all that taste of the pulse, or pottage, are killed.

Know then, that every natural man is a branch of a killing stock. Our natural root not only gives us no life, but it has a killing power, reaching to all the branches thereof. There are four things which the first Adam conveys to all his branches, and they are abiding in, and lying on, such of them as are not ingrafted in Christ. 1. A corrupt nature. He sinned, and his nature was thereby corrupted and depraved; and this corruption is conveyed to all his posterity. He was infected, and the contagion spread itself over all his seed. 2. Guilt, that is, an obligation to punishment (Rom 5.12), 'By one man sin entered into the world, and death by sin; and so death passed upon all men, for that all have sinned.' The threatenings of the law, as cords of death, are twisted about the branches of the old stock, to draw them over the hedge into the fire. And till they be cut off from this stock by the pruning-knife, the sword of vengeance hangs over their heads, to cut them down. 3. This killing stock transmits the curse into the branches. The stock, as the stock (for I speak not of Adam in his personal and private capacity), being cursed, so are the branches (Gal 3.10), 'For as many as are of the works of the law are under the curse.' The curse affects the whole man, and all that belongs to him, every thing he possesses, and works three ways. 1. As poison, infecting; thus their blessings are cursed (Mal 2.2). Whatever the man enjoys, it can do him no good, but evil, being thus poisoned by the curse. His prosperity in the world destroys him (Prov 1.32). The ministry of the gospel is a savour of death unto death to him (2 Cor 2.16). His seeming attainments in religion are cursed to him; his knowledge serves but to puff him up, and his duties to keep him back from Christ. 2. It works as a moth, consuming and wasting by little and little (Hos 5.12), 'Therefore will I be unto Ephraim as a moth.' There is a worm at the root, consuming them by degrees. Thus the curse pursued Saul, till it wormed him out of all his enjoyments, and out of the very show he had of religion. Sometimes they decay like the fat of lambs, and melt away as the snow in the sunshine. 3. It acts as a lion rampant (Hos 5.14), 'I will be unto Ephraim as a lion.' The Lord 'rains on them snares, fire and brimstone, and an horrible tempest,' in such a manner, that they are hurried away with the stream. He tears their enjoyments from them in His wrath, pursues them with terrors, rends their souls from their bodies, and throws the dead branch into the fire. Thus the curse devours like fire, which none can quench. 4. This killing stock transmits death to the branches upon it. Adam took the poisonous cup, and drank it off: this occasioned death to himself and us. We came into the world spiritually dead, thereby exposed to eternal death, and absolutely liable to temporal death. This root is to us like the Scythian river, which, they say, brings forth little bladders every day, out of which come certain small flies, that are bred in the morning, winged at noon, and dead at night: a very lively emblem of our mortal state.

Now, sirs, is it not absolutely necessary to be broken off from this our natural stock? What will our fair leaves of a profession, or our fruits of duties, avail, if we be still branches of the degenerate, dead, and killing stock? But, alas! of the many questions among us, few are taken up about these, 'Am I broken off from the old stock, or not? Am I ingrafted in Christ, or not?' Ah! wherefore all this waste of time? Why is there so much noise about religion among many, who can give no good account of their having laid a good foundation, being mere strangers to experimental religion? I fear, if God does not in mercy undermine the religion of many of us, and let us see that we have none at all, our root will be found rottenness, and our blossom go up as dust, in a dying hour. Therefore let us look to our state, that we be not found fools in our latter end.

11: Let us now view the supernatural stock, into which the branches cut off from the natural stock are ingrafted. Jesus Christ is sometimes called 'The Branch' (Zech 3.8). So He is in respect of His human nature, being a branch, and the top branch, of the house of David. Sometimes He is called a Root (Isa 11.10). We have both together (Rev 22.16), 'I am the root and the offspring of David;' David's root as God, and his offspring as man. The text tells us that He is the vine, that is, He as a Mediator, is the vine stock, whereof believers are the branches. As the sap comes from the earth into the root and stock, and from thence is diffused into the branches, so, by Christ as Mediator, divine life is conveyed from the fountain to those who are united to Him by faith (John 6.57), 'As the living Father hath sent me, and I live by the Father; so he that eateth me, even he shall live by me.' Now Christ is Mediator, not as God only, as some have asserted; nor yet as man only, as the papists generally hold: but He is Mediator as God-Man (Acts 20.28), 'The church of God, which he hath purchased with his own blood.' (Heb 9.14), 'Christ, who, through the eternal Spirit, offered himself without spot to God.' The divine and human natures have their distinct actings, yet a joint operation, in His discharging the office of Mediator. This is illustrated by the similitude of a fiery sword, which at once cuts and burns: cutting it burns, and burning it cuts; the steel cuts, and the fire burns. Wherefore Christ, God-man, is the stock, whereof believers are the branches: and they are united to a whole Christ. They are united to Him in His human nature, as being 'members of his body, of His flesh, and of His bones' (Eph 5.30). And they are united to Him in His divine nature; for so the apostle speaks of this union (Col 1.27), 'Christ in you, the hope of glory.' Those who are Christ's, have the Spirit of Christ (Rom 8.9); and by Him they are united to the Father, and to the Holy Ghost; (1 John 4.15), 'Whosoever shall confess that Jesus is the Son of God, God dwelleth in him, and he in God.' Faith, the bond of this union, receives a whole Christ, God-man, and so unites us to Him as such.

[266]

Behold here, O believers, your high privilege. You were once branches of a degenerate stock, even as others: but you are, by grace, become branches of the true vine (John 15.1). You are cut out of a dead and killing stock, and ingrafted in the last Adam, who was made a quickening spirit (1 Cor 15.45). Your loss by the first Adam is made up, with great advantage, by your union with the second. Adam, at his best estate, was but a shrub, in comparison with Christ, the tree of life. He was but a servant; Christ is the Son, the Heir, and Lord of all things, 'the Lord from heaven.' It cannot be denied, that grace was shown in the first covenant: but it is as far exceeded by the grace of the second covenant, as the twilight is by the light of the mid-day.

III: What branches are taken out of the natural stock, and grafted into this vine? *Answer:* These are the elect, and none other. They, and they only, are grafted into Christ; and consequently none but they are cut off from the killing stock. For them alone He intercedes, 'That they may be one in him and his Father' (John 17.9–23). Faith, the bond of this union, is given to none else; it is the faith of God's elect (Tit 1.1). The Lord passes by many branches growing on the natural stock, and cuts off only here one, and there one, and grafts them into the true vine, according as free love has determined. Often does He pitch upon the most unlikely branch, leaving the top boughs, passing by the mighty and the noble, and calling the weak, base, and despised (1 Cor 1.26,27). Yea, He often leaves the fair and smooth, and takes the rugged and knotty; 'and such were some of you, but ye are washed,' &c. (1 Cor 6.11). If we inquire, why so? we find no other reason but because they were chosen in Him (Eph 1.4); 'predestinated to the adoption of children by Jesus Christ' (verse 5). Thus are they gathered together in Christ, while the rest are left growing on their natural stock, to be afterwards bound up in bundles for the fire. Therefore, to whomsoever the Gospel may come in vain, it will have a blessed effect on God's elect (Acts 13.48), 'as many as were ordained to eternal life, believed.' Where the Lord has much people, the gospel will have much success, sooner or later. Such as are to be saved will be added to the mystical body of Christ.

IV: I am now to show how the branches are cut off from the natural stock, the first Adam, and grafted into the true vine, the Lord Jesus Christ. Thanks to the Husbandman, not to the branch, that is cut off from its natural stock, and grafted into a new one. The sinner, in his coming off from the first stock, is passive, and neither can nor will come off from it of his own accord, but clings to it, till almighty power makes him to fall off (John 6.44), 'No man can come unto me, except the Father, which hath sent me, draw him.' And (chap 5.40), 'Ye will not come to me, that ye might have life.' The ingrafted branches are 'God's husbandry' (1 Cor 3.9), 'The planting of the Lord' (Isa 61.3). The ordinary means He makes us of, in this work, is the ministry of the Word (1 Cor 3.9), 'We are labourers together with God.' But the efficacy thereof is wholly from Him, whatever the minister's abilities or piety be (verse 7), 'Neither is he that planteth any thing, neither he that watereth; but God that giveth the increase.' The apostles preached to the Jews, yet the body of that people remained in infidelity (Rom 10.16), 'Who hath believed our report?' Yea, Christ Himself, who spoke as never man spoke, says concerning the success of His own ministry, 'I have laboured in vain, I have spent my strength for nought' (Isa 49.4). The branches may be hacked by the preaching of the Word; but the stroke will never go through, till it is carried home by an omnipotent arm. However, God's ordinary way is, 'by the foolishness of preaching to save them that believe' (1 Cor 1.21).

The cutting of the branch from the natural stock is performed by the pruning knife of the law, in the hand of the Spirit of God (Gal 2.19), 'For I, through the law, am dead to the law.' It is by the bond of the covenant of works, as I said before, that we are knit to our natural stock. Therefore, as a wife, unwilling to be put away, pleads and hangs by the marriage tie, so do men by the covenant of works. They hold by it, like the man who held the ship with his hands, and when one hand was cut off, held it with the other, and when both were cut off, held it with his teeth. This will appear from a distinct view of the Lord's works on men, in bringing them off from the old stock; which I offer in the following particulars:

1: When the Spirit of the Lord comes to deal with a person, to bring him to Christ, he finds him in Laodicea's case, in a sound sleep of security, dreaming of heaven and the favour of God, though full of sin against the Holy One of Israel (Rev 3.17), 'Thou knowest not that thou art wretched, and miserable, and poor, and blind, and naked.' Therefore He darts in some beams of light into the dark soul and lets the man see that he is a lost man, if he turn not over a new leaf, and betake himself to a new course of life. Thus, by the Spirit of the Lord acting as a spirit of bondage, there is a criminal court erected in the man's breast, where he is arraigned, accused, and condemned for breaking the law of God, 'convicted of sin and judgment' (John 16.8). And now he can no longer sleep securely in his former course of life. This is the first stroke which the branch gets, in order to cutting off.

2: Hereupon the man forsakes his former profane courses, his lying, swearing, Sabbath-breaking, stealing, and such like practices; though they be dear to him as right eyes, he will rather quit them than ruin his soul. The ship is likely to sink, and therefore he throws his goods overboard, that he himself may not perish. Now he begins to bless himself in his heart, and looks joyfully on his evidences for heaven, thinking himself a better servant to God than many others (Luke 18.11), 'God, I thank thee, I am not as other men are, extortioners, unjust, adulterers,' &c. But he soon gets another stroke with the axe of the law, showing him that it is only he that does what is written in the law, that can be saved by it; and that his negative holiness is too scanty a covering from the storm of God's wrath. Thus, although his sins of commission only were heavy on him before, his sins of omission now crowd into his thoughts, attended with a train of law curses and vengeance. And each of the ten commandments discharges thunder-claps of wrath against him for his omission of required duties.

3 : Upon this he turns to a positively holy course of life. He not only is not profane, but he performs religious duties: he prays, seeks the knowledge of the principles of religion, strictly observes the Lord's day, and, like Herod, does many things, and hears sermons gladly. In one word, there is a great conformity, in his outward conversation, to the letter of both tables of the law. There is a mighty change in the man, which his neighbours cannot miss taking notice of. Hence he is cheerfully admitted by the godly into their society, as a praying person; and can confer with them about religious matters, yea, and about soul exercise, which some are not acquainted with. Their good opinion of him confirms his good opinion of himself. This step in religion is fatal to many, who never get beyond it. But here the Lord gives the elect branch a further stroke. Conscience flies in the man's face, for some wrong steps in his conversation, the neglect of some duty, or commission of some sin, which is a blot in his conversation; and then the flaming sword of the law appears again over his head, and the curse rings in his ears, for that he 'continueth not in *all things* written in the law, to do them' (Gal 3.10).

4 : On this account, he is obliged to seek another remedy for his disease. He goes to God, confesses his sin, seeks the pardon of it, promising to watch against it for the time to come; and so finds ease, and thinks he may very well take it, seeing the Scripture saith, 'If we confess our sins, he is faithful and just to forgive us our sins' (1 John 1.9); not considering that he grasps at a privilege, which is theirs only who are grafted into Christ, and under the covenant of grace, and which the branches yet growing on the old stock cannot plead. And here sometimes there are formal and express vows made against such and such sins, and binding to such and such duties. Thus many go on all their days, knowing no other religion than to perform duties, and to confess, and pray for pardon of that wherein they fail, promising themselves eternal happiness, though they are utter strangers to

Christ. Here many elect ones have been cast down wounded, and many reprobates have been slain, while the wounds of neither of them have been deep enough to cut them off from their natural stock. But the Spirit of the Lord gives yet a deeper stroke to the branch which is to be cut off, showing him, that, as yet, he is but an outside saint, and discovering to him the filthy lusts lodged in his heart, which he took no notice of before (Rom 7.9), 'When the commandment came, sin revived, and I died.' Then he sees his heart to be full of sinful lusts, covetousness, pride, malice, filthiness and the like. Now, as soon as the door of the chambers of his imagery is thus opened to him, and he sees what they do there in the dark, his outside religion is blown up as insufficient; and he learns a new lesson in religion, namely, 'That he is not a Jew, who is one outwardly' (Rom 2.28).

5: Upon this he goes further, even to inside religion; sets to work more vigorously than ever, mourns over the evils of his heart, and strives to bear down the weeds which he finds growing in that neglected garden. He labours to curb his pride and passion, and to banish speculative impurities; prays more fervently, hears attentively, and strives to get his heart affected in every religious duty he performs; and thus he comes to think himself, not only an outside, but an inside Christian. Wonder not at this, for there is nothing in it beyond the power of nature, or what one may attain to under a vigorous influence of the covenant of works; therefore another yet deeper stroke is given. The law charges home on the man's conscience, that he was a transgressor from the womb, that he came into the world a guilty creature and that in the time of his ignorance, and even since his eyes were opened, he has been guilty of many actual sins, either altogether overlooked by him or not sufficiently mourned over; for spiritual sores, not healed by the blood of Christ, but skinned over some other way, are easily irritated, and soon break out again. Therefore the law takes him by the throat, saying, 'Pay what thou owest.'

6: Then the sinner says in his heart, 'Have patience with me, and I will pay thee all;' and so falls to work to pacify an offended God, and to atone for these sins. He renews his repentance, such as it is; bears patiently the afflictions laid upon him; yea, he afflicts himself, denies himself the use of his lawful comforts, sighs deeply, mourns bitterly, cries with tears for a pardon, till he has wrought up his heart to a conceit of having obtained it. Having thus done penance for what is past, he resolves to be a good servant to God, and to hold on in outward and inward obedience, for the time to come. But the stroke must go nearer the heart yet, ere the branch falls off. The Lord discovers to him, in the glass of the law, how he sins in all he does, even when he does the best he can; and therefore the dreadful sound returns to his ears (Gal 3.10), 'Cursed is every one that continueth not in all things,' &c. 'When ye fasted and mourned,' says the Lord, 'did ye at all fast unto me, even to me?' Will muddy water make clean clothes? Will you satisfy for one sin with another? Did not your thoughts wander in such a duty? Were not your affections flat in another? Did not your heart give a sinful look to such an idol? And did it not rise in a fit of impatience under such an affliction? 'Should I accept this of your hands? Cursed be the deceiver, which sacrificeth to the Lord a corrupt thing' (Mal 1.13,14). And thus he becomes so far broken off, that he sees he is not able to satisfy the demands of the law.

7 : Hence, like a broken man, who finds he is not able to pay all his debt, he goes about to compound with his creditor. And, being in pursuit of ease and comfort, he does what he can to fulfil the law; and wherein he fails, he trusts that God will accept the will for the deed. Thus doing his duty, and having a will to do better, he cheats himself into persuasion of the goodness of his state and hereby thousands are ruined. But the elect get another stroke, which loosens their hold in this case. The doctrine of the law is borne in on their consciences, demonstrating to them that exact and perfect obedience is required by it, under pain of the curse; and that it is doing, and not wishing to do, which will avail. Wishing to do better will not answer the law's demands; and

therefore the curse sounds again, 'Cursed is every one that continueth not – to do them;' that is, actually to do them. In vain is
wishing then.

8: Being broken off from all hopes of compounding with the
law, he falls to borrowing. He sees that all he can do to obey the
law, and all his desires to be and to do better, will not save his
soul: therefore he goes to Christ, entreating that His righteousness may make up what is wanting in his own, and cover all the
defects of his doings and sufferings; that so God, for Christ's
sake, may accept them, and thereupon be reconciled. Thus doing
what he can to fulfil the law, and looking to Christ to make up
all his defects, he comes at length to sleep securely again. Many
persons are ruined this way. This was the error of the Galatians,
which Paul, in his epistle to them, disputes against. But the Spirit
of God breaks off the sinner from this hold also, by bringing
home to his conscience that great truth (Gal 3.12), 'The law is
not of faith, but the man that doeth them shall live in them.'
There is no mixing of the law and faith in this business; the sinner
must hold by one of them, and let the other go. The way of the
law, and the way of faith, are so far different, that it is not possible for a sinner to walk in the one, unless he comes off from the
other: and if he be for doing, he must do all alone; Christ will
not do a part for him, if He do not all. A garment pieced up of
sundry sorts of righteousness, is not a garment meet for the court
of heaven. Thus the man is like one in a dream who thought he
was eating, but being awakened by a stroke, behold his soul is
faint; his heart sinks in him like a stone, while he finds that he
can neither bear his burden himself alone, nor can he get help
under it.

9: What can he do who must needs pay, and yet has not enough
of his own to bring him out of debt; nor can borrow so much, and
is ashamed to beg? What can such a one do, I say, but sell himself, as the man under the law that was become poor? (Lev 25.47).
Therefore the sinner, beat off from so many holds, attempts to
make a bargain with Christ, and to sell himself to the Son of God,

[273]

if I may so speak, solemnly promising and vowing that he will be a servant to Christ as long as he lives, if He will save his soul. And here, the sinner often makes a personal covenant with Christ, resigning himself to Him on these terms; yea, and takes the sacrament, to make the bargain sure. Hereupon the man's great care is, how to obey Christ, keep His commandments, and so fulfil his bargain. In this the soul finds a false, unsound peace, for a while; till the Spirit of the Lord gives another stroke, to cut off the man from this refuge of lies likewise. And that happens in this manner: when he fails of the duties he engaged to perform, and falls again into the sin he covenanted against, it is powerfully carried home on his conscience, that his covenant is broken; so all his comfort goes, and terrors afresh seize on his soul, as one that has broken covenant with Christ. Commonly the man, to help himself, renews his covenant, but breaks it again as before. And how is it possible it should be otherwise, seeing he is still upon the old stock? Thus the work of many, all their days, as to their souls, is nothing but a making and breaking such covenants, over and over again.

Objection: Some perhaps will say, 'Who lives, and sins not? Who is there that fails not of the duties he has engaged to? If you reject this way as unsound, who then can be saved?' *Answer:* True believers will be saved, namely, all who do by faith take hold of God's covenant. But this kind of covenant is men's own covenant, devised of their own heart, not God's covenant, revealed in the Gospel of His grace. The making of it is nothing else but the making of a covenant of works with Christ, confounding the law and the Gospel; a covenant he will never subscribe to, though we should sign it with our heart's blood (Rom 4.14,16), 'For if they which are of the law be heirs, faith is made void, and the promise made of none effect. Therefore it is of faith, that it might be by grace; to the end the promise might be sure to all the seed' (chap 11.6), 'And if by grace, then is it no more of works: otherwise grace is no more grace. But if it be of works, then is it no more grace: otherwise work is no more work.' God's covenant is everlasting; once in, never out of it again; and the mercies of it are sure mercies (Isa 55.3). But that covenant of yours is a tottering covenant, never sure, but broken every day. It is a mere servile covenant, giving Christ service for salvation; but God's covenant is a filial covenant, in which the sinner takes Christ and His salvation freely offered, and so becomes a son (John 1.12), 'But as many as received him, to them gave he power to become the sons of God:' and becoming a son, he serves his Father, not that the inheritance may become his, but because it is his, through Jesus Christ. (See Gal 4.24, and onward.) To enter into that false covenant, is to buy from Christ with money; but to take hold of God's covenant, is to buy of Him without money and without price (Isa 55.1), that is to say, to beg of Him. In that covenant men work for life; in God's covenant they come to Christ for life, and work from life. When a person under that covenant fails in his duty, all is gone; the covenant must be made over again. But under God's covenant, although the man fail in his duty, and for his failure falls under the discipline of the covenant, and lies under the weight of it, till such time as he has recourse anew to the blood of Christ for pardon, and renews his repentance; yet all that he trusted to for life and salvation, namely, the righteousness of Christ, still stands entire, and the covenant remains firm. (See Rom 7.24,25; and chap 8.1.)

Now, though some men spend their lives in making and breaking such covenants of their own, the terror on the breaking of them becoming weaker and weaker, by degrees, till at last it creates in them little or no uneasiness: yet the man, in whom the good work is carried on, till it be accomplished in cutting him off from the old stock, finds these covenants to be as rotten cords, broken at every touch. The terror of God is thereupon redoubled on his spirit, and the waters at every turn get in unto his very soul, until he is obliged to cease from catching hold of such covenants and to seek help some other way.

10: Therefore the man comes at length to beg at Christ's door for mercy, but yet he is a proud beggar, standing on his personal worth. For, as the papists have mediators to plead for them with the one only Mediator, so the branches of the old stock have always something to produce which they think may commend them to Christ, and engage Him to take their cause in hand. They cannot think of coming to the spiritual market without money in their hand. They are like persons who have once had an estate of their own, but are reduced to extreme poverty, and forced to beg. When they come to beg, they still remember their former character, and though they have lost their substance, yet they retain much of their former spirit: therefore they cannot think that they ought to be treated as ordinary beggars, but deserve a particular regard; and, if that be not given them, their spirits rise against him to whom they address themselves for a supply. Thus God gives the unhumbled sinner many common mercies, and shuts him not up in the pit according to his deserving; but all this is nothing in his eyes. He must be set down at the children's table, otherwise he reckons himself hardly dealt with, and wronged: for he is not yet brought so low, as to think God may be justified when He speaks against him, and clear from all iniquity, when He judgeth him according to his real demerit (Psa 51.4). He thinks, perhaps, that, even before he was enlightened, he was better than many others; he considers his reformation of life, his repentance, the grief and tears which his sin has cost him, his earnest desires after Christ, his prayers and wrestlings for mercy; and uses all these now as bribes for mercy, laying no small weight upon them in his addresses to the throne of grace. But here the Spirit of the Lord shoots his arrows quickly into the man's heart, whereby his confidence in these things is sunk and destroyed; and, instead of thinking himself better than many, he is made to see himself worse than any. The faults in his reformation of life are discovered; his repentance appears to him no better than the repentance of Judas; his tears like Esau's, and his desires after Christ to be selfish and loathsome, like those who sought Christ because of the loaves (John 6.26). His answer from God seems now to be, Away, proud beggar, 'How shall I put thee among the children?'

[276]

He seems to look sternly on him for his slighting of Jesus Christ by unbelief, which is a sin he scarcely discerned before. But now at length he beholds it in its crimson colours, and is pierced to the heart, as with a thousand darts, while he sees how he has been going on blindly, sinning against the remedy of sin, and, in the whole course of his life, trampling on the blood of the Son of God. And now he is, in his own eyes, the miserable object of law vengeance, yea, and gospel vengeance too.

11: The man, being thus far humbled, will no more plead, 'he is worthy for whom Christ should do this thing;' but, on the contrary, looks on himself as unworthy of Christ, and unworthy of the favour of God. We may compare him, in this case, to the young man who followed Christ, 'having a linen cloth cast about his naked body; who, when the young men laid hold of him, left the linen cloth, and fled from them naked' (Mark 14.51,52). Even so, the man had been following Christ, in the thin and cold garment of his own personal worthiness: but by it, even by it, which he so much trusted to, the law catches hold of him, to make him prisoner; and then he is fain to leave it, and flees away naked – yet not to Christ, but from Him. If you now tell him he is welcome to Christ, if he will come to Him, he is apt to say, Can such a vile and unworthy wretch as I, be welcome to the holy Jesus? If a plaster be applied to his wounded soul, it will not stick. He says, 'depart from me, for I am a sinful man, O Lord' (Luke 5.8). No man needs speak to him of his repentance, for his comfort; he can quickly espy such faults in it as makes it naught; nor of his tears, for he is assured they have never come into the Lord's bottle. He disputes himself away from Christ and concludes now that he has been such a slighter of Christ, and is such an unholy and vile creature, that he cannot, he will not, he ought not to come to Christ; and that he must either be in better case, or else he will never believe. Hence he now makes the strongest efforts to amend what was amiss in his way before: he prays more earnestly than ever, mourns more bitterly, strives against sin in heart and life more vigorously, and watches more diligently, if by any means he may at length be fit to come to Christ. One would think the man is well humbled now: but, ah! deep pride lurks under the veil of this seeming humility. Like a kindly branch of the old stock, he adheres still, and will not submit to the righteousness of God (Rom 10.3). He will not come to the market of free grace, without money. He is bidden to the marriage of the King's Son, where the Bridegroom Himself furnishes all the guests with wedding garments, stripping them of their own: but he will not come, because he wants a wedding garment; although he is very busy in making one ready. This is sad work; and therefore he must have a deeper stroke yet, else he is ruined. This stroke is given him with the axe of the law, in its irritating power. Thus the law, girding the soul with cords of death, and holding it in with the rigorous commands of obedience, under the pain of the curse; and God, in His holy and wise conduct, withdrawing his restraining grace, corruption is irritated, lusts become violent; and the more they are striven against the more they rage, like a furious horse checked with the bit. Then corruptions set up their heads, which he never saw in himself before. Here oft-times, atheism, blasphemy, and, in one word, horrible things concerning God, terrible thoughts concerning the faith, arise in his breast; so that his heart is a very hell within him. Thus, while he is sweeping the house of his heart, not yet watered with gospel grace, those corruptions which lay quiet before, in neglected corners, fly up and down in it like dust. He is as one who is mending the bank of a river, and while he is repairing breaches in it, and strengthening every part of it, a mighty flood comes down, and overturns his works, and drives all away before it, both that which was newly laid, and what was laid before. (Read Rom 7.8–13.) This is a stroke which goes to the heart: and by it, his hope of making himself more fit to come to Christ, is cut off.

12: Now the time is come, when the man, between hope and despair, resolves to go to Christ as he is; and therefore, like a dying man, stretching himself just before his breath goes out, he rallies the broken forces of his soul, tries to believe, and in some sort lays hold on Jesus Christ. And now the branch hangs on the old stock by one single tack of a natural faith, produced by the natural vigour of one's own spirit, under a most pressing necessity (Psa 78.34,35), 'When he slew them, then they sought him, and they returned and inquired early after God. And they remembered that God was their rock, and the high God their redeemer.' (Hos 8.2), 'Israel shall cry unto me, My God, we know Thee.' But the Lord, never failing to perfect His work, fetches yet an-another stroke, whereby the branch falls quite off. The Spirit of God convincingly discovers to the sinner his utter inability to do any thing that is good, and so he dies (Rom 7.9). That voice powerfully strikes through his soul, 'How can ye believe?' (John 5.44). You can no more believe, than you can reach up your hand to heaven, and bring Christ down from thence. Thus at length he sees that he can neither help himself by working, nor by believing; and having no more to hang by on the old stock, he therefore falls off. While he is distressed thus, seeing himself likely to be swept away with the flood of God's wrath, and yet unable so much as to stretch forth a hand to lay hold of a twig of the tree of life, growing on the bank of the river, he is taken up, and ingrafted in the true vine, the Lord Jesus Christ giving him the spirit of faith.

By what has been said upon this head, I design not to rack or distress tender consciences; for though there are but a few such at this day, yet God forbid that I should offend any of Christ's little ones. But, alas! a dead sleep is fallen upon this generation, they will not be awakened, let us go ever so near to the quick: therefore I fear that there is another sort of awakening abiding this sermon-proof generation, which shall make the ears of them that hear it tingle. However, I would not have this to be looked upon as the sovereign God's stinted method of breaking off sinners from the old stock. But this I maintain as a certain truth, that all who are in Christ have been broken off from all these several confidences; and that they who were never broken off from them, are yet in their natural stock. Nevertheless, if the house be pulled down, and the old foundation rased, it is much the same whether it was taken down stone by stone, or whether it was undermined, and all fell down together.

Now it is that the branch is ingrafted in Jesus Christ. And as the law, in the hand of the Spirit of God, was the instrument to cut off the branch from the natural stock, so the Gospel, in the hand of the same Spirit, is the instrument used for ingrafting it into the supernatural stock (1 John 1.3). 'That which we have seen and heard declare we unto you, that ye also may have fellowship with us; and truly our fellowship is with the Father, and with his Son Jesus Christ.' (See Isa 61.1–3.) The Gospel is the silver cord let down from heaven, to draw perishing sinners to land. And though the preaching of the law prepares the way of the Lord; yet it is in the word of the Gospel that Christ and a sinner meet. Now, as in the natural grafting, the branch being taken up is put into the stock, and being put into it, becomes one with it, so that they are united; even so in the spiritual ingrafting, Christ apprehends the sinner, and the sinner, being apprehended of Christ, apprehends Him, and so they become one (Phil 3.12).

First, Christ apprehends the sinner by His Spirit, and draws him to Himself (1 Cor 12.13), 'For by one Spirit we are all baptized into one body.' The same Spirit which is in the Mediator Himself, He communicates to His elect in due time, never to depart from them, but to abide in them as a principle of life. The soul is now in the hands of the Lord of life, and possessed by the Spirit of life; how can it then but live? The man gets a ravishing sight of Christ's excellence in the glass of the Gospel: he sees Him a full, suitable, and willing Saviour; and gets a heart to take Him for and instead of all. The Spirit of faith furnishes him with feet to come to Christ and hands to receive Him. What by nature he could not do, by grace he can, the Holy Spirit working in him the work of faith with power.

Secondly, The sinner, thus apprehended, apprehends Christ by faith, and is one with the blessed stock (Eph 3.17), 'That Christ may dwell in your hearts by faith.' The soul that before tried many ways of escape, but all in vain, now looks with the eye of faith, which proves the healing look. As Aaron's rod, laid up in the tabernacle, budded, and brought forth buds (Numb 17.8); so the dead branch, apprehended by the Lord of life, put into, and bound up with the glorious quickening stock, by the Spirit of life buds forth in actual believing on Jesus Christ, whereby this union is completed. 'We having the same spirit of faith – believe' (2 Cor 4.13). Thus the stock and the graft are united, Christ and the Christian are married, faith being the soul's consent to the spiritual marriage covenant, which as it is proposed in the gospel to mankind-sinners indefinitely, so it is demonstrated, attested, and brought home to the man in particular, by the Holy Spirit: and so he, being joined to the Lord, is one spirit with Him. Hereby a believer lives in and for Christ, and Christ lives in and for the believer (Gal 2.20), 'I am crucified with Christ: nevertheless, I live; yet not I, but Christ liveth in me.' (Hos 3.3), 'Thou shalt not be for another man: so will I also be for thee.' The bonds, then, of this blessed union are, the Spirit on Christ's part, and faith on the believer's part.

Now both the souls and bodies of believers are united to Christ. 'He that is joined to the Lord is one spirit' (1 Cor 6.17). The very bodies of believers have this honour put upon them, that they are 'the temple of the Holy Ghost' (verse 19), and 'the members of Christ' (verse 15). When they sleep in the dust, they sleep in Jesus (1 Thess 4.14); and it is in virtue of this union they shall be raised up out of the dust again (Rom 8.11), 'He shall quicken your mortal bodies by his Spirit that dwelleth in you.' In token of this mystical union, the church of believers is called by the name of her Head and Husband (1 Cor 12.12), 'For as the body is one, and hath many members – so also is Christ.'

Use: From what is said, we may draw the following inferences:

1 : The preaching of the law is most necessary. He that would ingraft, must needs use the pruning-knife. Sinners have many contrivances to keep them from Christ; many things by which they keep their hold of the natural stock; therefore they have need

to be closely pursued, and hunted out of their skulking holes, and refuges of lies.

2 : Yet it is the Gospel that crowns the work: 'The law makes nothing perfect.' The law lays open the wound, but it is the Gospel that heals it. The law 'strips a man, wounds him and leaves him half dead:' the Gospel 'binds up his wounds, pouring in wine and oil,' to heal them. By the law we are broken off, but it is by the Gospel we are taken up and implanted in Christ.

3 : 'If any man have not the Spirit of Christ he is none of his' (Rom 8.9). We are told of a monster in nature, having two bodies differently animated, as appeared from contrary affections at one and the same time; but so united, that they were served with the self-same legs. Even so, however men may cleave to Christ, 'call themselves of the holy city, and stay themselves upon the God of Israel' (Isa 48.2), and may be bound up as branches in Him (John 15.2) by the outward ties of sacraments; yet if the Spirit that dwells in Christ dwell not in them, they are not one with Him. There is a great difference between adhesion and ingrafting. The ivy clasps and twists itself about the oak, but it is not one with it, for it still grows on its own root: so, to allude to Isa 4.1, many professors 'take hold' of Christ, 'and eat their own bread, and wear their own apparel, only they are called by his name.' They stay themselves upon Him, but grow upon their own root: they take Him to support their hopes, but their delights are elsewhere.

4 : The union between Christ and His mystical members is firm and indissoluble. Were it so that the believer only apprehended Christ, but Christ apprehended not him, we could promise little as to the stability of such a union, it might quickly be dissolved; but as the believer apprehends Christ by faith, so Christ apprehends him by His Spirit, and none shall pluck him out of His hand. Did the child only keep hold of the nurse, it might at length grow weary, and let go its hold, and so fall away: but if she have her arms about the child, it is in no hazard of falling away, even though it be not actually holding by her. So, whatever sinful intermissions may happen in the exercise of faith,

yet the union remains sure, by reason of the constant indwelling of the Spirit. Blessed Jesus! 'All his saints are in thy hand' (Deut 33.3). It is observed by some that the word Abba, is the same whether you read it forward or backward: whatever the believer's case be, the Lord is still to him Abba, Father.

5: They have an unsafe hold of Christ, whom He has not apprehended by His Spirit. There are many half marriages here, where the soul apprehends Christ, but is not apprehended of Him. Hence, many fall away, and never rise again; they let go their hold of Christ; and when that is gone, all is gone. These are 'the branches in Christ that bear not fruit, which the husbandman taketh away' (John 15.2). *Question:* How can that be? *Answer:* These branches are set in the stock by a profession, or an unsound hypocritical faith; they are bound up with it, in the external use of the sacraments; but the stock and they are never knit; therefore they cannot bear fruit. And they need not be cut off, nor broken off; they are by the Husbandman only taken away; or, as the word primarily signifies, lifted up, and so taken away, because there is nothing to hold them; they are indeed bound up with the stock, but were never united to it.

Question: How shall I know if I am apprehended of Christ? *Answer:* You may be satisfied in this inquiry, if you consider and apply these two things:

1: When Christ apprehends a man by His Spirit, he is so drawn, that he comes away to Christ with his whole heart: for true believing is believing with all the heart (Acts 8.37). Our Lord's followers are like those who followed Saul at first, men whose hearts God has touched (1 Sam 10.26). When the Spirit pours in overcoming grace, they pour out their hearts like water before Him (Psa 62.8). They flow unto Him like a river (Isa 2.2.), 'All nations shall flow unto it,' namely, to the 'mountain of the Lord's house.' It denotes not only the abundance of converts, but the disposition of their souls in coming to Christ; they come heartily and freely, as drawn with loving-kindness (Jer 31.3), 'Thy people shall be willing in the day of thy power' (Psa 110.3),

[283]

that is, free, ready, open-hearted, giving themselves to Thee as free-will offerings. When the bridegroom has the bride's heart, it is a right marriage; but some give their hand to Christ, who give Him not their heart. They that are only driven to Christ by terror, will surely leave Him again when that terror is gone. Terror may break a heart of stone, but the pieces into which it is broken still continue to be stone: terrors cannot soften it into a heart of flesh. Yet terrors may begin the work which love crowns. The strong wind, and the earthquake, and the fire going before, the still small voice, in which the Lord is, may come after them. When the blessed Jesus is seeking sinners to match with Him, they are bold and perverse: they will not speak with Him till He has wounded them, made them captives, and bound them with the cords of death. When this is done, then it is that He comes to them, and wins their hearts. The Lord tells us (Hos 2.16–20), that His chosen Israel shall be married unto Himself. But how will the bride's consent be won? Why, in the first place, He will bring her into the wilderness, as He did the people when He brought them out of Egypt (verse 14). There she will be hardly dealt with, scorched with thirst, and bitten of serpents: and then He will speak comfortably to her, or, as the expression is, He will speak unto her heart. The sinner is first driven, and then drawn unto Christ. It is with the soul as with Noah's dove; she was forced back again to the ark, because she could find nothing else to rest upon: but when she returned, she would have rested on the outside of it, if Noah had not 'put forth his hand and pulled her in' (Gen 8.9). The Lord sends His avenger of blood in pursuit of the criminal, who with a sad heart leaves his own city, and with tears in his eyes parts with his old acquaintances, because he dare not stay with them, and he flees for his life to the city of refuge. This is not at all his choice, it is forced work; necessity has no law. But when he comes to the gates, and sees the beauty of the place, the excellency and loveliness of it charm him; and then he enters it with heart and good-will, saying, 'This is my rest, and here I will stay;' and, as one said in another case, 'I had perished, unless I had perished.'

2: When Christ apprehends a soul, the heart is disengaged from, and turned against sin. As in cutting off the branch from the old stock, the great idol self is brought down, the man is powerfully taught to deny himself; so, in apprehending the sinner by the Spirit, that union is dissolved which was between the man and his lusts, while he was in the flesh, as the apostle expresses it (Rom 7.5). His heart is loosed from them, though formerly as dear to him as the members of his body, as his eyes, legs, or arms; and, instead of taking pleasure in them as before, he longs to be rid of them. When the Lord Jesus comes to a soul in the day of converting grace, he finds it like Jerusalem, in the day of her nativity (Ezek 16.4), with its navel not cut drawing its fulsome nourishment and satisfaction from its lusts: but He cuts off this communication, that He may impart to the soul His own consolations, and give it rest in Himself. And thus the Lord wounds the head and heart of sin, and the soul comes to Him, saying, 'Surely our fathers have inherited lies, vanity, and things wherein there is no profit' (Jer 16.19).

v: I proceed to speak of the benefits flowing to true believers from their union with Christ. The chief of the particular benefits which believers have by it, are justification, peace, adoption, sanctification, growth in grace, fruitfulness in good works, acceptance of these works, establishment in the state of grace, support, and a special conduct of providence about them. As for communion with Christ, it is such a benefit, being the immediate consequence of union with Him, as comprehends all the rest as mediate ones. For as the branch, immediately upon its union with the stock, has communion with the stock in all that is in it, so the believer, uniting with Christ, has communion with Him; in which he launches forth into an ocean of happiness, is led into a paradise of pleasures, and has a saving interest in the treasure hid in the field of the Gospel, the unsearchable riches of Christ. As soon as the believer is united to Christ, Christ Himself, in whom all fulness dwells, is his (Cant 2.16), 'My beloved is mine, and I am his.' And 'how shall he not with him freely give us all things?' (Rom 8.32), 'Whether Paul, or Apollos, or Cephas, or the world, or life, or death, or things present, or things to come, all are yours' (1 Cor. 3.22). This communion with Christ is the great comprehensive blessing necessarily flowing from our union with Him. Let us now consider the particular benefits flowing from it, before mentioned.

The first particular benefit that a sinner has by his union with Christ is justification; for, being united to Christ, he has communion with Him in His righteousness (1 Cor 1.30), 'But of him are ye in Christ Jesus, who of God is made unto us wisdom and righteousness.' He stands no more condemned, but justified before God, as being in Christ (Rom 8.1), 'There is therefore now no condemnation to them which are in Christ Jesus.' The branches hereof are pardon of sin, and personal acceptance.

1 : His sins are pardoned, the guilt of them is removed. The bond obliging him to pay his debt is cancelled. God the Father takes the pen, dips it in the blood of His Son, crosses the sinner's accounts, and blots them out of His debt-book. The sinner out of Christ is bound over to the wrath of God; he is under an obligation in law to go to the prison of hell, and there to lie till he has paid the utmost farthing. This arises from the terrible sanction with which the law is guarded, which is no less than death (Gen 2.17). So that the sinner, passing the bounds assigned him, is as Shimei in another case, a man of death (1 Kings 2.42). But now, being united to Christ, God says, 'Deliver him from going down to the pit; I have found a ransom' (Job 33.24). The sentence of condemnation is reversed, the believer is absolved, and set beyond the reach of the condemning law. His sins, which were set before the Lord (Psa 90.8), so that they could not be hid, God now takes and casts them all behind His back (Isa 38.17). Yea, He casts them into the depths of the sea (Micah 7.19). What falls into a brook may be got up again, but what is cast into the sea cannot be recovered. But there are some shallow places in the sea: true,

but their sins are not cast in there, but into the depths of the sea; and the depths of the sea are devouring depths, from whence they shall never come forth again. But what if they do not sink? He will cast them in with force, so that they shall go to the ground, and sink as lead in the mighty waters of the Redeemer's blood. They are not only forgiven, but forgotten (Jer 31.34), 'I will forgive their iniquity, and I will remember their sin no more.' And though their after-sins do in themselves deserve eternal wrath, and do actually make them liable to temporal strokes, and fatherly chastisements, according to the tenor of the covenant of grace (Psa 89.30–33), yet they can never be actually liable to eternal wrath, or the curse of the law; for they are dead to the law in Christ (Rom 7.4). They can never fall away from their union with Christ; neither can they be in Christ, and yet under condemnation at the same time (Rom 8.1), 'There is therefore now no condemnation to them which are in Christ Jesus.' This is an inference drawn from the doctrine of the believer's being dead to the law, set forth by the apostle (chap 7.1–6); as is clear from the second, third, and fourth verses of this eighth chapter. In this respect the justified man is the blessed man, to whom the Lord imputes not iniquity (Psa 32.2); as one who has no design to charge a debt on another, sets it not down in his account-book.

2 : The believer is accepted as righteous in God's sight (2 Cor 5.21). For he is 'found in Christ, not having his own righteousness, but that which is through the faith of Christ, the righteousness which is of God by faith' (Phil 3.9). He could never be accepted of God, as righteous, upon the account of his own righteousness; because, at best, it is but imperfect; and all righteousness, properly so called, which can abide a trial before the throne of God, is perfect. The very name of it implies perfection: for unless a work is perfectly conformed to the law, it is not right, but wrong, and so cannot make a man righteous before God, whose judgment is according to truth. Yet if justice demand a righteousness of one that is in Christ, upon which he may be accounted righteous before the Lord, 'Surely, shall' such a 'one

say, In the Lord have I righteousness' (Isa 45.24). The law is fulfilled, its commands are obeyed, its sanction is satisfied. The
believer's Surety has paid the debt. It was exacted, and He
answered for it.

Thus the person united to Christ is justified. You may conceive
of the whole proceeding herein, in this manner. The avenger of
blood pursuing the criminal, Christ, as the Saviour of lost sinners,
does by the Spirit apprehend him, and draw him to Himself, and
he, by faith, lays hold on Christ. So the Lord our Righteousness,
and the unrighteous creature, unite. From this union with Christ
results a communion with Him in His unsearchable riches, and
consequently in His righteousness, that white raiment which He
has for clothing of the naked (Rev 3.18). Thus the righteousness
of Christ becomes his; and because it is his by unquestionable
title, it is imputed to him; it is reckoned his in the judgment of
God, which is always according to truth. And so the believing
sinner, having a righteousness which fully answers the demands
of the law, is pardoned and accepted as righteous. (See Isa
45.22–25; Rom 3.24; and chap 5.1) Now he is a free man. Who
shall lay any thing to the charge of those whom God justifies?
Can justice lay any thing to their charge? No; for it is satisfied.
Can the law? No; for it has obtained all its demands on them in
Jesus Christ (Gal 2.20), 'I am crucified with Christ.' What can
the law require more, after it has wounded their head, poured in
wrath in full measure into their soul, and cut off their life, and
brought it into the dust of death, by doing all this to Jesus Christ,
who is their head (Eph 1.22), their soul (Acts 2.25-27), and
their life (Col 3.4)? What is become of the sinner's own hand-
writing, which would prove the debt upon him? Christ has
blotted it out (Col 2.14). But it may be, justice may get its eye
upon it again. No; He took it out of the way. But O that it had
been torn in pieces! may the sinner say. Yea, so it is; the nails
that pierced Christ's hands and feet are driven through it; He
nailed it. But what if the torn pieces be set together again?
They cannot be; for He nailed it to His cross, and His cross was

[288]

buried with Him, and will never rise again, seeing Christ dies no more. Where is the face-covering that was upon the condemned man? Christ has destroyed it (Isa 25.7). Where is death, that stood before the sinner with a grim face, and an open mouth, ready to devour him? Christ has swallowed it up in victory (verse 8), Glory, glory, glory to Him that thus 'loved us, and washed us from our sins in His own blood.'

The second benefit flowing from the same spring of union with Christ, and coming by way of justification, is peace; peace with God, and peace of conscience, according to the measure of the sense the justified have of their peace with God (Rom 5.1), 'Therefore being justified by faith, we have peace with God.' (Chap 14.17), 'For the kingdom of God is not meat and drink, but righteousness and peace, and joy in the Holy Ghost.' Whereas God was their enemy before, now He is reconciled to them in Christ: they are in a covenant of peace with him, and, as Abraham was, so are they the friends of God. He is well pleased with them in His beloved Son. His word, which spoke terror to them formerly, now speaks peace, if they rightly understand the language. And there is love in all dispensations towards them, which makes all work together for their good. Their consciences are purged of that guilt and filthiness which lay upon them: His conscience-purifying blood streams through their souls, by virtue of their union with Him (Heb 9.14), 'How much more shall the blood of Christ – purge your conscience from dead works to serve the living God!' The bonds laid on their consciences by the Spirit of God, acting as the spirit of bondage, are taken off, never more to be laid on (Rom 8.15), 'For ye have not received the spirit of bondage again to fear.' Hereby the conscience is quieted, as soon as the soul becomes conscious of the application of that blood; which falls out sooner or later, according to the measure of faith, and as the only wise God sees meet to time it. Unbelievers may have troubled consciences, which they may get quieted again: but, alas! their consciences become peaceable before they become pure; so their peace is but the seed of greater horror and confusion. Carelessness may give ease for a while to a sick conscience; men neglecting its wounds, they close again of their own accord, before the impure matter is removed. Many bury their guilt in the grave of an ill memory: conscience smarts a little; at length the man forgets his sin, and there is an end of it; but that is only an ease before death. Business, or the affairs of life, often give ease in this case. When Cain is banished from the presence of the Lord, he falls to building of cities. When the evil spirit came upon Saul, he calls not for his Bible, nor for the priests to converse with him about his case, but for music, to play it away. So many, when their consciences begin to be uneasy, fill their heads and hands with business, to divert themselves, and to regain ease at any rate. Yea, some will sin contrary to their convictions, and so get some ease to their consciences, as Hazael gave ease to his master by stifling him. Again, the performance of duties may give some ease to disquieted consciences; and this is all which legal professors have recourse to for quieting their consciences. When conscience is wounded they will pray, confess, mourn, and resolve to do so no more: and so they become whole again, without an application of the blood of Christ by faith. But they whose consciences are rightly quieted, come for peace and purification to the blood of sprinkling. Sin is a sweet morsel that makes God's elect sick souls, ere they get it vomited up. It leaves a sting behind it, which one time or other will create them no little pain.

Elihu shows us both the case and cure (Job 33). Behold the case which a man may be in, to whom God has thoughts of love. He darts convictions into his conscience, and makes them stick so fast that he cannot rid himself of them (verse 16), 'He openeth the ears of men, and sealeth their instruction.' His very body sickens (verse 19), 'He is chastened also with pain upon his bed, and the multitude of his bones with strong pain.' He loses his appetite (verse 20), 'His life abhorreth bread, and his soul dainty meat.' His body pines away, so that there is nothing on him but skin and bone (verse 21), 'His flesh is consumed away, that it cannot be seen, and his bones that were not seen stick out.'

Though he is not prepared for death, he has no hope of life (verse 22); 'His soul draweth near unto the grave, and', which is the height of his misery, 'his life to the destroyers;' he is looking every moment when devils, these destroyers (Rev 9.11), these murderers, or man-slayers (John 8.44), will come and carry away his soul to hell. O dreadful case! Is there any hope for such? Yes, there is hope. God designs to 'keep back his soul from the pit' (Job 33.18), although He bring him forward to the brink of it. Now, see how the sick man is cured. The physician's art cannot prevail here: the disease lies more inward than his medicines can reach. It is soul trouble that has brought the body into this disorder; and therefore the remedies must be applied to the sick man's soul and conscience. The physician for this case must be a spiritual physician; the remedies must be spiritual, a righteousness, a ransom, an atonement. Upon the application of these, the soul is cured, the conscience is quieted: and the body recovers (verses 23–26), 'If there be a messenger with him, an interpreter, one among a thousand, to show unto man his uprightness: then he is gracious unto him, and saith, Deliver him from going down into the pit, I have found a ransom. His flesh shall be fresher than a child's, he shall return to the days of his youth. He shall pray unto God, and he shall be favourable unto him, and he shall see his face with joy'. The proper physician for this patient is a messenger, an interpreter (verse 23), that is, as some expositors, not without ground, understand it, the great Physician, Jesus Christ, whom Job had called his Redeemer (chap 19.25). He is a messenger, the 'messenger of the covenant of peace' (Mal 3.1), who comes seasonably to the sick man. He is an interpreter, the great interpreter of God's counsels of love to sinners (Job 33.23), 'One among a thousand,' even 'the chief among ten thousand' (Cant 5.10), 'One chosen out of the people' (Psa 89.19), One to whom 'the Lord hath given the tongue of the learned – to speak a word in season to him that is weary' (Isa 50.4). It is He that is with him, by His Spirit, now, to 'convince him of righteousness' (John 16.8), as He was with him before, to 'convince him of sin and judgment.' His work now is, to show unto him His uprightness, or His righteousness, that is, the interpreter Christ's righteousness; which is the only righteousness arising from the paying of a ransom, and upon which a sinner is delivered from going down to the pit (Job 33.24). Thus Christ is said to declare God's name (Psa 22.22), and to preach righteousness (Psa 40.9). The phrase is remarkable: it is not to show to the man, but to man, His righteousness: (Job 33.23) which not obscurely intimates that He is more than a man, who shows or declares this righteousness. Compare Amos 4.13, 'He that formeth the mountains, and createth the wind, and declareth unto man what is his thought.' There seems to be in it a sweet allusion to the first declaration of this righteousness to man, or, as the word is, to Adam, after the fall, while he lay under terror from apprehensions of the wrath of God. This declaration was made by the messenger, the interpreter, namely, the eternal *Word*, the Son of God, called the voice of the Lord God (Gen 3.8), and by Him appearing, probably, in human shape. Now, while He by His Spirit, is the preacher of righteousness to the man, it is supposed that the man lays hold on the offered righteousness; whereupon the ransom is applied to him, and he is delivered from going down to the pit, for God has a ransom for him. This is intimated to him by the words, 'Deliver him' (Job 33.24). So his conscience, being purified by the blood of atonement, is pacified, and sweetly quieted. 'He shall pray unto God – and see his face with joy,' which before he beheld with horror (verse 26); that is, in New Testament language, 'Having an high priest over the house of God,' he shall 'draw near with a true heart, in full assurance of faith, having his heart sprinkled from an evil conscience' (Heb 10.21,22). But then, what becomes of the body, the weak and weary flesh? Why, 'his flesh shall be fresher than a child's, he shall return to the days of his youth' (verse 25). Yea, 'All his bones,' which were chastened with strong pain (verse 19), 'shall say, Lord, who is like unto thee?' (Psa 35.10).

A third benefit flowing from union with Christ, is adoption. Believers, being united to Christ, become children of God, and members of the family of heaven. By their union with Him, who is the Son of God by nature, they become the sons of God by grace (John 1.12). As when a branch is cut off from one tree, and grafted in the branch of another, the ingrafted branch, by means of its union with the adopting branch, as some not unfitly have called it, is made a branch of the same stock with that into which it is ingrafted: so sinners, being ingrafted into Jesus Christ, whose name is the *Branch*, His Father is their Father, His God their God (John 20.17). And thus they, who are by nature children of the devil, become the children of God. They have the Spirit of adoption (Rom 8.15), namely, the Spirit of His Son, which brings them to God, as children to a father, to pour out their complaints in His bosom, and to seek necessary supplies (Gal 4.6), 'Because ye are sons, God has sent forth the Spirit of his Son into your hearts, crying, Abba, Father.' Under all their weaknesses, they have fatherly pity and compassion shown them (Psalm 103.13), 'Like as a father pitieth his children; so the Lord pitieth them that fear him.' Although they were but foundlings, found in a desert land; yet now 'he keeps them as the apple of his eye' (Deut 32.10). Whoever pursues them, they have a refuge (Prov 14.26), 'His children shall have a place of refuge.' In a time of common calamity, they have chambers of protection, where they may be hid until the indignation is overpast (Isa 26.20). And He is not only their refuge for protection, but their portion for provision in that refuge (Psa 142.5); 'Thou art my refuge, and my portion in the land of the living.' They are provided for, for eternity (Heb 11.16), 'He hath prepared for them a city.' And what He sees they have need of for time, they shall not want (Matt 6.31,32), 'Take no thought, saying, What shall we eat? or what shall we drink? or wherewithal shall we be clothed? For your heavenly Father knoweth that ye have need of all these things.' Seasonable correction is likewise their privilege as sons: so they are not suffered to pass with their faults, as others who are not children but servants of the family, who at length will be turned out of doors for their miscarriages (Heb 12.7), 'If ye endure chastening,

[293]

God dealeth with you as with sons; for what son is he whom the father chasteneth not?' They are heirs of, and shall inherit the promises (Heb 6.12). Nay, they are heirs of God, who Himself is the portion of their inheritance (Psa 16.5), 'and joint-heirs with Christ' (Rom 8.17). And because they are the children of the great King, and heirs of glory, they have angels for their attendants, who are 'sent forth to minister for them who shall be heirs of salvation' (Heb 1.14).

A fourth benefit is sanctification (1 Cor 1.30), 'But of him are ye in Christ Jesus, who of God is made unto us wisdom, and righteousness, and sanctification.' Being united to Christ, they partake of His Spirit, which is the Spirit of holiness. There is a fulness of the Spirit in Christ, and it is not like the fulness of a vessel, which only retains what is poured into it; but it is the fulness of a fountain for diffusion and communication, which is always sending forth its waters, and yet is always full. The Spirit of Christ, that spiritual sap, which is in the stock, and from thence is communicated to the branches, is the Spirit of grace (Zech 12. 10). And where the Spirit of grace dwells, there will be found a confluence of all graces. Holiness is not one grace only, but all the graces of the Spirit; it is a constellation of graces; it is all the graces in their seed and root. And as the sap conveyed from the stock into the branch goes through it, and through every part of it; so the Spirit of Christ sanctifies the whole man. The poison of sin was diffused through the whole spirit, soul, and body of the man; and sanctifying grace pursues it into every corner (1 Thess 5.23). Every part of the man is sanctified, though no part is perfectly so. The truth we are sanctified by is not held in the head, as in a prison, but runs, with its sanctifying influences, through heart and life. There are indeed some graces in every believer which appear as top-branches above the rest, as meekness in Moses, patience in Job; but seeing there is in every child of God, a holy principle going along with the holy law, in all its parts, loving and approving of it, as it appears from their universal respect to the commands of God, it is evident that they are endowed with all the graces of the Spirit. There cannot be less in the effect, than there was in the cause.

Now, this sanctifying Spirit, whereof believers partake, is to them, 1. A spirit of mortification; 'through the Spirit they mortify the deeds of the body' (Rom 8.13). Sin is crucified in them (Gal 5.24). They are planted together with Christ in the likeness of His death, which was a lingering death (Rom 6.5). Sin in the saint, though not quite dead, yet is dying. If it were dead, it would be taken down from the cross, and buried out of his sight: but it hangs there as yet, working and struggling under its mortal wounds. As, when a tree has got such a stroke as reaches the heart of it, all the leaves and branches begin to fade and decay, so, where the sanctifying Spirit comes and breaks the power of sin, there is a gradual ceasing from it, and dying to it, in the whole man; so that he 'no longer lives in the flesh to the lusts of men.' He does not make sin his trade and business; it is not his great design to seek himself, and to satisfy his corrupt inclinations: but he is seeking for Immanuel's land and is walking in the highway to it, the way which is called the way of holiness, though the wind from hell, that was on his back before, blows now full in his face, makes his travelling uneasy, and often drives him off the highway. 2. This Spirit is a Spirit of vivification to them for He is the Spirit of life, and makes them live unto righteousness (Ezek 36.27), 'And I will put my Spirit within you, and cause you to walk in my statutes.' Those who have been 'planted together,' with Christ, 'in the likeness of his death, shall be also in the likeness of his resurrection' (Rom 6.5). At Christ's resurrection, when His soul was re-united with His body, every member of that blessed body was enabled again to perform the actions of life: so the soul, being influenced by the sanctifying Spirit of Christ, is enabled more and more to perform all the actions of spiritual life. And as the whole of the law, and not some scraps of it only, is written on the holy heart, so believers are enabled to transcribe that law in their life. Although they cannot write one line of it without blots, yet God, for Christ's sake, accepts of the performance, in point of sanctification, they being disciples to His own Son, and led by His own Spirit.

This sanctifying Spirit, communicated by the Lord Jesus to His members, is the spiritual nourishment the branches have from the stock into which they are ingrafted; whereby the life of grace, given them in regeneration, is preserved, continued, and actuated. It is the nourishment whereby the new creature lives, and is nourished up towards perfection. Spiritual life needs to be fed, and must have supply of nourishment: and believers derive the same from Christ their Head, whom the Father has appointed the Head of influences to all His members (Col 2.19), 'And not holding the head, from which all the body by joints and bands having nourishment ministered, or supplied,' &c. Now this supply is 'the supply of the Spirit of Jesus Christ' (Phil 1.19). The saints feed richly, 'eating Christ's flesh, and drinking His blood,' for their spiritual nourishment: yet our Lord himself teaches us, that 'it is the Spirit that quickeneth' (John 6.63), even that Spirit who dwells in His blessed body. The human nature is united to the divine nature in the person of the Son, and so, like the bowl in Zachariah's candlestick (chap 4) lies at the fountain head, as the glorious means of conveyance of influences from the fountain of Deity. He receives not the Spirit by measure, but ever hath a fulness of the Spirit, by reason of that personal union. Hence believers, being united to the man Christ, as the seven lamps to the bowl, by their seven pipes (Zech 4.2), His flesh is to them meat indeed, and His blood drink indeed: for, feeding on that blessed body, that is, effectually applying Christ to their souls by faith, they partake more and more of that Spirit who dwelleth therein, to their spiritual nourishment. The holiness of God can never admit of an immediate union with the sinful creature, nor, consequently, an immediate communion with it: yet the creature could not live the life of grace without communion with the fountain of life. Therefore, that the honour of God's holiness and the salvation of sinners might jointly be provided for, the second Person of the glorious Trinity took into a personal union with Himself a sinless

human nature; that so this holy, harmless, and undefiled human-
ity, might immediately receive a fulness of the Spirit, of which
He might communicate to His members, by His divine power and
efficacy. Suppose there were a tree, with its root in the earth, and
its branches reaching to heaven, the vast distance between the
root and the branches would not interrupt the communication
between the root and the top branch: even so, the distance between the man Christ, who is in heaven, and His members, who
are on earth, cannot hinder the communication between them.
What though the parts of mystical Christ, namely the Head and
the members, are not contiguous, as joined together in the way of
corporal union; the union is not therefore the less real and effectual. Yea, our Lord Himself shows us, that though we eat His
flesh in a corporeal and carnal manner, yet it would profit nothing
(John 6.63); we should not be one whit the holier thereby. But
the members of Christ on earth are united to their Head in
heaven, by the invisible bond of the self-same Spirit dwelling in
both; in Him as the Head, and in them as the members. The
wheels in Ezekiel's vision were not contiguous to the living creatures, yet were united to them by an invisible bond of one Spirit
in both; so that, 'when the living creatures went, the wheels went
by them, and when the living creatures were lifted up from the
earth, the wheels were lifted up' (Ezek 1.19); 'For,' says the
prophet, 'the Spirit of the living creature was in the wheels'
(verse 20).

Hence we may see the difference between true satisfaction, and
that shadow of it which is to be found among some strict professors of Christianity, who yet are not true Christians, are not
regenerated by the Spirit of Christ, and is of the same kind with
what has appeared in many sober heathens. True sanctification is
the result of the soul's union with the holy Jesus, the first and
immediate receptacle of the sanctifying Spirit, out of whose
fulness His members do, by virtue of their union with Him,
receive sanctifying influences. The other is the mere product of
the man's own spirit, which, whatever it has, or seems to

have, of the matter of true holiness, yet does not arise from the supernatural principles, nor to the high aims and ends thereof; for, as it comes from self, so it runs out into the dead sea of self again; and lies as wide of true holiness, as nature does of grace. They who have this species of holiness are like common boatmen, who serve themselves with their own oars: whereas the ship bound for Immanuel's land sails by the blowings of the divine Spirit. How is it possible there should be true satisfaction without Christ? Can there be true sanctification without partaking of the Spirit of holiness? Can we partake of that Spirit, but by Jesus Christ, 'the Way, the Truth, and the Life?' The falling dew shall as soon make its way through the flinty rock, as the influences of grace come from God to sinners any other way than through Him whom the Father has appointed the head of influences (Col 1.19), 'For it pleased the Father, that in him should all fulness dwell:' and (chap 2.19), 'And not holding the head, from which all the body by joints and bands having nourishment ministered and knit together, increaseth with the increase of God.' Hence see how it comes to pass, that many fall away from their seeming sanctification, and never recover: it is because they are not branches truly knit to the true vine. Meanwhile others recover from their decays, because of their union with the life-giving stock, by the quickening Spirit (1 John 2.19), 'They went out from us, but they were not of us; for if they had been of us, they would no doubt have continued with us.'

A fifth benefit is growth in grace. 'Having nourishment ministered, they increase with the increase of God' (Col 2.19); 'The righteous shall flourish like the palm-tree: he shall grow like a cedar in Lebanon' (Psa 92.12). Grace is of a growing nature; in the way to Zion they go from strength to strength. Though the holy man be at first a little child in grace, yet at length he becomes a young man, a father (1 John 2.13). Though he does but creep in the way to heaven sometimes, yet afterwards he walks, he runs, he mounts up with wings as eagles (Isa 40.31). If a branch grafted into a stock never grows, it is a plain evidence of its not having knit with the stock.

But some perhaps may say, 'If all true Christians be growing ones, what shall be said of those who, instead of growing, are going back?' I answer, There is a great difference between the Christian's growing simply, and his growing at all times. All true Christians do grow, but I do not say that they grow at all times. A tree that has life and nourishment grows to its perfection, yet it is not always growing; it grows not in the winter. Christians also have their winters, wherein the influences of grace, necessary for their growth, cease (Cant 5.2), 'I sleep.' It is by faith the believer derives gracious influences from Jesus Christ, as each lamp in the candlestick received oil from the bowl, by the pipe going between them (Zech 4.2). Now, if that pipe be stopped, if the saint's faith lie dormant and inactive, then all the rest of the graces will become dim, and seem ready to be extinguished. In consequence whereof, depraved nature will gather strength and become active. What then will become of the soul? Why, there is still one sure ground of hope. The saint's faith is not as the hypocrite's, like a pipe laid short of the fountain, whereby there can be no conveyance: it still remains a bond of union between Christ and the soul; and therefore, because Christ lives, the believer shall live also (John 14.19). The Lord Jesus 'puts in His hand by the hole of the door,' and clears the means of conveyance; and then influences for growth flow, and the believer's graces look fresh and green again (Hos 14.7), 'They that dwell under his shadow shall return: they shall revive as the corn, and grow as the vine.' In the worst of times, the saints have a principle of growth in them (1 John 3.9), 'His seed remaineth in him.' Therefore, after decays, they revive again: namely, when the winter is over, and the Sun of Righteousness returns to them with his warm influences. Mud thrown into a pool may lie there at ease; but if it be cast into a fountain, the spring will at length work it out, and run as clear as formerly. *Secondly*, Christians may mistake their growth, and that two ways. 1. By judging of their case according to their present feeling.

They observe themselves, and cannot perceive themselves to be growing; but there is no reason thence to conclude they are not growing (Mark 4.27), 'The seed springs and grows up, he knoweth not how.' Were a person to fix his eye never so steadfastly on a growing tree, he would not see it growing; but if he compare the tree as it now is, with what it was some years ago, he will certainly perceive that it has grown. In like manner may the Christian know whether he be in a growing or declining state, by comparing his present with his former condition. 2. Christians may mistake their case, by measuring their growth by the advances of the top only, not of the root. Though a man be not growing taller, he may be growing stronger. If a tree be uniting with the ground, fixing itself in the earth, and spreading out its roots, it is certainly growing, although it be not higher than formerly. So, although a Christian may want the sweet consolations and flashes of affection which he had; yet if he be growing in humility, self-denial, and sense of needy dependence on Jesus Christ, he is a growing Christian (Hos 14.5), 'I will be as the dew unto Israel; he shall cast forth his roots as Lebanon.'

Question: 'But do hypocrites grow at all? And if so, how shall we distinguish between their growth and true Christian growth?' *Answer:* To the first part of the question, hypocrites do grow. The tares have their growth, as well as the wheat: the seed that fell among thorns did spring up (Luke 8.7). Only it brought no fruit to perfection (verse 14). Yea, a true Christian may have a false growth. James and John seemed to grow in the grace of holy zeal, when their spirits grew so hot in the cause of Christ that they would have fired a whole village for not receiving their Lord and Master (Luke 9.54), 'They said, Lord, wilt thou that we command fire to come down from heaven and consume them, even as Elias did?' But it was indeed no such thing; and therefore he turned and rebuked them (verse 55), and said, 'Ye know not what manner of spirit ye are of.' To the second part of the question it is answered, that there is a peculiar beauty in the true Christian growth, distinguishing it from all false growth: it is universal, regular, proportionable. It is a 'growing up into him in all things, which is the head' (Eph 4.15). The growing Christian grows proportionably in all the parts of the new man. Under the kindly influences of the Sun of Righteousness, believers 'grow up as calves of the stall' (Mal 4.2). You would think it a monstrous growth in these creatures if you saw their heads grow, and not their bodies; or if you saw one leg grow, and another not; if all the parts do not grow proportionably. Aye, but such is the growth of many in religion. They grow like rickety children, who have a big head but a slender body; they get more knowledge into their heads, but not more holiness into their hearts and lives. They grow very hot outwardly, but very cold inwardly; like men in a fit of the ague. They are more taken up about the externals of religion than formerly, yet as great strangers to the power of godliness as ever. If a garden is watered with the hand, some of the plants will readily get much, some little, and some no water at all; and therefore some wither, while others are coming forward; but after a shower from the clouds, all come forward together. In like manner, all the graces of the Spirit grow proportionably, by the special influences of divine grace. The branches ingrafted in Christ, growing aright, grow in all the several ways of growth at once. They grow inward, growing into Christ (Eph 4.15), uniting more closely with Him; and cleaving more firmly to Him, as the Head of influences, which is the spring of all other true Christian growth. They grow outward in good works, in their life and conversation. They not only, with Naphtali, give goodly words, but, like Joseph, they are fruitful boughs. They grow upward in heavenly-mindedness, and contempt of the world; for their conversation is in heaven (Phil 3.20). And finally, they grow downward in humility and self-loathing. The branches of the largest growth in Christ, are, in their own eyes, 'less than the least of all saints' (Eph 3.8); 'the chief of sinners' (1 Tim 1.15); 'more brutish than any man' (Prov 30.2). They see that they can do nothing, no, not so much as 'think any thing, as of themselves' (2 Cor 3.5): that they deserve nothing, being 'not worthy of the least of all the mercies showed unto them' (Gen 32.10); and that they are nothing (2 Cor 12.11).

A sixth benefit is fruitfulness. The branch ingrafted into Christ is not barren, but brings forth fruit (John 15.5), 'He that abideth in me, and I in him, the same bringeth forth much fruit.' For that very end are souls united to Christ, that they may bring forth fruit unto God (Rom 7.4). They that are barren may be branches in Christ by profession, but not by real implantation. All who are united to Christ bring forth the fruit of Gospel-obedience and true holiness. Faith is always followed with good works. The believer is not only come out of the grave of his natural state, but he has put off his grave-clothes, namely, reigning lusts, in which he walked like a ghost; being dead while he lived in them (Col 3.7,8). For Christ has said of him, as of Lazarus, 'Loose him, and let him go.' Now that he has put on Christ, he personates Him, so to speak, as a beggar in borrowed robes represents a king on the stage, walking as he also walked. Now the fruit of the Spirit in him, is in all goodness (Eph 5.9). The fruits of holiness will be found in the hearts, lips, and lives of those who are united to Christ. The hidden man of the heart is not only a temple built for God, and consecrated to Him, but used and employed for Him, where love, fear, trust, and all the other parts of unseen religion, are exercised (Phil 3.3), 'For we are the circumcision which worship God in the Spirit.' The heart is no more the devil's common, where thoughts go free, for there even vain thoughts are hated (Psa 119.113); but it is God's enclosure, hedged about as a garden for Him (Cant 4.16). It is true, there are weeds of corruption there, because the ground is not yet perfectly cleared, but the man, in the day of his new creation, is set to dress it, and keep it. A live coal from the altar has touched his lips, and they are purified. (Psa 15.1–3), 'Lord, who shall abide in thy tabernacle? who shall dwell in thy holy hill? He that speaketh the truth in his heart; he that backbiteth not with his tongue, nor taketh up a reproach against his neighbour.' There may be, indeed, a smooth tongue, where there is a false heart.

The voice may be Jacob's, while the hands are Esau's. But, 'if any man among you seem to be religious, and bridleth not his tongue, but deceiveth his own heart, this man's religion is vain' (Jas 1.26). The power of godliness will rule over the tongue, though a world of iniquity. If one be a Galilean, his speech will bewray him; he will speak, not the language of Ashdod, but the language of Canaan. He will neither be dumb in religion, nor will his tongue walk at random, seeing, to the double guard which nature has given the tongue, grace has added a third. The fruits of holiness will be found in his outward conversation; for he has clean hands, as well as a pure heart (Psa 24.4). He is a godly man, and religiously discharges the duties of the first table of the law; he is a righteous man, and honestly performs the duties of the second table. In his conversation he is a good Christian, and a good neighbour too. He carries it towards God, as if men's eyes were upon him; and towards men, as believing God's eyes to be upon him. Those things which God hath joined in His law, he dares not put asunder in his practice.

Thus the branches in Christ are full of good fruits. And those fruits are a cluster of vital actions, whereof Jesus Christ is the principle and end. The principle: for He lives in them, and 'the life they live is by faith in the Son of God' (Gal 2.20). The end: for they live to Him, and 'to them to live is Christ' (Phil 1.21). The duties of religion are in the world, like fatherless children in rags; some will not take them in, because they never loved them nor their father; some take them in, because they may be serviceable to them: but the saints take them in for their Father's sake, that is for Christ's sake: and they are lovely in their eyes, because they are like Him. O! whence is this new life of the saints? Surely it could never have been hammered out of the natural powers of their souls, by the united force of all created power. In eternal barrenness would they have continued, but that being 'married to Christ, they bring forth fruit unto God' (Rom 7.4).

If you ask me, 'How can your nourishment, growth, and fruitfulness be forwarded?', I offer these few advices: 1. Make sure work as to your knitting with the stock by faith unfeigned, and beware of hypocrisy: a branch that is not sound at the heart will certainly wither. The trees of the Lord's planting are trees of righteousness (Isa 61.3). So, when others fade, they bring forth fruit. Hypocrisy is a disease in the vitals of religion, which will consume all at length; it is a leak in the ship, that will certainly sink it. Sincerity of grace will make it lasting, be it never so weak; as the smallest twig, that is sound at the heart, will draw nourishment from the stock and grow, while the greatest bough that is rotten can never recover, because it receives no nourishment. 2. Labour to be steadfast in the truths and way of God. An unsettled and wavering judgment is a great enemy to Christian growth and fruitfulness, as the apostle teaches (Eph 4.14,15), 'That we henceforth be no more children, tossed to and fro, and carried about with every wind of doctrine. But speaking the truth in love, may grow up into Him in all things, which is the head, even Christ.' A rolling stone gathers no moss, and a wavering judgment makes a fruitless life. Though a tree be never so sound, yet how can it grow, or be fruitful, if you be still removing it out of one soil into another? 3. Endeavour to cut off the suckers, as gardeners do, that their trees may thrive. These are unmortified lusts; therefore 'mortify your members that are upon the earth' (Col 3.5). When the Israelites got meat to their lusts, they got leanness to their souls. She that has many hungry children about her hand, and must be still putting into their mouths, will have much ado to get a bit put into her own. They must refuse the cravings of inordinate affections, who would have their souls to prosper. 4. Improve, for these ends, the ordinances of God. It is in the courts of our God where the trees of righteousness flourish (Psa 92.13). The waters of the sanctuary are the means appointed of God, to cause His people to grow as willows by the water courses. Therefore drink in with 'desire, the sincere milk of the word, that ye may grow thereby' (1 Pet 2.2). Come to these wells of salvation, not to look at them only, but to draw water out of them. The sacrament of the Lord's supper is in a special manner

[304]

appointed for these ends. It is not only a solemn public profession, and a seal of our union and communion with Christ, but it is a means of most intimate communion with Him, and strengthens our union with Him, our faith, love, repentance, and other graces (1 Cor 10.16), 'The cup of blessing, which we bless, is it not the communion of the blood of Christ? The bread which we break, is it not the communion of the body of Christ?' And (chapter 12.13), 'We have been all made to drink into one Spirit.' Give yourselves unto prayer; open your mouths wide, and He will fill them. By these means the branches in Christ may be further nourished, grow up, and bring forth much fruit.

A seventh benefit is, The acceptance of their fruits of holiness before the Lord. Though they may be imperfect, they are accepted, because they savour of Christ, the blessed stock, which the branches grow upon, while the fruits of others are rejected of God (Gen 4.4,5), 'And the Lord had respect unto Abel, and his offering; but unto Cain and his offering he had not respect.' Compare Heb 11.3, 'By faith, Abel offered unto God a more excellent sacrifice than Cain.' O how defective are the saints' duties in the eye of the law! The believer himself sees many faults in his best performances; yet the Lord graciously receives them. There is no grace planted in the heart, but there is a weed of corruption hard by its side, while the saints are in the lower world. Their very sincerity is not without a mixture of dissimulation or hypocrisy (Gal 2.13). Hence there are defects in the exercise of every grace, in the performance of every duty; depraved nature always drops something to stain their best works. There is still a mixture of darkness with their clearest light. Yet this does not mar their acceptance (Cant 6.10), 'Who is she that looketh forth as the morning?' or, 'as the dawning'? Behold how Christ's spouse is esteemed and accepted of her Lord, even when she looks forth as the morning, whose beauty is mixed with the blackness of the night! 'When the morning was looking out,' as the word is (Judges 19.26), that is, 'In the dawning of the day,' as we read it. So the very dawning of grace and good will to Christ, grace peeping out from under a mass of darkness in believers, is pleasant and acceptable to Him, as the break of day is to the weary traveller. Though the remains of unbelief make the hand of faith to shake and tremble, yet the Lord is so well pleased with it, that He employs it to carry away pardons and supplies of grace from the throne of grace and the fountain of grace. His faith was effectual, who 'cried out and said with tears, Lord, I believe, help thou mine unbelief!' (Mark 9.24). Though the remains of sensual affections make the flame of their love weak and smoky, He turns His eyes from the smoke, and beholds the flame, how fair it is (Cant 4.10), 'How fair is thy love, my sister, my spouse!' 'The smell of their' under 'garments' of inherent holiness, imperfect as it is, 'is like the smell of Lebanon' (verse 11); and that because they are covered with their elder brother's clothes, which make the sons of God to 'smell as a field which the Lord hath blessed.' Their good works are accepted; their cups of cold water given to a disciple, in the name of a disciple, shall not want a reward. Though they cannot offer for the tabernacle, gold, silver, and brass, and onyx stones, let them come forward with what they have; if it were but goats' hair, it shall not be rejected; if it were but rams' skins, they shall be kindly accepted; for they are dyed red, dipped by faith in the Mediator's blood, and so presented unto God. A very ordinary work done in faith, and from faith, if it were but the building of a wall about the holy city, is a great work (Neh 6.3). If it were but the bestowing of a box of ointment on Christ, it shall never be forgotten (Matt 26.13). Even 'a cup of cold water only given to one of Christ's little ones, in the name of a disciple, shall be rewarded' (Matt 10.42). Nay, not a good word for Christ shall drop from their mouths, but it shall be registered in God's 'book of remembrance' (Mal 3.16). Nor shall a tear drop from their eyes for Him, but He will 'put it in His bottle' (Psa 56.8). Their will is accepted for the deed; their sorrow for the want of will, for the will itself (2 Cor 8.12), 'For if there be first a willing mind, it is accepted according to that a man hath, and not according to that he hath not.' Their groanings,

[306]

when they cannot well express their desires, are heard in heaven; the meaning of those groans is well known there, and they will be returned like the dove with an olive branch of peace in her mouth. (See Rom 8.26,27.) Their mites are better than other men's talents. Their lisping and broken sentences are more pleasant to their Father in heaven, than the most fluent or flourishing speeches of those who are not in Christ. Their voice is sweet, even when they are ashamed it should be heard; their countenance is comely, even when they blush, and draw a veil over it (Cant 2.14). The Mediator takes their petitions, blots out some parts, rectifies others, and then presents them to the Father, in consequence whereof they pass in the court of heaven.

Every true Christian is a temple to God. If you look for sacrifices, they are not wanting there; they offer the sacrifice of praise, and do good: with such sacrifices God is well pleased (Heb 13.15,16). Christ Himself is the altar that sanctifies the gift (verse 10). If we look for incense, it is there too. The graces of the Spirit are found in their hearts, and the Spirit of the crucified Christ fires them, and puts them in exercise, as the fire was brought from the altar of burnt-offering, to set the insence aflame; then they mount heavenward, like pillars of smoke (Cant 3.6). But the best of incense will leave ashes behind it: yes, indeed; but as the priest took away the ashes of the incense in a golden dish, and threw them out, so our great High Priest takes away the ashes and refuse of all the saints' services, by His mediation in their behalf.

An eighth benefit flowing from union with Christ, is establishment. The Christian cannot fall away, but must persevere unto the end (John 10.28), 'they shall never perish, neither shall any man pluck them out of my hand.' Indeed, if a branch do not knit with the stock, it will fall away when shaking winds arise: but the branch knit to the stock stands fast whatever wind blows. Sometimes a stormy wind of temptation blows from hell, and shakes the branches in Christ the true vine: but their union with Him is their security; moved they may be, but removed they never can be. The Lord 'will with the temptation also make a way to escape' ((1 Cor 10.13). Calms are never of any continuance; there is almost always some wind blowing, and therefore branches are rarely altogether at rest. But sometimes violent winds arise, which threaten to rend them from off their stock. Even so it is with saints; they are daily put to it to keep their ground against temptation: sometimes the wind from hell rises so high, and blows so furiously, that it makes even top branches to sweep the ground; yet being knit to Christ their stock, they get up again, in spite of the most violent efforts of the prince of the power of the air (Psa 94.18), 'When I said, my foot slippeth, thy mercy, O Lord, held me up.' But the Christian improves by his trial, and is so far from being damaged that he is benefited by it, as it discovers what hold the soul has of Christ, and what hold Christ has of the soul. And look, as the wind in the bellows, which would blow out the candle, blows up the fire; even so it often comes to pass, that such temptations enliven the true Christian, awakening the graces of the Spirit in him; and by that means, discover both the reality and the strength of grace in him. And hence, as Luther, that great man of God, said, 'One Christian, who has had experience of temptation, is worth a thousand others.'

Sometimes a stormy wind of trouble and persecution from the men of the world blows upon the vine, that is, mystical Christ; but union with the stock is a sufficient security to the branches. In a time of the church's peace and outward prosperity, while the angels hold the winds that they blow not, there are a great many branches taken up and put into the stock, which never knit with it, nor live by it, though they be bound up with it by the bonds of external ordinances. Now, these may stand a while on the stock, and stand with great ease while the calm lasts; but when once the storms arise, and the winds blow, they will begin to fall off one after another; and the higher the wind rises, the greater will the number be that falls. Yea, some strong boughs of that sort, when they fall, will, by their weight, carry others of their own kind, quite down to the earth with them; and will bruise and press down some true branches in such a manner, that they would also fall off, were it not for that fast hold which the stock has of them. Then it is that many branches which before were high and eminent, are found lying on the earth withered, and fit to be gathered up and cast into the fire (Matt 13.6), 'When the sun was up, they were scorched: and because they had no root, they withered away.' (John 15.6), 'If a man abide not in me, he is cast forth as a branch, and is withered, and men gather them, and cast them into the fire, and they are burned.' But however violently the winds blow, none of the truly ingrafted branches that are knit with the stock are found missing, when the storm is changed into a calm (John 17.12), 'Those that thou gavest me, I have kept, and none of them is lost.' The least twig growing in Christ shall stand it out, and subsist, when the tallest cedars growing on their own root, shall be laid flat on the ground (Rom 8.35), 'Who shall separate us from the love of Christ? Shall tribulation, or distress, or persecution, or famine, or nakedness, or peril, or sword?' (See verses 36–39.) However severely Israel be 'sifted, yet shall not the least grain,' or, as it is in the original language, 'a little stone', 'fall upon the earth' (Amos 9.9). It is an allusion to the sifting of fine pebble stones from among heaps of dust and sand: though the sand and dust fall to the ground, to be blown away with the wind, and trampled under foot, yet there shall not fall on the earth so much as a little stone, such is the exactness of the sieve and the care of the sifter. There is nothing more ready to fall on the earth than a stone: yet, if professors of religion be lively stones, built on Christ the chief Corner-stone, although they be little stones, they shall not fall to the earth, whatever storm beats upon them. (See 1 Pet 2.4–6.) All the good grain in the church of Christ is of this kind; they are stones, in respect of solidity, and lively stones in respect of activity. If men be solid substantial Christians, they will not be like chaff tossed to and fro with every wind, having so much of the liveliness that they have nothing of the stone; and if they be lively Christians, whose spirits will stir in them, as Paul's did, when he saw the city wholly given to idolatry (Acts

17.16), they will not lie like stones, to be turned over, hither and thither, cut and carved, according to the lusts of men; having so much of the stone as leaves nothing of liveliness in them.

Our God's house is a great house, wherein are not only vessels of gold, but also of earth (2 Tim 2.20). Both these are apt to contract filthiness; and therefore when God brings trouble upon the church, he has an eye to both. As for the vessels of gold, they are not destroyed, but purified by a fiery trial in the furnace of affliction, as goldsmiths refine their gold (Isa 1.25), 'And I will turn my hand upon thee, and purely purge away thy dross.' But destruction is to the vessels of earth; they shall be broken in shivers, as a potter's vessel (verse 28), 'And the destruction,' or breaking 'of the transgressors, and of the sinners, shall be together.' It seems to be an allusion to that law for breaking the vessels of earth, when unclean; while vessels of wood, and consequently vessels of gold, were only to be rinsed (Lev 15.12).

A ninth benefit is support. If you are a branch ingrafted in Christ, the root bears you. The believer leans on Christ, as a weak woman in a journey leaning upon her beloved husband (Cant 8.5). He stays himself upon Him, as a feeble old man stays himself on his staff (Isa 50.10). He rolls himself on Him, as one rolls a burden he is not able to walk under, off his own back, upon another who is able to bear it (Psa 22.8, marg). There are many weights to hang upon and press down the branches in Christ the true vine. But you know, whatever weights hang on the branches, the stock bears all; it bears the branch, and the weight that is upon it too.

1: Christ supports believers in Him, under a weight of outward troubles. That is a large promise (Isa 43.2), 'When thou passest through the waters, I will be with thee: and through the rivers they shall not overflow thee.' See how David was supported under a heavy load (1 Sam 30.6). His city Ziglag was burnt, his wives were taken captives, his men spoke of stoning him: nothing was left him but his God and his faith; but by his faith, he encouraged himself in his God. The Lord comes, and lays His cross on His people's shoulders; it presses them down, and they are likely to sink under it, and therefore cry, 'Master, save us, we perish;' but He supports them under their burden; He bears them up, and they bear their cross. Thus the Christian, with a weight of outward troubles upon him, goes lightly under his burden, having the everlasting arms underneath him. The Christian has a spring of comfort which he cannot lose; and therefore never wants something to support him. If a man have all his riches in money, robbers may take these away; and then what has he more? But though the landed proprietor may be robbed of his money, yet his lands remain for his support. Those who build their comfort on worldly goods, may quickly be comfortless; but those who are united to Christ shall find comfort, when all the streams of worldly enjoyments are dried up (Job 6.13), 'Is not my help in me? and is wisdom driven quite from me?' that is, Though my substance is gone; though my servants, my children, my health, and soundness of body, are all gone; yet my grace is not gone too. Though the Sabeans have driven away my oxen and asses, and the Chaldeans have driven away my camels, they have not driven away my faith, and my hope too; these are yet in me; they are not driven from me; so that by them I can fetch comfort from heaven, when I can have none from earth.

2: Christ supports His people under a weight of inward troubles and discouragements. Many times 'heart and flesh fail them;' but then 'God is the strength of their heart' (Psa 73.26). They may have a weight of guilt pressing them. This is a load that will make their backs bend, and their spirits sink: but He takes it off, and puts a pardon into their hand, while they cast their burden upon Him. Christ takes the soul, as one marries a widow under a burden of debt: and so when the creditors come to Christ's spouse, she carries them to her Husband, confesses the debt, declares she is not able to pay, and lays all upon Him. The Christian sometimes, through carelessness, loses his discharge; he cannot find it, however he search for it. The law takes that opportunity, and proceeds against him for a debt paid already.

God hides His face, and the soul is distressed. Many arrows go through the heart now; many long accounts are laid before the man, which he reads and acknowledges. Often does he see the officers coming to apprehend him, and the prison door open to receive him. What else keeps him from sinking utterly under discouragements in this case, but that the everlasting arms of a Mediator underneath him, and that he relies upon the great Surety? Further, they may have a weight of strong lusts pressing them. They have a body of death upon them. Death is a weight that presses the soul out of the body. A leg or an arm of death, if I may so speak, would be a terrible load. One lively lust will sometimes lie so heavy on a child of God, that he can no more remove it than a child could throw a giant from off him. How then are they supported under a whole body of death? Their support is from that root which bears them, from the everlasting arm that is underneath them. 'His grace is sufficient for them' (2 Cor 12.9). The great stay of the believer is not the grace of God within him; that is a well whose streams sometimes run dry; but it is the grace of God without him, the grace that is in Jesus Christ, which is an ever-flowing fountain, to which the believer can never come amiss. For the apostle tells us in the same verse, it is 'the power of Christ.' 'Most gladly therefore,' says he, 'will I rather glory in my infirmities, that the power of Christ may rest upon me,' or 'tabernacle above me,' as the cloud of glory did on the Israelites, which God spread for a covering, or shelter, to them in the wilderness (Psa 105.39; compare Isa 4.5,6). So that the believer in this combat, like the eagle, first flies aloft by faith, and then comes down on the prey Psa 34.5), 'They looked to him, and were lightened.' Finally, they have a weight of weakness and wants upon them, but they 'cast over that burden on the Lord,' their strength, 'and He sustains them' (Psa 55.22). With all their wants and weakness they are cast upon Him; as the poor, weak, and naked babe coming out of the womb, is cast into the lap of one appointed to take care of it (Psa 22.10). Though they be destitute, as a shrub in the wilderness, which the foot of every beast may tread down, the Lord will regard them (Psa 102.17). It is not surprising that the weakest plant should be safe in a garden: but our Lord Jesus Christ is a hedge for protection to His weak and destitute ones, even in a wilderness.

Objection: 'But if the saints be so supported, how is it that they fall so often under temptations and discouragements?' *Answer:* 1. However low they fall at any time, they never fall off; and that is a great matter. They 'are kept by the power of God through faith unto salvation' (1 Pet 1.5). Hypocrites may fall, so as to fall off, and fall into the pit, as a bucket falls into a well when the chain breaks. But, though the child of God may fall, and that so low that the waters go over his head, yet there is still a bond of union between Christ and him; the chain is not broken; he will not go to the ground; he will be drawn up again (Luke 22.31,32), 'And the Lord said, Simon, Simon, Satan hath desired to have you, that he may sift you as wheat: but I have prayed for thee, that thy faith fail not.' 2. The falls of the saints flow from their not improving their union with Christ, their not making use of Him by faith, for staying or bearing them up (Psa 27.13), 'I had fainted, unless I had believed.' While the nurse holds the child in her arms, it cannot fall to the ground; yet if the unwary child hold not by her, it may fall backwards in her arms, to its great hurt. Thus David's fall broke his bones (Psa 51.8); but it did not break the bond of union between Christ and him; the Holy Spirit, the bond of that union, was not taken from him (verse 11).

The last benefit I shall name, is, the special care of the Husbandman (John 15.1,2), 'I am the true vine, and my Father is the husbandman. Every branch that beareth fruit, he purgeth it, that it may bring forth more fruit.' Believers, by virtue of their union with Christ, are the objects of God's special care and providence. Mystical Christ is God's vine; other societies in the world are but wild olive-trees. The men of the world are but God's out-field; the saints are his vineyard, which He has a special interest in, and a special concern for (Cant 8.12), 'My vineyard, which is mine, is before me.' He that slumbers not nor sleeps, is the keeper of it;

He does keep it; lest any hurt it, He will keep it night and day; He, in whose hand is the dew of heaven, will water it every moment (Isa 27.3). He dresses and weeds it, in order to further its fruitfulness (John 15.2). He cuts off the luxuriant twigs, that mar the fruitfulness of the branch. This is done, especially by the Word, and by the cross or afflictions; the saints need the ministry of the Word, as much as the vineyard needs one to dress and prune the vines (1 Cor 3.9), 'We are labourers together with God; ye are God's husbandry, ye are God's building.' And they need the cross too (1 Pet 1.6).

Therefore, if we were to reckon the cross amongst the benefits flowing to believers from their union with Christ, I judge that we should not reckon amiss. Sure I am, in their sufferings, they 'suffer with him' (Rom 8.17). The assurances which they have of the cross, have rather the nature of a promise, than of a threatening (Psa 89.30–33), 'If his children forsake My law – then will I visit their transgression with the rod, and their iniquity with stripes. Nevertheless, my loving-kindness will I not utterly take from him, nor suffer my faithfulness to fail.' This looks like a tutor's engaging to a dying father, to take care of the children left with him, and to give them both nurture and admonition for their good. The covenant of grace truly beats the spears of affliction into pruning-hooks, to them that are in Christ (Isa 27.9), 'By this therefore shall the iniquity of Jacob be purged, and this is all the fruit to take away his sin.' Why then should we be angry with our cross? why should we be frightened at it? The believer must take up his cross, and follow his leader, the Lord Jesus Christ. He must take up his every-day's cross (Luke 9.23), 'If any man will come after me, let him deny himself, and take up his cross daily:' Yea, he must take up holy-day's cross too (Lam 2.22), 'Thou hast called, as in a solemn day, my terrors round about.' The church of the Jews had of a long time many a pleasant meeting at the temple, on solemn days, for the worship of God; but they got a solemnity of another nature, when God called together, about the temple and city, the Chaldean army, that burnt the temple, and laid Jerusalem on heaps. And as the church of God is yet militant in this lower region, how can it be but the clouds will return after the rain? But the cross of Christ, by which appellation the saint's troubles are named, is a kindly name to the believer. It is a cross indeed, not to the believer's graces, but to his corruptions. The hypocrite's seeming graces may indeed breathe out their last on a cross, as those of the stony-ground hearers did (Matt 13.6), 'When the sun' of persecution (verse 21) 'was up, they were scorched; and because they had no root, they withered away;' but never did one of the real graces in a believer die upon the cross yet. Nay, as the candle shines brightest in the night, and the fire burns fiercest in intense frost, so the believer's graces are commonly most vigorous in a time of trouble.

There is a certain pleasure and sweetness in the cross, to those who have their senses exercised to discern and to find it out. There is a certain sweetness in a man's seeing himself upon his trials for heaven, and standing candidate for glory. There is a pleasure in travelling over those mountains, where the Christian can see the prints of Christ's own feet, and the footsteps of the flock, who have been there before him. How pleasant is it to a saint, in the exercise of grace, to see how a good God crosses his corrupt inclinations, and prevents his folly! How sweet is it to behold these thieves upon the cross! How refined a pleasure is there in observing how God draws away provision from unruly lusts, and so pinches them, that the Christian may get them governed! Of a truth, there is a paradise within this thorn-hedge. Many a time the people of God are in bonds, which are never loosed, till they are bound with cords of affliction. God takes them, and throws them into a fiery furnace, that burns off their bonds, and then, like the three children (Dan 3.25), they are 'loose walking in the midst of the fire.' God gives His children a potion, with one bitter ingredient: if that will not work upon them, He will put in a second, a third, and so on, as there is need, that they may work together for their good (Rom 8.28). With cross-winds He hastens them to their labour. They are often found in such ways, as that the cross is the happiest thing that they can meet with: and well may they salute it as David did Abigail, saying, 'Blessed be the Lord God of Israel, which sent thee this day to meet me' (1 Sam 25.32). Worldly things are often such a load to the Christian, that he moves but very slowly heavenward. God sends a wind of trouble, that blows the burden off the man's back; he then walks more speedily on his way, after God has drawn some gilded earth from him, that was drawing his heart away from God (Zeph 3.12), 'I will also leave in the midst of thee an afflicted and poor people, and they shall trust in the name of the Lord.' It was an observation of a heathen moralist, that 'no history makes mention of any man, who hath been made better by riches.' I doubt whether our modern histories can supply the defect of ancient histories in this point. But sure I am, many have been the worse for riches: thousands have been hugged to death in the embraces of a smiling world; and many good men have got wounds from outward prosperity, that must be cured by the cross. I remember to have read of one, who having an abscess in his breast, had in vain used the help of physicians: but being wounded with a sword, the abscess broke; and his life was saved by that accident, which threatened immediate death. Often have spiritual abscesses gathered in the breasts of God's people, in time of outward prosperity, and been thus broken and dispersed by the cross. It is kindly for believers to be healed by stripes, although they are usually so weak as to cry out for fear at the sight of the pruning-hook, as if it were the destroying axe, and to think that the Lord is coming to kill them, when He is indeed coming to cure them.

I shall now conclude, addressing myself in a few words, first, to saints, and next to sinners.

To you that are saints, I say,

First, Strive to obtain and keep up actual communion and fellowship with Jesus Christ; that is, to be still deriving fresh supplies of grace from the fountain thereof in Him, by faith, and making suitable returns of them, in the exercise of grace and holy obedience. Beware of estrangement between Christ and your

[316]

MYSTICAL UNION BETWEEN CHRIST AND BELIEVERS

souls. If it has got in already, which seems to be the case of many this day, endeavour to get it removed. There are multitudes in the world who slight Christ, though you should not slight Him; many that looked fair for heaven, have turned their backs upon Him. The warm sun of outward peace and prosperity has caused some to cast their cloak of religion from them, who held it fast when the wind of trouble was blowing upon them: and 'Will you also go away?' (John 6.67). The basest ingratitude is stamped on your slighting of communion with Christ (Jer 2.31), 'Have I been a wilderness unto Israel, a land of darkness? Wherefore say my people, We are lords, we will come no more unto thee?' Oh! beloved, 'Is this your kindness to your friend?' It is unbecoming any wife to slight converse with her husband, but her especially who was taken from a prison or a dunghill, as you were, by your Lord. Remember, I pray you, this is a very ill-chosen time to live at a distance from God. It is a time in which Divine providence frowns upon the land we live in; the clouds of wrath are gathering and are thick above our heads. It is not a time for you to be out of your chambers (Isa 26.20). They that now are walking most closely with God, may have enough to do to stand when the trial comes: how hard will it be for others then, who are like to be surprised with troubles, when guilt is lying on their consciences unremoved! To be awakened out of a sound sleep, and cast into a raging sea, as Jonah was, will be a fearful trial. To feel trouble before we see it coming, to be past hope before we have any fear, is a very sad case. Wherefore break down your idols of jealousy, mortify those lusts, those irregular appetites and desires, that have stolen away your hearts, and left you like Samson without his hair, and say, 'I will go and return to my first husband; for then was it better with me than now' (Hos 2.7).

Secondly, Walk as becomes those that are united to Christ. Prove your union with Him by 'walking as he also walked' (1 John 2.6). If you are brought from under the power of darkness, let your light shine before men. 'Shine as lights in the world, holding forth the Word of life;' as the lantern holds the candle, which being in it, shines through it (Phil 2.15,16). Now that you profess Christ to be in you, let His image shine forth in your conversation, and remember that the business of your lives is to prove, by practical arguments, what you profess.

1 : You know the character of a wife: 'She that is married careth how she may please her husband.' Go you, and do likewise; 'walk worthy of the Lord unto all pleasing' (Col 1.10). This is the great business of life; you must please Him, though it should displease all the world. What He hates must be hateful to you, because He hates it. Whatever lusts come to gain your hearts, deny them, seeing the grace of God has appeared, teaching us so to do, and you are joined to the Lord. Let Him be a covering to your eyes; for you have not your choice to make, it is made already, and you must not dishonour your Head. A man takes care of his feet, because, if he catch cold there, it flies up to his head. 'Shall I then take the members of Christ, and make them the members of a harlot? God forbid,' says the apostle (1 Cor 6.15). Will you take that heart of yours, which is Christ's dwelling-place, and lodge His enemies there? Will you take that body, which is His temple and defile it, by using the members thereof as instruments of sin?

2 : Be careful to bring forth fruit, and much fruit. The branch well laden with fruit, is the glory of the vine, and of the husbandman too (John 15.8), 'Herein is my Father glorified, that ye bear much fruit; so shall ye be my disciples.' A barren tree stands safer in a wood, than in an orchard; and branches in Christ that bring not forth fruit, will be taken away and cast into the fire.

3 : Be heavenly-minded, and maintain a holy contempt of the world. You are united to Christ; He is your Head and Husband, and is in heaven; wherefore your hearts should be there also (Col 3.1), 'If ye then be risen with Christ, seek those things which are above, where Christ sitteth on the right hand of God.' Let the serpent's seed go on their belly, and eat the dust of this earth: but let the members of Christ be ashamed to bow down and feed with them.

[318]

4: Live and act dependently, depending by faith on Jesus Christ. That which grows on its own root, is a tree, not a branch. It is of the nature of a branch to depend on the stock for all, and to derive all its sap from thence. Depend on Him for life, light, strength, and all spiritual benefits (Gal 2.20), 'I live, yet not I, but Christ liveth in me; and the life which I now live in the flesh, I live by the faith of the Son of God.' For this cause, in the mystical union, strength is united to weakness, life to death, and heaven to earth, that weakness, death and earth may mount up on borrowed wings. Depend on Him for temporal benefits also (Matt 6.11), 'Give us this day our daily bread.' If we have trusted Him with our eternal concerns, let us be ashamed to distrust Him in the matter of our provision in the world.

5: Be of a meek disposition, and a uniting temper with the fellow-members of Christ's body, as being united to the meek Jesus, the blessed centre of union. There is a prophecy to this purpose concerning the kingdom of Christ (Isa 11.6), 'The wolf shall dwell with the lamb; and the leopard shall lie down with the kid.' It is an allusion to the beasts in Noah's ark. The beasts of prey that were wont to kill and devour others, when once they came into the ark, lay down in peace with them; the lamb was in no hazard from the wolf there, nor the kid from the leopard. There was a beautiful accomplishment of it in the primitive church (Acts 4.32), 'And the multitude of them that believed were of one heart and of one soul.' And this prevails in all the members of Christ, according to the measure of the grace of God in them. Man is born naked; he comes naked into this world, as if God designed him for the picture of peace, and surely, when he is born again, he comes not into the new world of grace with claws to tear, a sword to wound, and a fire in his hand to burn up his fellow-members in Christ, because they cannot see with his light. Oh! it is sad to see Christ's lilies as thorns in one another's sides, Christ's lambs devouring one another like lions, and God's diamonds cutting one another: yet it must be remembered, that sin is no proper cement for the members of Christ, though

Herod and Pontius Pilate may be made friends that way. The apostle's rule is plain (Heb 12.14), 'Follow peace with all men, and holiness.' To follow peace no further than our humour, credit, and such like things will allow us, is too short: to pursue it further than holiness, that is, conformity to the Divine will, allows us, is too far. But otherwise it cannot be bought too dearly, wherefore we must rather want it, than purchase it at any expense of truth or holiness. But otherwise it cannot be bought too dearly, and it will always be precious in the eyes of the sons of peace.

And now, sinners, what shall I say to you? I have given you some view of the privileges of those in the state of grace. You have seen them afar off; but alas! they are not yours, because you are not Christ's. The sinfulness of an unregenerate state is yours, and the misery of it is yours also; you have neither part nor lot in this matter. The guilt of all your sins lies upon you; you have no part in the righteousness of Christ. There is no peace to you, no peace with God, no true peace of conscience, for you have no saving interest in the great Peace-maker. You are none of God's family; the adoption we spoke of, belongs not to you. You have no part in the Spirit of sanctification, and, in one word, you have no inheritance among them that are sanctified. All I can say to you in this matter, is, that the case is not desperate, they may yet be yours (Rev 3.20), 'Behold, I stand at the door and knock; if any man hear my voice, and open the door, I will come in to him, and will sup with him, and he with me.' Heaven is proposing a union with earth still; the potter is making suit to his own clay; and the gates of the city of refuge are not yet closed. O that we could compel you to come in!

Thus far of the state of grace.

IV

THE ETERNAL STATE

DEATH

For I know that thou wilt bring me to death, and to
the house appointed for all living   JOB 30.23

I come now to discourse of man's eternal state, into which he
enters by death. Of this entrance, Job takes a solemn serious view,
in the words of the text, which contain a general truth, and a
particular application of it. The general truth is supposed;
namely, that all men must, by death, remove out of this world,
they must die. But whither must they go? They must go to the
house appointed for all living; to the grave, that darksome,
gloomy, solitary house, in the land of forgetfulness. Wherever the
body is laid up till the resurrection, thither, as to a dwelling-
house, death brings us home. While we are in the body, we are
but in a lodging-house, in an inn, on our way homeward. When
we come to our grave, we come to our home, our long home
(Eccl 12.5). All living must be inhabitants of this house, good and
bad, old and young. Man's life is a stream, running into death's
devouring deeps. They who now live in palaces, must quit them,
and go home to this house; and they who have not where to lay
their heads, shall thus have a house at length. It is appointed for
all, by Him whose counsel shall stand. This appointment cannot
be shifted; it is a law which mortals cannot transgress. Job's
application of this general truth to himself, is expressed in these
words; 'I know that thou wilt bring me to death.' He knew that
he must meet with death; that his soul and body must needs part;
that God, who had set the time, would certainly see it kept.
Sometimes Job was inviting death to come to him, and carry him
home to its house; yea, he was in the hazard of running to it be-

fore the time (Job 7.15), 'My soul chooseth strangling, and death rather than my life.' But here he considers God would bring him to it; yea, bring him back to it, as the word imports. Whereby he seems to intimate, that we have no life in this world, but as runaways from death, which stretches out its cold arms, to receive us from the womb: but though we do then narrowly escape its clutches, we cannot escape long; we shall be brought back again to it. Job knew this, he had laid it down as a certainty, and was looking for it.

DOCTRINE: *All must die*

Although this doctrine be confirmed by the experience of all former generations, ever since Abel entered into the house appointed for all living, and though the living know that they shall die, yet it is needful to discourse of the certainty of death, that it may be impressed on the mind, and duly considered.

Wherefore consider, 1. There is an unalterable statute of death, under which men are concluded. 'It is appointed unto men once to die' (Heb 9.27). It is laid up for them, as parents lay up for their children; they may look for it, and cannot miss it, seeing God has designed and reserved it for them. There is no peradventure in it; 'we must needs die' (2 Sam 14.14). Though some men will not hear of death, yet every man must needs see death (Psa 89.48). Death is a champion all must grapple with: we must enter the lists with it, and it will have the mastery (Eccl 8.8), 'There is no man that hath power over the spirit, to retain the spirit; neither hath he power in the day of death.' They indeed who are found alive at Christ's coming, shall all be changed (1 Cor 15.51). But that change will be equivalent to death, will answer the purposes of it. All other persons must go the common road, the way of all flesh. 2. Let us consult daily observation. Every man 'seeth that wise men die, likewise the fool and brutish person' (Psa 49.10). There is room enough on this earth for us, notwithstanding the multitudes that were upon it before us. They are

[324]

gone, to make room for us, as we must depart to make room for others. It is long since death began to transport men into another world, and vast multitudes are gone thither already: yet the work is going on still; death is carrying off new inhabitants daily, to the house appointed for all living. Who could ever hear the grave say, It is enough! Long has it been getting, but still it asks. This world is like a great fair or market, where some are coming in, others going out; while the assembly that is in it is in confusion, and the most part know not wherefore they are come together; or, like a town situated on the road to a great city, through which some travellers have passed, some are passing, while others are only coming in (Eccl 1.4), 'One generation passeth away, and another generation cometh: but the earth abideth for ever.' Death is an inexorable, irresistible messenger, who cannot be diverted from executing his orders by the force of the mighty, the bribes of the rich, or the entreaties of the poor. It does not reverence the hoary head, nor pity the harmless babe. The bold and daring cannot outbrave it; nor can the faint-hearted obtain a discharge in this war. 3. The human body consists of perishing materials (Gen 3.19), 'Dust thou art, and unto dust shalt thou return.' The strongest are but brittle earthen vessels, easily broken in shivers. The soul is but meanly housed, while in this mortal body, which is not a house of stone but a house of clay. The mud walls cannot but moulder away, especially seeing the foundation is not on a rock, but in the dust; they are crushed before the moth, though this insect be so tender that the gentle touch of a finger will despatch it (Job 4.19). These principles are like gunpowder, a very small spark lighting on them will set them on fire, and blow up the house; the stone of a raisin, or a hair in milk, having choked men, and laid the house of clay in the dust. If we consider the frame and structure of our bodies, how fearfully and wonderfully we are made. On how regular and exact a motion of the fluids, and balance of humours, our life depends. Death has as many doors to enter in by, as the body has pores. If we compare the soul and body together, we may justly reckon, that there is somewhat more astonishing in our life than in our death; and that it is more strange to see dust walking up and down on the dust, than lying down in it. Though the lamp of our life be not violently blown out, yet the flame must go out at length for want of oil. What are those distempers and diseases which we are liable to, but death's harbingers, that come to prepare his way? They meet us, as soon as we set our foot on earth, to tell us at our entry, that we do but come into the world to go out again. Nevertheless, some are snatched away in a moment, without being warned by sickness or disease. 4. We have sinful souls, and therefore have dying bodies: death follows sin, as the shadow follows the body. The wicked must die, by virtue of the threatening of the covenant of works (Gen 2.17), 'In the day that thou eatest thereof, thou shalt surely die.' And the godly must die too, that as death entered by sin, sin may go out by death. Christ has taken away the sting of death, as to them, though He has not as yet removed death itself. Wherefore, though it fasten on them, as the viper did on Paul's hand, it shall do them no harm: but because the leprosy of sin is in the walls of the house, it must be broken down, and all the materials thereof carried forth. 5. Man's life in this world, according to the Scripture account of it, is but a few degrees removed from death. The Scripture represents it as a vain and empty thing, short in its continuance, and swift in its passing away.

First, Man's life is a vain and empty thing: while it is, it vanishes away; and, lo! it is not. (Job 7.16), 'My days are vanity.' If we suspect afflicted Job of partiality in this matter, hear the wise and prosperous Solomon's description of the days of his life (Eccl 7.15), 'All things have I seen in the days of my vanity,' that is, my vain days. Moses, who was a very active man, compares our days to a sleep (Psa 90.5), 'They are as a sleep,' which is not noticed till it is ended. The resemblance is just; few men have right apprehensions of life, until death awaken them; then we begin to know that we were living. 'We spend our years as a tale that is told' (verse 9). When an idle tale is a-telling it may affect

[326]

a little, but when it is ended, it is remembered no more: and so is man forgotten, when the fable of his life is ended. It is as a dream, or vision of the night, in which there is nothing solid; when one awakes, all vanishes (Job 20.8), 'He shall fly away as a dream, and shall not be found; yea, he shall be chased away as a vision of the night.' It is but a vain show or image (Psa 39.6), 'Surely every man walketh in a vain show.' Man, in this world, is but as it were a walking statue: his life is but an image of life, there is so much of death in it.

If we look on our life, in the several periods of it, we shall find it a heap of vanities. 'Childhood and youth are vanity' (Eccl 11.10). We come into the world the most helpless of all animals: young birds and beasts can do something for themselves, but infant man is altogether unable to help himself. Our childhood is spent in pitiful trifling pleasures, which become the scorn of our after-thoughts. Youth is a flower that soon withers, a blossom that quickly falls off; it is a space of time in which we are rash, foolish, and inconsiderate, pleasing ourselves with a variety of vanities, and swimming as it were through a flood of them. But before we are aware it is past, and we are, in middle age, encompassed with a thick cloud of cares, through which we must grope; and finding ourselves beset with pricking thorns of difficulties, through them we must force our way, to accomplish the projects and contrivances of our riper thoughts. The more we solace ourselves in any earthly enjoyment we attain to, the more bitterness do we find in parting with it. Then comes old age, attended with its own train of infirmities, labour, and sorrow (Psa 90.10), and sets us down next door to the grave. In a word, 'All flesh is grass' (Isa 40.6). Every stage or period of life is vanity. 'Man at his best state,' his middle age, when the heat of youth is spent, and the sorrows of old age have not yet overtaken him, 'is altogether vanity' (Psa 39.5). Death carries off some in the bud of childhood, others in the blossom of youth, and others when they are come to their fruit; few are left standing, till, like ripe corn, they forsake the ground; all die one time or other.

Secondly, Man's life is a short thing; it is not only a vanity, but a short-lived vanity. Consider, 1. How the life of man is reckoned in the Scriptures. It was indeed sometimes reckoned by hundreds of years: but no man ever arrived at a thousand, which yet bears no proportion to eternity. Now hundreds are brought down to scores; threescore and ten, or fourscore, is its utmost length (Psa 90.10). But few men arrive at that length of life. Death does but rarely wait, till men be bowing down, by reason of age, to meet the grave. Yet, as if years were too big a word for such a small thing as the life of man on earth, we find it counted by months (Job 14.5), 'The number of his months are with thee.' Our course, like that of the moon, is run in a little time: we are always waxing or waning, till we disappear. But frequently it is reckoned by days; and these but few (Job 14.1), 'Man, that is born of a woman, is of few days.' Nay, it is but one day, in Scripture account; and that a hireling's day, who will precisely observe when his day ends, and give over his work (verse 6), 'Till he shall accomplish as an hireling his day.' Yea, the Scripture brings it down to the shortest space of time, and calls it a moment (2 Cor 4.17), 'Our light affliction,' though it last all our life long, 'is but for a moment.' Elsewhere it is brought down yet to a lower pitch, further than which one cannot carry it (Psa 39.5), 'Mine age is as nothing before thee.' Agreeably to this, Solomon tells (Eccl 3.2), 'There is a time to be born, and a time to die;' but makes no mention of a time to live, as if our life were but a skip from the womb to the grave. 2. Consider the various similitudes by which the Scripture represents the shortness of man's life. Hear Hezekiah (Isa 38.12), 'Mine age is departed, and is removed from me as a shepherd's tent; I have cut off like a weaver my life.' The shepherd's tent is soon removed, for the flocks must not feed long in one place; such is a man's life on this earth, quickly gone. It is a web which he is incessantly working; he is not idle so much as for one moment: in a short time it is wrought, and then it is cut off. Every breathing is a thread in this web; when the last breath is drawn, the web is woven out; he expires, and then it is cut off, he breathes no more. Man is like grass, and like a flower (Isa 40.6). 'All flesh,' even the strongest and most healthy flesh, 'is grass, and all the goodliness thereof is as the flower of the field.' The grass is flourishing in the morning, but, being cut down by the mowers, in the evening it is withered; so man sometimes is walking up and down at ease in the morning, and in the evening is lying a corpse, being struck down by a sudden blow, with one or other of death's weapons. The flower, at best, is but a weak and tender thing, of short continuance wherever it grows, but observe, man is not compared to the flower of the garden but to the flower of the field, which the foot of every beast may tread down at any time. Thus is our life liable to a thousand accidents every day, any of which may cut us off. But though we should escape all these, yet at length this grass withereth, this flower fadeth of itself. It is carried off 'as the cloud is consumed, and vanisheth away' (Job 7.9). It looks big as the morning cloud, which promises great things, and raises the expectation of the husbandman; but the sun rises, and the cloud is scattered; death comes, and man vanishes. The apostle James proposes the question, 'What is your life?' (chap 4.14). Hear his own answer, 'It is even a vapour, that appeareth for a little time, and then vanisheth away.' It is frail, uncertain, and does not last. It is as smoke, which goes out of the chimney, as if it would darken the face of the heavens, but quickly it is scattered, and appears no more; thus departs man's life, and 'where is he?' It is wind (Job 7.7), 'O remember that my life is wind.' It is but a passing blast, a short puff, 'a wind that passeth away, and cometh not again' (Psa 78.39). Our breath is in our nostrils, as if it were always upon the wing to depart; ever passing and repassing, like a traveller, until it go away, not to return till the heavens be no more.

Thirdly, Man's life is a swift thing; not only a passing, but a flying vanity. Have you not observed how swiftly a shadow runs along the ground in a cloudy and a windy day, suddenly darkening the places beautified before with the beams of the sun, but as suddenly disappearing? Such is the life of man on the earth, for 'he fleeth as a shadow, and continueth not' (Job 14.2). A weaver's shuttle is very swift in its motion; in a moment it is thrown from one side of the web to the other; yet 'our days are swifter than a weaver's shuttle' (chap 7.6). How quickly is man tossed through time, into eternity! See how Job describes the swiftness of the time of life (chap 9.25,26). 'Now my days are swifter than a post; they flee away, they see no good. They are passed away as the swift ships; as the eagle that hasteth to the prey.' He compares his days with a post, a foot-post, a runner, who runs speedily to carry tidings, and will make no stay. But though the post were like Ahimaaz, who over-ran Cushi, our days would be swifter than he; for they flee away, like a man fleeing for his life before the pursuing enemy; he runs with his utmost vigour, yet our days run as fast as he. But this is not all; even he who is flee-ing for his life, cannot run always; he must needs sometimes stand still, lie down, or turn in somewhere, as Sisera did into Jael's tent, to refresh himself; but our time never halts. Therefore it is compared to ships, that can sail night and day without inter-mission, till they reach their port; and to swift ships, ships of desire, in which men quickly arrive at their desired haven, or ships of pleasure, that sail more swiftly than ships of burden. Yet the wind failing, the ship's course is checked: but our time always runs with a rapid course. Therefore it is compared to the eagle flying; not with his ordinary flight, for that is not sufficient to represent the swiftness of our days; but when he flies upon his prey, which is with an extraordinary swiftness. And thus, even thus, our days flee away.

Having thus discoursed of death, let us improve it in discern-ing the vanity of the world; in bearing up, with Christian con-tentment and patience under all troubles and difficulties in it; in mortifying our lusts; in cleaving unto the Lord with full purpose of heart, at all hazards, and in preparing for death's approach.

1 : Let us hence, as in a looking-glass, behold the vanity of the world, and of all those things in it, which men so much value and esteem, and therefore set their hearts upon. The rich and the

poor are equally intent upon this world; they bow the knee to it, yet it is but a clay god: they court this bulky vanity, and run eagerly to catch this shadow. The rich man is hugged to death in its embraces, and the poor man wearies himself in the fruitless pursuit. What wonder if the world's smiles overcome us, when we pursue it so eagerly, even while it frowns upon us! But look into the grave, O man! consider and be wise; listen to the doctrine of death and learn, that, 'hold as fast as thou canst, thou shalt be forced to let go thy hold of the world at length.' Though you load yourself with the fruits of this earth, yet all shall fall off when you come to creep into your hole, the house, under ground, appointed for all living. When death comes, you must bid an eternal farewell to your enjoyments in this world: you must leave your goods to another (Luke 12.20), 'Then whose shall those things be which thou hast provided?' Your portion of these things shall be very little ere long. If you lie down on the grass, and stretch yourself at full length, and observe the print of your body when you rise, you may see how much of this earth will fall to your share at last. It may be you will get a coffin, and a winding-sheet: but you are not sure of that; many who have had abundance of wealth, yet have not had so much when they took up their new house in the land of silence. But however that be, more you cannot expect. It was a mortifying lesson which Saladin, when dying, gave to his soldiers. He called for his standard-bearer, and ordered him to take his winding-sheet upon his pike, and go out to the camp with it, and tell them that of all his conquests, victories, and triumphs, he had nothing now left him but that piece of linen to wrap his body in for burial. 'This world is a false friend,' who leaves a man in time of greatest need, and flees from him when he has most to do. When you are lying on a deathbed, all your friends and relations cannot rescue you; all your substance cannot ransom you, nor procure you a reprieve for one day; nay, not for one hour. Yea, the more you possess of this world's goods, your sorrow at death is likely to be the greater; for though a man may live more commodiously in a palace than in a cottage, yet he may die more easily in the cottage, where he has very little to make him fond of life.

2 : It may serve as a storehouse for Christian contentment and patience under worldly losses and crosses. A close application of the doctrine of death is an excellent remedy against fretting, and gives some ease to a troubled heart. When Job had sustained very great losses, he sat down contented, with this meditation (Job 1.21), 'Naked came I out of my mother's womb, and naked shall I return thither: the Lord gave, and the Lord hath taken away: blessed be the name of the Lord.' When Providence brings a mortality or murrain among your cattle, how ready are you to fret and complain! but the serious consideration of your own death, to which you have a notable help from such providential occurrences, may be of use to silence your complaints, and quiet your spirits. Look to 'the house appointed for all living,' and learn, 1. 'That you must abide a more severe thrust than the loss of worldly goods.' Do not cry out for a thrust in the leg or arm: for before long there will be a home-thrust at the heart. You may lose your dearest relations; the wife may lose her husband, and the husband his wife; the parents may lose their dear children, and the children their parents; but if any of these trials happen to you, remember you must lose your own life at last; and 'Wherefore doth a living man complain?' (Lam 3.39). It is always profitable to consider, under affliction, that our case might have been worse than it is. Whatever is consumed, or taken from us, 'It is of the Lord's mercies that we' ourselves 'are not consumed' (verse 22). 2. 'It is but for a short space of time that we are in this world.' It is but little that our necessities require in so short a space of time: when death comes, we shall stand in need of none of these things. Why should men rack their heads with cares how to provide for to-morrow; while they know not if they shall then need any thing? Though a man's provision for his journey be nearly spent, he is not disquieted if he thinks he is near home. Are you working by candle light, and is there little of your candle left? It may be there is as little sand in your glass;

and if so, you have little use for it. 3. 'You have matters of great weight that challenge your care.' Death is at the door, beware you lose not your souls. If blood break out at one part of the body, they often open a vein in another part of it, to turn the stream of blood, and so to stop it. Thus the Spirit of God sometimes cures men of sorrow for earthly things, by opening the heart-vein to bleed for sin. Did we pursue heavenly things more vigorously when our affairs in this life prosper not, we should thereby gain a double advantage: our worldly sorrow would be diverted, and our best treasure increased. 4. 'Crosses of this nature will not last long.' The world's smiles and frowns will quickly be buried together in everlasting forgetfulness. Its smiles go away like foam on the water, and its frowns are as a passing stitch in a man's side. Time flies away with swift wings, and carries our earthly comforts, and crosses too, along with it: neither of them will accompany us into 'the house appointed for all living.' 'There the wicked cease from troubling; and there the weary be at rest. There the prisoners rest together; they hear not the voice of the oppressor. The small and great are there; and the servant is free from his master' (Job 3.17–19). Cast a look into eternity, and you will see that affliction here is but for a moment. The truth is, our time is so very short, that it will not allow either our joys or griefs to come to perfection. Wherefore, let them 'that weep be as though they wept not; and they that rejoice as though they rejoiced not,' &c. (1 Cor 7.29–31). 5. 'Death will put all men on a level.' The king and the beggar must dwell in one house, when they come to their journey's end; though their entertainment by the way be very different. 'The small and the great are there' (Job 3.19). We are all in this world as on a stage; it is no great matter whether a man act the part of a prince or a peasant, for when they have acted their parts, they must both get behind the curtain, and appear no more. 6. If you are not in Christ, whatever your afflictions now be, 'troubles a thousand times worse are abiding you in another world.' Death will turn your crosses into pure unmixed curses: and then, how gladly

[333]

would you return to your former afflicted state, and purchase it at any rate, were there any possibility of such a return. If you are in Christ, you may well bear your cross. Death will put an end to all your troubles. If a man on a journey be not well accommodated, where he lodges only for a night, he will not trouble himself much about the matter because he is not to stay there, it is not his home. You are on the road to eternity; let it not disquiet you that you meet with some hardships in the inn of this world; fret not, because it is not so well with you as with some others. One man travels with a cane in his hand; his fellow-traveller, perhaps, has but a common staff or stick: either of them will serve the turn. It is no great matter which of them be yours; both will be laid aside when you come to your journey's end.

3 : It may serve for a bridle, to curb all manner of lusts, particularly those dwelling about the body. A serious visit made to cold death, and that solitary mansion, the grave, might be of good use to repress them.

(1) It may be of use to cause men to cease from their inordinate care for the body, which is to many the bane of their souls. Often do these questions, 'What shall we eat? what shall we drink? and wherewithal shall we be clothed?' leave no room for another of more importance, namely, 'Wherewith shall I come before the Lord?' The soul is put on the rack, to answer these mean questions in favour of the body, while its own eternal interests are neglected. But ah! why are men so busy to repair the ruinous cottage, leaving the inhabitant to bleed to death of his wounds, unheeded, unregarded? Why so much care for the body, to the neglect of the concerns of the immortal soul? O be not so anxious for what can only serve your bodies, since, ere long, the clods of cold earth will serve for back and belly too.

(2) It may abate your pride on account of bodily endowments, which vain man is apt to glory in. Value not yourselves on the blossom of youth, for while you are in your blooming years, you are but ripening for a grave; death gives the fatal stroke, without

asking any body's age. Glory not in your strength, it will quickly be gone: the time will soon be, when you shall not be able to turn yourselves on a bed, and you must be carried by your grieving friends to your long home. And what signifies your healthful constitution? Death does not always enter in soonest where it begins soonest to knock at the door, but makes as great dispatch with some in a few hours, as with others in many years. Value not yourselves on your beauty, which 'shall consume in the grave' (Psa 49.14). Remember the change which death makes on the fairest face (Job 14.20), 'Thou changest his countenance, and sendest him away.' Death makes the greatest beauty so loath-some, that it must be buried out of sight. Could a looking-glass be used in 'the house appointed for all living,' it would be a terror to those who now look oftener into their glasses than into their Bibles. And what though the body be gorgeously arrayed? The finest clothes are but badges of our sin and shame, and in a little time will be exchanged for a winding-sheet, when the body will become a feast to the worms.

(3) It may be a check upon sensuality and fleshly lusts (1 Pet 2.11), 'I beseech you as strangers and pilgrims, abstain from fleshly lusts, which war against the soul.' It is hard to cause wet wood to take fire; and when the fire does take hold of it, it is soon extinguished. Sensuality makes men most unfit for divine communications, and is an effectual means to quench the Spirit. Intemperance in eating and drinking carries on the ruin of soul and body at once, and hastens death, while it makes the man most unmeet for it. Therefore, 'Take heed to yourselves lest at any time your hearts be overcharged with surfeiting and drunkenness, and so that day come upon you unawares' (Luke 21.34). But O how often is the soul struck through with a dart, in gratifying the senses! At these doors destruction enters in. Therefore Job 'made a covenant with his eyes' (chap 31.1). 'The mouth of a strange woman is a deep pit: he that is abhorred of the Lord shall fall therein' (Prov 22.14). 'Let him that thinketh he standeth, take heed lest he fall' (1 Cor 10.12). Beware of lasciviousness; study

modesty in your apparel, words, and actions. The ravens of the valley of death will at length pick out the wanton eye; the obscene filthy tongue will at length be quiet in the land of silence, and grim death, embracing the body in its cold arms, will effectually allay the heat of all fleshly lusts.

(4) In a word, it may check our earthly-mindedness; and at once knock down 'the lust of the flesh, the lust of the eyes, and the pride of life.' Ah! if we must die, why are we thus? Why so fond of temporal things, so anxious to get them, so eager in the embraces of them, so mightily touched with the loss of them? Let me, upon a view of 'the house appointed for all living,' address the worldling in the words of Solomon. (Prov 23.5), 'Wilt thou set thine eyes upon that which is not? For riches certainly make themselves wings; they fly away as an eagle toward heaven.' Riches and all worldly things are but a fair nothing; they are that which is not. They are not what they seem to be: they are but gilded vanities, that deceive the eye. Comparatively, they are not; there is infinitely more of nothingness and not being, than of being or reality, in the best of them. What is the world and all that is in it, but a fashion, or fair show, such as men make on the stage, a passing show? (1 Cor 7.31). Royal pomp is but gaudy show, or appearance, in God's account (Acts 25.23). The best name they get, is 'good things': but observe it, they are only the wicked man's 'good things' (Luke 16.25), 'Thou in thy lifetime receivedst thy good things,' says Abraham, in the parable, to the rich man in hell. Well may the men of the world call these things their goods; for there is no other good in them, about them, nor attending them. Now, will you set your eyes upon empty shadows and fancies? Will you cause your eyes to fly on them, as the word is? Shall men's hearts fly out at their eyes upon them, as a ravenous bird on its prey? if they do, let them know, that at length these shall flee as fast away from them, as their eyes flew upon them; like a flock of fair-feathered birds, that settle on a fool's ground, which, when he runs to catch them as his own, do immediately take wing, fly away, and sitting down on his neighbour's

ground, elude his expectation. (Luke 12.20), 'Thou fool, this night thy soul shall be required of thee; then whose shall those things be?' Though you do not make wings to them, as many do, they make themselves wings, and fly away; not as a tame house-bird, which may be caught again, but as an eagle, which quickly flies out of sight, and cannot be recalled. Forbear then to behold these things. O mortal! there is no good reason to be given why you should set your eyes upon them. This world is a great inn in the road to eternity to which you are travelling. You are attended by these things, as servants belonging to the inn where you lodge: they wait upon you while you are there; and when you go away, they will convoy you to the door. But they are not yours, they will not go away with you but return to wait on other strangers, as they did on you.

4: It may serve as a spring of Christian resolution to cleave to Christ, adhere to His truths, and continue in His ways, whatever we may suffer for so doing. It would much allay the fear of man, that brings a snare: 'Who art thou, that thou shouldest be afraid of a man that shall die?' (Isa 51.12). Look on persecutors as pieces of brittle clay that shall be dashed in pieces, for then shall you despise them as foes that are mortal, whose terror to others in the land of the living shall quickly die with themselves. The serious consideration of the shortness of our time, and the certainty of death, will teach us, that all the advantage which we can make by our apostasy in time of trial, is not worth the while; it is not worth going out of our way to get it; and what we refuse to forego for Christ's sake, may be quickly taken from us by death. But we can never lose it so honourably as for the cause of Christ and His Gospel: for what glory is it, that you give up what you have in the world, when God takes it away from you by death, whether you will or not? This consideration may teach us to undervalue life itself, and choose to forego it, rather than to sin. The worst that men can do is to take away that life which we cannot long keep, though all the world should conspire to help us to retain the spirit. If we refuse to offer it up to God when He calls for it in defence of His honour, He can take it from us another way; as it fared with him, who could not burn for Christ, but was afterwards burnt by an accidental fire in his house.

5: It may serve for a spur to incite us to prepare for death. Consider, 1. Your eternal state will be according to the state in which you die: death will open the doors of heaven or hell to you. As the tree falls, so it shall lie through eternity. If the infant be dead born, the whole world cannot raise it to life again: and if one die out of Christ, in an unregenerate state, there is no more hope of him for ever. 2. Seriously consider what it is to go into another world, a world of spirits, wherewith we are very little acquainted. How frightful is converse with spirits to poor mortals in this life! and how dreadful is the case, when men are hurried away into another world, not knowing but devils may be their companions for ever! Let us then give all diligence to make and advance our acquaintance with the Lord of that world. 3. It is but a short time you have to prepare for death: therefore now or never, seeing the time assigned for preparation will soon be over (Eccl 9.10), 'Whatsoever thy hand findeth to do, do it with thy might: for there is no work, nor device, nor knowledge, nor wisdom, in the grave, whither thou goest.' How can we be idle, having so great a work to do, and so little time to do it in? But if the time be short, the work of preparation for death, though hard work, will not last long. The shadows of the evening make the labourer work cheerfully, knowing the time to be at hand when he will be called in from his labour. 4. Much of our short time is over already; and the youngest of us all cannot assure himself that there is as much of his time to come as is past. Our life in the world is but a short preface to long eternity, and much of the tale is told. Oh! shall we not double our diligence, when so much of our time is spent, and so little of our great work is done? 5. The present time is flying away, and we cannot bring back time past, it has taken an eternal farewell of us; there is no kindling the fire again that is burnt to ashes. The time to come is not ours: and we have no assurance of a share in it when it comes.

We have nothing we can call ours, but the present moment; and that is flying away. How soon our time may be at an end, we know not. Die we must: but who can tell us when? If death kept one set time for all, we were in no hazard of a surprise: but daily observation shows us, that there is no such thing. Now the flying shadow of our life allows no time for loitering. The rivers run speedily into the sea, from whence they came, but not so speedily as man to dust, from whence he came. The stream of time is the swiftest current, and quickly runs out to eternity. 6. If once death carry us off, there is no coming back to mend our matters (Job 14.14), 'If a man die, shall he live again?' Dying is a thing we cannot get a trial of; it is what we can only do once (Heb. 9.27), 'It is appointed unto men *once* to die.' And that which can be but once done, and yet is of so much importance that our all depends on our doing it right, we have need to use the utmost diligence that we may do it well. Therefore prepare for death.

If you who are unregenerate ask me, what you shall do to prepare for death, that you may die safely, I answer, I have told you already what must be done. Your nature and state must be changed; you must be united to Jesus Christ by faith. Till this be done, you are not capable of other directions, which belong to a person's dying comfortably: whereof we may discourse afterwards in the due place.

2

THE DIFFERENCE BETWEEN THE RIGHTEOUS AND THE WICKED IN THEIR DEATH

The wicked is driven away in his wickedness: but the righteous hath hope in his death PROVERBS 14.32

This text looks like the cloud between the Israelites and Egyptians; having a dark side towards the latter, and a bright side towards the former. It represents death like Pharaoh's jailor, bringing the chief butler and the chief baker out of prison, the one to be restored to his office, and the other to be led to execution. It shows the difference between the godly and ungodly in their death; who, as they act a very different part in life, so, in death, have a vastly different exit.

As to the death of a wicked man, here is, 1. The manner of his passing out of the world. He is 'driven away;' namely, in his death, as is clear from the opposite clause. He is forcibly thrust out of his place in this world, driven away as chaff before the wind. 2. The state he passes away in. He dies also in a hopeless state; 'but the righteous hath hope in his death;' which plainly imports the hopelessness of the wicked in their death. Whereby is not meant, that no wicked man shall have any hope at all when he is dying, but shall die in despair. No: sometimes it is so indeed; but frequently it is otherwise; foolish virgins may, and often do, hope to the last breath. But the wicked man has no solid hope; as for the delusive hopes he entertains himself with, death will root them up, and he shall be for ever irretrievably miserable.

As to the death of a righteous man, he has hope in his death. This is ushered in with a 'but,' importing the removal of these dreadful circumstances with which the wicked man is attended, who is driven away in his wickedness. But the godly are not so in the manner of their passing out of the world; the righteous

[340]

are not driven away as chaff before the wind, but led away as a bride to the marriage chamber, carried away by the angels into Abraham's bosom (Luke 16.22). They are not so as to their state, when passing out of this life. The righteous man dies, not in a sinful, but in a holy state; he goes not away in his sin, but out of it. In his life he was putting off the old man, changing his prison garments; and now the remaining rags of them are removed, and he is adorned with robes of glory. They are not in a hopeless, but a hopeful state. He hath hope in his death; he has the grace of hope, and the well-founded expectation of better things than he ever had in this world, and though the stream of his hope at death may run shallow, yet he has still so much of it as makes him venture his eternal interests upon the Lord Jesus Christ.

DOCTRINE I: *The wicked, dying, are driven away in their wickedness, and in a hopeless state*

In speaking to this doctrine, I: I shall show how, and in what sense, the wicked are 'driven away in their wickedness' at death. II: I shall prove the hopelessness of their state at death. And then apply the whole.

I: How, and in what sense, the wicked are 'driven away in their wickedness.' In discoursing of this matter, I shall briefly inquire, 1. What is meant by their being 'driven away.' 2. Whence they shall be driven, and whither. 3. In what respects they may be said to be driven away 'in their wickedness.' But before I proceed, let me remark, that you are mistaken if you think that no persons are to be called wicked, but they who are avowedly vicious and profane, as if the devil could dwell in none but those whose name is Legion. In Scripture account, all who are not righteous, in the manner hereafter explained, are reckoned wicked. Therefore the text divides the whole world into two sorts, 'the righteous and the wicked:' and you will see the same thing in Mal 3.18, 'Then shall ye return, and discern between the righteous and the wicked.' Wherefore if you be not righteous, you are wicked. If you have not an imputed righteousness, and also an implanted righteousness, or holiness; if you be yet in your natural state, un-regenerated, not united to Christ by faith, however moral and blameless in the eyes of men your conversation may be, you are the wicked who shall be driven away in their wickedness, if death find you in that state. Now,

1 : As to the meaning of this phrase, 'driven away,' there are three things in it; the wicked shall be taken away suddenly, violently, and irresistibly.

(1) Unrenewed men shall be taken away suddenly at death. Not that all wicked men die suddenly; nor that they are all wicked that die so; God forbid! But, 1. Death commonly comes upon them unexpectedly, and so surprises them, as the deluge surprised the old world, though they were forewarned of it long before it came; and as travail comes on a woman with child, with sur-prising suddenness, although looked for and expected (1 Thess 5.3). Death seizes them, as a creditor doth his debtor, to hale him to prison (Psa 55.15), and that when they are not aware. Death comes in, as a thief, at the window, and finds them full of busy thoughts about this life which that very day perish. 2. Death always seizes them unprepared for it; the old house falls down about their ears, before they have another provided. When death casts them to the door, they have not where to lay their heads, unless it be on a bed of fire and brimstone. The soul and body are, as it were, hugging one another in mutual embraces when death comes like a whirlwind, and separates them. 3. Death hurries them away in a moment to destruction, and makes a most dismal change: the man for the most part never knows where he is, till 'in hell he lift up his eyes' (Luke 16.23). The floods of wrath suddenly overwhelm his soul, and before he is aware, he is plunged into the bottomless pit.

(2) The unrenewed man is taken away out of the world violently. Driving is a violent action; he is 'chased out of the world' (Job 18.18). Fain would he stay, if he could; but death drags him away, like a malefactor to the execution. He sought no

other portion than the profits and pleasures of this world: he has no other and he really desires no other: how can he then go away out of it, if he were not driven?

Question: 'But may not a wicked man be willing to die?' *Answer:* He may indeed be willing to die; but observe it is only in one of three cases. 1. In a fit of passion, by reason of some trouble that he is impatient to be rid of. Thus, many persons, when their passion has got the better of their reason, and when, on that account they are most unfit to die, will be ready to cry, 'O to be gone!' But should their desire be granted, and death come at their call, they would quickly show they were not in earnest; and that, if they go they must be driven away against their will. 2. When they are brim-full of despair they may be willing to die. Thus Saul murdered himself, and Spira wished to be in hell, that he might know the uttermost of what he believed he was to suffer. In this manner men may seek after death, while it flees from them. But fearful is the violence these undergo, whom the terrors of God do thus drive. 3. When they are dreaming of happiness after death. Foolish virgins, under the power of delusion as to their state, may be willing to die, having no fear of lying down in sorrow. How many are there, who can give no scriptural ground for their hope, who yet have no bands in their death! Many are driven to darkness sleeping: they go off like lambs, who would roar like lions, did they but know what place they are going to; though the chariot in which they are drives furiously to the depths of hell, yet they fear not, because they are fast asleep.

(3) The unregenerate man is taken away irresistibly. He must go, though sorely against his will. Death will take no refusal, nor admit of any delay; though the man has not lived half his days, according to his own computation. If he will not bow, it will break him. If he will not come forth, it will pull the house down about his ears; for there he must not stay. Although the physician help, friends groan, the wife and children cry, and he himself use his utmost efforts to retain the spirit, his soul is required of him;

yield he must, and go where he shall never more see light.

2. Let us consider, whence they are driven, and whither. When the wicked die (1) They are driven out of this world, where they sinned, into the other world, where they must be judged, and receive their particular sentences (Heb 9.27), 'It is appointed unto men once to die, but after this the judgment.' They shall no more return to their beloved earth. Though their hearts are wedded to their earthly enjoyments, they must leave them, they can carry nothing hence. How sorrowful must their departure be, when they have nothing in view so good as that which they leave behind them! (2) They are driven out of the society of the saints on earth, into the society of the damned in hell (Luke 16.22,23), 'The rich man also died, and was buried. And in hell he lift up his eyes.' What a multitude of the devil's goats do now take place among Christ's sheep! but at death they shall be 'led forth with the workers of iniquity' (Psa 125.5). There is a mixed multitude in this world, but no mixture in the other; each party is there set by themselves. Though hypocrites grow here as tares among the wheat, death will root them up, and they shall be bound in bundles for the fire. (3) They are driven out of time into eternity. While time lasts with them, there is hope; but when time goes, all hope goes with it. Precious time is now lavishly spent: it lies so heavy on the hands of many, that they think themselves obliged to take several ways to drive away time. But beware of being at a loss what to do in life; improve time for eternity, whilst you have it, for before long, death will drive it from you, and you from it, so as you shall never meet again. (4) They are driven out of their specious pretences to piety. Death strips them of the splendid robes of a fair profession, with which some of them are adorned; and turns them off the stage, in the rags of a wicked heart and life. The word 'hypocrite' properly signifies a stage-player, who appears to be what indeed he is not. This world is the stage on which these children of the devil personate the children of God. Their show of religion is the player's coat, under which one must look who will judge of them aright. Death turns them out of

their coat, and they appear in their native dress: it unveils them, and takes off their mask. There are none in the other world who pretend to be better than they really are. Depraved nature acts in the regions of horror undisguised. (5) They are driven away from all means of grace, and are set beyond the line, quite out of all prospect of mercy. There is no more an opportunity to buy oil for the lamp; it is gone out at death, and can never be lighted again. There may be offers of mercy and peace made, after they are gone; but they are to others, not to them: there are no such offers in the place to which they are driven; these offers are only made in that place from which they are driven away.

3: In what respects may they be said to be driven away in their wickedness? *Answer:* 1. In respect of their being driven away in their sinful unconverted state. Having lived enemies to God, they die in a state of enmity to Him: for none are brought into the eternal state of consummate happiness, but by the way of the state of grace in this life. The child that is dead in the womb, is born dead, and is cast out of the womb into the grave: so he who is dead while he lives, or is spiritually dead, is cast forth of the womb of time, in the same state of death, into the pit of utter misery. O miserable death, to die in the gall of bitterness, and bond of iniquity! it had been incomparably better for such as die thus, that they had never been born. 2. In regard that they die sinning, acting wickedly against God, in contradiction to the divine law. They can do nothing but sin while they live, so death takes them in the very act of sinning, violently draws them from the embraces of their lusts, and drives them away to the tribunal, to receive their sentence. It is a remarkable expression (Job 36.14), 'They die in youth:' the marginal reading is, 'their soul dieth in youth;' their lusts being lively, their desires vigorous, and expectations big, as is common in youth. 'And their life is among the unclean;' or, 'And the company' or herd 'of them' dieth 'among the Sodomites,' namely, is taken away in the heat of their sin and wickedness, as the men of Sodom were (Gen 19; Luke 17.28,29). 3. As they are driven away, loaded with the guilt of all their sins,

[345]

that is the winding-sheet that shall lie down with them in the dust (Job 20.11). Their works follow them into the other world; they go away with the yoke of their transgressions wreathed about their necks. Guilt is a bad companion in life, but how terrible will it be in death! It lies now, perhaps, like cold brimstone on their benumbed consciences: but when death opens the way for sparks of divine vengeance, like fire, to fall upon it, it will make dreadful flames in the conscience, in which the soul will be, as it were, wrapt up for ever. 4. The wicked are driven away in their wickedness, in so far as they die under the absolute power of their wickedness. While there is hope, there is some restraint on the worst of men. Those moral endowments, which God gives to a number of men, for the benefit of mankind in this life, are so many restraints upon the impetuous wickedness of human nature. But all hope being cut off, and these gifts withdrawn, the wickedness of the wicked will then arrive at its perfection. As the seeds of grace, sown in the hearts of the elect, come to their full maturity at death; so wicked and hellish dispositions in the reprobate, come then to their highest pitch. Their prayers to God will then be turned to horrible curses, and their praises to hideous blasphemies (Matt 22.13), 'There shall be weeping and gnashing of teeth.' This gives a dismal but correct view of the state of the wicked in another world.

11: I shall explain the hopelessness of the state of unrenewed men at death. It appears to be very hopeless, if we consider these four things.

1: Death cuts off their hopes and prospects of peace and pleasure in this life (Luke 12.19,20), 'Soul, thou hast much goods laid up for many years; take thine ease, eat, drink, and be merry. But God said unto him, Thou fool, this night thy soul shall be required of thee: then whose shall those things be which thou hast provided?' They look for great matters in this world, they hope to increase their wealth, to see their families prosper, and to live at ease; but death comes like a stormy wind, and shakes off all their fond hopes, like green fruit from off a tree. 'When he is

[346]

about to fill his belly, God shall cast the fury of his wrath upon him' (Job 20.23). He may begin a web of contrivances for advancing his worldly interest; but before he gets it wrought out, death comes and cuts it off. 'His breath goeth forth, he returneth to his earth; in that very day his thoughts perish' (Psa 146.4).

2: When death comes, they have no solid ground to hope for eternal happiness. 'For what is the hope of the hypocrite, though he hath gained, when God taketh away his soul?' (Job 27.8). Whatever hopes they fondly entertain, they are not founded on God's Word, which is the only sure ground of hope; if they knew their own case, they would see themselves only happy in a dream. And indeed what hope can they have? The law is plain against them, and condemns them. The curses of it, those cords of death, are about them already. The Saviour whom they slighted, is now their Judge; and their Judge is their enemy. How then can they hope? They have bolted the door of mercy against themselves by their unbelief. They have despised the remedy, and therefore must die without mercy. They have no saving interest in Jesus Christ, the only channel of conveyance through which mercy flows: and therefore they can never taste it. The sword of justice guards the door of mercy, so as none can enter in, but the members of the mystical body of Christ, over whose heads is a covert of atoning blood, the Mediator's blood. These indeed may pass without harm, for justice has nothing to require of them. But others cannot pass, since they are not in Christ: death comes to them with the sting in it, the sting of unpardoned guilt. It is armed against them with all the force which the sanction of a holy law can give it (1 Cor 15.56), 'The sting of death is sin, and the strength of sin is the law.' When that law was given on Sinai, 'the whole mount quaked greatly' (Exod 19.18). When the Redeemer was making satisfaction for the elect's breaking of it, 'the earth did quake, and the rocks rent' (Matt 27.51). What possible ground of hope, then, is there to the wicked man, when death comes upon him armed with the force of this law? How can he escape that fire, which 'burnt unto the midst of heaven?' (Deut

4.11). How shall he be able to stand in that smoke, that 'ascended as the smoke of a furnace?' (Exod 19.18). How will he endure the terrible 'thunders and lightnings' (verse 16), and dwell in 'the darkness, clouds, and thick darkness?' (Deut 4.11). All these comparisons heaped together do but faintly represent the fearful tempest of wrath and indignation which shall pursue the wicked to the lowest hell, and for ever abide on those who are driven to darkness at death.

3 : Death roots up their delusive hopes of eternal happiness; then it is that their covenant with death and agreement with hell is broken. They are awakened out of their golden dreams, and at length lift up their eyes (Job 8.14), 'Whose hope shall be cut off, and whose trust shall be a spider's web.' They trust that all shall be well with them after death: but their trust is as a web woven out of their own bowels, with a great deal of art and industry. They wrap themselves up in their hope, as the spider wraps herself in her web. But it is a weak and slender defence; for however it may withstand the threatenings of the Word of God, death, that besom of destruction, will sweep them and it both away, so as there shall not be the least shred of it left; and he, who this moment will not let his hope go, shall next moment be utterly hopeless. Death overturns the house built on the sand; it leaves no man under the power of delusion.

4 : Death makes their state absolutely and for ever hopeless. Matters cannot be retrieved and amended after death. For, 1. Time once gone can never be recalled. If cries or tears, price or pains, could bring time back again, the wicked man might have hope in his death. But tears of blood will not prevail; nor will his roaring for millions of ages cause it to return. The sun will not stand still for the sluggard to awake and enter on his journey; and when once it is gone down, he needs not expect the night to be turned into day for his sake: he must lodge through the long night of eternity, where his time left him. 2. There is no returning to this life, to amend what is amiss; it is a state of probation and trial, which terminates at death; therefore we cannot return

to it again; it is but once we thus live, and once we die. Death carries the wicked man to 'his own place' (Acts 1.25). This life is our working day. Death closes our day and our work together. We may admit the wicked might have some hope in their death, if, after death has opened their eyes, they could return to life, and have but the trial of one Sabbath, one offer of Christ, one day, or but one hour more, to make up their peace with God: but 'man lieth down, and riseth not till the heavens be no more; they shall not awake, nor be raised out of their sleep' (Job 14.12). 3. In the other world, men have no access to get their ruined state and condition retrieved, though they be ever so desirous of it. 'For there is no work, nor device, nor knowledge, nor wisdom, in the grave, whither thou goest' (Eccl 9.10). Now, a man may flee from the wrath to come, he may get into a refuge; but when once death has done its work, 'the door is shut;' there are no more offers of mercy, no more pardons: where the tree is fallen, there it must lie.

Let what has been said be carefully pondered; and that it may be of use, let me exhort you,

First, To take heed that you entertain no hopes of heaven but what are built on a solid foundation. Tremble to think what fair hopes of happiness death sweeps away, like cobwebs; how the hopes of many are cut off, when they seem to themselves to be at the very threshold of heaven; how, in the moment they expected to be carried by angels into Abraham's bosom, into the regions of bliss and peace, they are carried by devils into the society of the damned in hell, into the place of torment, and regions of horror. I beseech you to beware, 1. Of a hope built upon ground that was never cleared. The wise builder digged deep (Luke 6.48). Were your hopes of heaven never shaken? but have you had good hopes all your days? Alas for it! you may see the mystery of your case explained (Luke 11.21), 'When a strong man armed keepeth his palace, his goods are in peace.' But if they have been shaken, take heed lest some breaches only have been made in the old building, which you have got repaired again by ways and means of your own. I assure you, that your hope, however fair a building it is, is not fit to trust to, unless your old hopes have been razed, and you have built on a foundation quite new. 2. Beware of that hope which looks bright in the dark, but loses all its lustre when it is set in the light of God's Word, when it is examined and tried by the touchstone of divine revelation (John 3.20,21), 'For every one that doeth evil hateth the light, neither cometh to the light, lest his deeds should be reproved. But he that doeth truth cometh to the light, that his deeds may be made manifest, that they are wrought in God.' That hope, which cannot abide Scripture trial, but sinks when searched into by sacred truth, is a delusion, and not a true hope: for God's Word is always a friend to the graces of God's Spirit, and an enemy to delusion. 3. Beware of that hope, which stands without being supported by Scriptural evidences. Alas! many are big with hopes, who cannot give, because they really have not, any Scripture grounds for them. You hope that all will be well with you after death: but what word of God is it, on which you have been caused to hope (Psa 119.49)? What Scriptural evidence have you to prove that your hope is not the hope of the hypocrite? What have you, after impartial self-examination, as in the sight of God, found in yourself, which the Word of God determines to be a sure evidence of his right to eternal life who is possessed of it? Numbers are ruined with such hopes as stand unsupported by Scriptural evidence. Men are fond and tenacious of these hopes; but death will throw them down, and leave the self-deceiver hopeless. 4. Beware of that hope of heaven, which does not prepare and dispose you for heaven, which never makes your soul more holy (1 John 3.3), 'Every man that hath this hope in him, purifieth himself, even as he is pure.' The hope of the most part of men, is rather a hope to be free from pain and torment in another life, than a hope of true happiness, the nature whereof is not understood and discerned: therefore it rests in sloth and indolence, and does not excite to mortification and a heavenly life. So far are they from hoping aright for heaven, that they must own, if they speak their genuine sentiments, that removing out of this world into any other place whatsoever, is rather their fear than their hope. The glory of the heavenly city does not at all draw their hearts upwards to it, nor do they lift up their heads with joy, in the prospect of arriving at it. If they had the true hope of the marriage day, they would, as the bride, the 'Lamb's wife,' be 'making themselves ready for it' (Rev 19.7). But their hopes are produced by their sloth, and their sloth is nourished by their hopes. O, Sirs, as you would not be driven away helpless in your death, beware of these hopes! Raze them now, and build on a new foundation, lest death leave not one stone of them upon another, and you never be able to hope any more.

Secondly, Hasten, O sinners, out of your wickedness, out of your sinful state, and out of your wicked life, if you would not at death be driven away in your wickedness. Remember the fatal end of the wicked as the text represents it. I know there is a great difference in the death of the wicked, as to some circumstances: but all of them, in their death, agree in this, that they are driven away in their wickedness. Some of them die resolutely, as if they scorned to be afraid; some in raging despair, so filled with horror that they cry out as if they were already in hell; others in sullen despondency, oppressed with fears, so that their hearts sink within them, at the remembrance of mis-spent time, and the view which they have of eternity, having neither head nor heart to do anything for their own relief. And others die stupidly; they live like beasts, and they die like beasts, without any concern on their spirits about their eternal state. They groan under their bodily distress but have no sense of the danger of their soul. One may, with almost as much prospect of success, speak to a stone, as speak to them; vain is the attempt to teach them; nothing that can be said moves them. To discourse to them, either of the joys of heaven or the torments of hell, is to plough on a rock, or beat the air. Some die like the foolish virgins, dreaming of heaven; their foreheads are steeled against the fears of hell, with presumptuous hopes of heaven. The business of those who would be useful to them, is not to answer doubts about the case of their souls, but to discover to them their own false hopes. But whichever way the unconverted man dies, he is 'driven away in his wickedness.' O dreadful case! Oh, let the consideration of so horrid a departure out of this world, move you to flee to Jesus Christ as the all-sufficient Saviour, an almighty Redeemer. Let it prevail to drive you out of your wickedness, to holiness of heart and life. Though you reckon it pleasant to live in wickedness, yet you cannot but own, it is bitter to die in it. And if you leave it not in time, you must go on in your wickedness to hell, the proper place of it, that it may be set there on its own base. For when you are passing out of this world, all your sins, from the first to the last of them, will swarm about you, hang upon you, accompany you to the other world, and, as so many furies, surround you there for ever.

Thirdly, O be concerned for others, especially for your relations, that they may not continue in their sinful natural state, but be brought into a state of salvation, lest they be driven away in their wickedness at death. What would you not do to prevent any of your friends dying an untimely and violent death? But, alas! do you not see them in hazard of being driven away in their wickedness? Is not death approaching them, even the youngest of them? And are they not strangers to true Christianity, remaining in that state in which they came into the world? Oh! make haste to pluck the brand out of the fire, lest it be burned to ashes. The death of relations often leaves a sting in the hearts of those they leave behind them, because they did not do for their souls as they had opportunity; and because the opportunity is for ever taken out of their hands.

DOCTRINE II: *The state of the godly in death is a hopeful state*

We have seen the dark side of the cloud looking towards ungodly men, as they pass out of the world; let us now take a view of the bright side of it, shining on the godly as they enter on their eternal state. In discoursing on this subject, I shall confirm this doctrine, answer an objection against it, and then make some practical improvement of the whole.

For confirmation, let it be observed, that although the passage out of this world by death has a frightful aspect to poor mortals, and to miscarry in it must needs be of fatal consequence, yet the following circumstances make the state of the godly in their death, happy and hopeful.

1 : They have a trusty good Friend before them in the other world. Jesus Christ, their best Friend, is Lord of the land to which death carries them. When Joseph sent for his father to come down to him to Egypt, telling him, 'God hath made me lord of all Egypt' (Gen 45.9), 'And when Jacob saw the wagons Joseph had sent to carry him, the spirit of Jacob revived' (verse 27). He resolves to undertake the journey. I think, when the Lord calls a godly man out of the world, He sends him such glad tidings, and such a kind invitation into the other world, that, having faith to believe it, his spirit must revive, when he sees the wagon of death which comes to carry him thither. It is true, indeed, he has a weighty trial to undergo; after death the judgment. But the case of the godly is altogether hopeful; for the Lord of the land is their Husband, and their Husband is the Judge; 'The Father hath committed all judgment unto the Son' (John 5.22). Surely the case of the wife is hopeful, when her own husband is her judge, even such a husband as hates putting away. No husband is so loving and so tender of his spouse, as the Lord Christ is of His. One would think it would be a very bad land; which a wife would not willingly go to, where her husband is the ruler and judge. Moreover, their Judge is the Advocate (1 John 2.1), 'We have an advocate with the Father, Jesus Christ the righteous.' Therefore they need not fear their being put back, and falling into condemnation. What can be more favourable? Can they think, that He who pleads their cause will Himself pass sentence against them? Yet further, their advocate is their Redeemer; they are 'redeemed with the precious blood of Christ' (1 Pet 1.18,19).

[353]

So when He pleads for them, He is pleading His own cause. Though an advocate may be careless of the interest of one who employs him, yet surely he will do his utmost to defend his own right, which he has purchased with his money: and shall not their advocate defend the purchase of His own blood? But more than all that, their Redeemer is their head, and they are His members (Eph 5.23,30). Though one were so silly as to let his own purchase go, without standing up to defend his right, yet surely he will not part with a limb of his own body. Is not their case then hopeful in death, who are so closely linked and allied to the Lord of the other world, who has 'the keys of hell and of death?'

2: They shall have a safe passage to another world. They must indeed go through 'the valley of the shadow of death;' but though it be in itself a dark and shady vale, it shall be a valley of hope to them: they shall not be driven through it, but be as men in perfect safety, who fear no evil (Psa 23.4). Why should they fear? They have the Lord of the land's safe conduct, His pass sealed with His own blood: namely, the blessed covenant, which is the saint's death-bed comfort (2 Sam 23.5), 'Although my house be not so with God, yet he hath made with me an everlasting covenant, ordered in all things and sure: for this is all my salvation, and all my desire, although he make it not to grow.' Who then can harm them? It is safe riding in Christ's chariot (Cant 3.9), both through life and death. They have good and honourable attendants, a guard, even a guard of angels. These encamp about them in the time of their life; and surely will not leave them in the day of their death. These happy ministering spirits are attendants on their Lord's bride, and will doubtless convey her safe home to His house. When friends in mournful mood stand by the saint's bedside, waiting to see him draw his last breath, his soul is waited for by angels, to be carried into Abraham's bosom (Luke 16.22). The Captain of the saints' salvation is the Captain of this holy guard: He was their guide even unto death, and He will be their guide through it too (Psa 23.4), 'Yea, though I walk through the valley of the shadow of death,

I will fear no evil; for thou art with me.' They may, without fear, pass that river, being confident it shall not overflow them; and they may walk through that fire, being sure they shall not be burnt by it.

Death can do them no harm. It cannot even hurt their bodies: for though it separate the soul from the body, it cannot separate the body from the Lord Jesus Christ. Even death is to them but sleep in Jesus (1 Thess 4.14). They continue members of Christ, though in a grave. Their dust is precious dust, laid up in the grave as in their Lord's cabinet. They lie in a grave mellowing, as precious fruit laid up to be brought forth to Him at the resurrection. The husbandman has corn in his barn, and corn lying in the ground: the latter is more precious to him than the former, because he looks to get it returned with increase. Even so the dead bodies of the saints are valued by their Saviour: they are 'sown in corruption,' to be 'raised in incorruption;' 'sown in dishonour,' to be 'raised in glory' (1 Cor 15.42,43). It cannot hurt their souls. It is with the souls of the saints at death, as with Paul and his company in their voyage, whereof we have the history (Acts, chap 27). The ship was broken to pieces, but the passengers got all safe to land. When the dying saint's speech is stopped, his eyes set, and his last breath drawn, the soul gets safe away into the heavenly paradise, leaving the body to return to its earth, but in the joyful hope of a re-union at its glorious resurrection. But how can death hurt the godly? it is a foiled enemy: if it cast them down, it is only that they may rise more glorious. 'Our Saviour Jesus Christ hath abolished death' (2 Tim 1.10). The soul and life of it is gone: it is but a walking shade that may fright, but cannot hurt saints: it is only the shadow of death to them, it is not the thing itself; their dying is but as dying, or somewhat like dying. The apostle tells us, 'It is Christ that died' (Rom 8.34). Stephen, the first Christian martyr, though stoned to death, yet only fell asleep (Acts 7.60). Certainly the nature of death is quite changed, with respect to the saints. It is not to them, what it was to Jesus Christ their Head: it is not the venomed ruining thing, wrapt up in the sanction of the first covenant (Gen 2.17), 'In the day thou eatest thereof, thou shalt surely die.' It comes to the godly without a sting: they may meet it with that salutation, 'O death, where is thy sting?' Is this *Marah*? Is this bitter death? It went out full into the world, when the first Adam opened the door to it, but the second Adam has brought it again empty to His own people. I feel a sting, may the dying saint say, yet it is but a bee-sting, stinging only through the skin; but, O death, where is thy sting, thine old sting, the serpent's sting, that stings to the heart and soul? The sting of death is sin: but that is taken away. If death arrest the saint, and carry him before the Judge to answer for the debt he contracted, the debt will be found paid by the glorious Surety; and he has the discharge to show. The thorn of guilt is pulled out of the man's conscience, and his name is blotted out of the black roll, and written among the living in Jerusalem. It is true, it is a great journey through the valley of the shadow of death: but the saint's burden is taken away from his back, his iniquity pardoned, he may walk at ease: 'No lion shall be there, nor any ravenous beast:' the redeemed may walk at leisure there, free from all apprehensions of danger.

3: They shall have a joyful entrance into the other world. Their arrival in the regions of bliss will be celebrated with rapturous hymns of praise to their glorious Redeemer. A dying day is a good day to a godly man. Yea, it is his best day; it is better to him than his birth-day, or than the most joyous day which he ever had on earth. 'A good name,' says the wise man, is 'better than precious ointment: and the day of death than the day of one's birth' (Eccl 7.1). The notion of the immortality of the soul, and of future happiness, which obtained among some pagan nations, had wonderful effects on them. Some of them, when they mourned for the dead, did it in women's apparel; that, being moved with the indecency of the garb, they might the sooner lay aside their mourning. Others buried them without any lamentation or mourning; but had a sacrifice, and a feast for friends, upon that occasion. Some were wont to mourn at births, and rejoice at burials. But the practice of some Indian nations is yet more strange, where, upon the husband's decease, his wives were accustomed to contend, before the judges, which of them was the most beloved wife. She in whose favour it was determined, thereupon, with a cheerful countenance, threw herself into the flames prepared for her husband's corpse, was burned with it, and was reckoned happy, while the rest lived in grief and were accounted miserable. But however much false notions of a future state, assisted by pride, love of applause, apprehensions of difficulties in this life, and such like principles proper to depraved human nature, may influence rude uncultivated minds, when strengthened by the arts of hell, O what solid joy and consolation may they have who are true Christians, being in Christ, who 'hath brought life and immortality to light through the Gospel!' (2 Tim 1.10). Death is one of those 'all things,' that 'work together for good to them that love God' (Rom 8.28). When the body dies, the soul is perfected; the body of death goes off, at the death of the body. What harm did the jailer to Pharaoh's butler, when he opened the prison door to him, and let him out? Is the bird in worse case, when at liberty, than when confined in a cage? Thus, and no worse, are the souls of the saints treated by death. It comes to the godly, as Haman came to Mordecai, with the royal apparel and the horse (Esther 6.11), with commission to do them honour, however awkwardly it be performed. I question not but Haman performed the ceremony with a very ill mien, a pale face, a downcast look, and a cloudy countenance, and like one who came to hang him, rather than to honour him. But he whom the king delighted to honour, must be honoured; and Haman, Mordecai's grand enemy, must be the man employed to put this honour upon him. Glory, glory, glory, blessing and praise to our Redeemer, our Saviour, our Mediator, by whose death, grim devouring death is made to do such a good office to those whom it might otherwise have hurried away in their wickedness, to utter and eternal destruction! A dying day is, in itself, a joyful day to the godly; it is their redemption day, when the captives are delivered, when the prisoners are set free. It is the day of the pilgrims coming home from their pilgrimage; the day in which the heirs of glory return from their travels, to their own country, and their Father's house, and enter into actual possession of the glorious inheritance. It is their marriage day; now is the time of espousals, but then the marriage is consummated, and a marriage feast begun, which has no end. If so, is not the state of the godly in death a hopeful state?

Objection. 'But if the state of the godly in their death be so hopeful, how comes it to pass that many of them, when dying, are full of fears, and have little hope?' *Answer:* It must be owned, that saints do not all die in one and the same manner; there is a diversity among them, as well as among the wicked; yet the worst case of a dying saint is indeed a hopeful one. Some die triumphantly, in a full assurance of faith. (2 Tim 4.6–8), 'The time of my departure is at hand. I have fought a good fight, I have finished my course, I have kept the faith. Henceforth there is laid up for me a crown of righteousness.' They get a taste of the joys of heaven, while here on earth, and begin the songs of Zion, while yet in a strange land. Others die in a solid dependence of faith on their Lord and Saviour: though they cannot sing triumphantly, yet they can, and will say confidently, 'The Lord is their God.' Though they cannot triumph over death like old Simeon, having Christ in his arms, and saying, 'Lord now lettest thou thy servant depart in peace, according to thy word: for mine eyes have seen thy salvation' (Luke 2.29,30); yet they can say with dying Jacob, 'I have waited for thy salvation, O Lord' (Gen 49.18). His left hand is under their head, to support them, though his right hand does not embrace them: they firmly believe, though they are not filled with joy in believing. They can plead the covenant, and cling to the promise, although their house is not so with God as they could wish. But the dying day

[358]

of some saints may be like that day mentioned in Zechariah 14.7, 'Not day, nor night.' They may die under great doubts and fears; setting as it were in a cloud, and going to heaven in a mist. They may go mourning without the sun, and never put off their spirit of heaviness, till death strips them of it. They may be carried to heaven through the confines of hell; and may be pursued by the devouring lion, even to the very gates of the new Jerusalem; and may be compared to a ship almost wrecked in sight of the harbour, which yet gets safe into her port (1 Cor 3.15), 'If any man's work shall be burnt, he shall suffer loss: but he himself shall be saved, yet so as by fire.' There is safety amidst their fears, but danger in the strong confidence of the wicked; and there is a blessed seed of gladness in their greatest sorrows: 'Light is sown for the righteous, and gladness for the upright in heart' (Psa 97.11).

Now, saints are liable to such perplexity in their death, because, though they are Christians indeed, yet they are men of like passions with others, and death is a frightful object in itself, whatever dress it appears in; the stern countenance with which it looks at mortals, can hardly fail of causing them to shrink. Moreover, the saints are of all men the most jealous of themselves. They think of eternity, and of a tribunal, more deeply than others do; with them it is a more serious thing to die than the rest of mankind are aware of. They know the deceits of the heart, the subtleties of depraved human nature, better than others do. Therefore they may have much to do to keep up hope on a death-bed, while others pass off quietly, like sheep to the slaughter; and the rather, that Satan, who uses all his art to support the hopes of the hypocrite, will do his utmost to mar the peace, and increase the fears, of the saints. And finally, the bad frame of spirit, and ill condition, in which death sometimes seizes a true Christian, may cause this perplexity. By his being in the state of grace, he is indeed always habitually prepared for death, and his dying safely is ensured: but yet there is more requisite to his actual preparation and dying comfortably; his spirit must be in good condition too.

Wherefore there are three cases in which death cannot but be very uncomfortable to a child of God. 1. If it seize him at a time when the guilt of some particular sin, unrepented of, is lying on his conscience; and death comes on that very account, to take him out of the land of the living, as was the case with many of the Corinthian professors (1 Cor 11.30), 'For this cause,' namely, of unworthy communicating, 'many are weak and sickly among you, and many sleep.' If a person is surprised by the approach of death, while lying under the guilt of some unpardoned sin, it cannot but cause a mighty consternation. 2. When death catches him sleeping. The midnight cry must be frightful to sleeping virgins. The man who lies in a ruinous house, and awakes not till the timbers begin to crack, and the stones to drop down about his ears, may indeed get out of it safely, but not without fears of being crushed by its fall. When a Christian has been going on in a course of security and backsliding, and awakens not till death comes to his bedside, it is no wonder that he gets a fearful awakening. 3. When he has lost sight of his saving interest in Christ, and cannot produce evidences of his title to heaven. It is hard to meet death without some evidence of a title to eternal life at hand; hard to go through the dark valley without the candle of the Lord shining upon the head. It is a terrible adventure to launch out into eternity, when a man can make no better of it than a leap in the dark, not knowing where he shall light, whether in heaven or hell.

Nevertheless the state of the saints, in their death, is always in itself hopeful. The presumptuous hopes of the ungodly, in their death, cannot make their state hopeful, neither can the fears of a saint make his state hopeless, for God judgeth according to the truth of the thing, not according to men's opinions about it. Therefore the saints can no more be altogether without hope, than they can be altogether without faith. Their faith may be very weak, but it fails not; and their hope very low, yet they will, and do hope to the end. Even while the godly seem to be carried away with the stream of doubts and fears, there remains still as much hope as determines them to lay hold on the tree of life that grows on the banks of the river (Jonah 2.4), 'Then I said, I am cast out of thy sight: yet I will look again toward thy temple.'

Use: This speaks comfort to the godly against the fear of death. A godly man may be called a happy man before his death, because, whatever befalls him in life, he shall certainly be happy at death. You who are in Christ, who are true Christians, have hope in your end, and such a hope as may comfort you against all those fears which arise from the consideration of a dying hour. This I shall branch out, in answering some cases briefly:

Case 1: 'The prospect of death,' some of the saints will say, 'is uneasy to me, not knowing what shall become of my family when I am gone.' *Answer:* The righteous hath hope in his death as to his family, as well as himself. Although you have little, for the present, to live upon, which has been the condition of many of God's chosen ones (1 Cor 4.11), 'We,' namely, the apostles, 'both hunger and thirst, and are naked, and are buffeted, and have no certain dwelling-place;' and though you have nothing to leave them, as was the case of that son of the prophets, who feared the Lord, and yet died in debt which he was unable to pay, as his poor widow represents (2 Kings 4.1); yet you have a good Friend to leave them to, a covenant God, to whom you may confidently commit them (Jer 49.11), 'Leave thy fatherless children, I will preserve them alive; and let thy widows trust in me.' The world can bear witness of signal settlements made upon the children of providence; such as by their pious parents have been cast upon God's providential care. It has been often remarked that they wanted neither provision nor education. Moses is an eminent instance of this. He, though he was an outcast infant (Exod 2.3), yet became learned in all the wisdom of the Egyptians (Acts 7.22), and became king in Jeshurun (Deut 33.5). O! may we not be ashamed, that we do not confidently trust Him with the concerns of our families, to whom, as our Saviour and Redeemer, we have committed our eternal interests?

Case 2 : 'Death will take us away from our dear friends; yea, we shall not see the Lord in the land of the living, in the blessed ordinances.' *Answer:* It will take you to your best Friend, the Lord Christ. The friends you leave behind you, if they be indeed persons of worth, you will meet again, when they come to heaven: and you will never be separated any more. If death take you away from the temple below, it will carry you to the temple above. It will indeed take you from the streams, but it will set you down by the fountain. If it put out your candle, it will carry you where there is no night, where there is an eternal day.

Case 3 : 'I have so much ado, in time of health, to satisfy myself as to my interest in Christ, about my being a real Christian, a regenerate man, that I judge it is almost impossible I should die comfortably.' *Answer:* If it is thus with you, then double your diligence to make your calling and election sure. Endeavour to grow in knowledge, and walk closely with God; be diligent in self-examination, and pray earnestly for the Holy Spirit, whereby you may know the things freely given you of God. If you are enabled, by the power and Spirit of Christ, thus diligently to prosecute your spiritual concerns, though the time of your life be neither day nor night, yet at evening time it may be light. Many weak Christians indulge doubts and fears about their spiritual state, as if they placed at least some part of religion in this imprudent practice; but towards the end of life, they think and act in another manner. The traveller, who reckons that he has time to spare, may stand still debating with himself, whether this or the other be the right way : but when the sun begins to set, he is forced to lay aside his scruples, and resolutely to go forward in the road which he judges to be the right one, lest he lie all night in the open fields. Thus some Christians, who perplex themselves much, throughout the course of their lives, with jealous doubts and fears, content themselves when they come to die, with such evidences of the safety of their state as they could not be satisfied with before; and by disputing less against themselves, and believing more, court the peace they formerly rejected, and gain it too.

Case 4: 'I am under a sad decay, in respect of my spiritual condition.' *Answer:* Bodily consumptions may make death easy: but it is not so in spiritual decays. I will not say that a godly man cannot be in such a case, when he dies, but I believe it is rarely so. Ordinarily, I suppose a cry comes to awaken sleeping virgins, before death comes. Samson is set to grind in the prison till his locks grow again. David and Solomon fell under great spiritual decays; but before they died they recovered their spiritual strength and vigour. However, bestir yourselves without delay, to strengthen the things that remain: your fright will be the less, for being awakened from spiritual sleep before death comes to your bedside: and you ought to lose no time, seeing you know not how soon death may seize you.

Case 5: 'It is terrible to think of the other world, that world of spirits, which I have so little acquaintance with.' *Answer:* Your best friend is Lord of that other world. Abraham's bosom is kindly even to those who never saw his face. After death, your soul becomes capable of converse with the blessed inhabitants of that other world. The spirits of just men made perfect were once such as your spirit now is. And as for the angels, however superior their nature in the rank of beings, yet our nature is dignified above theirs, in the man Christ, and they are all of them your Lord's servants, and so your fellow-servants.

Case 6: 'The pangs of death are terrible' *Answer:* Yet not so terrible as pangs of conscience, caused by a piercing sense of guilt, and apprehensions of divine wrath, with which I suppose you to be not altogether unacquainted. But who would not endure bodily sickness, that the soul may become sound, and every whit whole? Each pang of death will set sin a step nearer the door; and with the last breath, the body of sin will breathe out its last. The pains of death will not last long; and the Lord your God will not leave, but support you under them.

Case 7: 'But I am like to be cut off in the midst of my days.' *Answer:* Do not complain, you will be the sooner at home: you thereby have the advantage of your fellow-labourers, who were at work before you in the vineyard. God, in the course of His providence, hides some of His saints early in the grave, that they may be taken away from the evil to come. An early removal out of this world prevents sin and misery. They have no ground of complaint who get the residue of their years in Immanuel's land. Surely you will live as long as you have work cut out for you by the great Master, to be done for Him in this world: and when that is at an end, it is high time to be gone.

Case 8: 'I am afraid of sudden death.' *Answer:* You may indeed die so. Good Eli died suddenly (1 Sam 4.18). Yet death found him watching (verse 13): 'Watch, therefore, for ye know not what hour your Lord doth come' (Matt 24.42). Be not afraid. It is an inexpressible comfort, that death, come when it will, can never catch you out of Christ; and therefore can never seize you, as a jailor, to hurry you into the prison of hell. Sudden death may hasten and facilitate your passage to heaven, but can do you no prejudice.

Case 9: 'I am afraid it will be my lot to die wanting the exercise of reason.' *Answer:* I make no question but a child of God, a true Christian, may die in this case. But what harm? There is no hazard in it, as to his eternal state: a disease at death may divest him of his reason, but not of his religion. When a man, going a long voyage, has put his affairs in order, and put all his goods aboard, he himself may be carried on board the ship sleeping: all is safe with him, although he knows not where he is, till he awake in the ship. Even so the godly man, who dies in this case, may die uncomfortably, but not unsafely.

Case 10: 'I am naturally timorous, and the very thoughts of death are terrible to me.' *Answer:* The less you think on death, the thoughts of it will be the more frightful; make it familiar to you by frequent meditations upon it, and you may thereby quiet your fears. Look at the white and bright side of the cloud; take faith's view of the city that hath foundations, so shall you see hope in your death. Be duly affected with the body of sin and death, the frequent interruptions of your communion with God, and with the glory which dwells on the other side of death: this will contribute much to remove slavish fear.

It is a pity that saints should be so fond of life as they often are: they ought to be always on good terms with death. When matters are duly considered, it might be well expected that every child of God, every regenerate man, should generously profess concerning this life, what Job did (chap 7.16), 'I loathe it, I would not live alway.' In order to gain their hearts to this desirable temper, I offer the following additional considerations.

1 : Consider the sinfulness that attends life in this world. While you live here, you sin, and see others sinning. You breathe infectious air, you live in a pest-house. Is it at all strange to loathe such a life? 1. Your own plague-sores are running on you. Does not the sin of your nature make you groan daily? Are you not sensible, that though the cure is begun, it is far from being perfected? Has not the leprosy got into the wall of the house, which cannot be removed without pulling it down? Is not your nature so vitiated, that no less than the separation of the soul from the body can root out the disease? Have you not your sores without, as well as your sickness within? Do you not leave marks of your pollution on whatever passes through your hands? Are not all your actions tainted and blemished with defects and imperfections? Who, then, should be so much in love with life, but those whose sickness is their health, and who glory in their shame? 2. The loathsome sores of others are always before your eyes, go where you will. The follies and wickedness of men are everywhere conspicuous, and make but an unpleasant scene. This sinful world is but an unsightly company, a disagreeable crowd, in which the most loathsome are the most numerous. 3. Are not your own sores often breaking out again after healing? Frequent relapses may well cause us to grow less fond of this life. To be ever struggling, and anon falling into the mire again, makes

[365]

weary work. Do you never wish for cold death, thereby effectually to cool the heat of these lusts, which so often take fire again, even after a flood of godly sorrow has gone over them? Do not you sometimes infect others, and others infect you? There is no society in the world, in which every member of it does not sometimes lay a stumbling-block before the rest. The best carry about with them the tinder of a corrupt nature, which they cannot be rid of while they live, and which is liable to be kindled at all times, and in all places: yea, they are apt to inflame others, and become the occasions of sinning. Certainly these things are apt to embitter this life to the saints.

2: Consider the misery and troubles that attend it. Rest is desirable, but it is not to be found on this side of the grave. Worldly troubles attend all men in this life. This world is a sea of trouble, where one wave rolls upon another. They who fancy themselves beyond the reach of trouble are mistaken; no state, no change of life, is exempted from it. The crowned head is surrounded by thorny cares. Honour many times paves the way to deep disgrace: riches, for the most part, are kept to the hurt of the owners. The fairest rose wants not prickles, and the heaviest cross is sometimes wrapt up in the greatest earthly comfort. Spiritual troubles attend the saints in this life. They are like travellers journeying in a cloudy night, in which the moon sometimes breaks out from under one cloud, but quickly hides her head again under another: no wonder they long to be at their journey's end. The sudden alterations which the best frame of spirit is liable to, the perplexing doubts, confounding fears, short-lived joys, and long-running sorrows, which have a certain affinity with the present life, must needs create in the saints a desire to be with Christ, which is best of all.

3: Consider the great imperfections attending this life. While the soul is lodged in this cottage of clay, the necessities of the body are many: it is always craving. The mud walls must be repaired and patched up daily, till the clay cottage fall down for good and all. Eating, drinking, sleeping, and the like, are, in themselves, but mean employments for a rational creature; and will be reputed such by the heaven-born soul. They are badges of imperfection, and, as such, unpleasant to the mind aspiring to that life and immortality which is brought to light through the gospel; and would be very grievous, if this state of things were of long continuance. Does not the gracious soul often find itself yoked with the body, as with a companion in travel unable to keep pace with it? When the spirit is willing, the flesh is weak. When the soul would mount upward, the body is a clog upon it, and as a stone tied to the foot of a bird attempting to fly. The truth is, O believer, your soul in this body is, at best, but like a diamond in a ring, where much of it is obscured; it is far sunk in the vile clay, till relieved by death.

I conclude this subject with a few directions, how to prepare for death, so that we may die comfortably. I speak not here of habitual preparation for death, which a true Christian, in virtue of his gracious state, never wants, from the time he is born again and united to Christ; but of actual preparation, or readiness in respect of his particular case, frame, and disposition of mind and spirit, the want of which makes even a saint very unfit to die.

First, Let it be your constant care to keep a clean conscience, 'a conscience void of offence toward God, and toward men' (Acts 24.16). Beware of a standing controversy between God and you, on the account of some iniquity regarded in the heart. When an honest man is about to leave his country, and not to return, he settles accounts with those he has had dealings with, and lays down methods for paying his debts in due time, lest he be reckoned a bankrupt, and attacked by an officer when he is going off. Guilt lying on the conscience, is a fountain of fears, and will readily sting severely, when death stares the criminal in the face. Hence it is, that many, even of God's children, when dying, wish passionately, and desire eagerly, that they may live to do what they ought to have done before that time. Wherefore, walk closely with God; be diligent, strict, and exact in your course: beware of loose, careless, and irregular conversation, as you would not lay up for yourselves anguish and bitterness of spirit in a dying hour. And because, through the infirmity cleaving to us, in our present state of imperfection, in many things we offend all, renew your repentance daily, and be ever washing in the Redeemer's blood. As long as you are in the world, you will need to wash your feet (John 13.10), that is, to make application of the blood of Christ anew, for purging your consciences from the guilt of daily miscarriages. Let death find you at the fountain; and, if so, it will find you ready to answer at its call.

Secondly, Be always watchful, waiting for your change, 'like unto men that wait for their Lord – that when he cometh and knocketh, they may open unto him immediately' (Luke 12.36). Beware of slumbering and sleeping, while the bridegroom tarries. To be awakened out of spiritual slumber, by a surprising call to pass into another world, is a very frightful thing: but he who is daily waiting for the coming of his Lord, will comfortably receive the grim messenger, while he beholds him ushering in Him, of whom he may confidently say, 'This is my God, and I have waited for Him.' The way to die comfortably, is, to die daily. Be often essaying, as it were, to die. Bring yourselves familiarly acquainted with death, by making many visits to the grave, in serious meditations upon it. This was Job's practice (chap 17.13,14), 'I have made my bed in the darkness.' Go thou and do likewise; and when death comes, you will have nothing to do but to lie down. 'I have said to corruption, Thou art my father: to the worm, Thou art my mother and my sister.' Do you say so too; and you will be the fitter to go home to their house. Be frequently reflecting upon your conduct, and considering what course of life you wish to be found in, when death arrests you, and act accordingly. When you do the duties of your station in life, or are employed in acts of worship, think with yourselves, that, it may be, this is the last opportunity; and therefore do it as if you were never to do more of that kind. When you lie down at night, compose your spirits, as if you were not to awake till the heavens be no more. And when you awake in the morning, consider that new day as your last; and live accordingly. Surely that night cometh, of which you will never see the morning; or that morning, of which you will never see the night. But which of your mornings or nights will be such, you know not.

Thirdly, Employ yourselves much in weaning your hearts from the world. The man who is making ready to go abroad, busies himself in taking leave of his friends. Let the mantle of earthly enjoyments hang loose about you, that it may be easily dropped, when death comes to carry you away into another world. Moderate your affections towards your lawful comforts of life: let not your hearts be too much taken with them. The traveller acts unwisely, who suffers himself to be so allured with the conveniences of the inn where he lodges, as to make his necessary departure from it grievous. Feed with fear, and walk through the world as pilgrims and strangers. When the corn is forsaking the ground, it is ready for the sickle; when the fruit is ripe, it falls off the tree easily; likewise, when a Christian's heart is truly weaned from the world, he is prepared for death, and it will be the more easy to him. A heart disengaged from the world is a heavenly one: we are ready for heaven when our heart is there before us (Matt 6.21).

Fourthly, Be diligent in gathering and laying up evidences of your title to heaven, for your support and comfort at the hour of death. The neglect hereof mars the joy and consolation which some Christians might otherwise have at their death. Wherefore, examine yourselves frequently as to your spiritual state, that evidences which lie hid and unobserved, may be brought to light and taken notice of. And if you would manage this work successfully, make solemn, serious work of it. Set apart some time for it. And, after earnest prayer to God, through Jesus Christ, for the enlightening influences of His Holy Spirit, whereby you are enabled to understand His own Word, and to discern His own work in your souls, examine yourselves before the tribunal of your own consciences, that you may judge yourselves in this weighty matter.

And, in the first place, let the marks of a regenerate state be fixed from the Lord's Word: have recourse to some particular text for that purpose such as (Prov 8.17), 'I love them that love me.' Compare (Luke 14.26), 'If any man come to me, and hate not his father, and mother, and wife, and children, and brethren, and sisters, yea, and his own life also, he cannot be my disciple.' (Psa 119.6), 'Then shall I not be ashamed, when I have respect unto all thy commandments.' (Psa 18.23), 'I was also upright before him; and I kept myself from mine iniquity.' Compare (Rom 7.22,23), 'For I delight in the law of God after the inward man: but I see another law in my members, warring against the law of my mind.' (1 John 3.3), 'Every man that hath this hope in him, purifieth himself, even as he is pure.' (Matt 5.3), 'Blessed are the poor in spirit: for theirs is the kingdom of heaven.' (Phil 3.3), 'For we are the circumcision, which worship,' or serve 'God in the Spirit, and rejoice in Christ Jesus, and have no confidence in the flesh.' The sum of the evidence arising from these texts lies here: a real Christian is one who loves God for Himself, as well as for His benefits, and that with a supreme love, above all persons, and all things; he has an awful and impartial regard to God's commands; he opposes and wrestles against that sin, which of all others most easily besets him: he approves and loves the holy law, even in that very point wherein it strikes against his own beloved lust; his hope of heaven engages him in the study of universal holiness, in which he aims at perfection, though he cannot reach it in this life. He serves the Lord, not only in acts of worship, but in the whole of his conversation, and as to both, is spiritual in the principle, motives, aims, and ends of his service; yet he sees nothing in himself to trust to, before the Lord; Christ and His fulness are the stay of his soul; his confidence is cut off from all that is not Christ, or in Christ, in point of justification or acceptance with God, and in point of sanctification too. Every one, in whom these characters are found, has a title to heaven, according to the Word. It is convenient and profitable to mark such texts, for this special use, as they occur, while you read the Scriptures, or hear sermons. The marks of a regenerate state being thus fixed, in the next place impartially search and try your own hearts thereby, as in the sight of God, with dependence on Him for spiritual discernment, that you may know whether they be in you or not. When you find them, form the conclusion deliberately and distinctly; namely, that therefore you are regenerated, and have a title to heaven. Thus you may gather evidences. But be sure to have recourse to God in Christ, by earnest prayer, for the testimony of the Spirit, whose office it is to 'bear witness with our spirit, that we are the children of God' (Rom. 8.16). Moreover, carefully observe the course and method of providence towards you; and likewise, how your soul is affected under the same, in the various steps thereof; compare both with Scripture doctrines, promises, threatenings, and examples, so shall you perceive if the Lord deals with you as He used to do unto those that love His name, and if you are going forth by the footsteps of the flock. This may afford you comfortable evidence. Walk tenderly and circumspectly, and the Lord will manifest Himself to you, according to His promise (John 14.21), 'He that hath my commandments, and keepeth them, he it is that loveth me; and he that loveth me, shall be loved of my Father; and I will love him, and will manifest myself to him.' But it is in vain to think of successful self-examination, if you be loose and irregular in your conversation.

Lastly, Despatch the work of your day and generation with speed and diligence. 'David, after he had served his own generation by the will of God, fell on sleep' (Acts 13.36). God has allotted us certain pieces of work of this kind, which ought to be despatched before the time of working be over (Eccl 9.10), 'Whatsoever thy hand findeth to do, do it with thy might: for there is no work, nor knowledge, nor wisdom in the grave, whither thou goest.' (Gal 6.10), 'As we have therefore opportunity, let us do good unto all men, especially unto them who are of the household of faith.' If a passenger, after he is got on shipboard, and the ship is getting under sail, remember that he has omitted to despatch a piece of necessary business when he was ashore, it must needs be uneasy to him: even so, reflection in a dying hour upon neglected seasons, and lost opportunities, cannot fail to disquiet a Christian. Wherefore, whatever is incumbent upon you to do for God's honour, and the good of others, either as the duty of your station, or by special opportunity put into your hand, perform it seasonably, if you would die comfortably.

3

THE RESURRECTION

Marvel not at this: for the hour is coming, in the
which all that are in the graves shall hear his voice,
and shall come forth: they that have done good unto
the resurrection of life; and they that have done evil
unto the resurrection of damnation.   JOHN 5.28,29

These words are part of the defence which our Lord Jesus Christ
makes for Himself, when persecuted by the Jews for curing the
impotent man and ordering him to carry away his bed on the
Sabbath; and for vindicating His conduct, when accused by them
of having thereby profaned that day. On this occasion He professes
Himself not only the Lord of the Sabbath, but also Lord of life
and death; declaring, in the words of the text, the resurrection of
the dead to be brought to pass by His power. This He introduces
with these words, as with a solemn preface, 'Marvel not at this,'
namely, at this strange discourse of Mine: do not wonder to hear
Me, whose appearance is so very mean in your eyes, talk at this
rate; for the day is coming in which the dead shall be raised by
My power.

Observe in this text, 1. The doctrine of the resurrection asserted, 'All that are in the graves shall hear his voice, and shall
come forth.' The dead bodies, which are reduced to dust, shall
revive, and evidence life by hearing and moving. 2. The author of
it, Jesus Christ, 'the Son of man' (verse 27). The dead shall hear
His voice, and be raised thereby. 3. The number that shall be
raised, 'All that are in the graves,' that is, all the dead bodies of
men, however differently disposed of, in different kinds of graves;
or all the dead, good and bad. They are not all buried in graves,
properly so called: some are burnt to ashes: some drowned, and
buried in the bellies of fishes; but, wherever the matter or sub-

stance of which the body was composed is to be found, thence they shall come forth. 4. The great distinction that shall be made between the godly and the wicked: they shall both rise again in the resurrection. None of the godly shall be missing, though, perhaps, they either had no burial, or a very obscure one; and all the wicked shall come forth; their vaulted tombs shall hold them no longer than the voice is uttered. But the former have a joyful resurrection to life, whilst the latter have a dreadful resurrection to damnation. 5. The set time of this great event: there is an hour, or certain fixed period of time, appointed of God for it. We are not told when that hour will be, but that it is coming; for this, among other reasons, that we may always be ready.

DOCTRINE: *There shall be a resurrection of the dead*

In discoursing of this subject, I shall: 1. Show the certainty of the resurrection. 2. I shall inquire into the nature of it. And, *Lastly,* make some practical improvement of the whole.

1: In showing the certainty of the resurrection, I shall evince, 1. That God can raise the dead. 2. That He will do it; which are the two grounds or topics laid down by Christ Himself, when disputing with the Sadducees (Matt 22.29), 'Jesus answered and said unto them, Ye do err, not knowing the Scriptures nor the power of God.'

1: Seeing God is almighty, surely He can raise the dead. We have instances of this powerful work of God, both in the Old and New Testament. The son of the widow in Sarepta was raised from the dead (1 Kings 17.22); the Shunammite's son (2 Kings 4.35); and the man 'cast into the sepulchre of Elisha' (chap 13.21). In which we may observe a gradation, the second of these miraculous events being more illustrious than the first, and the third than the second. The first of these persons was raised when he was but newly dead, the prophet Elijah who raised him being present at his decease. The second, when he had lain dead a considerable time; namely, while his mother travelled from Shunem, to mount

[374]

Carmel, reckoned about the distance of sixteen miles, and returned from thence to her house, with Elisha, who raised him. The last, not till they were burying him, and the corpse was cast into the prophet's grave. In like manner, in the New Testament, Jairus's daughter (Mark 5.41), and Dorcas (Acts 9.40), were both raised to life, when lately dead; the widow's son in Nain, when they were carrying him out to bury him (Luke 7.11–15); and Lazarus, when stinking in the grave (John 11.39–44).

Can men make curious glasses out of ashes, and cannot the great Creator, who made all things of nothing, raise man's body, after it is resolved into dust? If it be objected, 'How can men's bodies be raised up again, after they are reduced to dust, and the ashes of many generations are mingled together?', Scripture and reason furnish the answer, 'With men it is impossible, but not with God.' It is absurd for men to deny that God can do a thing, because they see not how it may be done. How small a portion do we know of His ways! How absolutely incapable are we of conceiving distinctly of the extent of almighty power, and much more of comprehending its actings, and method of procedure! I question not, but many illiterate men are as great unbelievers as to many chemical experiments, as some learned men are to the doctrine of the resurrection: and as these last are ready to deride the former, so 'the Lord will have them in derision.' What a mystery was it to the Indians, that the Europeans could, by a piece of paper, converse together at the distance of some hundreds of miles! How much were they astonished to see them, with their guns, produce as it were thunder and lightning in a moment, and at pleasure kill men afar off! Shall some men do such things as are wonders in the eyes of others because they cannot comprehend them, and shall men confine the infinite power of God within the narrow boundaries of their own shallow capacities, in a matter no ways contrary to reason! An inferior nature has but a very imperfect conception of the power of a superior. Brutes do not conceive of the actings of reason in men; and men have but imperfect notions of the power of angels: how low and inadequate a con-

[375]

ception, then, must a finite nature have of the power of that which is infinite! Though we cannot conceive how God acts, yet we ought to believe He can do above what we can think or conceive.

Wherefore, let the bodies of men be laid in the grave; let them rot there, and be reduced into the most minute particles: or let them be burnt, and the ashes cast into rivers, or thrown up into the air, to be scattered by the wind: let the dust of a thousand generations be mingled, and the streams of the dead bodies wander to and fro in the air: let birds or wild beasts eat the bodies, or the fishes of the sea devour them, so that the parts of human bodies, thus destroyed, pass into substantial parts of birds, beasts or fishes. Then let our modern Sadducees propose the question in these cases, as the ancient Sadducees did in the case of the woman who had been married to seven husbands successively (Matt 22.28). We answer, as our blessed Lord and Saviour did (verse 29), 'Ye do err, not knowing the Scriptures, nor the power of God.' We believe God to be omniscient and omnipotent, infinite in knowledge and in power; and hence, agreeably to the dictates of reason, we conclude the possibility of the resurrection, even in the cases supposed.

Material things may change their forms and shapes, may be reduced to the principles of which they are formed: but they are not annihilated, or reduced to nothing; nor can they be so, by any created power. God is omniscient, His understanding is infinite; therefore He knows all things, what they were at any time, what they are, and where they are to be found. Though the countryman, who comes into the apothecary's shop, cannot find out the drug he wants; yet the apothecary himself knows what he has in his shop, whence it came, and where it is to be found. And, in a mixture of many different seeds, the expert gardener can distinguish between each of them. Why then may not Omniscience distinguish between dust and dust? Can He, who knows all things to perfection, be liable to any mistake about His own creatures? Whoso believes an infinite understanding, must needs own, that no mass of dust is so jumbled together, but God perfectly comprehends, and infallibly knows, how the most minute particle, and every one of them, is to be matched. Therefore He knows where the particles of each dead body are; whether in the earth, sea, or air, however they are now scattered. It is certain the bodies of men, as of all other animals or living creatures, are in a continual change: they grow and are sustained by daily food; so small a part whereof becomes nourishment, that the most part is evacuated. It is reckoned also that much of the food is evacuated insensibly by perspiration. Yea, the nourishing part of the food, when assimilated, and thereby become a part of the body, is evacuated by perspiration, through the pores of the skin, and is again supplied by the use of other food: yet the body is still reckoned one and the same body. Whence we may conclude, that it is not essential to the resurrection of the body, that every particle of the matter which at any time was part of a human body, should be restored to it, when it is raised up from death to life. Were it so, the bodies of men would become of so huge a size, that they would bear no resemblance to the persons. It is sufficient to denominate it the same body that died, when it is risen again, if the body that is raised be formed in its former proportions, of the same particles of matter, which at any time were its constituent parts, howsoever it be refined: just as we reckon it is the same body that has pined away by long sickness, which becomes fat and fair again after recovery.

Now, to this infinite understanding join infinite power, whereby He is able to subdue all things unto Himself, and this gloriously great work appears most reasonable. If Omniscience discover every little particle of dust, where it is, and how it is to be matched, cannot Omnipotence bring them, and join them together, in their order? Can the watchmaker take up the several pieces of a watch, lying in a confused heap before him, and set each in its proper place; and cannot God put the human body into order, after its dissolution? Did He speak this world into being, out of nothing: and can He not form man's body out of its pre-existent matter? If He calls those things which be not, as though they were, surely He can call things that are dissolved, to be as they were before the compound was resolved into its parts and principles. Wherefore, God can raise the dead. And 'Why should it be thought a thing incredible with you, that God should raise the dead?' (Acts 26.8).

2: God will do it. He not only can do it, but He certainly will do it, because He has said it. Our text is very full to this purpose, 'All that are in the graves shall hear his voice, and shall come forth; they that have done good, unto the resurrection of life, and they that have done evil, unto the resurrection of damnation.' These words relate to, and are an explanation of, that part of Daniel's prophecy (Dan 12.2), 'And many of them that sleep in the dust of the earth shall awake, some to everlasting life, and some to shame and everlasting contempt.' This appears to be calculated to confront the doctrine of the Sadducees, which the Holy Ghost knew was to be at a great height in the Jewish church, under the persecution of Antiochus. There are many other texts in the Old and New Testament, that might here be adduced; such as Acts 24.15, 'And have hope towards God, which they themselves also allow, that there shall be a resurrection of the dead, both of the just and unjust.' And (Job 19.26,27), 'Though after my skin, worms destroy this body, yet in my flesh shall I see God: whom I shall see for myself, and mine eyes shall behold, and not another; though my reins be consumed within me.' But I need not multiply testimonies, in a matter so clearly and frequently taught in sacred Scripture. Our Lord and Saviour Himself proves it, against the Sadducees, in that remarkable text (Luke 20.37,38), 'Now that the dead are raised, even Moses showed at the bush, when he calleth the Lord, the God of Abraham, the God of Isaac, and the God of Jacob; for he is not a God of the dead, but of the living; for all live unto him.' These holy patriarchs were dead; nevertheless, the Lord Jehovah is called their God, namely, in virtue of the covenant of grace, and in the sense thereof; in which sense the phrase comprehends all blessedness, as that which, by the covenant, is secured to those who are in it; (Heb 11.16), 'God

[378]

is not ashamed to be called their God; for he has prepared for them a city.' He is not called the God of their souls only; but their God, the God of their persons, souls, and bodies; which, by virtue of His truth and faithfulness, must have its full effect. Now, it cannot have its full effect on the dead, who, in as far as they are dead, are far from all blessedness; but on the living, who alone are capable of it. Therefore, since God is still called their God, they are living in respect of God,[1] although their bodies are yet in the grave; for, in respect of Him, who by His power can restore them to life, and in His covenant has declared His will and purpose so to do, and whose promise cannot fail, they are all to be reckoned to live; and, consistent with the covenant, their death is but a sleep, out of which, in virtue of the said covenant, securing all blessedness to their persons, their whole man, they must and shall certainly be awakened. The apostle Paul proves the resurrection at large (1 Cor chap 15), and shows it to be a fundamental article, the denial whereof is subversive of Christianity (verses 13,14), 'If there be no resurrection of the dead, then is Christ not risen. And if Christ be not risen, then is our preaching vain, and your faith is also vain.'

To assist us in conceiving of it, the Scripture gives us types of the resurrection of the dead; as the dry bones living (Ezek, chap 37); Jonah's coming out of the whale's belly (Matt 12.40). And nature affords us emblems and resemblances of it; as the sun's setting and rising again, night and day, winter and summer, sleeping and waking; swallows in winter lying without any appearance of life, in ruinous buildings and subterraneous caverns, and reviving again in the spring season; the seed dying under the clod, and springing up again: all which, and the like, may justly be admitted as designed by the God of nature, though not for proofs, yet for memorials of the resurrection; whereof we have assurance

---

[1] Their souls are actually so, and enjoy communion with Him, and with saints and angels.

from the Scripture (1 Cor 15.36), 'Thou fool, that which thou sowest is not quickened, except it die.'

11 : I shall inquire into the nature of the resurrection, showing, 1. Who shall be raised. 2. What shall be raised. 3. How the dead shall be raised.

1 : Who shall be raised? Our text tells us who they are; namely 'all that are in the graves,' that is, all mankind who are dead. As for those persons who are found alive at the second coming of Christ, they shall not die, and soon thereafter be raised again; but such a change shall suddenly pass upon them as shall be to them instead of dying and rising again; so that their bodies shall become like to those bodies which are raised out of the graves (1 Cor 15.51,52), 'We shall not all sleep, but we shall all be changed: in a moment, in the twinkling of an eye.' Hence those that are to be judged at the great day, are distinguished into *quick* and *dead* (Acts 10.42). All the dead shall arise, whether godly or wicked, just or unjust (Acts 24.15), old or young; the whole race of mankind, even those who never saw the sun (Rev 20.12), 'And I saw the dead, small and great, stand before God.' The sea and earth shall give up their dead without reserve, none shall be kept back.

2 : What shall be raised? The bodies of mankind. A man is said to die, when the soul is separated from the body, 'and returns unto God who gave it' (Eccl 12.7). But it is the body only which is laid in the grave, and can be properly said to be raised: wherefore the resurrection, strictly speaking, applies to the body only. Moreover, it is the same body that dies, which shall rise again. At the resurrection, men shall not appear with other bodies, as to substance, than those which they now have, and which are laid down in the grave; but with the self-same bodies, endowed with other qualities. The very notion of a resurrection implies this, since nothing can be said to rise again, but that which falls. But to illustrate it a little, 1. It is plain from Scripture testimony. The apostle asserts, that it is 'this mortal' which 'must put on immortality' (1 Cor 15.53); and that Christ 'shall change our vile body, that it may be fashioned like unto his glorious body' (Phil 3.21).

[380]

Death, in Scripture language, is a sleep, and the resurrection an awaking out of that sleep (Job 14.12); which shows the body rising up, to be the self-same that died. 2. The equity of the divine procedure, both with respect to the godly and the wicked, proves this. It is not reckoned equal among men, that one do the work, and another get the reward. Though the glorifying of the bodies of the saints is not, properly speaking, and in a strict sense, the reward of their services or sufferings on earth; yet this is evident, that it is not at all agreeable to the manner of the divine dispensation, that one body should serve Him, and another be glorified; that one should fight, and another receive the crown. How can it be imagined, that 'the temples of the Holy Ghost,' as the bodies of believers are termed (1 Cor 6.19), should always lie in rubbish, and others be reared up in their stead? that these members of Christ (verse 15), should perish utterly, and other bodies come in their room? No, surely, as the bodies of the saints now bear a part in glorifying God, and some of them suffer in His cause, so they shall partake of the glory that is to be revealed. And these bodies of the wicked, which are laid in the dust, shall be raised again, that the same body which sinned may suffer. Shall one body sin here, and another suffer in hell for that sin? Shall that body which was the soul's companion in sin, lie for ever hid in the dust; and another body which did not act any part in sinning, be its companion in torment? No, no; it is that body which now takes up all their thoughts to provide for its back and belly, that shall be raised up, to suffer in hell. It is that tongue, which is now the swearing, lying tongue, that will need water to cool it, in eternal flames. The same feet that now stand in the way of sinners, and carry men in their ungodly courses, shall stand in the burning lake. And the same covetous and lascivious eyes shall receive the fire and smoke of the pit.

3: How shall the dead be raised? The same Jesus, who was crucified within the gates of Jerusalem, shall, at the last day, to the conviction of all, be declared both Lord and Christ: appearing as Judge of the world, attended with His mighty angels (2 Thess

1.7), 'He shall descend from heaven with a shout, with the voice of the archangel, and with the trump of God' (1 Thess 4.16), 'The trumpet shall sound, and the dead shall be raised' and those who are alive, changed (1 Cor 15.52). Whether this shout, voice, and trumpet, denote some audible voice, or only the workings of Divine power, for the raising of the dead, and other awful purposes of that day, though the former seems probable, I will not positively determine. There is no question but this coming of the Judge of the world will be in greater majesty and terror than we can conceive: yet that awful grandeur, majesty, and state, which was displayed at the giving of the law, namely, thunders heard, lightnings, and a thick cloud upon the mount seen, the Lord descending in fire, the whole mount quaking greatly, and the voice of the trumpet waxing louder and louder (Exod 19.16–19), may help us to form a becoming thought of it. However, the sound of this trumpet shall be heard all the world over; it shall reach the depths of the sea, and of the earth. At this loud alarm, bones shall come together, bone to his bone: the scattered dust of all the dead shall be gathered together, dust to his dust: 'neither shall one thrust another, they shall walk every one in his path;' and, meeting together again, shall make up that very same body which crumbled into dust in the grave. At the same alarming voice shall every soul come into its own body, never more to be separated. The dead can stay no longer in their graves, but must bid an eternal farewell to their long homes: they hear His voice, and must come forth, and receive their final sentence.

Now as there is a great difference between the godly and the wicked, in their life, and in their death; so will there be also in their resurrection.

The godly shall be raised out of their graves, by virtue of the Spirit of Christ, the blessed bond of their union with him (Rom 8.11), 'He that raised up Christ from the dead, shall also quicken your mortal bodies, by His Spirit that dwelleth in you.' Jesus Christ arose from the dead, as the 'first-fruits of them that slept' (1 Cor 15.20), so they that are Christ's shall follow at His coming

[382]

(verse 23). The mystical Head having got above the waters of death, He cannot but bring forth the members after Him, in due time.

They shall come forth with inexpressible joy; for then shall that passage of Scripture, which, in its immediate scope, respected the Babylonish captivity, be fully accomplished in its most extensive meaning (Isa 26.19), 'Awake and sing, ye that dwell in the dust.' As a bride adorned for her husband goes forth of her bedchamber unto the marriage: so shall the saints go forth of their graves, unto the marriage of the Lamb. Joseph had a joyful coming out from the prison, Daniel from the lions' den, and Jonah from the whale's belly: yet these are but faint representations of the saints' coming forth from the grave, at the resurrection. Then shall they sing the song of Moses and of the Lamb, in highest strains, death being quite swallowed up in victory. They had, while in this life, sometimes sung by faith the triumphant song over death and the grave, 'O death, where is thy sting? O grave where is thy victory?' (1 Cor 15.55). But then they sing the same from sight and sense; the black band of doubts and fears, which frequently disturbed them, and disquieted their minds, is for ever dispersed and driven away.

May we not suppose the soul and body of every saint, as in mutual embraces, to rejoice in each other, and triumph in their happy meeting again? and the body to address the soul thus? 'O my soul, have we got together again, after so long a separation! art thou come back to thine old habitation, never more to remove! O joyful meeting! how unlike is our present state to what our case was, when a separation was made between us at death! Now is our mourning turned into joy; the light and gladness sown before, are now sprung up; and there is a perpetual spring in Immanuel's land. Blessed be the day in which I was united to thee, whose chief care was to get Christ in us the hope of glory, and to make me a temple for His Holy Spirit. O blessed soul, which in the time of our pilgrimage, kept thine eye on the land then afar off, but now near at hand! thou tookest me into secret places, and there madest

[383]

me to bow these knees before the Lord, that I might bear a part in our humiliation before Him: and now is the time that I am lifted up. Thou didst employ this tongue in confessions, petitions, and thanksgivings, which henceforth shall be employed in praising for evermore. Thou madest these sometimes weeping eyes sow that seed of tears, which is now sprung up in joy that shall never end. I was happily beat down by thee, and kept in subjection, while others pampered their flesh, and made their bellies their gods, to their own destruction; but now I gloriously arise, to take my place in the mansions of glory, whilst they are dragged out of their graves to be cast into fiery flames. Now, my soul, thou shalt complain no more of a sick and pained body; thou shalt be no more clogged with weak and weary flesh; I shall now keep pace with thee in the praises of our God for evermore.' And may not the soul say, 'O happy day in which I return to dwell in that blessed body, which was, and is, and will be for ever, a member of Christ, a temple of the Holy Spirit! Now I shall be eternally knit to thee: the silver cord shall never be loosed more: death shall never make another separation between us. Arise then, my body, and come away! and let these eyes, which were wont to weep over my sins, behold with joy the face of our glorious Redeemer; lo! this is our God, and we have waited for Him. Let these ears, which were wont to hear the Word of life in the temple below, come and hear the hallelujahs in the temple above. Let these feet, that carried me to the congregation of saints on earth, take their place among those in heaven. And let this tongue, which confessed Christ before men, and used to be still dropping something to His commendation, join the choir of the upper house in His praises for evermore. You will fast no more, but keep an everlasting feast; you will weep no more, neither shall your countenance be overclouded; but you will shine for ever as a star in the firmament. We took part together in the fight, come, let us go together to receive and wear the crown.'

But on the other hand, the wicked shall be raised by the power of Christ, as a just Judge, who is to render vengeance to His

[384]

enemies. The same divine power which shut up their souls in hell, and kept their bodies in the grave, as in the prison, shall bring them forth, that soul and body together may receive the dreadful sentence of eternal damnation, and be shut up together in the prison of hell.

They shall come forth from their graves with unspeakable horror and consternation. They shall be dragged forth, as so many malefactors out of a dungeon, to be led to execution; crying to the mountains and to the rocks to fall on them, and hide them from the face of the Lamb. Fearful was the cry in Egypt, the night on which the destroying angel went through, and slew their first-born. Dreadful were the shouts, at the earth opening her mouth, and swallowing up Dathan and Abiram, and all that appertained to them. What hideous crying then must there be, when at the sound of the last trumpet, the earth and sea shall open their mouths, and cast forth all the wicked world, delivering them up to the dreadful Judge! How will they cry, roar, and tear themselves! How will the jovial companions weep and howl, and curse one another! How will the earth be filled with their doleful shrieks and lamentations, while they are pulled out like sheep for the slaughter! They who, while they lived in this world, were profane, debauchees, covetous worldlings, or formal hypocrites, shall then, in anguish of mind, wring their hands, beat their breasts, and bitterly lament their case, roaring forth their complaints, and calling themselves beasts, fools, and madmen, for having acted so mad a part in this life, in not believing what they then heard. They were driven away in their wickedness, at death: and now all their sins rise with them; and, like so many serpents, twist themselves about their wretched souls, and bodies too, which have a frightful meeting, after a long separation.

Then we may suppose the miserable body thus to accost the soul, 'Hast thou again found me, O mine enemy, my worst enemy, savage soul, more cruel than a thousand tigers. Cursed be the day that ever we met. O that I had never received sense, life, and motion! O that I had rather been the body of a toad, or serpent, than thy body; for then had I lain still, and had not seen this terrible day! If I was to be necessarily thine, O that I had been thy ass, or one of thy dogs, rather than thy body; for then wouldst thou have taken more true care of me than thou didst! O cruel kindness! hast thou thus hugged me to death, thus nourished me to the slaughter? Is this the effect of thy tenderness for me? Is this what I am to reap of thy pains and concern about me? What do riches and pleasures avail now, when this fearful reckoning is come of which thou hadst fair warning? O cruel grave! why didst thou not close thy mouth upon me for ever? Why didst thou not hold fast thy prisoner? Why hast thou shaken me out, while I lay still and was at rest? Cursed soul, wherefore didst thou not abide in thy place, wrapped up in flames of fire? Wherefore art thou come back to take me also down to the bars of the pit? Thou madest me an instrument of unrighteousness; and now I must be thrown into the fire. This tongue was by thee employed in mocking at religion, cursing, swearing, lying, backbiting, and boasting; and withheld from glorifying God: and now it must not have so much as a drop of water to cool it in the flames. Thou didst withdraw mine ears from hearing the sermons which gave warning of this day. Thou foundest ways and means to stop them from attending to seasonable exhortations, admonitions, and reproofs. But why didst thou not stop them from hearing the sound of this dreadful trumpet? Why dost thou not rove and fly away on the wings of imagination, thereby, as it were, transporting me during these frightful transactions, as thou wast wont to do, when I was set down at sermons, communions, prayers, and godly conferences; that I might now have as little sense of the one, as I formerly had of the other? But ah! I must burn for ever, for thy love to thy lusts, thy profanity, thy sensuality, thy unbelief, and hypocrisy.' But may not the soul answer – 'Wretched and vile carcase! I am now driven back into thee. O that thou hadst lain for ever in thy grave! Had I not torment enough before? Must I be knit to thee again, that, being joined together as two dry sticks for the fire, the wrath of God may burn us up? It was by caring for

[386]

you, that I lost myself. It was your back and your belly, and the gratifying of your senses, which ruined me. How often was I ensnared by your ears! how often betrayed by your eyes! It was to spare you, that I neglected opportunities of making peace with God, loitered away Sabbaths, lived in the neglect of prayer; went to the house of mirth, rather than to the house of mourning; and that I chose to deny Christ, and forsake His cause and interest in the world; and so am fallen a sacrifice to your cursed ease. When at any time my conscience began to awake, and I was setting myself to think of my sins, and the misery which I have felt since we parted, and now feel, it was you that diverted me from these thoughts, and drew me off to make provision for you. O wretched flesh! by your silken cords of fleshly lusts I was drawn to destruction, in defiance of my light and conscience: but now they are turned into iron chains, with which I am to be held under wrath for evermore. Ah wretched profits! ah cursed pleasures! for which I must lie for ever in utter darkness!' – But no complaints will then avail. O that men were wise, that they understood this, that they would consider their latter end!

As to the qualities with which the bodies of the saints shall be endowed at the resurrection, the apostle tells us, they shall be raised incorruptible, glorious, powerful, and spiritual (1 Cor 15.42–44), 'It is sown in corruption, it is raised in incorruption: it is sown in dishonour, it is raised in glory: it is sown in weakness, it is raised in power: it is sown a natural body, it is raised a spiritual body.'

1: The bodies of the saints shall be raised incorruptible. They are now, as the bodies of others, a mass of corruption, full of the seeds of diseases and death; and, when dead, become so offensive, even to their dearest friends, that they must be buried out of their sight, and cast into the grave: yea, loathsome sores and diseases make some of them very unsightly, even while alive. But, at the resurrection, they leave all the seeds of corruption behind them in the grave; and rise incorruptible, incapable of the least indisposition, sickness, or sore, and much more, of dying. External

[387]

violences and inward causes of pain, shall for ever cease; they shall feel it no more, yea, they shall have an everlasting youth and vigour, being no more subject to the decays which age produced in this life.

2: They shall be glorious bodies; not only beautiful, comely, and well-proportioned, but full of splendour and brightness. The most beautiful face, and best proportioned body, that now appears in the world, is not to be named in comparison with the body of the meanest saint at the resurrection; for 'then shall the righteous shine forth as the sun' (Matt 13.43). If there was a dazzling glory on Moses' face, when he came down from the mount; and if Stephen's face was 'as it had been the face of an angel,' when he stood before the council, how much more shall the faces of the saints be beautiful and glorious, full of sweet agreeable majesty, when they have put off all corruption, and shine as the sun! But observe, this beauty of the saints is not restricted to their faces, but diffuses itself through their whole bodies: for the whole body is raised in glory, and shall be fashioned like unto their Lord and Saviour's glorious body, in whose transfiguration, not only did His face shine as the sun, but His raiment also was white as the light (Matt 17.2). Whatever defects or deformities the bodies of the saints had when laid in the grave, occasioned by accidents in life, or arising from secret causes in their formation, they shall rise out of the grave free of all these. But suppose the marks of the Lord Jesus, the scars or prints of the wounds and bruises which some of the saints received while on earth, for His sake, should remain in their bodies after the resurrection; the same as the print of the nails remained in the Lord Jesus's body after His resurrection: these marks will rather be badges of distinction, and add to their glory, than detract from their beauty. But however that be, surely Isaac's eyes shall not then be dim, nor will Jacob halt: Leah shall not be tender-eyed, nor Mephibosheth lame of his legs. For as the goldsmith melts down the old cracked vessel, and casts it over again in a new mould, bringing it forth with a new lustre, so shall the vile body, which lay dissolved in the grave, come forth at the resurrection, in perfect beauty and comely proportion.

3: They shall be powerful and strong bodies. The strongest men on earth, being frail and mortal, may justly be reckoned weak and feeble, for their strength, however great, is quickly worn out and consumed. Many of the saints now have weaker bodies than others; but 'the feeble among them,' to allude to Zech 12.8, at that day shall be 'as David, and the house of David shall be as God.' A grave divine says, that one shall be stronger at the resurrection than a hundred, yea, than thousands are now. Certainly great, and vastly great, must the strength of glorified bodies be; for they shall bear up under an exceeding and eternal weight of glory. The mortal body is not at all adapted to such a state. Do transports of joy occasion death, as well as excessive grief. And can it bear up under a weight of glory? Can it subsist in union with a soul filled with heaven's rapture? Surely not. The mortal body would sink under that load, and such fulness of joy would make the earthen pitcher to fly all in pieces.

The Scripture has plainly told us, 'That flesh and blood,' namely, in their present frail state, though it were the flesh and blood of a giant, 'cannot inherit the kingdom of God' (1 Cor 15.50). How strong must the bodily eyes be, which, to the soul's eternal comfort, shall behold the dazzling glory and splendour of the New Jerusalem, and steadfastly look at the transcendent glory and brightness of the man Christ, the Lamb, who is the light of that city, the inhabitants whereof shall shine as the sun! The Lord of heaven doth now in mercy 'hold back the face of his throne, and spreadeth his cloud upon it;' (Job 26.9) that mortals may not be confounded with the rays of glory which shine forth from it. But then the veil shall be removed, and they made able to behold it, to their unspeakable joy. How strong must their bodies be, who shall not rest night nor day, but be, without intermission, for ever employed in the heavenly temple, to sing and proclaim the praises of God without weariness, which is a weakness incident to the frail mortal, but not to the glorified body!

4. They shall be spiritual bodies. Not that they shall be changed into spirits, but they shall be spiritual as to their spirit-like qualities and endowments. The body shall be absolutely subservient to the soul, subject to it, and influenced by it, and therefore no more a clog to its activity, nor the animal appetites a snare to it. There will be no need to beat it down, nor to drag it to the service of God. The soul in this life is so much influenced by the body, that, in Scripture style, it is said to be carnal; but then the body shall be spiritual, readily serving the soul in the business of heaven, and in that only, as if it had no more relation to earth than a spirit. It will have no further need of the now necessary supports of life, namely, food, and raiment, and the like. 'They shall hunger no more, neither thirst any more' (Rev 7.16). 'For in the resurrection, they neither marry, nor are given in marriage, but are as the angels of God in heaven.' Then shall the saints be strong without meat or drink, warm without clothes, ever in perfect health without medicine, and ever fresh and vigorous, though they shall never sleep, but serve Him night and day in His temple (Rev 7.15). They will need none of these things, any more than spirits do. They will be nimble and active as spirits, and of a most refined constitution. The body, that is now lumpish and heavy, shall then be most sprightly. No such thing as melancholy shall be found to make the heart heavy, and the spirits flag and sink. I shall not further dip into this matter: the day will declare it.

As to the qualities of the bodies of the wicked at the resurrection, I find the Scripture speaks but little of them. Whatever they may need, they shall not get a drop of water to cool their tongues (Luke 16.24,25). Whatever may be said of their weakness, it is certain they will be continued for ever in life, that they may be ever dying; they shall bear up, however unwillingly, under the load of God's wrath, and shall not faint away under it. 'The smoke of their torment ascendeth up for ever and ever. And they have no rest day nor night.' Surely they shall not partake of the glory and beauty of the saints. All their glory dies with them, and shall never rise again. Daniel tells us, they shall awake to shame and everlasting contempt (chap 12.2). Shame follows sin, as the shadow follows the body: but the wicked in this world walk in the dark, and often under a disguise: nevertheless, when the Judge comes in flaming fire at the last day, they will be brought to the light; their mask will be taken off, and the shame of their nakedness will clearly appear to themselves and others, and fill their faces with confusion. Their shame will be too deep for blushes: all faces shall gather blackness at that day, when they shall go forth from their graves, as malefactors out of their prisons, to execution: for their resurrection is the resurrection of damnation. The greatest beauties, who now pride themselves in their comeliness of body, not regarding their deformed souls, will then appear with a ghastly countenance, a grim and death-like visage. Their looks will be frightful, and they will be horrible spectacles, coming forth from their graves, like infernal furies out of the pit. They shall rise also to everlasting contempt. They shall then be the most contemptible creatures, filled with contempt from God, as vessels of dishonour, whatever honourable employments they had in this world; and filled also with contempt from men. They will be most despicable in the eyes of the saints; even of those saints who gave them honour here, either for their high station, the gifts of God in them, or because they were of the same human nature with themselves. But then their bodies shall be as so many loathsome carcases, which they shall go forth and look upon with abhorrence; yea, 'They shall be an abhorring unto all flesh' (Isa 66.24). The word here rendered 'an abhorring,' is the same which in the other text is rendered 'contempt,' and Isaiah and Daniel point at one and the same thing, namely, the loathsomeness of the wicked at the resurrection. They will be loathsome in the eyes of one another. The unclean wretches were never so lovely to each other as then they will be loathsome; dear companions in sin will then abhor one another; and the great and honourable men who were wicked, shall be no more regarded by their wicked subjects, their servants, their slaves, than the mire in the streets.

Use 1: Of comfort to the people of God. The doctrine of the resurrection is a spring of consolation and joy unto you. Think on it, O believers, when you are in the house of mourning for the loss of your godly relations or friends, 'that ye sorrow not, even as others which have no hope;' for you will meet again (1 Thess 4.13,14). They are but laid down to rest in their beds for a little while (Isa 57.2); but in the morning of the resurrection they will awake again, and come forth out of their graves. The vessel of honour was but coarse, it had much alloy of base metal in it; it was too weak, too dim and inglorious, for the upper house, whatever lustre it had in the lower one. It was cracked, it was polluted; and therefore it must be melted down, to be refined and fashioned more gloriously. Do but wait a while, and you shall see it come forth out of the furnace of earth, vying with the stars in brightness; nay, as the sun when he goes forth in his might. Have you laid your infant children in the grave? You will see them again. Your God calls himself 'the God of your seed;' which, according to our Saviour's exposition, secures the glorious resurrection of the body. Wherefore, let the covenant you embraced for yourself, and your babes now in the dust, comfort your heart, in the joyful expectation that, by virtue thereof, they shall be raised up in glory; and that, as being no more infants of days, but brought to a full and perfect stature, as is generally supposed. Be not discouraged by reason of a weak and sickly body: there is a day coming, when you shall be every whit whole. At the resurrection, Timothy shall be no more liable to his often infirmities; his body, that was weak and sickly, even in youth, shall be raised in power: Lazarus shall be healthy and sound, his body being raised incorruptible. Although perhaps your weakness will not allow you now to go one furlong to meet the Lord in public ordinances, yet the day is coming, when your body shall be no more a clog to you, but you shall 'meet the Lord in the air' (1 Thess 4.17). It will be with the saints coming up from the grave, as with the Israelites when they came out of Egypt. (Psa 105.37), 'There was not one feeble person among their tribes.' Have you an uncomely or deformed body? There is a

glory within, which will then set all right without, according
to all the desire of your heart. It shall rise a glorious, beautiful, handsome, and well-proportioned body. Its uncomeliness
or deformities may go with it to the grave, but they shall not
come back with it. O that those who are now so desirous to be
beautiful and handsome, would not be too hasty to effect it with
their foolish and sinful arts, but wait and study the heavenly art
of beautifying the body, by endeavouring now to become all
glorious within, with the graces of God's Spirit! This would at
length make them admirable and everlasting beauties. You must
indeed, O believer, grapple with death, and will get the first fall:
but you will rise again, and come off victorious at last. You must
go down to the grave; but, though it be your long home, it will not
be your everlasting home. You will not hear the voice of your
friends there; but you will hear the voice of Christ there. You
may be carried thither with mourning, but you will come up from
it rejoicing. Your friends, indeed, will leave you there, but your
God will not. What God said to Jacob, concerning his going down
to Egypt (Gen 46.3,4), he says to you, concerning your going down
to the grave, 'Fear not to go down – I will go down with thee –
and I will also surely bring thee up again.' O solid comfort! O
glorious hopes! 'Wherefore comfort' yourselves, and 'one another
with these words' (1 Thess 4.18).

Use 2: Of terror to all unregenerate men. You who are yet in
your natural state, look at this view of the eternal state; and consider what will be your part in it, if you be not in time brought
into a state of grace. Think, O sinner, on that day when the trumpet shall sound, at the voice of which the bars of the pit shall be
broken asunder, the doors of the grave shall fly open, the devouring depths of the sea shall throw up their dead, the earth cast forth
hers; and death everywhere, in the excess of astonishment, shall
let go its prisoners; and your wretched soul and body shall be
re-united, to be summoned before the tribunal of God. Then, if
you had a thousand worlds at your disposal, you would gladly

give them all away, on condition that you might lie still in your grave, with the hundredth part of that ease wherewith you have sometimes lain at home on the Lord's day; or, if that cannot be obtained, that you might be but a spectator of the transactions of that day; as you have been at some solemn occasions, and rich gospel feasts; or, if even that is not to be purchased, that a mountain or a rock might fall on you, and cover you from the face of the Lamb. Ah! how are men bewitched, thus to trifle away the precious time of life, in almost as little concern about death as if they were like the beasts that perish! Some will be telling where their corpses must be laid; while yet they have not seriously considered whether their graves shall be their beds, where they shall awake with joy, in the morning of the resurrection; or their prisons, out of which they shall be brought to receive the fearful sentence. Remember, now is your seed-time; and as you sow, so shall you reap. God's seed-time begins at death; and at the resurrection the bodies of the wicked, that were sown 'full of sins, that lie down with them in the dust' (Job 20.11), shall spring up again, sinful, wretched, and vile. Your bodies, which are now instruments of sin, the Lord will lay aside for the fire at death, and bring them forth for the fire at the resurrection. That body, which is not employed in God's service, but is abused by uncleanness and lasciviousness, will then be brought forth in all its vileness, thenceforth to lodge with unclean spirits. The body of the drunkard shall then stagger, by reason of the wine of the wrath of God poured out to him, and poured into him, without mixture. Those who now please themselves in their revellings will reel to and fro at another rate, when, instead of their songs and music, they shall hear the sound of the last trumpet. Many weary their bodies for worldly gain, who will be loath to distress them for the benefit of their souls; by labour, unreasonably hard, they will quite unfit them for the service of God; and, when they have done, will reckon it a very good reason for shifting duty, that they are already tired out with other business; but the day is com-

[394]

ing, when they will be made to abide a yet greater distress. Many will go several miles for back and belly, who will not go half the way for the good of their immortal souls; many will be sickly and unable on the Lord's day, who will be tolerably well all the rest of the week. But when that trumpet sounds, the dead shall find their feet, and none shall be missing in that great congregation. When the bodies of the saints shine as the sun, frightful will the looks of their persecutors be. Fearful will their condition be, who shut up the saints in prison, stigmatized, burnt them to ashes, hanged them, and stuck up their heads and hands in public places, to frighten others from the way of righteousness for which they suffered. Many faces, now fair, will then gather blackness. They shall be no more admired and caressed for that beauty which has a worm at the root, that will cause it to issue in loathsomeness and deformity. Ah! what is that beauty, under which there lurks a monstrous, deformed, and graceless heart? What, but a sorry paint, a slight varnish; which will leave the body so much the more ugly before that flaming fire, in which the Judge shall be 'revealed from heaven, taking vengeance on them that know not God, and that obey not the gospel?' (2 Thess 1.7,8). They shall be stripped of all their ornaments, and not have a rag to cover their nakedness: but their carcases shall be an abhorrence to all flesh, and serve as a foil to set off the beauty and glory of the righteous, and make it appear the brighter.

Now is the time to secure, for yourselves, a part in the resurrection of the just: which if you would do, unite with Jesus Christ by faith, rising spiritually from sin, and glorifying God with your bodies. He is the 'resurrection and the life' (John 11.25). If your bodies be members of Christ, temples of the Holy Ghost, they shall certainly arise in glory. Get into this ark now, and you shall come forth with joy into the new world. Rise from your sins; cast away these grave-clothes, putting off your former lusts. How can any one imagine, that those who continue dead while they live, shall come forth, at the last day, unto the resurrection of life?

But that will be the privilege of all those who, having first consecrated their souls and bodies to the Lord by faith, do glorify
Him with their bodies, as well as their souls; living and acting to
Him, and for Him, yea, and suffering for Him too, when He calls
them to it.

4

THE GENERAL JUDGMENT

When the Son of man shall come in his glory, and
all the holy angels with him, then shall he sit upon
the throne of his glory. And before him shall be
gathered all nations; and he shall separate them one
from another, as a shepherd divideth his sheep from
the goats: and he shall set the sheep on his right
hand, but the goats on the left. Then shall the King
say unto them on his right hand, Come, ye blessed,
&c. – Unto them on the left hand, Depart from me,
ye cursed, &c. – And these shall go away into everlasting punishment; but the righteous into life
eternal.   MATTHEW 25.31–34,41,46

The dead being raised, and those found alive at the coming of the
Judge changed, then follows the general judgment, plainly and
awfully described in this portion of Scripture; in which we shall
take notice of the following particulars: 1. The coming of the
Judge: 'When the Son of man shall come in his glory,' &c. The
Judge is Jesus Christ, 'the Son of man;' the same by whose
almighty power, as He is God, the dead will be raised. He is also
called the King (verse 34), the judging of the world being an act
of the royal Mediator's kingly office. He will come in glory;
glorious in His own person, and having a glorious retinue, even
all the holy angels with Him, to minister to Him at this great
solemnity. 2. The Judge's mounting the tribunal. He is a King,
and therefore it is a throne, a glorious throne: 'He shall sit upon
the throne of his glory' (verse 31). 3. The attendance of the parties.
These are, all nations; all and every one, small and great, of whatever nation, who ever were, are, or shall be on the face of the
earth; all shall be gathered before Him, summoned before His
tribunal. 4. The sorting of them. He shall separate the elect sheep
and reprobate goats, setting each party by themselves, as a

shepherd, who feeds his sheep and goats together all the day, separates them at night (verse 32). The godly He will set on His right hand, as the most honourable place; the wicked on the left (verse 33). Yet so as they shall be both before Him (verse 32). It seems to be an allusion to a custom in the Jewish courts, in which one sat on the right hand of the judges, who wrote the sentence of absolution; another at their left, who wrote the sentence of condemnation. 5. The sentencing of the parties, and that according to their works, the righteous being absolved, and the wicked condemned (verses 34–41). 6. The execution of both sentences, in the driving away of the wicked into hell, and carrying the godly to heaven (verse 46).

DOCTRINE: *There shall be a general judgment*

This doctrine I shall, 1: Confirm; 2: Explain; and then Apply.

1: For confirmation of this great truth, that there shall be a general judgment.

1: It is evident from plain Scripture testimonies. The world has in all ages been told of it. Enoch, before the flood, taught it in his prophecy, related in Jude (verses 14, 15), 'Behold the Lord cometh with ten thousands of his saints, to execute judgment upon all,' &c. Daniel describes it (chapter 7.9,10), 'I beheld till the thrones were cast down, and the Ancient of days did sit, whose garment was white as snow, and the hair of his head like the pure wool: his throne was like a fiery flame, and his wheels as burning fire. A fiery stream issued and came forth from before him: thousand thousands ministered unto him and ten thousand times ten thousand stood before him: the judgment was set, and the books were opened.' The apostle is very express (Acts 17.31), 'He hath appointed a day, in the which he will judge the world in righteousness, by that man whom he hath ordained.' (See Matt 16.27; 2 Cor 5.10; 2 Thess 1.7–10; Rev. 20.11–15.) God has not only said it, but He has sworn it (Rom 14.10,11), 'We must all stand before the judgment seat of Christ. For it is written, As I

[398]

live, saith the Lord, every knee shall bow to me, and every tongue shall confess to God.' So that the truth of God is most solemnly plighted for it.

2: The perfect justice and goodness of God, the sovereign Ruler of the world, necessarily require it, inasmuch as they require its being well with the righteous, and ill with the wicked. Yet we often see wickedness exalted, while truth and righteousness fall in the streets; piety oppressed, while profanity and irreligion triumph. This is so very common, that every one who sincerely embraces the way of holiness, must and does lay his account with the loss of all he has, which the world can take away from him (Luke 14.26), 'If any man come to me, and hate not his father, and mother, and wife, and children, and brethren, and sisters, yea, and his own life also, he cannot be my disciple.' But it is inconsistent with the justice and goodness of God that the affairs of men should always continue in the state which they appear in from one generation to another, and that every man should not be rewarded according to his works: and since that is not done in this life, there must be a judgment to come; 'Seeing it is a righteous thing with God to recompense tribulation to them that trouble you; and to you who are troubled, rest with us, when the Lord Jesus shall be revealed from heaven' (2 Thess 1.6,7). There will be a day in which the tables will be turned, and the wicked shall be called to an account for all their sins, suffering the due punishment of them; and the pious shall be the prosperous: for, as the apostle argues for the happy resurrection of the saints, 'If in this life only we have hope in Christ, we are of all men most miserable' (1 Cor 15.19). It is true, God sometimes punishes the wicked in this life: that men may know, 'He is a God that judgeth in the earth:' but yet much wickedness remains unpunished and undiscovered, to be a pledge of the judgment to come. If none of the wicked were punished here, they would conclude that God had utterly forsaken the earth; if all of them were punished in this life, men would be apt to think there is no after reckoning. Therefore, in the wisdom of God some are punished now, and some not. Sometimes the Lord smites sinners in the very act of sin, to show unto the world that He is witness to all their wickedness, and will call them to an account for it. Sometimes He delays long before He strikes, that He may discover to the world that He forgets not men's ill deeds, though He does not immediately punish them. Besides all this, the sins of many outlive them; and the impure fountain opened by them, runs long after they are dead and gone. As in the case of Jeroboam, the first king of the ten tribes, whose sin ran all along unto the end of that unhappy kingdom (2 Kings 17.22,23), 'The children of Israel walked in all the sins of Jeroboam, which he did; they departed not from them; until the Lord removed Israel out of his sight.'

3 : The resurrection of Christ is a certain proof that there shall be a day of judgment. This argument Paul uses to convince the Athenians that Jesus Christ will be the Judge of the world; 'Whereof,' says he, 'he hath given assurance to all men, in that he hath raised him from the dead' (Acts 17.31). The Judge is already named, His patent written and sealed, yea, and read before all men, in His rising again from the dead. Hereby God has given assurance of it : by raising Christ from the dead, He has exhibited His credentials as Judge of the world. When, in the days of His humiliation, He was cited before a tribunal, arraigned, accused, and condemned of men, He plainly told them of this judgment, and that He Himself would be the Judge (Matt 26.64), 'Hereafter shall ye see the Son of man sitting on the right hand of power, and coming in the clouds of heaven.' And now that He is raised from the dead, though condemned as a blasphemer on this very head, is it not an undeniable proof from Heaven of the truth of what He asserted? Moreover, this was one of the great ends of Christ's death and resurrection : 'For to this end Christ both died, and rose, and revived, that He might be the Lord,' that is, 'the Lord Judge,' as is evident from the context, 'both of the dead and of the living' (Rom 14.9).

4 : Every man bears about with him a witness to this within his own breast (Rom 2.15), 'Which show the work of the law

written in their hearts, their conscience also bearing witness, and their thoughts the meanwhile accusing, or else excusing one another.' There is a tribunal erected within every man, where conscience is accuser, witness, and judge, binding over the sinner to the judgment of God. This fills the most profligate wretches with horror, and inwardly stings them, upon the commission of some atrocious crime; in effect summoning them to answer for it before the Judge of the quick and dead. And this it does, even when the crime is secret, and hid from the eyes of the world. It reaches those whom the laws of men cannot reach, because of their power or craft. Men have fled from the judgment of their fellow-creatures; yet go where they will, conscience, as the supreme Judge's officer, still keeps hold of them, reserving them in its chains, to the judgment of the great day. And whether they escape punishment from men, or fall by the hand of public justice, when they perceive death's approach, they hear from within of this after reckoning; being constrained to hearken to it, in these the most serious minutes of their lives. If there be some in whom nothing of this appears, we have no more ground thence to conclude against it, than we have to conclude, that because some men do not groan, therefore they have no pain; or that dying is a mere jest, because there have been some who seemed to make little else of it. A good face may be put upon an ill conscience; the more hopeless men's case is, they reckon it the more their interest to make no reflections on their state and case. But every one, who will consult himself seriously, will find in himself the witness to the judgment to come. Even the heathens wanted not a notion of it, though mixed with fictions of their own. Hence, though some of the Athenians, 'when they heard of the resurrection of the dead, mocked,' yet there is no account of their mocking, when they heard of the general judgment (Acts 17.31,32).

11: For explication, the following particulars may serve to give some view of the transactions of that great day.

1: God shall judge the world by Jesus Christ. 'He will judge the world in righteousness by that man whom he hath ordained'

(Acts 17.31). The psalmist tells us, that God is Judge Himself (Psa 50.6). The holy blessed Trinity, Father, Son, and Holy Ghost is Judge, in respect to judicial authority, dominion, and power: but the Son incarnate is the Judge in respect of dispensation, and special exercise of that power. The judgment shall be exercised or performed by Him as the royal Mediator; for He has delegated power of judgment from the Father, as His Servant, 'his King,' whom He hath 'set upon his holy hill of Zion' (Psa 2.6), and to whom He 'hath committed all judgment' (John 5.22). This is a part of the Mediator's exaltation, given Him in consequence of His voluntary humiliation (Phil 2.8–10), 'He humbled himself, and became obedient unto death, even the death of the cross. Wherefore God also hath highly exalted him, and given him a name which is above every name,' that is, power and authority over all, 'that at,' or in, 'the name of Jesus,' – not the name Jesus; that is not the name above every name; being common to others, as to Justus (Col 4.11); and Joshua (Heb 4.8), 'every knee shall bow.' This is explained by the apostle himself, of 'standing before the judgment-seat of Christ' (Rom 14.10,11). So He who was judged and condemned of men, shall be the Judge of men and angels.

2 : Jesus Christ the Judge, descending from heaven into the air (1 Thess 4.16,17), 'shall come in the clouds of heaven, with power and great glory' (Matt 24.30). This His coming will be a mighty surprise to the world, which will be found in deep security, foolish virgins sleeping, and the wise slumbering. There will then be much luxury and debauchery in the world, little sobriety and watchfulness; much business, but a great scarcity of faith and holiness. 'As it was in the days of Noah, so also shall it be in the days of the Son of man. They did eat, they drank, they married wives, they were given in marriage, until the day that Noe entered into the ark: and the flood came, and destroyed them all. Likewise also as it was in the days of Lot: they did eat, they drank, they bought, they sold, they planted, they builded. Even thus shall it be in the day when the Son of man is revealed'

(Luke 17.26–30). The coming of the Judge will surprise some at markets, buying and selling; others at table, eating and drinking, and making merry; others busy with their new plantings; some building new houses; nay, the wedding-day of some will be their own and the world's judgment-day. But the Judge cometh! the markets are marred; the buyer throws away what he has bought; the seller casts down his money; they are raised from the table, and their mirth is extinguished in a moment. Though the tree be set in the earth, the gardener cannot stay to cast the earth about it; the workmen throw away their tools, when the house is half built, and the owner regards it no more; the bridegroom, bride, and guests, must leave the wedding feast, and appear before the tribunal; for, 'Behold, he cometh with clouds, and every eye shall see him' (Rev 1.7). He shall come most gloriously; for He will 'come in the glory of his Father, with the holy angels' (Mark 8.38). When He came in the flesh, to die for sinners, He laid aside the robes of His glory, and was despised and rejected of men: but when He comes again, to judge the world, such shall be His visible glory and majesty, that it shall cast an eternal veil over all earthly glory, and fill His greatest enemies with fear and dread. Never had prince and potentate in the world such a glorious train as will accompany this Judge: all the holy angels shall come with Him, for His honour and service. Then He, who was led to the cross with a band of soldiers, will be gloriously attended to the place of judgment, by 'not a multitude of the heavenly host,' but the whole host of angels: 'all His holy angels,' says the text.

3: At the coming of the Judge, the summons is given to the parties by the sound of the last trumpet, at which the dead are raised, and those found alive are changed (see 1 Thess 4.16,17). O loud trumpet, that shall be heard at once in all corners of the earth and of the sea! O wonderful voice, that will not only disturb those who sleep in the dust, but effectually awaken, rouse them out of their sleep, and raise them from death! Were trumpets sounding now, drums beating, furious soldiers crying and killing men, women and children running and shrieking, the wounded groaning and dying; those who are in the graves would have no more disturbance than if the world were in most profound peace. Yea, were stormy winds casting down the lofty oaks, the seas roaring and swallowing up the ships, the most dreadful thunders going along the heavens, lightnings everywhere flashing, the earth quaking, trembling, opening, and swallowing up whole cities, and burying multitudes at once; the dead would still enjoy a perfect repose, and sleep soundly in the dust, though their own dust should be thrown out of its place. But at the sound of this trumpet they shall all awake. The morning is come, they can sleep no longer; the time for the dead to be judged: they must get out of their graves, and appear before the Judge.

4 : The Judge shall sit down on the tribunal; He shall sit on the throne of His glory. He stood before a tribunal on earth, and was condemned as a malefactor: now He shall sit on His own tribunal, and judge the world. He once hung upon the cross, covered with shame; now He shall sit on a throne of glory. What this throne shall be, whether a bright cloud, or what else, I shall not inquire. Our eyes will give an answer to that question at length. John 'saw a great white throne' (Rev 20.11). 'His throne,' says Daniel, 'was like the fiery flame, and his wheels as burning fire' (chapter 7.9). Whatever it be, doubtless it will be a throne glorious beyond expression, in comparison with which the most glorious throne on the earth is but a seat on a dunghill; and the sight of it will equally surprise kings who sat on thrones in this life, and beggars who sat on dunghills. It will be a throne, for stateliness and glory, suited to the quality of Him who shall sit on it. Never had a judge such a throne, and never had a throne such a Judge on it.

Leaving the discovery of the nature of the throne until that day, it concerns us more nearly to consider what a Judge will sit on it; a point on which we are not left to uncertain conjectures. The Judge on the throne will be (1) A Judge visible to our bodily eyes (Rev 1.7), 'Every eye shall see Him.' When God gave the

[404]

law on mount Sinai, the people 'saw no similitude, only they heard a voice:' but when He calls the world to an account, how they have observed His law, the man Christ being Judge, we shall see our Judge with our eyes, either to our eternal comfort, or to our eternal confusion, according to the entertainment which we give Him now. That very body which was crucified without the gates of Jerusalem, between two thieves, shall then be seen on the throne, shining in glory. We now see Him symbolically in the sacrament of His supper; the saints see Him by the eye of faith; then, all shall see Him with those eyes now in their heads. (2) A Judge having full authority and power to render unto every one according to his works. Christ, as God, has authority of Himself; and as Mediator He has a judicial power and authority, which His father has invested Him with, according to the covenant between the Father and the Son for the redemption of sinners. His divine glory will be a light, by which all men shall see clearly to read His commission for this great and honourable employment. 'All power is given unto me in heaven and in earth (Matt 28.18). He has 'the keys of hell and of death' (Rev 1.18). There can be no appeal from His tribunal: sentence once passed there, must stand for ever; there is no reversing it. All appeals are from an inferior to a superior court: but when God gives sentence against a man, where can he find a higher court to bring his suit to? This judgment is the Mediator's judgment, and therefore the last judgment. If the Intercessor be against us, who can be for us? If Christ condemn us, who will absolve us? (3) A Judge of infinite wisdom. His eyes will pierce into, and clearly discern the most intricate cases. His omniscience qualifies Him for judging the most retired thoughts, as well as the words and works. The most subtle sinner shall not be able to deceive Him, nor, by any artful management, to palliate the crime. He is the searcher of hearts, to whom nothing can be hid or perplexed; but all things are naked and open to His eyes (Heb 4.13). (4) A most just Judge; a Judge of perfect integrity. He is the righteous Judge (2 Tim 4.8), and His throne a great white throne (Rev 20.11), from

[405]

whence no judgment shall proceed but what is pure and spotless. The Thebans painted Justice blind, and without hands; because judges ought not to respect persons, nor take bribes. The Areopagites judged in the dark; that they might not regard who spoke, but what was spoken. With the Judge on His throne, there will be no respect of persons; He will neither regard the person of the rich, nor of the poor: but just judgment shall go forth, in every one's cause. (5) An omnipotent Judge, able to put His sentence in execution. The united force of devils and wicked men will be altogether unable to withstand Him. They cannot retard the execution of the sentence against them one moment; far less can they stop it altogether. 'Thousand thousands of angels minister unto him' (Dan 7.10). And, by the breath of His mouth, He can drive the cursed herd whither He pleases.

5: The parties shall appear. These are men and devils. Although the fallen angels were, from the first moment of their sinning, subjected to the wrath of God, and were cast down to hell, and wherever they go they carry their hell about with them; yet it is evident that they are reserved unto judgment (2 Pet 2.4), namely, unto the judgment of the great day (Jude, verse 6). Then they shall be solemnly and publicly judged (1 Cor 6.3), 'Know ye not that we shall judge angels?' At that day they shall answer for their trade of sinning, and tempting to sin, which they have been carrying on from the beginning. Then many a hellish brat, which Satan has laid down at the saints' door, but not adopted by them shall be laid at the door of the true father of it, that is the devil. And he shall receive the due reward of all the dishonour which he has done to God, and of all the mischief which he has done to men. Those wicked spirits now in chains, though not in such strait custody but that they go about, like roaring lions, seeking whom they may devour, shall then receive their final sentence, and be shut up in their den, in the prison; where they shall be held in extreme and unspeakable torment, through all eternity (Rev 20.10). 'And the devil, that deceived them, was cast into the lake of fire and brimstone, where the beast and the false prophet are, and shall be tormented day and night for ever and ever.' In prospect of which, the devils said to Christ, 'Art thou come hither to torment us before the time?' (Matt 8.29).

But what we are chiefly concerned to take notice of, is the case of men at that day. All men must appear before this tribunal. All of each sex, of every age, quality, and condition; the great and small, noble and ignoble; none are excepted. Adam and Eve, with all their sons and daughters, every one who has had or, to the end of the world, shall have a living soul united to a body, will make up this great congregation. Even those who refused to come to the throne of grace, shall be forced to the bar of justice: for there can be no hiding from the all-seeing Judge, no flying from Him who is present every where, no resisting of Him who is armed with almighty power, 'We must all stand before the judgment-seat of Christ' (2 Cor 5.10). 'Before Him shall be gathered all nations,' says the text. This is to be done by the ministry of angels. By them shall the elect be gathered (Mark 13.27), 'Then shall he send his angels, and shall gather together his elect from the four winds.' And they also shall gather the reprobate (Matt 13.40,41), 'So shall it be in the end of this world. The Son of man shall send forth his angels, and they shall gather out of his kingdom all things that offend, and them which do iniquity'. From all corners of the world shall the inhabitants thereof be gathered unto the place where He shall set His throne for judgment.

6: There shall be a separation made between the righteous and the wicked; the fair company of the elect sheep being set on Christ's right hand, and the reprobate goats on His left. There is no necessity to wait for this separation till the trial is over; since the parties will rise out of their graves with plain outward marks of distinction, as was mentioned before. The separation seems to be effected by that double gathering, before mentioned; the one of the elect (Mark 13.27): the other of them that do iniquity (Matt 13.41). The elect, being 'caught up together in the clouds, meet the Lord in the air' (1 Thess 4.17), and so are set on His right hand; and the reprobate left on the earth, are placed upon the

Judge's left hand. Here is now a total separation of two parties, who were always opposite to each other in their principles, aims, and manner of life; who, when together, were a burden the one to the other, under which the one groaned, and the other raged; but now they are finally parted, never to come together any more. The righteous and wicked, like the iron and clay, which could never mix (see Dan 2.41–43), are quite separated; the one being drawn up into the air, by the attractive virtue of 'the stone cut out of the mountain,' namely, Jesus Christ; and the other left upon its earth, to be trod under foot.

Now let us look to the right hand, and there we shall see a glorious company of saints shining, as so many stars in their orbs, and with a cheerful countenance beholding Him who sits upon the throne. Here will be two wonderful sights, which the world never saw. 1. A great congregation of saints, in which there will not be so much as one hypocrite. There was a bloody Cain in Adam's family; a cursed Ham in Noah's family, in the ark; a treacherous Judas in Christ's own family; but in that company there will be none but sealed ones, members of Christ, having all one Father. This is a sight reserved for that day. 2. All the godly upon one side. Seldom or never do the saints on earth make such harmony, but there are some jarring strings among them. It is not to be expected, that men who see but in part, though they are all going to one city, should agree as to every step in the way: no, we must not look for it, in this state of imperfection. But at that day, Paul and Barnabas shall meet in peace and unity, though once 'the contention was so sharp between them, that they departed asunder, the one from the other' (Acts 15.39). There shall be no more divisions, no more separate standing amongst those who belong to Christ. All the godly, of the different parties, shall then be upon one side; seeing, whatever were their differences in lesser things, while in the world, yet even then they all met in one Lord Jesus Christ as their true centre, by a true and lively faith, and in the one way of holiness, or practical godliness.

And vile hypocrites, of whatsoever party, shall be led forth with the workers of iniquity.

Look to the left hand, and there you will see the cursed goats, all the wicked ones, from Cain to the last ungodly person who shall be in the world, gathered together into one most miserable congregation. There are many assemblies of the wicked now; then there shall be but one. But all of them shall be present there, brought together, as one herd for the slaughter, bellowing and roaring, weeping and howling, for the miseries come, and that are coming on them. And remember, you shall not be a mere spectator, to look at these two such different companies; but must yourself take your place in one of the two, and will share with the company, whatever hand it be on. Those who now abhor no society so much as that of the saints, would then be glad to be allowed to get in among them, though it were but to lie at their feet. But then not one tare shall be found with the wheat; He will thoroughly purge His floor. Many of the right-hand men of this world will be left-hand men in that day. Many, who must have the door and the right hand of those who are better than they, if the righteous be more excellent than his neighbour, shall then be turned to the left hand, as most despicable wretches! O how terrible will this separation be to the ungodly! How dreadful will this gathering them together into one company be! What they will not believe, they will then see, namely, that but few are saved. They think it enough now to be neighbour-like, and can securely follow the multitude: but the multitude on the left hand will yield them no comfort. How will it sting the ungodly Christian, to see himself set on the same hand with Turks and Pagans! How will it gall profane Protestants, to stand with idolatrous Papists; praying people, with their profane neighbours who mocked at religious exercises; formal professors, strangers to the new birth and the power of godliness, with persecutors! Now there are many opposite societies in the world; but then all the ungodly shall be in one society. And how dreadful will the faces of companions in sin be to one another there! What doleful shrieks, when the whoremonger and his whore shall meet; when the drunkards, who have had many a jovial day together, shall see one another in the face; when the husband and the wife, the parents and children, masters and servants, and neighbours, who have been snares and stumbling-blocks to one another, to the ruin of their own souls and those of their relatives, shall meet again in that miserable society! Then there will be curses instead of salutations; and tearing of themselves, and raging against one another, instead of the wonted embraces.

7: The parties shall be tried. The trial cannot be difficult, seeing the Judge is omniscient, and nothing can be hid from Him. But, that His righteous judgment may be made evident to all, He will set the hidden things of darkness in the clearest light at that trial (1 Cor 4.5).

Men shall be tried, 1. Upon their works; for 'God shall bring every work into judgment, with every secret thing, whether it be good, or whether it be evil' (Eccl 12.14). The Judge will try every man's conversation, and set his deeds done in the body, with all the circumstances thereof, in a true light. Then will many actions, commended and applauded of men, as good and just, be discovered to have been evil and abominable in the sight of God; and many works, now condemned by the world, will be approved and commended by the great Judge, as good and just. Secret things will be brought to light; and what was hid from the view of the world, shall be laid open. Wickedness, which has kept its lurking place in spite of all human search, will then be brought forth to the glory of God, and the confusion of impenitent sinners, who hid it. The world appears now very vile in the eyes of those who are exercised to godliness; but it will then appear a thousand times more vile, when that which is done of men in secret comes to be discovered. Every good action shall then be remembered; and the hidden religion and good works, most industriously concealed by the saints from the eyes of men, shall no more lie hid: for though the Lord will not allow men to proclaim every one his own goodness, yet He Himself will do it in due

[410]

time. 2. Their words shall be judged (Matt 12.37), 'For by thy words thou shalt be justified, and by thy words thou shalt be condemned.' Not a word spoken for God and His cause in the world, from love to Himself, shall be forgotten. They are all kept in remembrance, and shall be brought forth as evidences of faith, and of an interest in Christ. (Mal 3.16,17), 'Then they that feared the Lord spake often one to another, and the Lord hearkened and heard it; and a book of remembrance was written before him. And they shall be mine, saith the Lord of hosts, in that day when I make up my jewels.' The tongue, which did run at random, shall then confess to God; and the speaker shall find it to have been followed, and every word noted that dropped from the unsanctified lips. 'Every idle word that men shall speak, they shall give account thereof in the day of judgment (Matt 12.36). And if they shall give account of idle words, that is, words spoken to no good purpose, neither for God's glory, nor their own nor their neighbours' good; how much more shall men's wicked words, their sinful oaths, curses, lies, filthy communications, and bitter words, be called over again in that day! The tongues of many shall then fall upon themselves, and ruin them. 3. Men's thoughts shall be brought into judgment: the Judge will make manifest the counsels of the hearts (1 Cor 4.5). Thoughts go free from man's judgment, but not from the judgment of the heart-searching God, who knows men's thoughts, without the help of signs to discern them by. The secret springs of men's actions will then be brought to light; and the sins that never came further than the heart, will then be laid open. O what a figure will man's corrupt nature present, when his inside is turned out, and all his speculative impurities are exposed! The rottenness that is within many a whited sepulchre, the speculative filthiness and wantonness, murder and malignity, now lurking in the hearts of men as in the chambers of imagery, will then be discovered, and what good was in the hearts of any shall no more lie concealed. If it was in their hearts to build a house to the Lord, they shall hear that they did well that it was in their heart.

This trial will be righteous and impartial, accurate and searching, clear and evident. The Judge is the righteous Judge, and He will do right to every one. He has a just balance for good and evil actions, and for honest and false hearts. The fig-leaf cover of hypocrisy will then be blown aside, and the hypocrite's nakedness will appear; as when the Lord came to judge Adam and Eve 'in the cool,' or, as the word is, 'in the wind of the day' (Gen 3.8). 'The fire,' which tries things most exquisitely, 'shall try every man's work, of what sort it is' (1 Cor 3.13). Man's judgment is often perplexed and confused: but here the whole process shall be clear and evident, as written with a sunbeam. It shall be clear to the Judge, to whom no case can be intricate; to the parties, who shall be convinced (Jude, verse 15). And the multitudes on both sides shall see that the Judge is clear when He judges; for then 'the heavens shall declare His righteousness,' in the audience of all the world; and so it shall be universally known (Psa 50.6).

On these accounts it is, that this trial is held out in the Scripture, under the notion of 'opening of books;' and men are said to be 'judged out of those things written in the books' (Rev 20.12). The Judge of the world, who infallibly knows all things, has no need of books to be laid before Him, to prevent mistakes in any point of law or fact; but the expression points at His proceeding as most nice, accurate, just and well-grounded, in every step of it. Now, there are four books that shall be opened in that day.

(1) The book of God's remembrance, or omniscience (Mal 3.16). This is an exact record of every man's state, thoughts, words, and deeds, good or evil: it is, as it were, a day-book, in which the Lord puts down all that passes in men's hearts, lips, and lives; and it is a reckoning up every day that one lives. In it are recorded men's sins and good works, secret and open, with all their circumstances. Here are registered all their privileges, temporal and spiritual mercies, often made ready to their hand; the checks, admonitions, and rebukes, given by teachers, neighbours, afflictions, and men's own consciences; every thing in its due order. This book will serve only as a bill of indictment, in

respect of the ungodly; but it will be for another use in respect of the godly, namely, for a memorial of their good. The opening of it is the Judge's bringing to light what is written in it; the reading as it were, of the bill and memorial, respectively, in their hearing.

(2) The book of conscience will be opened, which shall be as a thousand witnesses to prove the fact (Rom 2.15), 'Which show the work of the law written in their hearts, their conscience also bearing witness.' Conscience is a censor going with every man wherever he goes, taking an account of his deeds done in the body, and, as it were, noting them in a book. Much is written in it which cannot be read now; the writing of conscience being, in many cases, like to that which is made with the juice of lemons, not to be read till it is held before the fire; but then men shall read it clearly and distinctly. The fire which is to try every man's work will make the book of conscience legible in every point.

Though the book be sealed now, the conscience blind, dumb, and deaf, the seals will then be broken, and the book opened. There shall be no more a silent conscience, and far less a seared conscience, amongst all the ungodly crew: but their consciences shall be most quick-sighted, and most lively, in that day. None shall then call good evil, or evil good. Ignorance of what sin is, and what things are sins, will have no place among them: and the subtle reasonings of men, in favour of their lusts, will then be for ever baffled by their own conscience. None shall have the favour, if I may so speak, of lying under the soft cover of delusion; but they shall all be convicted by their conscience. Whether they will or not, they must look on this book, read, be confounded, and stand speechless, knowing that nothing is charged upon them by mistake; since this is a book which was always in their own custody. Thus shall the Judge make every man see himself in the glass of his own conscience, which will make quick work.

(3) The book of the law shall be opened. This book is the standard and rule, by which is known what is right and what is

wrong; as also, what sentence is to be passed accordingly on those who are under it. As to the opening of this book, in its statutory part, which shows what is sin, and what is duty, it agrees with the opening of the book of conscience: for conscience is set, by the sovereign Law-giver, in every man's breast, to be his private teacher, to show him the law; and his private pastor, to make application of the same; and at that day, it will be perfectly fit for its office, so that the conscience, which is most stupid now, shall then read to the man most accurate, but dreadful lectures on the law. But what seems principally pointed at by the opening of this book, is the opening of that part of it which determines the reward of men's works. Now the law promises life, upon perfect obedience: but none can be found on the right hand, or on the left, who will pretend to that, when once the book of conscience is opened. It threatens death upon disobedience, and will effectually bring it upon all under its dominion. And this part of the book of the law, determining the reward of men's works, is opened, only to show what must be the portion of the ungodly, and that there they may read their sentence before it is pronounced. But it is not opened for the sentence of the saints; for no sentence absolving a sinner could ever be drawn out of it. The law promises life, not as it is a rule of actions, but as a covenant of works; therefore innocent man could not have demanded life upon his obedience, till the law was reduced into the form of a covenant, as was shown before. But the saints, having been, in this life, brought under a new covenant, namely, the covenant of grace, were dead to the law as a covenant of works, and it was dead to them. Wherefore, as they shall not now have any fear of death from it, so they can have no hope of life from it, since 'they are not under the law, but under grace' (Rom 6.14). But, for their sentence, 'another book is opened.'

Thus the book of the law is opened, for the sentence against all those on the left hand: and by it they will clearly see the justice of the judgment against them, and how the Judge proceeds therein according to law. Nevertheless, there will be this difference,

[414]

namely, that those who had only the natural law, and lived not under any special revelation, shall be judged by that law of nature they had in their hearts; which law declares 'that they which commit such things' as they will stand convicted of, 'are worthy of death' (Rom 1.32). But those who had the written law, to whom the Word of God came, sounding in the visible church, shall be judged by that written law. So says the apostle (Rom 2.12), 'For as many as have sinned without' the written 'law, shall also perish without' the written 'law: and as many as have sinned in the law,' that is, under the written law, 'shall also be judged by the' written 'law.'

(4) 'Another book' shall be 'opened, which is the book of life' (Rev 20.12). In this the names of all the elect are written, as Christ said to His disciples (Luke 10.20), 'Your names are written in heaven.' This book contains God's gracious and unchangeable purpose, to bring all the elect to eternal life; and that, in order thereto, they be redeemed by the blood of His Son, effectually called, justified, adopted, sanctified, and raised up by Him at the last day without sin. It is now lodged in the Mediator's hand, as the book of 'the manner of the kingdom:' and having perfected the work the Father gave Him to do, He shall, on the great day, produce and open the book, and present the persons therein named, 'faultless before the presence of his glory (Jude, verse 24); not having spot, or wrinkle, or any such thing' (Eph 5.27). Not one of those who are named in the book will be missing. They shall be found qualified, according to the order of the book, re- deemed, called, justified, sanctified, raised up, without spot. What remains then, but, according to the same book, they obtain the great end, namely, everlasting life? This may be gathered from that precious promise (Rev 3.5), 'He that overcometh, the same shall be clothed in white raiment,' being raised in glory; and I will not blot out his name out of the book of life, but I will confess his name before my Father:' – it shall be as it were, read out among the rest of God's elect – 'and before his angels.' Here is now the ground of the saints' absolution, the ground of the

blessed sentence they shall receive. The book of life being opened, it will be known to all, who are elected, and who are not. Thus far of the trial of the parties.

8: Then shall the Judge pronounce this blessed sentence on the saints, 'Come, ye blessed of my Father, inherit the kingdom prepared for you from the foundation of the world' (Matt 25.34). It is most probable, the man Christ will pronounce it with an audible voice: which not only all the saints, but all the wicked likewise, shall hear and understand. Who can conceive the inexpressible joy with which these happy ones will hear these words? Who can imagine that fulness of joy which will be poured into their hearts with these words reaching their ears? And who can conceive how much of hell shall break forth into the hearts of all the ungodly crew, by these words of heaven? It is certain that this sentence shall be pronounced before the sentence of damnation. 'Then shall the King say unto them on his right hand, Come, ye blessed,' &c. (Matt 25.34). 'Then shall he say also to them on the left hand, Depart from me, ye cursed,' &c. (verse 41). There is no need of this order, that the saints may, without fear, hear the other sentence on the reprobate: they who are raised in glory, caught up to meet the Lord in the air, presented without spot, and whose souls, for the far greater part of them, have been so long in heaven before, shall not be capable of any such fear. But hereby they will be brought in orderly, to sit in judgment, as Christ's assessors, against the ungodly, whose torment will be aggravated by it. It will be a hell to them to be kept out of hell, till they see the doors of heaven opened to receive the saints, who once dwelt in the same world with them; and perhaps in the same country, parish, or town, and sat under the same ministry with themselves. Thus will they see heaven afar off, to make their hell the hotter, like that unbelieving lord (2 Kings 7.19,20). They 'shall see' the plenty 'with their eyes, but shall not eat thereof.' Every word of the blessed sentence shall be like an envenomed arrow shot into their hearts while they see what they have lost, and from thence gather what they are to expect.

This sentence is passed on the saints, 'according to their works' (Rev 20.12); but not for their works, nor for their faith, as if eternal life were merited by them. The sentence itself overthrows this absurd conceit. The kingdom which they are called to, was 'prepared for them, from the foundation of the world:' not left to be merited by themselves, who were but of yesterday. They inherit it as sons, but procure it not to themselves as servants do the reward of their work. They were redeemed by the blood of Christ, and clothed with His spotless righteousness, which is the proper cause of the sentence. They were also qualified for heaven by the sanctification of His Spirit; and hence it is 'according to their works:' so that the ungodly world shall see now, that the Judge of the quick and dead does good to those who were good. Therefore it is added to the sentence, 'For I was an hungred, and ye gave me meat,' &c. (verses 35, 36); which does not denote the ground, but the evidence of their right to heaven; as if a judge should say he absolves a man pursued for debt, for the witnesses attest that it is paid already. So the apostle says (1 Cor 10.5), 'But with many of them God was not well pleased; for they were overthrown in the wilderness.' Their overthrow in the wilderness was not the ground of God's displeasure with them, but it was an evidence of it. And thus our Lord teaches us the necessary connection between glory and good works, namely works evangelically good; works having a respect to Jesus Christ, and done out of faith in Him, and love to Him, without which they will not be regarded in that day. And the saints will so far be judged according to such works, that the degrees of glory amongst them shall be according to these works. For it is an eternal truth, 'He that soweth sparingly, shall reap also sparingly' (2 Cor 9.6).

Thus shall the good works of the godly have a glorious, but a gratuitous reward; a reward of grace, not of debt; which will fill them with wonder at the riches of free grace, and at the Lord's condescending to take any notice, especially such public notice, of their poor worthless works; which seems to be the import of what they are said to answer, 'saying, Lord, when saw we thee an hungred?' (verses 37–39). And may they not justly wonder to see themselves set down at the marriage supper of the Lamb, and to hear Him acknowledge a dinner or supper, a little meat or drink, such as they had, which they gave to a hungry member of Christ, for His sake? O plentiful harvest, following upon the seed of good works! Rivers of pleasure, in exchange for a cup of cold water given to a disciple in the name of a disciple! Eternal mansions of glory, in exchange for a night's lodging given to a saint who was a stranger! Everlasting robes of glory, in exchange for a new coat, or, it may be, an old one, bestowed on some saint who had not necessary clothing! A visit to the sick saint, repaid by Christ Himself, coming in the glory of His Father, with all His holy angels! A visit made to a poor prisoner for the cause of Christ, repaid with a visit from the Judge of all, taking away the visitant with Him to the palace of heaven, there to be for ever with Himself! These things will be matter of everlasting wonder; and should stir up all to sow liberally in time, while the seed-time of good works lasts. But it is Christ's stamp on good works, that puts a value on them, in the eye of a gracious God; which seems to be the import of our Lord's reply (verse 40), 'Inasmuch as ye have done it unto one of the least of these my brethren, ye have done it unto me.'

9: Now the saints having received their own sentence, 'they shall judge the world' (1 Cor 6.2). This was not fulfilled when the empire became Christian, and Christians were made magistrates. No, the psalmist tells us, 'This honour have all his saints' (Psa 149.9). And the apostle in the forecited place, adds, 'And if the world shall be judged by you, are ye unworthy to judge the smallest matters?' (verse 3), 'Know ye not that we shall judge angels?' Being called, they come to receive their kingdom, in the view of angels and men: they go, as it were, from the bar to the throne, 'To him that overcometh will I grant to sit with me in my throne' (Rev 3.21). They shall not only judge the world, in

[418]

Christ their Head, by way of communion with Him, by their works compared with those of the ungodly, or by way of testimony against them, but they shall be assessors of Jesus Christ the Judge, giving their voice against them, consenting to His judgment as just, and saying *Amen* to the doom pronounced against all the ungodly: as is said of the saints, upon the judgment of the great whore (Rev 19.1,2), 'Hallelujah – for true and righteous are his judgements.' Thus, the upright shall have dominion over them in the morning,' of the resurrection (Psa 49.14). Then, and not till then, shall that be fully accomplished (Psa 149.6–9), 'Let the high praises of God be in their mouth, and a two-edged sword in their hand: to execute vengeance upon the heathen, and punishments upon the people: this honour have all his saints.' O! What a strange turn of affairs will appear here! What an astonishing sight will it be, to see wicked churchmen and statesmen standing as criminals before the saints whom formerly they condemned as heretics, rebels, and traitors! To see men of riches and power stand pale-faced before those whom they oppressed! To see the mocker stand trembling before those whom he mocked! the worldly-wise man, before those whom he accounted fools! Then shall the despised faces of the saints be dreadful faces to the wicked; and those, who sometimes were the song of the drunkards, shall then be a terror to them. All wrongs must be righted at length, and every one set in his proper place.

10: The Judge will pronounce the sentence of damnation on all the ungodly multitude. 'Then shall he say also unto them on the left hand, depart from me, ye cursed, into everlasting fire, prepared for the devil and his angels' (verse 41). Fearful doom! and that from the same mouth from whence proceeded the sentence of absolution before. It was an aggravation of the misery of the Jews, when their city was destroyed, that they were ruined by one who was accounted the darling of the world. O what an aggravation of the misery of the wicked will it be that Christ will pronounce this sentence also! To hear the curse from mount Zion must needs be most terrible. To be damned by Him who came to save sinners, must be double damnation. But thus it will be. The Lamb of God shall roar, as a lion, against them: he shall excommunicate, and cast them out of His presence for ever, by a sentence from the throne, saying, 'Depart from me, ye cursed.' He shall adjudge them to everlasting fire, and the society of devils for evermore. And this sentence also, we suppose, will be pronounced with an audible voice, by the man Christ. And all the saints shall say, 'Hallelujah, true and righteous are his judgments.' None were so compassionate as the saints when on earth, during the time of God's patience. But now that time is at an end, their compassion for the ungodly is swallowed up in joy in the Mediator's glory, and His executing of just judgment, by which His enemies are made His footstool. Though, when on earth, the righteous man wept in secret places for their pride, and because they would not hear; yet then he 'shall rejoice when he seeth the vengeance: he shall wash his feet in the blood of the wicked' (Psa 58.10). No pity shall then be shown them from their nearest relations. The godly wife shall applaud the justice of the Judge in the condemnation of her ungodly husband: the godly husband shall say *Amen* to the damnation of her who lay in his bosom: the godly parents shall say *Hallelujah*, at the passing of the sentence against their ungodly child: and the godly child shall, from the bottom of his heart, approve the damnation of his wicked parents, the father who begat him, and the mother who bore him. The sentence is just; they are judged 'according to their works' (Rev 20.12).

There is no wrong done them, 'For I was an hungred,' says our Lord,' and ye gave me no meat: I was thirsty, and ye gave me no drink: I was a stranger, and ye took me not in; naked, and ye clothed me not; sick, and in prison, and ye visited me not' (verses 42,43). These are not only evidences of their ungodly and cursed state, but most proper causes and grounds of their condemnation: for though good works do not merit salvation, yet evil works merit damnation. Sins of one kind only, namely, of omission, are here mentioned; not that these alone shall then be discovered (for

[420]

the books lays all open), but because these, though there were no more, are sufficient to condemn unpardoned sinners. And if men are condemned for sins of omission, much more for sins of commission. The omission of works of charity and mercy is mentioned in particular, to stop the mouths of the wicked; for it is most just that he 'have judgment without mercy, that hath shewed no mercy' (James 2.13). The taking notice of the omission of acts of charity and mercy towards the distressed members of Christ, intimates, that it is the judgment of those who have heard of Christ in the Gospel that is principally intended in this portion of Scripture, and that the slighting of Christ will be the great cause of the ruin of those who hear the Gospel: but the enmity of the hearts of the wicked against Christ Himself is discovered by the entertainment they now give to His members.

In vain will they say, 'When saw we thee an hungred or athirst?' &c. (verse 44). For the Lord reckons, and will reckon, the world's unkindness to His people, unkindness to Himself: 'Inasmuch as ye did it not to one of the least of these, ye did it not to me' (verse 45). O meat and drink unhappily withheld, when a member of Christ was in need of it! O wretched neglect, that the stranger saint was not taken in! It had been better for them if they had quitted their own room, and their own bed, than that he wanted lodging. O cursed clothing, may the wicked say, that was in my house, locked up in my chest, or hanging in my wardrobe, and was not brought out to clothe such a one! O that I had stripped myself, rather than he had gone away without clothing! Cursed business that diverted me from visiting such a saint! O that I had rather watched whole nights with him! Wretch that I was ! Why did I sit at ease in my house, when he was in prison, and did not visit him? But now the tables are turned: Christ's servants shall eat, but I shall be hungry; His servants shall drink, but I shall be thirsty; they rejoice, but I am ashamed (Isa 65.13). They are taken in, but I am cast out, and bid to depart; they are clothed with robes of glory, but I 'walk naked, and they see my shame' (Rev 16.15). They are now raised up on high, beyond the reach of sickness or pain; but I must now 'lie down in sorrow' (Isa 50.11). Now they will go to the palace of heaven, but I must go to the prison of hell.

But if our Lord thus resents men's neglecting to help His people under these, and the like distresses; what may they expect who are the authors and instruments of them? If they shall be fed with wrath, who fed them not when they were hungry; what shall become of those who robbed and spoiled them? What a full cup of wrath shall be the portion of those, who were so far from giving them meat or drink when hungry or thirsty, that they made it a crime for others to entertain them, and made themselves drunken with their blood! They must lodge with devils for evermore, who took not in the Lord's people when strangers: then, what a lodging shall those have, who drove them out of their own houses, out of their native land, and made them strangers! Men will be condemned for not clothing them, when naked: then, how heavy must the sentence of those be, who have stripped them, and made them go without clothing! Surely, if not visiting them in sickness, or in prison, shall be so severely punished, those shall not escape a most heavy doom who have cast them into prisons, and have put them under such hardships as have impaired their health, brought sickness on them, and cut short their days in prison, or out of prison.

To put a face upon such wicked practices, men will pretend to retain an honour for Christ and religion, while they thus treat His members, walking in His way and keeping the truth. They are here represented to say, 'When saw we thee an hungred, or athirst, or a stranger, or naked, or sick, or in prison, and did not minister unto thee?' (verse 44). As if they should say, Our bread, drink, lodging, clothing, and visits, were indeed refused, but not to Christ; but to a set of men of a bad character, men who 'turned the world upside down' (Acts 17.6); who troubled Israel (1 Kings 18.17); a humorous and fantastic sort of people, having laws diverse from all people, factious and rebellious; they did not keep the king's laws, and were therefore a dangerous set of men; it was

[422]

not for the king's profit to suffer them (Esther 3.8). But although men cast iniquity upon the godly, and give them ill names, that they may treat them as criminals, all these pretences will avail them nothing in the great day before the righteous Judge, nor before their own consciences, but the real ground of their enmity against the saints will be found, to their own conviction, to be their enmity against Christ Himself. This seems to be the import of the objection of the damned (verse 44), and of the answer to it (verse 45), 'Inasmuch as ye did it not to one of the least of these, ye did it not to me.'

11: Sentence being passed on both parties, the full execution of the same follows (verse 46), 'And these shall go away into everlasting punishment; but the righteous into life eternal.' The damned shall get no reprieve, but go to their place without delay; they shall be driven away from the judgment-seat into hell: and the saints 'shall enter into the King's palace' (Psa 45.15), namely, into heaven, the seat of the blessed. But our Lord Christ and His glorious company shall keep the field that day, and see the backs of all their enemies; for the damned go off first.

In this day of the Lord, the great day, shall be the general conflagration; by which these visible heavens, the earth, and sea, shall pass away. Not that they shall be annihilated, or reduced to nothing, that is not the operation of fire; but they shall be dissolved, and purified by that fire, from all the effects of sin, and of the curse, upon them; and then renewed, and made more glorious and stable. Of this conflagration, the apostle Peter speaks (2 Pet 3.10), 'But the day of the Lord will come as a thief in the night; in the which the heavens shall pass away with a great noise, and the elements shall melt with fervent heat; the earth also, and the works that are therein shall be burnt up.' (See also verses 7,12.) And of the renewing of the world, he adds (verse 13), 'Nevertheless we, according to his promise, look for new heavens, and a new earth, wherein dwelleth righteousness.'

It seems most agreeable to the Scriptures, and to the nature of the thing, to conceive this conflagration to follow after the general judgment; sentence being passed on both parties before it. And I judge it probable, that it will fall in with the putting of the sentence in execution against the damned; so as they shall, according to their sentence, depart, and the heavens and the earth pass away, together and at once, at that furious rebuke from the throne, driving them away, out of the world (in this fire) to the everlasting fire prepared for the devil and his angels. Even as, in the deluge, with which the apostle Peter compares the conflagration, or burning of the world (2 Pet 3.6,7), the world itself, and the wicked upon it, perished together; the same water which destroyed the earth, sweeping away the inhabitants. For it is not likely that the wicked shall at all stand on the new earth, 'wherein dwelleth righteousness' (2 Pet 3.13). And as for this earth, it shall 'flee away,' which seems to denote a very quick despatch, and it shall 'flee from His face, who sits on the throne' (Rev 20.11), 'And I saw a great white throne, and him that sat on it, from whose face the earth and the heaven fled away.' The execution of the sentence on the wicked is also thus expressed; they 'shall be punished with everlasting destruction from the presence,' or 'from the face of the Lord' (2 Thess 1.9). The original word is the same in both texts, which, being compared, seem to say, that these created things, abused by the wicked, being left to stand as witnesses against them, in the judgment, are, after sentence passed on their abusers, made to pass away with them from the face of the Judge. It is true, the fleeing away of the earth and the heavens is narrated (Rev 20.11), before the judgment; but that does not prove its going before the judgment, any more than the narrating of the judgment (verse 12), before the resurrection (verse 13), will prove the judgment to be before it. Further, it is remarkable, in the execution of the sentence (Rev 20.14,15), that not only the reprobate are 'cast into the lake,' but 'death and hell' are cast into it likewise: all effects of sin and of the curse are removed out of the world, for which very cause shall the conflagration be, and they are confined to the place of the damned. Besides all this, it is evident that the end of the world is by the conflagration: and the apostle tells us (1 Cor 15.24,25), 'Then cometh the end, when he shall have delivered up the kingdom to God, even the Father; when he shall have put down all rule, and all authority and power. For he must reign till he hath put all enemies under his feet.' Which last, as it must be done before the end, so it seems not to be done but by putting the sentence in execution, passed in the day of judgment, against the wicked.

Now, if the burning of Sodom and Gomorrah, that are set forth for an example (Jude, verse 7), was so dreadful, how terrible will that day be, when the whole world shall be at once in flames! How will wretched worldlings look, when their darling world shall be all on fire! Then shall strong castles and towering palaces, with all their rich furniture, go up together in one flame with the lowest cottages. What heart can fully conceive the terror of that day to the wicked, when the whole fabric of heaven and earth shall at once be dissolved by that fire! when that miserable company shall be driven from the tribunal to the pit with fire within them, and fire without them, and fire behind them, and on every hand of them, and fire before them, awaiting them in the lake; whither this fire, for aught that appears, may also follow them.

As for the particular place of this judgment, though some point us to the valley of Jehoshaphat for it: yet our Lord, who infallibly knew it, being asked the question by his disciples, 'Where, Lord?' only said, 'Wheresoever the body is, thither will the eagles be gathered together' (Luke 17.37). After which answer, it is too much for men to renew the question. As for the time when it shall be, in vain do men search for what the Lord has purposely kept secret (Act 1.7), 'It is not for you to know the times or the seasons, which the Father has put in his own power.' The apostle Paul, after having very plainly described the second coming of Christ (1 Thess 4.16,17), adds (chapter 5.1,2), 'But of the times and seasons, brethren, you have no need that I write unto you: for yourselves know perfectly that the day of the Lord so cometh as a thief in the night.' Nevertheless, some, in several ages, have made very bold with the time; and several particular years, which are now past, have been given out to the world, for the time of the end, by men who have pried into the secrets of God. Time has proclaimed to the world their rashness and folly; and it is probable they will be no more happy in their conjectures, whose determinate time is yet to come. Let us rest in that 'He cometh.' God has kept the day hid from us, that we may be every day ready for it (Matt 25.13), 'Watch, therefore; for ye know neither the day nor the hour wherein the Son of man cometh.' And let us remember, that the last day of our life will determine our state in the last day of the world: and as we die, so shall we be judged.

III: I shall now conclude this subject, with some application of what has been said.

Use I: Of comfort to all the saints. Here is abundance of consolation to all who are in the state of grace. Whatever be your afflictions in the world, this day will make up all your losses. 'Though ye have lien among the pots, yet shall ye be as the wings of a dove covered with silver, and her feathers with yellow gold' (Psa 68.13). Though the world reproach, judge, and condemn you, the Judge will at that day absolve you, and bring forth your righteousness as the light. The world's fools will then appear to have been the only wise men who were in it. Though the cross be heavy, you may well bear it, in expectation of the crown of righteousness, which the righteous Judge will then give you. If the world despise you, and treat you with the utmost contempt, regard it not: the day is coming wherein you shall sit with Christ in His throne. Be not discouraged by reason of manifold temptations. But resist the devil in confidence of a full and complete victory; for you shall judge the tempter at last. Though you have hard wrestling now with the body of sin and death, yet you shall get all your enemies under your feet at length, and be presented faultless before the presence of His glory. Let not the terror of that day dispirit you, when you think upon it; let those who have slighted the Judge, and continue enemies to Him, and to the way of holiness, droop and hang down their heads, when they think

[426]

of His coming: but lift you up your heads with joy, for the last day will be your best day. The Judge is your Head and Husband, your Redeemer, and your Advocate. You must appear before the judgment-seat, but you 'shall not come into condemnation' (John 5.24). His coming will not be against you but for you. He came in the flesh, to remove the lawful impediments of the spiritual marriage, by His death: He came in the Gospel to you, to espouse you to Himself; He will come, at last, to solemnize the marriage, and take the bride home to His Father's house. 'Even so, come, Lord Jesus.'

Use 2: Of terror to all unbelievers. This may serve to awaken a secure generation, a world lying in wickedness, as if they were never to be called to an account for it; and slighting the Mediator, as if He were not to judge them. Ah! how few have lively impressions of the judgment to come! Most men live as if what is said of it from the Word were but idle tales. The profane lives of many speak the thoughts of it to be far from their hearts, and in every deed make a mock of it before the world, saying, in effect, 'Where is the promise of his coming?' The hypocrisy of others, who blind the eyes of the world with a splendid profession, being in appearance Christ's sheep, while they are indeed the devil's goats, proves that the great separation of the sheep from the goats is very little laid to heart. How do many indulge themselves in secret wickedness, of which they would be ashamed before witnesses; not considering, that their most secret thoughts and actions will, at that day, be discovered before the great congregation! How eagerly are men's hearts set on the world, as if it were to be their everlasting habitation! The solemn assemblies, and public ordinances, wherein the Judge is upon a transaction of peace with the criminals, are undervalued: men's hearts swim like feathers in the waters of the sanctuary, that sink like stones to the bottom in cares of this life; they will be very serious in trifles of this world, and trifle in the most serious and weighty things of another world. O consider the day that is approaching, in which Christ will come to judgment! the world shall be summoned, by the sound of the last trumpet, to appear before His tribunal. The Judge will sit on His throne, and all nations will be summoned before Him; the separation will be made between the godly and the wicked; the books opened, and the dead judged out of them; one party will be adjudged to everlasting life, and the other to everlasting fire, according to their works.

It would be a sight of admirable curiosity, if you could wrap up yourself in some dark cloud, or hide yourself in the cleft of some high rock, from whence you might see wicked kings, princes, judges, and great ones of the earth, rising out of their marble tombs, and brought to the bar, to answer for all their cruelty, injustice, oppression and profanity, without any marks of distinction, but what their wickedness puts upon them. Profane, unholy, and unfaithful ministers, pursued with the curses of their ruined people from their graves to the judgment seat, and charged with the blood of souls, to whom they gave not faithful warning! mighty men standing trembling before the Judge, unable to recover their wonted boldness, to outwit Him with their subtleties, or defend themselves by their strength! delicate women cast forth of their graves, as abominable branches, dragged to the tribunal, to answer for their ungodly lives! the ignorant, suddenly taught in the law to their cost; and the learned declared before the world, fools and laborious triflers: the atheist convinced, the hypocrite unmasked; and the profane at length turned serious about his eternal state: secret murders, adulteries, thefts, cheats, and other works of darkness, which defied all human search, discovered and laid open before the world, with their most minute circumstances: no regard had to the rich, no pity shown to the poor: the scales of the world turned; oppressed and despised piety set on high, and prosperous wickedness at last brought low: all not found in Christ, arraigned, convicted, and condemned without respect of persons, and driven from the tribunal to the pit; while those found in Him, at that day, being absolved before the world, go with Him into heaven. Nay, but you cannot so escape. Whoever you are, not being in Christ, you must bear a part in this tragical and alarming scene.

Sinner, that same Lord Christ, whom you now despise, whom you wound through the sides of His messengers, and before whom you prefer your lusts, will be your Judge. The neglected Saviour will be a severe Judge. O! what mountain, what rock, will you get to fall on you, and hide you from the face of Him who sits on the throne? You have now a rock within you, a heart of adamant, so that you can count the darts of the Word as stubble, and laugh at the shaking of the spear: but that rock will rend at the sight of the Judge: that hard heart will then break, and you will weep and wail, when weeping and wailing will be to no purpose. Death's bands will fall off, the grave will cast you out; and the mountains shall skip from you, and the rocks refuse to grind you to powder. How will these cursed eyes abide the sight of the Juge? Behold, He cometh! Where is the profane swearer, who tore His wounds? The wretched worldling, now abandoned of his God? The formal hypocrite, who kissed Him and betrayed Him? The despiser of the Gospel, who sent Him away in His messengers groaning, profaned His ordinances, and trampled under foot His precious blood? O murderer, the slain man is thy Judge: there is He whom you did so maltreat. Behold the neglected Lamb of God appearing as a lion against you. How will your heart endure the darts of His fiery looks? That rocky heart, which now holds out against Him, shall then be blown up; that face, which refuses to blush now, shall then gather blackness: arrows of wrath shall pierce where arrows of conviction cannot enter now. What will you answer Him, when He rises up, and charges you with your unbelief and impenitence? Will you say, you were not warned? Conscience within you will give you the lie; the secret groans and weariness of those who warned you, will witness the contrary. If a child or a fool did tell you that your house was on fire, you would immediately run to quench it: but, in matters of eternal concern, men will first fill their hearts with prejudices against the messengers, and then cast their message behind their backs. But these silly excuses and pretences will not avail in the day of the Lord. How will these cursed ears, now deaf to the call of the Gospel inviting sinners to come to Christ, hear the fearful sentence, 'Depart from me, ye cursed, into ever-lasting fire, prepared for the devil and his angels!' No sleepy hearer shall be there; no man's heart will then wander; their hearts and eyes will then be fixed on their misery, which they will not now believe. O that we knew, in this our day, the things that belong to our peace!

Lastly, Be exhorted to believe this great truth; and believe it so that you may prepare for the judgment betimes. Set up a secret tribunal in your own breasts, and often call yourselves to an account there. Make the Judge your friend in time, by closing with Him in the offer of the Gospel; and give all diligence, that you may be found in Christ at that day. Cast off the works of darkness; and live, as believing you are, at all times, and in all places, under the eye of your Judge, who will bring every work into judgment, with every secret thing! Be fruitful in good works, knowing that as you sow, you shall reap. Study piety to-wards God, righteousness and charity towards men. Lay up in store plenty of works of charity and mercy towards those who are in distress, especially such as are of the household of faith; that they may be produced, at that day, as evidences that you belong to Christ. Shut not up your bowels of mercy, now, towards the needy, lest you then find no mercy. Take heed, that in all your works you be single and sincere; aiming, in them all, at the glory of the Lord, a testimony of your love to Him, and in obedience to His command. Leave it to hypocrites, who have their reward, to proclaim every man his own goodness; and to sound a trumpet when they do their alms. It is a base and unchristian spirit which cannot have satisfaction in a good work unless it be exposed to the view of others: it is utterly unworthy of one who believes that the last trumpet shall call together the whole world, before whom the Judge Himself shall publish works truly good, how secretly soever they were done. Live in a believing expectation of the coming of the Lord. Let your loins be always girt, and your lamps burning; so when He comes, whether in the last day of your life, or in the last day of the world, ye shall be able to say with joy, 'Lo, this is our God, and we have waited for Him.'

5

THE KINGDOM OF HEAVEN

Then shall the King say unto them on his right hand,
Come, ye blessed of my Father, inherit the kingdom
prepared for you from the foundation of the world.
MATTHEW 25.34

Having from this portion of Scripture, which the text is a part of, discoursed of the general judgment; and having now to speak of the everlasting happiness of the saints, and the everlasting misery of the wicked, from the respective sentences to be pronounced upon them in the great day, I shall take them in the order wherein they lie before us; and the rather that, as sentence is first passed upon the righteous, so the execution thereof is first begun, though probably the other may be fully executed before it is completed.

The words of the text contain the joyful sentence itself, together with an historical introduction thereto, which gives us an account of the Judge pronouncing the sentence; 'the King,' Jesus Christ; the parties on whom it is given, 'them on His right hand;' and the time when, 'then,' as soon as the trial is over. Of these I have spoken already. It is the sentence itself we are now to consider, 'Come, ye blessed of my Father,' &c. Stand back, O ye profane goats! away all unregenerate souls, not united to Jesus Christ! this is not for you. Come, O ye saints, brought out of your natural state into the state of grace! behold here the state of glory awaiting you. Here is glory let down to us in words and syllables; a looking-glass, in which you may see your everlasting happiness; a scheme or draft of Christ's Father's house, wherein there are many mansions.

This glorious sentence bears two things. 1. The complete happiness to which the saints are adjudged, 'the kingdom.' 2. Their solemn admission to it, 'Come, ye blessed of my Father, inherit,'

[432]

&c. 1. Their complete happiness is a kingdom. A kingdom is the height of world felicity; there is nothing on earth greater than a kingdom: therefore the hidden weight of the glory in heaven is held forth to us under that notion. But it is not an ordinary kingdom, it is 'the kingdom;' the kingdom of heaven, surpassing all the kingdoms of the earth in glory, honour, profit, and pleasure, infinitely more than they do in these excel the low and inglorious condition of a beggar in rags, and on a dunghill. 2. There is a solemn admission of the saints into this their kingdom, 'Come ye, inherit the kingdom.' In view of angels, men, and devils, they are invested with royalty, and solemnly inaugurated before the whole world, by Jesus Christ, the Heir of all things, who hath 'all power in heaven and in earth.' Their right to the kingdom is solemnly recognised and owned. They are admitted to it as undoubted heirs of the kingdom, to possess it by inheritance, or lot, as the word properly signifies, because, of old, inheritances were designed by lot, as Canaan to Israel, God's 'first-born,' as they are called (Exod 4.22). And because this kingdom is the Father's kingdom, therefore they are openly acknowledged, in their admission to it, to be the blessed of Christ's Father: which blessing was given them long before this sentence, but it is now solemnly recognised and confirmed to them by the Mediator, in His Father's name. It is observable, He says not, Ye blessed of *the* Father, but, Ye blessed of *my* Father; to show us, that all blessings are derived by us from the Father, the fountain of blessing, as He is 'the God and Father of our Lord Jesus Christ,' through whom we are blessed (Eph 1.3). And, finally, they are admitted to this kingdom, as that which was 'prepared for them from the foundation of the world,' in God's eternal purpose, before they, or any of them, were; that all the world may see eternal life to be the free gift of God.

DOCTRINE: *The saints shall be made completely happy in the possession of the kingdom of heaven*

[433]

Two things I shall here inquire into: 1: The nature of this kingdom. 11: The admission of the saints thereto. And then I shall make some practical improvement of the whole.

1: As to the nature of the kingdom of heaven, our knowledge of it is very imperfect; for 'eye hath not seen, nor ear heard, neither have entered into the heart of man, the things which God hath prepared for them that love him' (1 Cor 2.9). As, by familiar resemblances, parents instruct their little children concerning things of which otherwise they can have no tolerable notion; so our gracious God, in consideration of our weakness, is pleased to represent to us heaven's happiness under similitudes taken from earthly things, glorious in the eyes of men; since discoveries of the heavenly glory, divested of earthly resemblances, would be too bright for our weak eyes, and we would but lose ourselves in them. Wherefore now we can but speak as children of these things, which the day will fully discover.

The state of glory is represented under the idea of a kingdom, a kingdom, among men, being that in which the greatest number of earthly good things centre. Now, every saint shall, as a king, inherit a kingdom. All Christ's subjects shall be kings, each one with his crown upon his head: not that the great King shall divest himself of His royalty, but He will make all His children partakers of His kingdom.

1: The saints shall have kingly power and authority given them. Our Lord gives not empty titles to His favourites; He makes them kings indeed. The dominion of the saints will be a dominion far exceeding that of the greatest monarch who ever was on earth. They will be absolute masters over sin, which had the dominion over them. They will have a complete rule over their own spirits; an entire management of all their affections and inclinations, which now create them so much molestation: the turbulent root of corrupt affections shall be for ever expelled out of that kingdom, and never be able any more to give them the least disturbance. They shall have power over the nations, the ungodly of all nations, 'and shall rule them with a rod of iron' (Rev

[434]

2.26,27). The whole world of the wicked shall be broken before them: 'Satan shall be bruised under their feet' (Rom 16.20). He shall never be able to fasten a temptation on them any more: but he will be judged by them, and, in their sight, cast with the reprobate crew into the lake of fire and brimstone. So shall they rule over their oppressors. Having fought the good fight, and got the victory, Christ will entertain them as Joshua did his captains, causing them to 'come near, and put their feet on the necks of kings' (Joshua 10.24).

2: They shall have the ensigns of royalty. For a throne, Christ will grant them 'to sit with Him in his throne' (Rev 3.21). They will be advanced to the highest honour and dignity that they are capable of; and in the enjoyment of it, they will have an eternal undisturbed repose, after all the tossings which they met with in the world, in their way to the throne. For a crown, they shall 'receive a crown of glory, that fadeth not away' (1 Pet 5.4). Not a crown of flowers, as subjects, being conquerors or victors, sometimes have got; such a crown quickly fades, but their crown never fades. Not a crown of gold, such as earthly kings wear; even a crown of gold is often stained, and at best can never make those who wear it happy. But it shall be 'a crown of glory.' A crown of glory is 'a crown of life' (Rev 2.10), that life which knows no end: a crown which death can never make to fall off one's head. It must be an abiding crown; for it is a 'crown of righteousness'(2 Tim 4.8). It was purchased for them by 'Christ's righteousness,' which is imputed to them; they are qualified for it by inherent righteousness; God's righteousness, or faithfulness, secures it to them. They shall have 'a sceptre, a rod of iron' (Rev 2.27), terrible to all the wicked world. And a sword too, 'a two-edged sword in their hand, to execute vengeance upon the heathen, and punishments upon the people' (Psa 149.6,7). They shall have royal apparel. The royal robes in this kingdom are white robes (Rev 3.4), 'They shall walk with me in white,' which, in a very particular manner, points at the inconceivable glory of the state of the saints in heaven.

[435]

The Lord is pleased often to represent to us the glorious state of the saints, by speaking of them as clothed in 'white garments.' It is promised to the conqueror, that he shall be 'clothed in white raiment' (Rev 3.5). The elders about the throne are 'clothed in white raiment' (chap 4.4). The multitude before the throne are 'clothed with white robes' (chap 7.9); 'arrayed in white robes' (verse 13); 'made white in the blood of the Lamb' (verse 14). I own, the last two testimonies respect the state of the saints on earth; yet the terms are borrowed from the state of the church in heaven. All garments, properly so called, being badges of sin and shame, shall be laid aside by the saints when they come to their state of glory. But if we consider on what occasions white garments were wont to be put on, we shall find much of heaven under them.

(1) The Romans, when they set their bond-servants free, gave them a white garment as a badge of their freedom. So shall the saints that day receive their white robes; for it is the day of 'the glorious liberty of the children of God' (Rom 8.21), the day of 'the redemption of their body' (verse 23). They shall no more see the house of bondage, nor lie any more among the pots. If we compare the state of the saints on earth with that of the wicked, it is indeed a state of freedom, whereas the other is a state of slavery: but, in comparison with their state in heaven, it is but a servitude. A saint on earth is indeed a young prince, and heir to the crown; but his motto may be, 'I serve;' 'for he differeth nothing from a servant, though he be lord of all' (Gal 4.1). What are the groans of a saint, the sordid and base work which he is sometimes found employed in, the black and tattered garments which he walks in, but the badges of this comparative servitude? But from the day the saints come to the crown, they receive their complete freedom, and serve no more. They shall be fully freed from sin, which of all evils is the worst, both in itself, and in their apprehension too; how great then must that freedom be, when these 'Egyptians, whom they see to-day,' they 'shall see them again no more for ever!' They shall be free from all temptation

[436]

to sin: Satan can have no access to tempt them any more, by himself, or by his agents. A full answer will then be given to that petition they have so often repeated, 'Lead us not into temptation.' No hissing serpent can come into the paradise above: no snare or trap can be laid there, to catch the feet of the saints: they may walk there without fear, for they can be in no hazard: there are no lions' dens, no mountains of leopards, in the promised land. Nay, they shall be set beyond the possibility of sinning, for they shall be confirmed in goodness. It will be the consummate freedom of their will, to be for ever unalterably determined to good. And they shall be freed from all the effects of sin: 'There shall be no more death, neither sorrow, nor crying, neither shall there be any more pain' (Rev 21.4). What kingdom is like unto this? Death makes its way now into a palace, as easily as into a cottage: sorrow fills the heart of one who wears a crown on his head: royal robes are no defence against pain, and crying by reason of pain. But in this kingdom no misery can have place. All reproaches shall be wiped off, and never shall a tear drop any more from their eyes. They shall not complain of desertions again; the Lord will never hide His face from them: but the Sun of Righteousness shining upon them in his meridian brightness, will dispel all clouds, and give them an everlasting day, without the least mixture of darkness. A deluge of wrath, after a fearful thunder-clap from the throne, will sweep away the wicked from before the judgment-seat, into the lake of fire: but the righteous are, in the first place, like Noah, brought into the ark, and out of harm's way.

(2) White raiment was a token of purity. Therefore 'the Lamb's wife is arrayed in fine linen, clean and white' (Rev 19.8). And those who stood before the throne 'washed their robes, and made them white in the blood of the Lamb' (chap 7.14). The saints shall then put on the robes of perfect purity, and shine in spotless holiness, like the sun in its strength, without the least cloud to intercept its light. Absolute innocence shall then be restored, and every appearance of sin banished far from this kingdom. The

guilt of sin, and the reigning power of it are even now taken away in the saints; nevertheless, sin dwells in them (Rom 7.20). But then it shall be no more in them: the corrupt nature will be quite removed; that root of bitterness will be plucked up, and no vestiges of it left in their souls: their nature shall be altogether pure and sinless. There shall be no darkness in their minds, but the understanding of every saint, when he is come to his kingdom, will be as a globe of pure and unmixed light. There shall not be the least aversion to good, nor the least inclination to evil, in their wills, but they will be brought to a perfect conformity to the will of God; blessed with angelic purity, and fixed therein. Their affections shall not be liable to the least disorder or irregularity; it will cost no trouble to keep them right: they will get such a fixed habit of purity, as they can never lose. They will be so refined from all earthly dross, as never to savour more of any thing but of heaven. Were it possible for them to be set again amidst the ensnaring objects of an evil world, they would walk among them without the least defilement; as the sun shines on the dung-hill, yet is untainted, and as the angels preserved their purity in the midst of Sodom. Their graces shall then be perfected; and all the imperfections now cleaving to them done away. There will be no more ground for complaints of weakness of grace: none in that kingdom shall complain of an ill heart, or a corrupt nature. 'It doth not yet appear what we shall be, but when He shall appear, we shall be like Him' (1 John 3.2).

(3) Among the Jews, those who desired to be admitted into the priestly office, being tried, and found to be of the priest's line and without blemish, were clothed in white, and enrolled among the priests. This seems to be alluded to (Rev 3.5), 'He that overcometh, the same shall be clothed in white raiment, and I will not blot out his name out of the book of life.' So the saints shall not be kings only, but priests also; for they are a 'royal priesthood' (1 Pet 2.9). They will be priests upon their thrones. They are judicially found descended from the Great High Priest of their profession, begotten of Him by His Spirit, of the incorruptible

seed of the Word, and without blemish: so the trial being over, they are admitted to be priests in the temple above, that they may dwell in the house of the Lord for ever. There is nothing upon earth more glorious than a kingdom; nothing more venerable than the priesthood; and both meet together in the glorified state of the saints. 'The general assembly of the first-born' (Heb 12.23), whose is the priesthood and the double portion, appearing in their white robes of glory, will be a reverend and glorious company. That day will show them to be the persons whom the Lord has chosen out of all the tribes of the earth, to be near unto Him, and to enter into His temple, even into His holy place. Their priesthood, begun on earth, shall be brought to its perfection, when they shall be employed in offering the sacrifice of praise to God and the Lamb for ever and ever. They got not their portion in the earth with the rest of the tribes; but the Lord Himself was their portion, and will be their double portion, through the ages of eternity.

(4) They were wont to wear white raiment in a time of triumph; to which also there seems to be an allusion (Rev 3.5), 'He that overcometh, the same shall be clothed in white raiment.' And what is heaven but an everlasting triumph? None get thither but such as fight, and overcome too. Though Canaan was given to the Israelites as an inheritance, they were required to conquer it, before they could be possessors of it. The saints, in this world, are in the field of battle; often in red garments, garments rolled in blood, but the day approaches in which they shall 'stand before the throne, and before the Lamb, clothed with white robes, and palms in their hands' (Rev 7.9), having obtained a complete victory over all their enemies. The palm was used as a sign of victory, because that tree, though oppressed with weights, yet yields not, but rather shoots upwards. And palm trees were carved on the doors of the most holy place (1 Kings 6.32), which was a special type of heaven; for heaven is the place which the saints are received into as conquerors.

Behold the joy and peace of the saints in their white robes!

The joys arising from the view of past dangers, and of riches and honours gained at the very door of death, do most sensibly touch one's heart: and this will be an ingredient in the everlasting happiness of the saints, which could have had no place in the heaven of innocent Adam, and his sinless offspring, supposing him to have stood. Surely the glorified saints will not forget the entertainment which they met with in the world; it will be to the glory of God to remember it, and will also heighten their joy. The Sicilian king, by birth the son of a potter, acted a wise part, in that he would be served at his table with earthen vessels; which could not but put an additional sweetness in his meals, not to be relished by one born heir to the crown. Can ever meat be so sweet to any as to the hungry man? Or can any have such a relish of plenty as he who has been under pinching straits? The more difficulties the saints have passed through in their way to heaven, the place will be the sweeter to them when they come to it. Every happy stroke, struck in the spiritual warfare, will be a jewel in their crown of glory. Each victory obtained against sin, Satan, and the world, will raise their triumphant joy the higher. The remembrance of the cross will sweeten the crown; and the remembrance of their travel through the wilderness will put an additional verdure on the fields of glory, while they walk through them, looking back on the day when they went mourning without the sun.

And now that they appear triumphing in white robes, it is a sign they have obtained an honourable peace; such a peace as their enemies can disturb no more. So every thing peculiarly adapted to their militant condition is laid aside. The sword is laid down; and they betake themselves to the pen of a ready writer, to commemorate the praises of Him by whom they overcame. Public ordinances, preaching, sacraments, shall be honourably laid aside; there is no temple there (Rev 21.22). On earth these were sweet to them: but the travellers being all got home, the inns, appointed for their entertainment by the way, are shut up; the candles are put out when the sun is risen; and the tabernacle used in the wilderness is folded up, when the temple of glory is come in its room. Many of the saints' duties will then be laid aside, as one gives his staff out of his hand, when he is come to the end of his journey. Praying shall then be turned to praising: and there being no sin to confess, no wants to seek the supply of, confession and petition shall be swallowed up in everlasting thanksgiving. There will be no mourning in heaven. They have sown in tears : the reaping time of joy is come, and, 'God shall wipe all tears from their eyes' (Rev 21.4). No need of mortification there; and self-examination is then at an end. They will not need to watch any more; the danger is over. Patience has had its perfect work, and there is no use for it there. Faith is turned into sight, and hope is swallowed up in the ocean of sensible and full enjoyment. All the rebels are subdued, and the saints quietly sit on their throne. The forces, needful in the time of the spiritual warfare, are disbanded, and they carry on their triumph in the profoundest peace.

(5) White garments were worn on festival days, in token of joy. And so shall the saints be clothed in white raiment; for they shall keep an everlasting Sabbath to the Lord (Heb 4.9), 'There remaineth therefore a rest,' or keeping of a Sabbath, 'to the people of God.' The Sabbath, in the esteem of saints, is the queen of days; and they shall have an endless Sabbatism in the kingdom of heaven, so shall their garments be always white. They will have an eternal rest, with an uninterrupted joy; for heaven is not a resting place, where men may sleep out an eternity; there they rest not day nor night, but their work is their rest, and continual recreation, and toil and weariness have no place there. They rest there in God, who is the centre of their souls. Here they find the completion, or satisfaction, of all their desires, having the full enjoyment of God, and uninterrupted communion with Him. This is the point to which, till the soul come, it will always be restless : but that point reached, it rests; for God is the last end, and the soul can go no further. It cannot understand, will, nor desire more; but in Him it has what is commensurable to its

boundless desires. This is the happy end of all the labours of the saints; their toil and sorrows issue in a joyful rest. The Chaldeans, measuring the natural day, put the day first, and the night last: but the Jews counted the night first, and the day last. Even so the wicked begin with a day of rest and pleasure, but end with a night of everlasting toil and sorrow: but God's people have their gloomy night first, and then comes their day of eternal rest. This, Abraham, in the parable, observed to the rich man in hell (Luke 16.25), 'Son, remember that thou in thy lifetime receivedst thy good things, and likewise Lazarus evil things: but now he is comforted, and thou art tormented.'

3: If any inquire where the kingdom of the saints lies, it is not in this world; it lies in a better country, 'that is, an heavenly' (Heb 11.16), a country better than the best of this world; namely, the heavenly Canaan, Immanuel's land, where nothing is wanting to complete the happiness of the inhabitants. This is the happy country, blessed with a perpetual spring, and yielding all things for necessity, convenience, and delight. There men shall eat angels' food; they shall be entertained with the hidden manna (Rev 2.17), without being set to the painful task of gathering it: they will be fed to the full, with the product of the land falling into their mouths, without the least toil to them. That land enjoys everlasting day, for there is 'no night there' (Rev 21.25). Eternal sunshine beautifies this better country, but there is no scorching heat there. No clouds shall be seen there for ever: yet it is not a land of drought; the trees of the Lord's planting are set by the rivers of water, and shall never want moisture, for they will have an eternal supply of the Spirit, by Jesus Christ, from His Father. This is the country from whence our Lord came, and whither He is gone again; the country which all the holy patriarchs and prophets had their eye upon while on earth; and which all the saints, who have gone before us, have fought their way to; and to which the martyrs have joyfully swum through a sea of blood. This earth is the place of the saints' pilgrimage; that is their country, where they find their everlasting rest.

4: The royal city is that great city, the holy Jerusalem, described at large (Rev 21.10, to the end of the chapter). It is true, some learned divines place this city in the earth: but the particulars of this description seem to me to favour those most, who point us to the other world for it. The saints shall reign in that city, whose wall is of 'jasper' (verse 18); 'and the foundations of the wall garnished with all manner of precious stones' (verse 19); and 'the street of pure gold' (verse 21). So that their feet shall be set on that which the men of this world set their hearts upon. This is the city which God 'has prepared for them.' (Heb 11.16); 'a city that hath foundations' (verse 19); 'a continuing city' (chap 13.14), which shall stand and flourish, when all the cities of the world are laid in ashes; and which shall not be moved, when the foundations of the world are overturned. It is a city that never changes its inhabitants: none of them shall ever be removed out of it; for life and immortality reign there, and no death can enter into it. It is blessed with a perfect and perpetual peace, and can never be in the least disturbed. Nothing from without can annoy it; the gates therefore are not shut at all by day, and there is no night there (Rev 21.25). There can nothing from within trouble it. No want of provision there, no scarcity, no discord among the inhabitants. Whatever contentions are among the saints now, no vestige of their former jarrings shall remain there. Love to God and to one another shall be perfected; and those of them who stood at the greatest distance here, will joyfully embrace and delight in one another there.

5: The royal palace is Christ's Father's house, in which 'are many mansions' (John 14.2). There shall the saints dwell for ever. This is the house prepared for all the heirs of glory, even those of them who dwell in the meanest cottage now, or have not where to lay their heads. As the Lord calls His saints to a kingdom, He will provide them a house suitable to the dignity He puts upon them. Heaven will be a convenient, spacious, and glorious house, for those whom the King delights to honour. Never was a house purchased at so great a rate as this, being the purchase of the

Mediator's blood; and for no less could it be afforded to them: never was there so much to do, to fit the inhabitants for a house. The saints were, by nature, utterly unfit for this house, and human art and industry could not make them meet for it. But the Father gives the designed inhabitants to the Son, to be by Him redeemed: the Son pays the price of their redemption, even His own precious blood; justice gives them access to the house; and the Holy Spirit sanctifies them by His grace; that they may be meet to come in thither, where no unclean thing can enter. And no wonder, for it is the King's palace they enter into (Psa 45.15), the house of the kingdom, where the great King keeps his court, where He has set His throne, and shows forth His glory in a singular manner, beyond what mortals can conceive.

6: Paradise is their palace garden. 'This day shalt thou be with me in paradise,' said our Saviour to the penitent thief on the cross (Luke 23.43). Heaven is a paradise for pleasure and delight, where there is both wood and water: 'A pure river of water of life, clear as crystal, proceeding out of the throne of God and of the Lamb; and on either side of the river, the tree of life, which bears twelve manner of fruits, and yields her fruits every month, (Rev 22.1,2). How happy might innocent Adam have been in the earthly paradise, where there was nothing wanting for use or delight! Eden was the most pleasant spot of the uncorrupted earth, and paradise the most pleasant spot of Eden: but what is earth in comparison of heaven? The glorified saints are advanced to the heavenly paradise. There they shall not only see, but 'eat of the tree of life, which is in the midst of the paradise of God' (Rev 2.7). They shall behold the Mediator's glory, and be satisfied with His goodness. No flaming sword shall be there, to keep the way of that tree of life; but they shall freely eat of it, and live for ever. They shall 'drink of the river of pleasures' (Psa 36.8), the sweetest and purest pleasures which Immanuel's land affords, and shall swim in an ocean of unmixed delight for evermore.

7: They shall have royal treasures, sufficient to support the dignity to which they are advanced. Since the street of the royal

[444]

city is pure gold, and the twelve gates thereof are twelve pearls, their treasure must be of that which is better than gold or pearl. It is an 'eternal weight of glory' (2 Cor 4.17). O precious treasure! a treasure not liable to insensible corruption, by moths or rust; a treasure which none can steal from them (Matt 6.20). Never did any kingdom afford such a precious treasure, nor a treasure of such variety; for 'he that ovecometh, shall inherit all things' (Rev 21.7). No treasures on earth are stored with all things: if they were all put together in one, there would be far more valuable things wanting in that one, than found in it. This then is the peculiar treasure of the kings who inherit the kingdom of heaven. They shall want nothing that may contribute to their full satisfaction. Now they are rich in hope; but then they will have their riches in hand. Now all things are theirs in respect of right; then all shall be theirs in possession. They may go for ever through Immanuel's land, and behold the glory and riches thereof, with the satisfying thought that all they see is their own. It is a pity those should ever be uneasy under the want of earthly good things, who may be sure they shall inherit all things at length.

8: Though there is no material temple therein, no serving of God in the use of ordinances, as here on earth; yet, as for this kingdom, 'The Lord God Almighty, and the Lamb, are the temple of it' (Rev 21.22). As the temple was the glory of Canaan, so will the celestial temple be the glory of heaven. The saints shall be brought in thither as a royal priesthood, to dwell in the house of the Lord for ever; for Jesus Christ will then make every saint 'a pillar in the temple of God, and he shall go no more out' (Rev 3.12), as the priests and Levites did, in their courses, go out of the material temple. There the saints shall have the cloud of glory, the divine presence, with most intimate, uninterrupted communion with God. There they shall have Jesus Christ, as the true Ark, wherein the fiery law shall be for ever hid from their eyes: and the mercy-seat, from which nothing shall be breathed but everlasting peace and good will towards them: the cherubim, the society of holy angels, who shall join with them in eternal admiration of the mystery of Christ: the golden candlestick, with its seven lamps, for 'the glory of God' doth 'lighten it, and the Lamb is the light thereof' (Rev 21.23): the incense altar, in the intercession of Christ, who 'ever liveth to make intercession for them' (Heb 7.25), eternally exhibiting the manner of His death and suffering, and efficaciously willing for ever, that those whom the Father has given Him, be with Him: and the shewbread table, in the perpetual feast they shall have together in the enjoyment of God. This leads me more practically to consider,

9: The society in this kingdom. What would royal power and authority, ensigns of royalty, richest treasures, and all other advantages of a kingdom, avail, without comfortable society? Some crowned heads have had but a wretched life, through the want of it: their palaces have been unto them as prisons, and their badges of honour, as chains on a prisoner: while, hated of all, they had none they could trust in, or whom they could have comfortable fellowship with. But the chief part of heaven's happiness lies in the blessed society which the saints shall have there.

(1) The society of the saints, among themselves, will be no small part of heaven's happiness. The communion of saints on earth is highly prized by all those who are travelling through the world to Zion; companions in sin can never have such true pleasure and delight in one another as sometimes the Lord's people have in praying together, and in conversing about those things to which the world is a stranger. Here the saints are but few in a company at best: and some of them are so situated, as that they seem to themselves to dwell alone, having no access to such as they would freely embosom themselves to, in spiritual matters. They sigh and say, 'Woe is me! for I am as when they have gathered the summer-fruits – there is no cluster to eat – the good man is perished out of the earth' (Micah 7.1,2). But in the general assembly of the first-born in heaven, none of all the saints, who ever were or will be on the earth, shall be missing. They will be all of them together in one place, all possess one kingdom, and all sit down together to the marriage supper of the Lamb. Here

[446]

the best of the saints want not their sinful imperfections, making their society less comfortable: but there they shall be perfect, without 'spot or wrinkle, or any such thing' (Eph 5.27). All natural, as well as sinful imperfections, will be done away; they 'shall shine as the brightness of the firmament' (Dan 12.3).

There we shall see Adam and Eve in the heavenly paradise freely eating of the tree of life; Abraham, Isaac, and Jacob, and all the holy patriarchs, no more wandering from land to land, but come to their everlasting rest; all the prophets feasting their eyes on the glory of Him of whose coming they prophesied; the twelve apostles of the Lamb, sitting on their twelve thrones; all the holy martyrs in their long white robes, with their crowns on their heads; the godly kings advanced to a kingdom which cannot be moved; and those that turn many to righteousness, shining as the stars for ever and ever. There we shall see our godly friends, relations, and acquaintances, pillars in the temple of God, to go no more out from us. And it is more than probable that the saints will know one another in heaven; at least they will know their friends, relatives, and those they were acquainted with on earth, and such as have been most eminent in the Church; yet that knowledge will be purified from all earthly thoughts and affections. This seems to be included in that perfection of happiness to which the saints shall be advanced. If Adam knew who and what Eve was, at first sight, when the Lord God brought her to him (Gen 2.23,24), why should one question but husbands and wives, parents and children, will know one another in glory? If the Thessalonians, converted by Paul's ministry, shall be his 'crown of rejoicing in the presence of our Lord Jesus Christ at his coming' (1 Thess 2.19), why may we not conclude that ministers shall know their people, and people their ministers, in heaven? And if the disciples, on the mount of transfiguration, knew Moses and Elias, whom they had never seen before (Matt 17.4), we have reason to think that we shall know them too, and such as them, when we come to heaven. The communion of saints shall be most intimate there; 'they shall sit down with Abraham, Isaac, and Jacob, in the kingdom of heaven' (Matt 8.11). Lazarus was carried by the angels into Abraham's bosom (Luke 16.23), which denotes most intimate and familiar society. And though diversity of tongues shall cease (1 Cor 13.8), I make no question, but there will be the use of speech in heaven; and that the saints will glorify God in their bodies there, as well as in their spirits, speaking forth His praises with an audible voice. As for the language, we shall understand what it is, when we come thither. When Paul was caught up to the third heaven, the seat of the blessed, he heard there unspeakable words, which it is not lawful for a man to utter (2 Cor 12.4). Moses and Elias, on the mount with Christ, 'talked with Him' (Matt 17.3), and 'spake of his decease which he should accomplish at Jerusalem' (Luke 9.31).

(2) The saints will have the society of all the holy angels there. An innumerable company of angels shall be companions to them in their glorified state. Happy were the shepherds who heard the song of the heavenly host when Christ was born! but thrice happy they, who shall join their voices with them in the choir of saints and angels in heaven, when He shall be glorified in all who shall be about Him there! Then shall we be brought acquainted with those blessed spirits who never sinned. How bright will those morning stars shine in the holy place! they were ministering spirits to the heirs of salvation: loved them for their Lord and Master's sake; encamped round about them, to preserve them from danger. How joyfully will they welcome them to their everlasting habitations, and rejoice to see them come at length to their kingdom, as the tutor does in the prosperity of his pupils! The saints shall be no more afraid of them, as at times they were wont to be: they shall then have put off mortality, and the infirmities of the flesh, and be themselves as the angels of God, fit to enjoy communion and fellowship with them. And both being brought under one head, the Lord Jesus Christ, they shall join in the praises of God and of the Lamb, 'saying, with a loud voice, Worthy is the Lamb that was slain,' &c. (Rev 5.11,12). Whether the angels shall, as some think, assume ethereal bodies,

[448]

that they may be seen by the bodily eyes of the saints, and be in a nearer capacity to converse with them, I know not: but, as they want not ways of converse among themselves, we have reason to think that conversation between them and the saints shall not be for ever blocked up.

(3) They shall have society with the Lord Himself in Heaven, glorious communion with God in Christ, which is the perfection of happiness. I choose to speak of communion with God and the man Christ, together; because, as we derive our grace from the Lamb, so we shall derive our glory from Him too, the man Christ being, if I may be allowed the expression, the centre of the divine glory in heaven, from whence it is diffused unto all the saints. This seems to be taught us by the Scriptures which express heaven's happiness by 'being with Christ' (Luke 23.43), 'This day thou shalt be with me in paradise.' (John 17.24), 'Father, I will that they also, whom thou hast given me, be with me,' and remarkably to this purpose is what follows, 'that they may behold my glory.' (1 Thess 4.17), 'So shall we ever be with the Lord,' that is, the Lord Christ, whom we shall meet in the air. This also seems to be the import of the Scriptures wherein God and the Lamb, the slain Saviour, are jointly spoken of, in point of the happiness of the saints in heaven (Rev 7.17), 'For the Lamb which is in the midst of the throne shall feed them, and shall lead them unto living fountains of waters: and God shall wipe away all tears from their eyes.' (Chapter 21.3), 'Behold, the tabernacle of God is with men, and He will dwell with them,' as in a tabernacle, so the word signifies, that is, in the flesh of Christ: (compare John 1.14; and verse 22), 'The Lord God Almighty, and the Lamb are the temple of it.' Here lies the chief happiness of the saints in heaven, without which they never could be happy, though lodged in that glorious place, and blessed with the society of angels there. What I will venture to say of it, shall be comprised in three things:

First, The saints in heaven shall have the glorious presence of God and of the Lamb: God Himself shall be with them (Rev

21.3), and they shall ever be with the Lord. God is every where present in respect of His essence: the saints militant have His special gracious presence; but in heaven they have His glorious presence. There they are brought near to the throne of the great King, and stand before Him, where he shows His inconceivable glory. There they have the tabernacle of God, on which the cloud of glory rests, the all-glorious human nature of Christ, wherein the fulness of the Godhead dwells; not veiled, as in the days of His humiliation, but shining through that blessed flesh, that all His saints may behold His glory, and making that body more glorious than a thousand suns: so that the city has no need of the sun, nor of the moon but 'the glory of God doth lighten it, and the Lamb is the light thereof,' properly 'the candle thereof' (Rev 21.23), that is, the Lamb is the luminary or luminous body, which gives light to the city; as the sun and moon now give light to the world, or as a candle lightens a dark room: and the light proceeeding from the glorious luminary of the city is the glory of God. Sometimes on earth that candle burned very dimly; it was hid under a bushel in the time of His humiliation; only now and then it darted out some rays of this light, which dazzled the eyes of the spectators: but now it is set on high, in the city of God, where it shines, and shall shine for ever in perfection of glory. It was sometimes laid aside, as a stone disallowed of the builders: but now it is and for ever will be, 'the light,' or luminary of that city; and that, 'like unto a stone most precious, even like a jasper stone, clear as crystal' (verse 11).

Who can conceive the happiness of the saints in the presence chamber of the great King, where He sits in His chair of state, making His glory eminently to appear in the man Christ? His gracious presence makes a mighty change upon the saints in this world: His glorious presence in heaven, then, must needs raise their graces to perfection, and elevate their capacities. The saints experience that the presence of God, now with them in His grace, can make a little heaven of a sort of hell. How great then must the glory of heaven be, by His presence there in His glory! If a candle, in some sort, beautifies a cottage or prison, how will the shining sun beautify a palace or paradise! The gracious presence of God made a wilderness lightsome to Moses; the valley of the shadow of death, to David; a fiery furnace, to the three children: what a ravishing beauty then shall arise from the Sun of Righteousness, shining in His meridian brightness on the street of the city paved with pure gold! This glorious presence of God in heaven, will put a glory on the saints themselves. The most pleasing garden is devoid of beauty when the darkness of the night sits down on it; but the shining sun puts a glory on the blackest mountains: so those who are now as bottles in the smoke, when set in the glorious presence of God, will be glorious both in soul and body.

Secondly, The saints in heaven shall have the full enjoyment of God and of the Lamb. This is it that perfectly satisfies the rational creature; and here is the saints' everlasting rest. This will make up all their wants, and fill the desires of their souls, which, after all here obtained, still cry, 'Give, give,' not without some anxiety, because though they do enjoy God, yet they do not enjoy Him fully. As to the way and manner of this enjoyment, our Lord tells us (John 17.3), 'This is life eternal, that they might know thee, the only true God, and Jesus Christ, whom thou hast sent.' Now there are two ways in which a desirable object is known most perfectly and satisfyingly; the one is by sight, the other by experience: sight satisfies the understanding, and experience satisfies the will. Accordingly, one may say that the saints enjoy God and the Lamb in heaven, 1. By an intuitive knowledge; 2. By an experimental knowledge; both of them perfect, I mean in respect of the capacity of the creature; for otherwise a creature's perfect knowledge of an infinite Being is impossible. The saints below enjoy God, in that knowledge they have of Him by report, from His holy Word, which they believe; they see Him likewise darkly in the glass of ordinances, which do, as it were, represent the Bridegroom's picture, or shadow, while He is absent: they have also some experimental knowledge of Him; they taste that God is good, and that the Lord is gracious. But the saints above shall not need a good report of the King, they shall see Him; therefore faith ceaseth: they will behold His own face; therefore ordinances are no more: there is no need of a glass. They shall drink, and drink abundantly, of that whereof they have tasted; and so hope ceaseth, for they are at the utmost bounds of their desires.

(1) The saints in heaven shall enjoy God and the Lamb, by sight, and that in a most perfect manner (1 Cor 13.12), 'For now we see through a glass, darkly; but then face to face.' Here our sight is but mediate, as by a glass, in which we see not things themselves, but the images of things! but there we shall have an immediate view of God and the Lamb. Here our knowledge is but obscure: there it shall be clear, without the least mixture of darkness. The Lord now converses with His saints through the lattices of ordinances; but then shall they be in the presence chamber with Him. There is a veil now on the glorious face, as to us: but when we come to the upper house, that veil, through which some rays of beauty are now darted, will be found entirely taken off; and then shall glorious excellencies and perfections, not seen in Him by mortals, be clearly discovered, for we shall see His face (Rev 22.4). The phrase seems to be borrowed from the honour put on some in the courts of monarchs, to be attendants on the king's person. We read (Jer 52.25), of 'seven men that were' (Heb) 'seers of the king's face,' that is, as we read it, 'near the king's person.' O unspeakable glory! the great King keeps His court in heaven: and the saints shall all be His courtiers ever near the King's person, seeing His face. 'The throne of God and of the Lamb shall be in it, and his servants shall serve him; and they shall see his face' (Rev 22.3,4).

They shall see Jesus Christ, God and man, with their bodily eyes, as He will never lay aside the human nature. They will behold that glorious blessed body, which is personally united to the divine nature, and exalted above principalities and powers and every name that is named. There we shall see, with our eyes,

that very body which was born of Mary at Bethlehem, and crucified at Jerusalem between two thieves: the blessed head that
was crowned with thorns; the face that was spit upon; the hands
and feet that were nailed to the cross; all shining with inconceivable glory. The glory of the man Christ will attract the eyes
of all the saints, and He will be for ever admired in all them that
believe (2 Thess 1.10). Were each star in the heavens shining as
the sun in its meridian brightness, and the light of the sun so
increased, as the stars, in that case, should bear the same proportion to the sun, in point of light, that they do now; it might
possibly be some faint resemblance of the glory of the man
Christ in comparison with that of the saints; for though the
saints 'shine forth as the sun,' yet not they but the Lamb shall
be 'the light of the city.' The wise men fell down, and worshipped
Him, when they saw Him 'a young child, with Mary His mother
in the house.' But O what a ravishing sight will it be to see Him
in His Kingdom, on His throne, at the Father's right hand! 'The
Word was made flesh' (John 1.14), and the glory of God shall
shine through that flesh, and the joys of heaven spring out from
it, unto the saints, who shall see and enjoy God in Christ. For
since the union between Christ and the saints is never dissolved,
but they continue His members for ever; and the members cannot draw their life but from their head, seeing that which is
independent of the head, as to vital influence, is no member;
therefore Jesus Christ will remain the everlasting bond of union
betwixt God and the saints; from whence their eternal life shall
spring (John 17.2,3), 'Thou hast given him power over all flesh,
that he should give eternal life to as many as thou hast given
him. And this is life eternal that they might know thee the
only true God, &c. (verses 22,23), 'And the glory which thou
gavest me, I have given them, that they may be one, even as we
are one: I in them and thou in me, that they may be made
perfect in one.' Wherefore the immediate enjoyment of God in
heaven, is to be understood in respect of the laying aside of
Word and sacraments, and such external means as we enjoy God

by in this world; but not as if the saints should then cast off their dependence on their Head for vital influences: nay, 'the Lamb which is in the midst of the throne shall feed them, and lead them unto living fountains of waters' (Rev 7.17).

Now when we shall behold Him, who died for us, that we might live for evermore, whose matchless love made Him swim through the Red Sea of God's wrath, to make a path in the midst of it for us, by which we might pass safely to Canaan's land; then we shall see what a glorious One he was, who suffered all this for us; what entertainment He had in the upper house; what hallelujahs of angels could not hinder Him from hearing the groans of a perishing multitude on earth, and from coming down for their help; and what glory He laid aside for us. Then shall we be more 'able to comprehend with all saints, what is the breadth, and length, and depth, and height; and to know the love of Christ, which passeth knowledge' (Eph 3.18,19). When the saints shall remember that the waters of wrath which He was plunged into are the wells of salvation from whence they draw all their joy; that they have got the cup of salvation in exchange for the cup of wrath His Father gave Him to drink, which His sinless human nature shivered at; how will their hearts leap within them, burn with seraphic love, like coals of juniper, and the arch of heaven ring with their songs of salvation! The Jews, celebrating the feast of tabernacles, which was the most joyful of all their feasts, and lasted seven days, went once every day about the altar, singing hosanna, with their myrtle, palm, and willow branches in their hands, the two former being signs of victory, the last, of chastity; in the meantime bending their boughs towards the altar. When the saints are presented as a chaste virgin to Christ, and as conquerors have got their palms in their hands, how joyfully will they compass the altar evermore, and sing their hosannas, or rather their hallelujahs about it, bending their palms towards it, acknowledging themselves to owe all unto the Lamb that was slain, and who redeemed them with His blood! To this agrees what John saw (Rev 7.9,10), 'A great multitude – stood before

[454]

the throne, and before the Lamb, clothed with white robes, and palms in their hands; and cried with a loud voice, saying, Salvation to our God, which sitteth upon the throne, and unto the Lamb.'

They shall see God (Matt 5.8). They will be happy in seeing the Father, Son, and Holy Ghost, not with their bodily eyes, in respect of which, God is invisible (1 Tim 1.17), but with the eyes of their understanding; being blessed with the most perfect, full, and clear knowledge of God, and of divine things, which the creature is capable of. This is called the beatific vision, and is the perfection of understanding, the utmost term thereof. It is but an obscure delineation of the glory of God, that mortals can have on earth; a sight, as it were, of 'his back parts' (Exod 33.23). But there they will see His face (Rev 22.4). They shall see Him in the fulness of His glory, and behold Him fixedly; whereas it is but a passing view they can have of Him here (Exod 34.6). There is a vast difference between the sight of a king in his undress, quickly passing by us; and a fixed leisurely view of him, sitting on his throne in his royal robes, his crown on his head, and his sceptre in his hand: such a difference will there be between the greatest manifestation of God that ever a saint had on earth, and the display of His glory in heaven. There the saints shall eternally, without interruption, feast their eyes upon Him, and be ever viewing His glorious perfections. And as their bodily eyes shall be strengthened, and fitted to behold the glorious majesty of the man Christ, as eagles gaze on the sun without being blinded thereby, so their minds shall have such an elevation as will fit them to see God in His glory: their capacities shall be enlarged, according to the measure in which He shall be pleased to communicate Himself to them, for their complete happiness.

This blissful sight of God being quite above our present capacities, we must needs be much in the dark about it. But it seems to be something else than the sight of that glory, which we shall see with our bodily eyes, in the saints, and in the man Christ, or any other splendour or refulgence from the Godhead whatever;

[455]

for no created thing can be our chief good and happiness, nor fully satisfy our souls; and it is plain that these things are somewhat different from God Himself. Therefore I conceive, that the souls of the saints shall see God Himself: so the Scriptures teach us, that we shall 'see face to face, and know even as we are known' (1 Cor 13.12); and that 'we shall see Him as He is' (1 John 3.2). Yet the saints can never have an adequate conception of God: they cannot comprehend that which is infinite. They may touch the mountain, but cannot grasp it in their arms. They cannot, with one glance of their eye, behold what grows on every side: but the divine perfections will be an unbounded field, in which the glorified shall walk eternally, seeing more and more of God; since they can never come to the end of that which is infinite. They may bring their vessels to this ocean every moment, and fill them with new waters. What a ravishing sight would it be, to see all the perfections and lovely qualities that are scattered here and there among the creatures, gathered together into one! But even such a sight would be infinitely below this blissful sight the saints shall have in heaven. For they shall see God, in whom all these perfections shall eminently appear infinitely more, whereof there is no vestige to be found in the creatures. In Him shall they see every thing desirable, and nothing but what is desirable.

Then shall they be perfectly satisfied as to the love of God towards them, which they are now ready to question on every turn. They will no more find any difficulty to persuade themselves of it, by marks, signs, and testimonies: they will have an intuitive knowledge of it. They shall, with the profoundest reverence be it spoken, look into the heart of God, and there see the love He bore to them from all eternity, and the love and goodness He will bear to them for evermore. The glorified shall have a most clear and distinct understanding of divine truths, for in His light we shall see light (Psa 36.9). The light of glory will be a complete commentary on the Bible, and untie all the hard and knotty questions in divinity. There is no joy on earth comparable to

[456]

that which arises from the discovery of truth, no discovery of truth comparable to the discovery of Scripture truth, made by the Spirit of the Lord to the soul. 'I rejoice at thy word,' says the psalmist, 'as one that findeth great spoil' (Psa 119.162). Yet, while here, it is but an imperfect discovery. How ravishing then will it be, to see the opening of all the treasure hid in that field! They shall also be led into the understanding of the works of God. The beauty of the works of creation and providence will then be set in due light. Natural knowledge will be brought to perfection by the light of glory. The web of providence, concerning the church, and all men whatever, will then be cut out, and laid before the eyes of the saints: and it will appear a most beautiful mixture; so as they shall all say together, on the view of it, 'He hath done all things well.' But, in a special manner, the work of redemption shall be the eternal wonder of the saints, and they will admire and praise the glorious contrivance for ever. Then shall they get a full view of its suitableness to the divine perfections and to the case of sinners; and clearly read the covenant that passed between the Father and the Son from all eternity concerning their salvation. They shall for ever wonder and praise, and praise and wonder, at the mystery of wisdom and love, goodness and holiness, mercy and justice appearing in the glorious scheme. Their souls shall be eternally satisfied with the sight of God Himself, of their election by the Father, their redemption by the Son, and application thereof to them by the Holy Spirit.

(2) The saints in heaven shall enjoy God in Christ by experimental knowledge, which is, when the object itself is given and possessed. This is the participation of the divine goodness in full measure; which is the perfection of the will, and utmost term thereof. 'The Lamb shall lead them unto living fountains of waters' (Rev 7.17). These are no other but God Himself, 'the fountain of living waters,' who will fully and freely communicate Himself to them. He will pour out of His goodness eternally into their souls: then shall they have a most lively sensation, in the

innermost part of their souls, of all that goodness they heard of, and believe to be in Him, and of what they shall see in Him by the light of glory. This will be an everlasting practical exposition of that word which men and angels cannot sufficiently unfold, namely, 'God Himself shall be their God' (Rev 21.3). God will communicate Himself to them fully: they will no more be set to taste of the streams of divine goodness in ordinances, as they were wont, but shall drink at the fountain head. They will be no more entertained with sips and drops, but filled with all the fulness of God. And this will be the entertainment of every saint: for though, in created things, what is given to one is withheld from another, yet this infinite good can fully communicate itself to all, and fill all. Those who are heirs of God, the great heritage, shall then enter into a full possession of their inheritance: and the Lord will open His treasures of goodness to them, that their enjoyment may be full. They shall not be stinted in any measure: but the enjoyment shall go as far as their enlarged capacities can reach. As a narrow vessel cannot contain the ocean, so neither can the finite creature comprehend the infinite good: but no measure shall be set to the enjoyment, but what ariseth from the capacity of the creature. So that, although there be degrees of glory, yet all shall be filled, and have what they can hold; though some will be able to hold more than others. There will be no want to any of them; all shall be fully satisfied, and perfectly blessed in the full enjoyment of divine goodness, according to their enlarged capacities. As when bottles of different sizes are filled, some contain more, others less; yet all of them have what they can contain. The glorified shall have all in God, for the satisfaction of all their desires. No created thing can afford satisfaction to all our desires; clothes may warm us, but they cannot feed us; the light is comfortable, but cannot nourish us: but in God we shall have all our desires, and we shall desire nothing without Him. They shall be the happy ones, that desire nothing but what is truly desirable; they shall have all they desire. God will be all in all to the saints: He will be their life, health, riches, honour, peace, and all good things. He will communicate Himself freely to them: the door of access to Him shall never be shut again for one moment. They may, when they will, take of the fruits of the tree of life, for they will find it on each side of the river (Rev 22.2). There will be no veil between God and them, to be drawn aside; but His fulness shall ever stand open to them. No door to knock at in heaven; no asking to go before receiving; the Lord will allow His people an unrestrained familiarity with Himself there.

Now they are in part made 'partakers of the divine nature!' but then they shall perfectly partake of it; that is to say, God will communicate to them His own image, make all His goodness not only pass before them, but pass into them, and stamp the image of all His own perfections upon them, so far as the creature is capable of receiving the same; from whence shall result a perfect likeness to Him in all things in or about them; which completes the happiness of the creature. This is what the psalmist seems to have had in view (Psa 17.15), 'I shall be satisfied, when I awake, with thy likeness;' the perfection of God's image following upon the beatific vision. And so says John (1 John 3.2), 'We shall be like him; for we shall see him as he is.' Hence there shall be a most close and intimate union between God and the saints: God shall be in them, and they in God, in a glorious and most perfect union: for then shall their dwelling in love be made perfect. 'God is love; and he that dwelleth in love, dwelleth in God, and God in him' (1 John 4.16). How will the saints be united to God and He to them, when He shall see nothing in them but His own image; when their love shall arrive at its perfection, no nature but the divine nature being left in them; and all imperfection being swallowed up in their glorious transformation into the likeness of God! Their love to the Lord, being purified from the dross of self-love, shall be most pure; so as they shall love nothing but God, and in God. It shall no more be faint and languishing, but burn like coals of juniper. It will be a light without darkness, a flaming fire without smoke. As the live coal, when all the moisture is gone out of it, is all fire, so will

[459]

the saints be all love, when they come to the full enjoyment of God in heaven, by intuitive and experimental knowledge of Him, by sight and full participation of the divine goodness.

Thirdly, From this glorious presence and enjoyment shall arise an unspeakable joy, which the saints shall be filled with. 'In thy presence is fulness of joy' (Psa 16.11). The saints sometimes enjoy God in the world; but when their eyes are held, so as not to perceive it, they have not the comfort of the enjoyment: but then, all mistakes being removed, they shall not only enjoy God, but rest in the enjoyment with inexpressible delight and satisfaction. The desire of earthly things causes torment, and the enjoyment of them often ends in loathing. But though the glorified saints shall ever desire more and more of God, their desires shall not be mixed with the least anxiety, since the fulness of the Godhead stands always open to them. Therefore they shall hunger no more, they shall not have the least uneasiness in their eternal appetite after the hidden manna; neither shall continued enjoyment cause loathing; they shall never think they have too much; therefore it is added, 'neither shall the sun light on them, nor any heat' (Rev 7.16). The enjoyment of God and the Lamb will be ever fresh and new to them, through the ages of eternity: for they shall drink of living fountains of waters, where new waters are continually springing up in abundance (verse 17). They shall eat of the tree of life, which, for variety, affords twelve manner of fruits, and these always new and fresh, for it yields every month (Rev 22.2). Their joy shall be pure and unmixed, without any dregs of sorrow; not slight and momentary, but solid and everlasting, without interruption. They will enter into joy (Matt 25.21), 'Enter thou into the joy of thy Lord.' The expression is somewhat unusual, and brings to my recollection this word of our suffering Redeemer (Mark 14.34), 'My soul is exceeding sorrowful unto death.' His soul was beset with sorrows, as the word there used will bear; the floods of sorrow went round about Him, encompassing Him on every hand: wherever He turned His eyes, sorrow was before Him; it flowed in upon Him from heaven,

[460]

earth, and hell, all at once: thus was He entered into sorrow, and therefore saith (Psa 69.2), 'I am come into deep waters, where the floods overflow me.' Now, wherefore all this, but that His own might enter into joy? Joy sometimes enters into us now, but has much to do to get access, while we are encompassed with sorrows: but then joy shall not only enter into us, but we shall enter into it, and swim for ever in an ocean of joy, where we shall see nothing but joy wherever we turn our eyes. The presence and enjoyment of God and the Lamb will satisfy us with pleasures for evermore: and the glory of our souls and bodies, arising from thence, will afford us everlasting delight. The spirit of heaviness, however closely it cleaves to any of the saints now, shall drop off then: their weeping shall be turned into songs of joy, and bottles of tears shall issue in rivers of pleasure. Happy they who now sow in tears, which shall spring up in joy in heaven, and will encircle their heads with a weight of glory.

Thus far of the society in this kingdom of the saints.

10: In the last place, the kingdom shall endure for ever. As every thing in it is eternal, so the saints shall have undoubted certainty, and full assurance, of the eternal duration of the same. This is a necessary ingredient in perfect happiness; for the least uncertainty as to the continuance of any good with one, is not without some fear, anxiety, and torment, and therefore is utterly inconsistent with perfect happiness. But the glorified shall never have fear, nor cause of fear, of any loss: they shall be 'ever with the Lord' (1 Thess 4.17). They shall all attain the full persuasion, that nothing shall be able to separate them from the love of God, nor from the full enjoyment of Him for ever. The inheritance 'reserved in heaven is incorruptible;' it has no principle of corruption in itself, to make it liable to decay, but endures for evermore; it is undefiled, nothing from without can mar its beauty, nor is there any thing in itself to offend those who enjoy it. Therefore it fadeth not away; but ever remains in its native lustre, and primitive beauty (1 Pet 1.4). Hitherto of the nature of the kingdom of heaven.

11: We now proceed to speak of the admission of the saints into this their new kingdom. I shall briefly touch upon two things: 1. The formal admission, in the call upon them from the Judge to come into their kingdom. 2. The quality in which they are admitted and introduced to it.

1: Their admission the text shows, is by a voice from the throne: the King calling to them, from the throne, before angels and men, to come to their kingdom. *Come* and *go* are but short words: but they will be such as will afford matter of thought to all mankind, through the ages of eternity; since everlasting happiness turns upon one, and everlasting misery on the other.

Now, our Lord bids the worst of sinners, who hear the Gospel, Come; but the most part will not come unto Him. Some few, whose hearts are touched by His Spirit, embrace the call, and their souls within them say, 'Behold, we come unto Thee:' they give themselves to the Lord, forsake the world and their lusts for Him: they bear His yoke, and cast it not off, no, not in the heat of the day when the weight of it, perhaps, makes them sweat the blood out of their bodies. Behold the fools! says the carnal world, whither are they going? But stay a little, O foolish world! From the same mouth whence they had the call they are now following, another call shall come, that will make amends for all: 'Come ye blessed of my Father, inherit the kingdom.'

The saints shall find an inexpressible sweetness in this call, Come. 1. Hereby Jesus Christ shows His desire for their society in the upper house, that they may be ever with Him there. Thus He will open His heart to them, as sometimes He did to His Father concerning them, saying, 'Father, I will they be with me, where I am' (John 17.24). Now, the travail of His soul stands before the throne, not only the souls, but the bodies He has redeemed; and they must come, for He must be completely satisfied. 2. Hereby they are solemnly invited to the marriage supper of the Lamb. They were invited to the lower table by the voice of the servants, and the sacred workings of the Spirit within them; and they came, and did partake of the feast of divine communications in the lower house: but Jesus Christ in person shall invite them, before all the world, to the higher table. 3. By this He admits them into the mansions of glory. The keys of heaven hang at the girdle of our royal Mediator. 'All power in heaven' is given to Him (Matt 28.18): and none get in thither but whom He admits. When they were living on earth with the rest of the world, He opened the doors of their hearts, entered into them, and shut them again, so that sin could never re-enter, to reign there as formerly: now He opens heaven's doors to them, draws His doves into the ark, and shuts them in; so that the law, death, and hell, can never get them out again. The saints in this life were still labouring to enter into that rest; but Satan was always pulling them back, their corruptions always drawing them down, insomuch that they have sometimes been left to hang by a hair of promise, if I may be allowed the expression, not without fear of falling into the lake of fire: but now Christ gives the word for their admission, they are brought in, and put beyond all hazard. 4. He speaks to them as the person introducing them into the kingdom, into the presence-chamber of the great King, and to the throne. Jesus Christ is the great Secretary of heaven, whose office it is to bring the saints into the gracious presence of God now, and to whom alone it belongs to bring them into the glorious presence of God in heaven. Truly heaven would be a strange place to them if Jesus were not there; but the Son will introduce His brethren into His Father's kingdom; they shall go in 'with Him to the marriage' (Matt 25.10).

2: Let us consider in what *quality* they are introduced by Him.

(1) He brings them in as the blessed of His Father; so runs the call from the throne, 'Come, ye blessed of my Father,' &c. It is Christ's Father's house they are to come into: therefore He puts them in mind that they are blessed of the Father, dear to the Father, as well as Himself. This it is that makes heaven home to them, namely, that it is Christ's Father's house, where they may be assured of welcome, being married to the Son, and being His Father's choice for that very end. He brings them in for His

[463]

Father's sake, as well as for His own: they are the blessed of His Father; who, as He is the fountain of the Deity, is also the fountain of all blessings conferred on the children of men. They are those whom God loved from eternity. They were blessed in the eternal purpose of God, being elected to everlasting life. At the opening of the book of life, their names were found written therein: so that by bringing them to the kingdom, He does but bring them to what the Father, from all eternity, designed for them: being saved by the Son, they are saved according to His, that is, the Father's purpose (2 Tim 1.9). They are those to whom the Father has spoken well. He spoke well to them in His Word, which must now receive its full accomplishment. They had His promise of the kingdom, lived and died in the faith of it; and now they come to receive the thing promised. Unto them He has done well. A gift is often in Scripture called a blessing; and God's blessing is ever real, like Isaac's blessing, by which Jacob became his heir: they were all by grace justified, sanctified, and enabled to persevere to the end; now they are raised up in glory, and being tried, stand in the judgment. What remains, then, but that God should crown His work of grace in them, in giving them their kingdom, in the full enjoyment of Himself for ever? Finally, they are those whom God has consecrated; the which also is a Scripture term of blessing (1 Cor 10.16). God set them apart for Himself, to be kings and priests unto Him; and the Mediator introduces them, as such, to their kingdom and priesthood.

(2) Christ introduces them, as heirs of the kingdom, to the actual possession of it. 'Come, ye blessed, inherit the kingdom.' They are the children of God by regeneration and adoption; 'And if children, then heirs, heirs of God, and joint-heirs with Christ' (Rom 8.17). Now is the general assembly of the first-born before the throne: their minority is overpast; and the time appointed of the Father for their receiving their inheritance is come. The Mediator purchased the inheritance for them with His own blood; their rights and evidences were drawn long ago, and registered in the Bible; nay, they have investment of their inheritance in the

person of Christ, as their proxy, when He ascended into heaven, 'Whither the forerunner is for us entered' (Heb 6.20). Nothing remains, but that they enter into personal possession thereof, which, begun at death, is perfected at the last day, when the saints in their bodies, as well as their souls, go into their kingdom.

(3) They are introduced to it as those it was prepared for, from the foundation of the world. The kingdom was prepared for them in the eternal purpose of God, before they, or any of them, had a being; which shows it to be a gift of free grace to them. It was from eternity the divine purpose that there should be such a kingdom for the elect; and that all impediments which might oppose their access to it should be removed out of the way. By the same eternal decree, every one's place in it was determined and set apart, to be reserved for him, that each of the children coming home at length into their Father's house, might find his own place awaiting him, and ready for him, as at Saul's table David's place was empty when he was not there to occupy it himself (1 Sam 20.25). And now the appointed time is come, they are brought in, to take their several places in glory.

III: *Use:* I shall conclude my discourse on this subject with a word of application. 1. To all who claim a right to this kingdom. 2. To those who have indeed a right to it. 3. To those who have no right thereto.

1: Since it is evident there is no promiscuous admission into the kingdom of heaven, and none obtain it but those whose claim to it is solemnly tried by the great Judge, and, after trial, supported as good and valid; it is necessary that all of us impartially try and examine whether, according to the laws of the kingdom contained in the Holy Scriptures, we can verify and make good our claim to this kingdom. The hopes of heaven which most men have, are built on such sandy foundations as can never abide the trial. Having no ground whatever but in their own deluded fancy, such hopes will leave those who entertain them miserably disappointed at last. Wherefore, it is not only our duty, but our interest, to put the matter to a fair trial in time. If we find we have no right to heaven, we are yet in the way, and what we have not, we may obtain; but if we find we have a right to it, we shall then have the comfort of a happy prospect into eternity, which is the greatest comfort one is capable of in the world. If you inquire how you may know whether you have a right to heaven or not, I answer, You may know that by the state you are now in. If you are yet in your natural state, you are children of wrath, and not children of this kingdom; for that state, to those who live and die in it, issues in eternal misery. If you are brought into the state of grace, you have a just claim to the state of glory; for grace will certainly issue in glory at length. This kingdom is an inheritance which none but the children of God can justly claim. Now, we become the children of God by regeneration, and union with Christ His Son; 'And if children, then heirs, heirs of God, and joint-heirs with Christ (Rom 8.17). These, then, are the great points upon which our evidences for the state of glory depend. Therefore, I refer you to what is said on the state of grace, for satisfying you as to your right to glory.

If you be heirs of glory, 'the kingdom of God is within you,' by virtue of your regeneration and union with Christ. 1. The kingdom of heaven has the throne in your heart, if you have a right to that kingdom: Christ is in you, and God is in you; and having chosen Him for your portion, your soul has taken up its everlasting rest in Him, and gets no true rest but in Him; as the dove, until she came into the ark. To Him the soul habitually inclines, by virtue of the new nature, the divine nature, which the heirs of glory are partakers of (Psa 73.25), 'Whom have I in heaven but thee? and there is none upon earth that I desire beside thee.' 2. The laws of heaven are in your heart, if you are an heir of heaven (Heb 8.10), 'I will put my laws into their mind, and write them in their hearts.' Your mind is enlightened in the knowledge of the laws of the kingdom by the Spirit of the Lord, the instructor of all the heirs of glory; for whoever may want instruction, surely an heir to a crown shall not want it. 'It is written in the prophets, And they shall be all taught of God' (John 6.45). Therefore, though father and mother leave them early, or be in no concern about their Christian education, and they be soon put to work for their daily bread, yet they shall not lack teaching. Withal, your heart is changed, and you bear God's image, which consists in 'righteousness and true holiness' (Eph 4.24). Your soul is reconciled to the whole law of God, and at war with all known sin. In vain do they pretend to the holy kingdom, who are not holy in heart and life; for 'without holiness no man shall see the Lord' (Heb 12.14). If heaven is a rest, it is for spiritual labourers, not for loiterers. If it is an eternal triumph, they are not in the way to it who avoid the spiritual warfare, and are in no care to subdue corruption, resist temptation, and to cut their way to it through the opposition made by the devil, the world, and the flesh. 3. The treasure in heaven is the chief in your esteem and desire; for it is your treasure, and 'where your treasure is, there will your heart be also' (Matt 6.21). If it is not the things that are seen, but the things that are not seen, which your heart is in the greatest care and concern to obtain; if you are driving a trade with heaven, and your chief business lies there; it is a sign that your treasure is there, for your heart is there. But if you are of those who wonder why so much ado is made about heaven and eternal life, as if less might serve the turn, you are like to have nothing to do with it at all. Carnal men value themselves most on their treasures upon earth; with them, the things that are not seen are weighed down by the things that are seen, and no losses so much affect them as earthly losses: but the heirs of the crown of glory value themselves most on their treasures in heaven, and will not put their private estate in the balance with their kingdom; nor will the loss of the former go so near their hearts as the thoughts of the loss of the latter. Where these first-fruits of heaven are to be found, the eternal weight of glory will surely follow after; while the want of them must be admitted according to the Word, to be an incontestible evidence of an heir of wrath.

2. Let the heirs of the kingdom behave themselves suitably to their character and dignity. Live as having the faith and hope of

this glorious kingdom: let your conversation be in heaven (Phil 3.20). Let your souls delight in communion with God while you are on earth, since you look for your happiness in communion with Him in heaven. Let your speech and actions savour of heaven; and in your manner of life, look like the country to which you are going: that it may be said of you, as of Gideon's brethren (Judges 8.18), 'Each one resembled the children of a king.' Maintain a holy contempt of the world, and of the things of the world. Although others, whose earthly things are their best things, set their hearts upon them, yet it becomes you to set your feet on them, since your best things are above. This world is but the country through which lies your road to Immanuel's land. Therefore pass through it as pilgrims and strangers; and dip not into the encumbrances of it, so as to retard you in your journey. It is unworthy of one born to a palace, to set his heart on a cottage to dwell there; and of one running for a prize of gold, to go off his way to gather the stones of the brook: but much more it is unworthy of an heir of the kingdom of heaven to be hid among the stuff of this world, when he should be going on to receive his crown. The prize set before you challenges your utmost zeal, activity, and diligence; and holy courage, resolution, and magnanimity become those who are to inherit the crown. You cannot come at it without fighting your way to it, through difficulties from without and from within: but the kingdom before you is sufficient to balance them all, though you should be called to resist even unto blood. Prefer Christ's cross before the world's crown, and wants in the way of duty, before ease and wealth in the way of sin: 'Choose rather to suffer affliction with the people of God, than to enjoy the pleasures of sin for a season' (Heb 11.25). In a common inn, strangers perhaps fare better than the children; but here lies the difference, the children are to pay nothing for what they have got; but the strangers get their bill, and must pay completely for all they have had. Did we consider the after-reckoning of the wicked for all the smiles of common providence they meet with in the world, we should not grudge

[468]

them their good things here, nor take it amiss that God keeps our best things last. Heaven will make up all the saints' losses, and there all tears will be wiped away from their eyes.

It is worth observing, that there is such a variety of Scripture notions of heaven's happiness, as may suit every afflicted case of the saints. Are they oppressed? The day cometh in which they shall have the dominion. Is their honour laid in the dust? A throne to sit upon, a crown on their head, and a sceptre in their hand, will raise it up again. Are they reduced to poverty? Heaven is a treasure. If they be forced to quit their own habitations, yet Christ's Father's house is ready for them. Are they driven to the wilderness? There is a city prepared for them. Are they banished from their native country? They shall inherit a better country. If they are deprived of public ordinances, the Lord God Almighty and the Lamb are the temple there, whither they are going; a temple, the doors of which none can shut. If their life be full of bitterness, heaven is a paradise for pleasure. If they groan under the remains of spiritual bondage, there is glorious liberty abiding them. Do their defiled garments make them ashamed? The day is coming in which their robes shall be white, pure, and spotless. The battle against flesh and blood, principalities and powers, is indeed sore: but a glorious triumph awaits them. If the toil and labours of the Christian life be great, there is an everlasting rest for them in heaven. Are they judged unworthy of the society of angels in heaven? Do they complain of frequent interruptions of their communion with God? There they shall go no more out, but shall see His face for evermore. If they are in darkness here, eternal light is there. If they grapple with death, there they shall have everlasting life. And, to sum up all in one word, 'He that overcometh shall inherit all things' (Rev 21.7). He shall have peace and plenty, profit and pleasure, everything desirable; full satisfaction to his most enlarged desires. Let the expectants of heaven, then, lift up their heads with joy; let them gird up their loins, and so run that they may obtain, trampling on every thing that may hinder them in their way to the kingdom. Let them never account any duty too hard, nor any cross too heavy, nor any pains too great, so that they may attain the crown of glory.

3: Let those who have no right to the kingdom of heaven be stirred up to seek it with all diligence. Now is the time wherein the children of wrath may become heirs of glory: when the way to everlasting happiness is opened, it is no time to sit still and loiter. Raise up your hearts towards the glory that is to be revealed; and be not always in search of rest in this perishing earth. What can all your worldly enjoyments avail you, while you have no solid ground to expect heaven after this life is gone? The riches and honours, profits and pleasures, that must be buried with us, and cannot accompany us into another world, are but a wretched portion, and will leave men comfortless at length. Ah! why are men so eager in their lifetime to receive their good things? Why are they not rather careful to secure an interest in the kingdom of heaven, which would never be taken from them, but afford them a portion to make them happy through the ages of eternity? If you desire honour, there you may have the highest honour, which will last when the world's honours are laid in the dust; if riches, heaven will yield you a treasure; and there are pleasures for evermore. O! be not despisers of the pleasant land, neither judge yourselves unworthy of eternal life; close with Christ, as He is offered to you in the Gospel, and you shall inherit all things. Walk in the way of holiness, and it will lead you to the kingdom. Fight against sin and Satan, and you shall receive the crown. Forsake the world, and the doors of heaven will be opened to receive you.

6

HELL

Then shall he say also unto them on the left hand,
Depart from me, ye cursed, into everlasting fire, prepared for the devil and his angels.   MATTHEW 25.41

Were there no other place of eternal lodging but heaven, I should
here have closed my discourse of man's eternal state; but as in the
other world there is a prison for the wicked, as well as a palace
for saints, we must also inquire into that state of everlasting
misery; which the worst of men may well bear with, without
crying, 'Art thou come to torment us before the time?' since there
is yet access to flee from the wrath to come; and all that can be
said of it comes short of what the damned will feel; for 'who
knoweth the power of God's anger?'

The last thing which our Lord did, before He left the earth,
was, 'He lifted up his hands, and blessed his disciples' (Luke
24.50,51). But the last thing He will do, before He leaves the
throne, is to curse and condemn His enemies; as we learn from
the text which contains the dreadful sentence wherein the everlasting misery of the wicked is declared. In which, three things
may be taken notice of: 1. The quality of the condemned: 'ye
cursed.' The Judge finds the curse of the law upon them as transgressors, and sends them away with it, from His presence, into
hell, there to be fully executed upon them. 2. The punishment
which they are adjudged to, and to which they were always
bound over by virtue of the curse. And it is twofold, the punishment of loss, in separation from God and Christ, 'Depart from
Me;' and the punishment of sense, in most exquisite and extreme
torments, 'Depart from Me into fire.' 3. The aggravations of their
torments. 1. They are ready for them, they are not to expect a

moment's respite. The fire is prepared and ready to catch hold of those who are thrown into it. 2. They will have the society of devils in their torments, being shut up with them in hell. They must depart into the same fire, prepared for Beelzebub, the prince of devils, and his angels; namely, other reprobate angels who fell with him, and became devils. It is said to be prepared for them; because they sinned and were condemned to hell before man sinned. This speaks further terror to the damned, that they must go into the same torments, and place of torment, with the devil and his angels. They hearkened to his temptations, and they must partake in his torments: his works they would do, and they must receive the wages, which is death. In this life they joined with devils, in enmity against God and Christ, and the way of holiness; and in the other, they must lodge with them. Thus all the goats shall be shut up together; for that name is common to devils and wicked men, in Scripture (Lev 17.7), where the word rendered devils properly signifies hairy ones, or goats, in the shape of which creatures devils delighted much to appear to their worshippers. 3. The last aggravation of their torment is the eternal duration thereof; they must depart into everlasting fire. This is what puts the top-stone upon their misery, namely, that it shall never have an end.

DOCTRINE: *The wicked shall be shut up under the curse of God, in everlasting misery, with the devils in hell*

After having proved that there shall be a resurrection of the body and a general judgment, I think it is not needful to insist on proving the truth of future punishment. The same conscience there is in men of a future judgment, bears witness also of the truth of future punishment. (And that the punishment of the damned shall not be annihilation, or a reducing them to nothing, will be clear in the progress of our discourse.) In treating of this awful subject I shall inquire into these four things: I. The curse under which the damned shall be shut up. II. Their misery under that curse. III. Their society with devils in this miserable state. IV. The eternity of the whole.

I: As to the curse under which the damned shall be shut up in hell, it is the terrible sentence of the law, by which they are bound over to the wrath of God, as transgressors. This curse does not first seize them when standing before the tribunal to receive their sentence; but they were born under it, they led their lives under it in this world, they died under it, rose with it out of their graves; and the Judge finding it upon them, sends them away with it into the pit, where it shall lie on them through all the ages of eternity. By nature all men are under the curse; but it is removed from the elect by virtue of their union with Christ. It abides on the rest of sinful mankind, and by it they are devoted to destruction, separated to evil, as one describes the curse (from Deut 29.21), 'And the Lord shall separate him unto evil.' Thus shall the damned for ever be persons devoted to destruction; separate and set apart from the rest of mankind, unto evil, as vessels of wrath; set up as marks for the arrows of divine wrath; and made the common receptacle and shore of vengeance.

This curse has its first-fruits on earth, which are a pledge of the whole lump that is to follow. Hence it is, that as temporal and eternal benefits are bound up together, under the same expressions, in the promise to the Lord's people (as Isa 35.10), 'And the ransomed of the Lord shall return, and come to Zion,' &c., relating both to return from Babylon, and to the saints' going to their eternal rest in heaven; even so, temporal and eternal miseries, on the enemies of God, are sometimes included under one and the same expression in the threatening (as Isa 30.33), 'For Tophet is ordained of old; yea, for the king it is prepared; he hath made it deep and large: the pile thereof is fire and much wood; the breath of the Lord, like a stream of brimstone, doth kindle it.' Which relates both to the temporal and eternal destruction of the Assyrians, who fell by the hand of the angel before Jerusalem. (See also Isa 66.24.) What is that judicial blindness to which many are given up, 'whom the god of this world hath blinded' (2 Cor 4.4), but the first fruits of hell and of the curse? Their sun is going down at noon-day, their darkness increasing, as if it would not stop till it issue in utter darkness. Many a lash in the dark doth conscience give the wicked, which the world doth not hear of: and what is that but the never-dying worm already begun to gnaw them? And there is not one of these but they may call it Joseph, for 'the Lord shall add another;' or rather God, for 'a troop cometh.' These drops of wrath are terrible forebodings of the full shower which is to follow. Sometimes they are given up to their vile affections, that they have no more command over them (Rom 1.26). So their lusts grow up more and more towards perfection, if I may so speak.

As in heaven grace comes to its perfection, so in hell sin arrives at its highest pitch; and as sin is thus advancing upon the man, he is the nearer and liker to hell. There are three things that have a fearful aspect here. 1. When every thing that might do good to men's souls, is blasted to them; so that their blessings are cursed (Mal 2.2); sermons, prayers, admonitions, and reproofs, which are powerful towards others, are quite inefficacious to them. 2. When men go on in sinning still, in the face of plain rebukes from the Lord, in ordinances and providences. God meets them with rods in the way of their sin, as it were striking them back; yet they rush forward. What can be more like hell, where the Lord is always smiting and the damned always sinning against Him? 3. When every thing in one's lot is turned into fuel to one's lusts. Thus, adversity and prosperity, poverty and wealth, the want of ordinances and the enjoyment of them, do all but nourish the corruptions of many. Their vicious stomachs corrupt whatever they receive, and all does but increase noxious humours.

But the full harvest follows, in that misery which they shall for ever lie under in hell; that wrath which, by virtue of the curse, shall come upon them to the uttermost; which is the curse fully executed. This black cloud opens upon them, and the terrible thunderbolt strikes them, by that dreadful voice from the throne, 'Depart from me, ye cursed,' &c. Which will give the

[474]

whole wicked world a dismal view of what is in the bosom of the curse. It is, 1. A voice of extreme indignation and wrath, a furious rebuke from the Lion of the tribe of Judah. His looks will be most terrible to them; His eyes will cast flames of fire on them; and His words will pierce their hearts, like envenomed arrows. When He will thus speak them out of His presence for ever, and by His word chase them away from before the throne, they will see how keenly wrath burns in His heart against them for their sins. 2. It is a voice of extreme disdain and contempt from the Lord. Time was when they were pitied, admonished to pity themselves, and to be the Lord's; yet they despised Him, they would have none of Him: but now they shall be buried out of His sight, under everlasting contempt. 3. It is a voice of extreme hatred. Hereby the Lord shuts them out of His bowels of love and mercy. 'Depart, ye cursed.' I cannot endure to look at you; there is not one purpose of good to you in Mine heart; nor shall you ever hear one word more of hope from Me. 4. It is a voice of eternal rejection from the Lord. He commands them to be gone, and so casts them off for ever. Thus the doors of heaven are shut against them; the gulf is fixed between them and it, and they are driven to the pit. Now, were they to cry with all possible earnestness, 'Lord, Lord, open to us;' they will hear nothing but, 'Depart, depart ye cursed.' Thus shall the damned be shut up under the curse.

Use 1 : Let all those who, being yet in their natural state, are under the curse, consider this, and flee to Jesus Christ in time, that they may be delivered from it. How can you sleep in that state, being under the curse! Jesus Christ is now saying unto you, 'Come ye cursed, I will take the curse from off you, and give you the blessing.' The waters of the sanctuary are now running, to heal the cursed ground; take heed to improve them for that end to your own souls, and fear it as hell to get no spiritual advantage thereby. Remember that 'the miry places,' which are neither sea nor dry land, a fit emblem of hypocrites, 'and the marshes,' that neither breed fishes, nor bear trees, but the waters

[475]

of the sanctuary leave them, as they find them, in their barrenness, 'shall not be healed,' seeing they spurn the only remedy; 'they shall be given to salt,' left under eternal barrenness, set up for the monuments of the wrath of God, and concluded for ever under the curse (Ezek 47.11). 2. Let all cursers consider this, whose mouths are filled with cursing themselves and others. He who 'clothes himself with cursing,' shall find the curse 'come into his bowels like water, and oil into his bones' (Psa 109.18), if repentance prevent it not. He shall get all his imprecations against himself fully answered, in the day wherein he stands before the tribunal of God: and shall find the killing weight of the curse of God, which he now makes light of.

11: I proceed to speak of the misery of the damned, under that curse; a misery which the tongues of men and angels cannot sufficiently express. God always acts like Himself: no favours can be compared to His, and His wrath and terrors are without a parallel. As the saints in heaven are advanced to the highest pitch of happiness, so the damned in hell arrive at the height of misery. Two things here I shall soberly inquire into – the punishment of loss, and the punishment of sense, in hell. But since these also are such things as eye hath not seen, nor ear heard, we must, as geographers do, leave a large void for the unknown land, which the day will discover.

1: The punishment of loss which the damned shall undergo, is separation from the Lord, as we learn from the text, 'Depart from me, ye cursed.' This will be a stone upon their grave's mouth, as 'the talent of lead' (Zech 5.7,8), that will hold them down for ever. They shall be eternally separated from God and Christ. Christ is the way to the Father: but the way, as to them, shall be everlastingly blocked up, the bridge shall be drawn, and the great gulf fixed; so shall they be shut up in a state of eternal separation from God the Father, Son, and Holy Ghost. They will be locally separated from the man Christ, and shall never come into the seat of the blessed, where He appears in His glory, but be cast out into outer darkness (Matt 22.13). They cannot indeed be

[476]

locally separated from God, they cannot be in a place where He is not; since He is, and will be present every where: 'If I make my bed in hell,' says the psalmist, 'behold thou art there' (Psa 139.8). But they shall be miserable beyond expression, in a relative separation from God. Though He will be present in the very centre of their souls, if I may so express it, while they are wrapped up in fiery flames, in utter darkness, it shall only be to feed them with the vinegar of His wrath, and to punish them with the emanations of His revenging justice: they shall never more taste of His goodness and bounty, nor have the least glimpse of hope from Him. They will see His heart to be absolutely alienated from them, and that it cannot be towards them; that they are the party against whom the Lord will have indignation for ever. They shall be deprived of the glorious presence and enjoyment of God: they shall have no part in the beatific vision; nor see any thing in God towards them, but one wave of wrath rolling after another. This will bring upon them overwhelming floods of sorrow for evermore. They shall never taste of the rivers of pleasures which the saints in heaven enjoy; but shall have an everlasting winter and a perpetual night, because the Sun of Righteousness has departed from them, and so they are left in utter darkness. So great as heaven's happiness is, so great will their loss be: for they can have none of it for ever.

This separation of the wicked from God will be, 1. An involuntary separation. Now they depart from Him, they will not come to Him, though they are called and entreated to come: but then they shall be driven away from Him, when they would gladly abide with Him. Although the question 'What is thy beloved more than another beloved?' is frequent now amongst the despisers of the Gospel, there will be no such question among all the damned; for then they will see that man's happiness is only to be found in the enjoyment of God, and that the loss of Him is a loss that can never be balanced. 2. It will be a total and utter separation. Though the wicked are, in this life, separated from God, yet there is a kind of intercourse between them: He gives them many good gifts, and they give Him, at least, some good words; so that the peace is not altogether hopeless. But then there shall be a total separation, the damned being cast into utter darkness, where there will not be the least gleam of light and favour from the Lord; which will put an end to all their fair words to Him. 3. It shall be a final separation; they will part with Him, never more to meet, being shut up under everlasting horror and despair. The match between Jesus Christ and unbelievers, which has so often been carried forward, and put back again, shall then be broken up for ever; and never shall one message of favour or good-will go between the parties any more.

This punishment of loss, in a total and final separation from God, is a misery beyond what mortals can conceive, and which the dreadful experience of the damned can only sufficiently unfold. But that we may have some conception of the horror of it, let these following things be considered.

(1) God is the chief good; therefore, to be separated from Him, must be the chief evil. Our native country, our relations, and our life, are good, and therefore to be deprived of them we reckon a great evil; and the better any thing is, so much the greater evil is the loss of it. Wherefore, God being the chief good, and no good comparable to Him, there can be no loss so great as the loss of God. The full enjoyment of Him is the highest pinnacle of happiness the creature is capable of arriving at: to be fully and finally separated from Him, must then be the lowest step of misery which the rational creature can be reduced to. To be cast off by men, by good men, is distressing; what must it then be, to be rejected of God, of goodness itself?

(2) God is the fountain of all goodness, from which all goodness flows unto the creatures, and by which it is continued in them, and to them. Whatever goodness or perfection, natural as well as moral, is in any creature, it is from God, and depends upon Him, as the light is from, and depends on, the sun; for every created being, as such, is a dependent one. Wherefore, a total separation from God, wherein all comfortable communication be-

[478]

tween God and a rational creature is absolutely blocked up, must of necessity bring along with it a total eclipse of all light of comfort and ease whatsoever. If there is but one window, or open place, in a house, and that be quite shut up, it is evident there can be nothing but darkness in that house. Our Lord tells us (Matt 19.17), 'There is none good but one, that is, God.' Nothing good or comfortable is originally from the creature: whatever good or comfortable thing one finds in one's self, as health of body, peace of mind; whatever sweetness, rest, pleasure, or delight, one finds in other creatures, as in meat, drink, arts and sciences; all these are but some faint rays of Divine perfections, communicated from God unto the creature, and depending on a constant influence from Him for their conversation, which failing, they would immediately be gone; for it is impossible that any created thing can be to us more or better than what God makes it to be. All the rivulets of comfort we drink of, within or without ourselves, come from God as their spring-head; the course of which towards us being stopped, of necessity they must all dry up. So that when God goes, all that is good and comfortable goes with Him, all ease and quiet of body and mind (Hos 9.12), 'Woe also to them, when I depart from them.' When the wicked are totally and finally separated from Him, all that is comfortable in them, or about them, returns to its fountain; as the light goes away with the sun, and darkness succeeds in the room thereof. Thus, in their separation from God, all peace is removed far away from them, and pain in body and anguish of soul, succeed to it: all joy goes, and unmixed sorrow settles in them: all quiet and rest separate from them, and they are filled with horror and rage: hope flies away, and despair seizes them; common operations of the Spirit, which now restrain them, are withdrawn for ever, and sin comes to its utmost height. Thus we have a dismal view of the horrible spectacle of sin and misery, which a creature proves when totally separated from God and left to itself; and we may see this separation to be the very hell of hell.

Being separated from God, they are deprived of all good. The

[479]

good things which they set their hearts upon in this world are beyond their reach there. The covetous man cannot enjoy his wealth there, nor the ambitious man his honours, nor the sensual man his pleasures, no, not a drop of water to cool his tongue (Luke 16.24,25). No meat or drink there to strengthen the faint; no sleep to refresh the weary: and no music, or pleasant company, to comfort and cheer up the sorrowful. And as for those good things they despised in the world, they shall never more hear of them, nor see them. No offer of Christ there, no pardon, no peace; no wells of salvation in the pit of destruction. In one word, they shall be deprived of whatever might comfort them, being totally and finally separated from God, the fountain of all goodness and comfort.

(3) Man naturally desires to be happy, being conscious to himself that he is not self-sufficient: he has ever a desire of something without himself, to make him happy; and the soul being, by its natural make and constitution, capable of enjoying God, and nothing else being commensurable to its desires, it can never have true and solid rest till it rests in the enjoyment of God. This desire of happiness the rational creature can never lay aside, no, not in hell. Now, while the wicked are on earth, they seek their satisfaction in the creature: and when one fails, they go to another: thus they spend their time in the world, deceiving their own souls with vain hopes. But, in the other world, all comfort in the creatures failing, and the shadows which they are now pursuing having all of them vanished in a moment, they shall be totally and finally separated from God, and see they have thus lost Him. So the doors of earth and heaven both are shut against them at once. This will create them unspeakable anguish, while they shall live under an eternal gnawing hunger after happiness, which they certainly know shall never be in the least measure satisfied, all doors being closed on them. Who then can imagine how this separation from God shall cut the damned to the heart! how they will roar and rage under it! and how it will sting and gnaw them through the ages of eternity!

[480]

(4) The damned shall know that some are perfectly happy, in the enjoyment of that God from whom they themselves are separated; and this will aggravate the sense of their loss, that they can never have any share with those happy ones. Being separated from God, they are separated from the society of the glorified saints and angels. They may see Abraham afar off, and Lazarus in his bosom (Luke 16.23), but can never come into their company; being, as unclean lepers, thrust out without the camp, and excommunicated from the presence of the Lord, and of all His holy ones. It is the opinion of some, that every person in heaven or hell shall hear and see all that passes in either state. Whatever is to be said of this, we have ground from the Word to conclude that the damned shall have a very exquisite knowledge of the happiness of the saints in heaven; for what else can be meant of the rich man in hell seeing Lazarus in Abraham's bosom? One thing is plain in this case, that their own torments will give them such notions of the happiness of the saints, as a sick man has of health, or a prisoner has of liberty. And as they cannot fail of reflecting on the happiness of those in heaven, without any hope of attaining to contentment with their own lot, so every thought of that happiness will aggravate their loss. It would be a mighty torment to a hungry man to see others liberally feasting, while he is so chained up as not to have one crumb to stay his gnawing appetite. To bring music and dancing before a man labouring under extreme pains would but increase his anguish: how then will the songs of the blessed, in their enjoyment of God, make the damned mourn under their separation from Him!

(5) They will remember that time was when they might have been made partakers of the blessed company of saints, in their enjoyment of God: and this will aggravate their sense of the loss. All may remember that there was once a possibility of it; that they were once in the world, in some corners of which the way of salvation was laid open to men's view, and may wish they had gone round the world, till they had found it out. Despisers of

the Gospel will remember, with bitterness, that Jesus Christ, with all His benefits, was offered to them: that they were exhorted, entreated, and pressed to accept, but would not; and that they were warned of the misery they feel, and exhorted to flee from the wrath to come, but they would not hearken. The Gospel offer slighted will make a hot hell, and the loss of an offered heaven will be a sinking weight on the spirits of unbelievers in the pit. Some will remember that there was a probability of their being eternally happy; that once they seemed to stand fair for it, and were not far from the kingdom of God; that they had once almost consented to the blessed bargain; the pen was in their hand, as it were, to sign the marriage contract between Christ and their souls; but unhappily they dropped it, and turned back from the Lord to their lusts again. Others will remember that they thought themselves sure of heaven, but, being blinded with pride and self-conceit, they were above ordinances, and beyond instruction, and would not examine their state, which was their ruin: but then they will in vain wish that they had reputed themselves the worst of the congregation, and curse the fond conceit they had of themselves, and that others had of them too. Thus it will sting the damned, that they might have escaped this loss.

(6) They will see the loss to be irrecoverable; that they must eternally lie under it, never, never to be repaired. Might the damned, after millions of ages in hell, regain what they have lost, it would be some ground of hope; but the prize is gone, and never can be recovered. There are two things which will pierce them to the heart: 1. That they never knew the worth of it, till it was irrecoverably lost. Should a man give away an earthen pot full of gold for a trifle, not knowing what was in it till it were quite gone from him, and past recovery, how would this foolish action gall him, upon the discovery of the riches in it! Such a one's case may be a faint resemblance of the case of despisers of the Gospel, when in hell they lift up their eyes, and behold that to their torment, which they will not see now to their salvation. 2. That they have lost it for dross and dung; sold their part of

heaven, and not enriched themselves with the price. They have lost heaven for earthly profits and pleasures, and now both are gone together from them. The drunkard's cups are gone, the covetous man's gain, the voluptuous man's carnal delights, and the sluggard's ease: nothing is left to comfort them now. The happiness they lost remains indeed, but they can have no part in it for ever.

Use: Sinners, be persuaded to come to God through Jesus Christ, uniting with Him through the Mediator; that you may be preserved from this fearful separation from Him. O be afraid to live in a state of separation from God, lest that which you now make your choice become your eternal punishment hereafter. Do not reject communion with God, cast not off the communion of saints, for it will be the misery of the damned to be driven out from that communion. Cease to build up the wall of separation between God and you, by continuing in your sinful courses; repent rather in time, and so pull it down, lest the topstone be laid upon it, and it stand for ever between you and happiness. Tremble at the thought of rejection and separation from God. By whomsoever men are rejected upon earth, they ordinarily find some pity; but, if you be thus separated from God, you will find all doors shut against you. You will find no pity from any in heaven; neither saints nor angels will pity them whom God has utterly cast off; none will pity you in hell, where there is no love, but loathing; all being loathed of God, loathing Him, and loathing one another. This is a day of losses and fears. I show you a loss you would do well to fear in time; be afraid lest you lose God; if you do, eternity will be spent in roaring out lamentations for this loss. O horrid stupidity! Men are in a mighty care and concern to prevent worldly losses; but they are in danger of losing the enjoyment of God for ever and ever; in danger of losing heaven, the communion of the blessed, and all good things for soul and body in another world; yet as careless in that matter as if they were incapable of thought. O compare this day with the day our text aims at. To-day heaven is opened for those who hitherto have rejected Christ; and yet there is room, if they will come: but that day the doors shall be shut. Now Christ is saying unto you, 'Come:' then he will say: 'Depart,' seeing you would not come when you were invited. Now pity is shown; the Lord pities you, His servants pity you, and tell you that the pit is before you, and cry to you, that you do yourselves no harm: but then shall you have no pity from God or man.

2: The damned shall be punished in hell with the punishment of sense; they must depart from God into everlasting fire. I am not disposed to dispute what kind of fire it is into which they shall depart, to be tormented for ever, whether a material fire or not: experience will more than satisfy the curiosity of those who are disposed rather to dispute about it than to seek how to escape it. Neither will I meddle with the question, Where is it? It is enough that the worm that never dieth, and the fire that is never quenched, will be found somewhere by impenitent sinners. But, first, I shall prove that, whatever kind of fire it is, it is more vehement and terrible than any fire we on earth are acquainted with. Secondly, I shall state some of the properties of these fiery torments.

As to the first of these, burning is the most terrible punishment, and brings the most exquisite pain and torment with it. By what reward could a man be induced to hold but his hand in the flame of a candle for one hour? All imaginable pleasures on earth will never prevail with the most voluptuous man, to venture to lodge but one half hour in a burning fiery furnace; nor would all the wealth in the world prevail with the most covetous to do it: yet, on much lower terms do most men, in effect, expose themselves to everlasting fire in hell, which is more vehement and terrible than any fire we on earth are acquainted with; as will appear by the following considerations.

(1) As in heaven, grace being brought to its perfection, profit and pleasure also arrive at their height there, so sin, being come to its height in hell, the evil of punishment also arrives at its perfection there. Wherefore, as the joys of heaven are far greater

than any joys which the saints obtain on earth, so the punishments of hell must be greater than any earthly torments whatsoever; not only in respect of the continuance of them, but also in respect of vehemency and exquisiteness.

(2) Why are the things of another world represented to us in an earthly dress, in the Word, but because the weakness of our capacities in such matters, which the Lord is pleased to condescend unto, requires it; it being always supposed, that the things of the other world are in their kind more perfect than those by which they are represented. When heaven is represented to us under the notion of a city, with gates of pearl and the street of gold, we expect not to find gold and pearls there, which are so mightily prized on earth, but something more excellent than the finest and most precious things in the world: when, therefore, we hear of hell-fire, it is necessary we understand by it something more vehement, piercing, and tormenting, than any fire ever seen by our eyes. And here it is worth considering, that the torments of hell are held forth under several other notions than that of fire simply: and the reason of it is plain; namely, that hereby what of horror is wanting in one notion of hell, is supplied by another. Why is heaven's happiness represented under the various notions of 'a treasure, a paradise, a feast, a rest,' &c., but that there is not one of these things sufficient to express it? Even so, hell-torments are represented under the notion of fire, which the damned are cast into. A dreadful representation indeed! yet not sufficient to express the misery of the state of sinners in them. Wherefore, we hear also of 'the second death' (Rev 20.6), for the damned in hell shall be ever dying, of the 'wine-press of the wrath of God' (chap 14.19), wherein they will be trodden in anger, trampled in the Lord's fury (Isa 63.3); pressed, broken, and bruised, without end: 'the worm that dieth not' (Mark 9.44), which shall eternally gnaw them: 'a bottomless pit,' where they will be ever sinking (Rev 20.3). It is not simply called 'a fire,' but 'the lake of fire and brimstone' (verse 10), 'a lake of fire burning with brimstone' (chap 19.20); than which one can imagine nothing more dread-

ful. Yet, because fire gives light, and light, as Solomon observes (Eccl 11.7), is sweet, there is no light there, but darkness, utter darkness (Matt 25.30). For they must have an everlasting night, since nothing can be there which is in any measure comfortable or refreshing.

(3) Our fire cannot affect a spirit, but by way of sympathy with the body to which it is united; but hell-fire will not only pierce into the bodies, but directly into the souls of the damned, for it is 'prepared for the devil and his angels,' those wicked spirits, whom no fire on earth can hurt. Job complains heavily, under the chastisements of God's fatherly hand, saying, 'The arrows of the Almighty are within me, the poison whereof drinketh up my spirit' (Job 6.4). But how will the spirits of the damned be pierced with the arrows of revenging justice! how will they be drunk up with the poison of the curse of these arrows! how vehement must that fire be which pierces directly into the soul, and makes an everlasting burning in the spirit, the most lively and tender part of a man, wherein wounds or pains are most intolerable!

(4) The preparation of this fire proves the inexpressible vehemency and dreadfulness of it. The text calls it, 'prepared fire,' yea, '*the* prepared fire,' by way of eminence. As the three children were not cast into ordinary fire, but a fire prepared for a particular purpose which therefore was exceeding hot, the furnace being heated seven times more than ordinary (Dan 3.19–22), so the damned shall find in hell a prepared fire, the like to which was never prepared by human art. It is a fire of God's own preparing, the product of infinite wisdom, with a particular purpose, to demonstrate the most strict and severe divine justice against sin; which may sufficiently evidence to us the inconceivably exquisiteness thereof. God always acts in a peculiar way, becoming His infinite greatness, whether for or against the creature: therefore, as the things He has prepared for them that love Him are great and good beyond expression or conception, so one may conclude that the things He has prepared against those who hate Him are great and terrible beyond what men can either say or think of

them. The pile of Tophet is 'fire, and much wood;' the coals of that fire are 'coals of juniper,' a kind of wood which, set on fire, burns most fiercely (Psa 120.4); 'and the breath of the Lord, like a stream of brimstone, doth kindle it' (Isa 30.33). Fire is more or less violent, according to the matter of it, and the breath by which it is blown. What heart, then, can fully conceive the horror of coals of juniper, blown up with the breath of the Lord? Nay, God Himself will be a consuming fire (Deut 4.24) to the damned; intimately present, as a devouring fire, in the souls and bodies. It is a fearful thing to fall into a fire, or to be shut up in a fiery furnace, on earth; but the terror of these vanishes, when we consider how fearful it is to fall into the hands of the living God, which is the lot of the damned; for 'Who shall dwell with devouring fire? Who shall dwell with everlasting burnings?' (Isa 33.14).

As to the second point proposed, namely, the properties of the fiery torments in hell:

(1) They will be universal torments, every part of the creature being tormented in that flame. When one is cast into a fiery furnace, the fire makes its way into the very heart, and leaves no member untouched: what part, then, can have ease, when the damned swim in a lake of fire, burning with brimstone? There will their bodies be tormented and scorched for ever. And as they sinned, so shall they be tormented, in all the parts thereof, that they shall have no sound side to turn them to; for what soundness or ease can be to any part of that body, which being separated from God, and all refreshment from Him, is still in the pangs of the second death, ever dying, but never dead? But as the soul was chief in sinning, it will be chief in suffering too, being filled quite full of the wrath of a sin-avenging God. The damned shall be ever under the deepest impressions of God's vindictive justice against them: and this fire will melt their souls within them, like wax. Who knows the power of that wrath which had such an effect on the Mediator standing in the room of sinners (Psa 22.14). 'My heart is like wax, it is melted in the midst of my bowels?' Their minds shall be filled with the terrible appre-

hensions of God's implacable wrath: and whatever they can think upon, past, present, or to come, will aggravate their torment and anguish. Their will shall be crossed in all things for evermore; as their will was ever contrary to the will of God's precepts, so God, in His dealing with them in the other world, shall have war with their will for ever. What they would have, they shall not in the least obtain: but what they would not, shall be bound upon them without remedy. Hence, no pleasant affection shall ever spring up in their hearts any more; their love of complacency, joy, and delight, in any object whatever, shall be plucked up by the root, and they will be filled with hatred, fury, and rage against God, themselves, and their fellow-creatures, whether happy in heaven, or miserable in hell, as they themselves are. They will be sunk in sorrow, racked with anxiety, filled with horror, galled to the heart with fretting, and continually darted with despair: which will make them weep, gnash their teeth, and blaspheme for ever. 'Bind him hand and foot, and take him away, and cast him into outer darkness; there shall be weeping and gnashing of teeth' (Matt 22.13). 'And there fell upon men a great hail out of heaven, every stone about the weight of a talent: and men blasphemed God because of the hail; for the plague thereof was exceeding great' (Rev 16.21). Conscience will be a worm to gnaw and prey upon them; remorse for their sins shall seize them and torment them for ever, and they shall not be able to shake it off, as once they did; for 'in hell their worm dieth not' (Mark 9.44,46). Their memory will serve but to aggravate their torment, and every new reflection will bring another pang of anguish (Luke 16.25), 'But Abraham said,' to the rich man in hell, 'Son, remember that thou in thy lifetime receivedst thy good things.'

(2) The torments in hell are manifold. Put the case that a man were, at one and the same time, under the violence of the gout, gravel, and whatever diseases and pains have ever met together in one body; the torment of such a one would be but light in comparison of the torments of the damned. For, as in hell there is an absence of all that is good and desirable, so there is the confluence

of all evils there; since all the effects of sin and of the curse take their place in it, after the last judgment (Rev 20.14), 'And death and hell were cast into the lake of fire.' There they will find a prison they can never escape out of; a lake of fire, where they will be ever swimming and burning; a pit, whereof they will never find a bottom. The worm that dieth not shall feed on them, as on bodies which are interred; the fire that is not quenched shall devour them, as dead bodies which are burned. Their eyes shall be kept in blackness of darkness, without the least comfortable gleam of light; their ears filled with frightful yellings of the infernal crew. They shall taste nothing but the sharpness of God's wrath, the dregs of the cup of His fury. The stench of the burning lake of brimstone will be the smell there; and they shall feel extreme pains for evermore.

(3) They will be most exquisite and vehement torments, causing 'weeping, wailing, and gnashing of teeth' (Matt 13.42, and 22.13). They are represented to us under the notion of pangs in travail, which are very sharp and exquisite. So says the rich man in hell (Luke 16.24), 'I am tormented,' that is, as one in the pangs of child-bearing, 'in this flame.' Ah! dreadful pangs! horrible travail, in which both soul and body are in pangs together! helpless travail, hopeless and endless! The word used for hell (Matt 5.22), and in various other places of the New Testament, properly denotes the valley of Hinnom, the name being taken from the valley of the children of Hinnom, in which was Tophet (2 Kings 23.10), where idolaters offered their children to Moloch. This is said to have been a great brazen idol, with arms like a man's: which being heated by fire within it, the child was set in the burning arms of the idol, and, that the parent might not hear the shrieks of the child burning to death, they beat drums in the time of the horrible sacrifice; whence the place had the name of Tophet. Thus the exquisiteness of the torments in hell are pointed out to us. Some have endured grievous tortures on earth with surprising obstinacy and undaunted courage: but men's courage will fail them there, when they find themselves fallen into the

hands of the living God; and no escape to be expected for ever. It is true, there will be degrees of torments in hell; 'It shall be more tolerable for Tyre and Sidon than for Chorazin and Bethsaida' (Matt 11.21,22). But the least load of wrath there will be insupportable; for how can the heart of the creature endure, or his hands be strong, when God Himself is a consuming fire to him? When the tares are bound in bundles for the fire, there will be bundles of covetous persons, of drunkards, profane swearers, unclean persons, formal hypocrites, unbelievers, and despisers of the Gospel, and the like. The several bundles being cast into hell-fire, some will burn more vehemently than others, according as their sins have been more heinous than those of others: a fiercer flame shall seize the bundle of the profane than the bundle of unsanctified moralists; the furnace will be hotter to those who have sinned against light, than to those who lived in darkness; (Luke 12.47,48), 'That servant which knew his lord's will, and prepared not himself, neither did according to his will, shall be beaten with many stripes. But he that knew not, and did commit things worthy of stripes, shall be beaten with few stripes.' But the sentence common to them all (Matt 13.30), 'Bind them in bundles to burn them,' speaks the great vehemency and exquisiteness of the lowest degree of torment in hell.

(4) They will be uninterrupted; there is no intermission there; no ease, no, not for a moment. They 'shall be tormented day and night for ever and ever' (Rev 20.10). Few are so tossed in this world, but sometimes they get rest; but the damned shall get none; they took their rest in the time appointed of God for their labour. Storms are rarely seen, without some space between showers; but there is no intermission in the storm that falls on the wicked in hell. There, deep will be calling unto deep, and the waves of wrath continually rolling over them. There, the heavens will be always black to them, and they shall have a perpetual night, but no rest (Rev 14.11), 'They have no rest day nor night.'

(5) They will be unpitied. The punishments inflicted on the

[490]

greatest malefactors on earth draw forth some compassion from the spectators; but the damned shall have none to pity them. God will not pity them, but laugh at their calamity (Prov 1.26). The blessed company in heaven shall rejoice in the execution of God's righteous judgment, and sing while the smoke rises up for ever and ever (Rev 19.3), 'And again they said, Hallelujah; and her smoke rose up for ever and ever.' No compassion can be expected from the devil and his angels, who delight in the ruin of the children of men, and are and will be for ever void of pity. Neither will one pity another there, where every one is weeping and gnashing his teeth, under his own insupportable anguish and pain. There, natural affection will be extinguished; parents will not love their children, nor children their parents; the mother will not pity the daughter in these flames, nor will the daughter pity the mother; the son will show no regard to his father there, nor the servant to his master, where every one will be groaning under his own torment.

(6) To complete their misery, their torments shall be eternal (Rev 14.11), 'And the smoke of their torments ascendeth up for ever and ever.' Ah! what a frightful case is this, to be tormented in the whole body and soul, and that not with one kind of torment, but many; all of these most exquisite, and all this without any intermission, and without pity from any! What heart can conceive those things without horror? Nevertheless, if this most miserable case were at length to have an end, that would afford some comfort; but the torments of the damned will have no end; of which more afterwards.

Use: Learn from this, 1. The evil of sin. It is a stream that will carry down the sinner, till he be swallowed up in the ocean of wrath. The pleasures of sin are bought too dear, at the rate of everlasting burnings. What availed the rich man's purple clothing and sumptuous fare, when in hell he was encircled by purple flames, and could not have a drop of water to cool his tongue? Alas! that men should indulge themselves in sin which will be such bitterness in the end! that they should drink so greedily of the poisonous cup, and hug that serpent in their bosom that will sting them to the heart. 2. What a God He is with whom we have to do! What hatred He bears to sin, and how severely He punishes it! Know the Lord to be most just, as well as most merciful, and think not that He is such an one as you are; away with the fatal mistake before it be too late (Psa 50.21,22), 'Thou thoughtest that I was altogether such an one as thyself; but I will reprove thee, and set them in order before thine eyes. Now consider this, ye that forget God, lest I tear you in pieces, and there be none to deliver.' The fire prepared for the devil and his angels, dark as it is, will discover God to be a severe revenger of sin. 3. The absolute necessity of fleeing to the Lord Jesus Christ by faith; the same necessity of repentance, and holiness of heart and life. The avenger of blood is pursuing you, O sinner; haste and escape to the city of refuge. Wash now in the fountain of the Mediator's blood, that you may not perish in the lake of fire. Open your heart to Him, lest the pit close its mouth on you. Leave your sins, else they will ruin you; kill them, else they will be your death for ever.

Let not the terror of hell-fire put you upon hardening your heart more, as it may do, if you entertain that wicked thought, 'There is no hope' (Jer 2.25), which, perhaps, is more common among the hearers of the gospel than many are aware of. But there is hope for the worst of sinners, who will come to Jesus Christ. If there are no good qualifications in you, as certainly there can be none in a natural man, none in any man, but what are received from Christ, know that He has not suspended your welcome on any good qualifications: do you take Him and His salvation freely offered to all to whom the Gospel comes. 'Whosoever will, let him take the water of life freely' (Rev 22.17). 'Him that cometh to me I will in no wise cast out' (John 6.37). It is true, you are a sinful creature, and cannot repent; you are unholy, and cannot make yourself holy: nay, you have attempted to repent, to forsake sin, and to be holy, but still failed of repentance, reformation, and holiness; and therefore, 'Thou saidst,

There is no hope. No, for I have loved strangers, and after them will I go.' Truly, no wonder that the success has not answered your expectation, since you have always begun your work amiss. But do you first of all honour God, by believing the testimony He has given of His Son, namely, that eternal life is in Him: and honour the Son of God, by believing in Him, that is, embracing and falling in with the free offer of Christ, and of His salvation from sin and from wrath, made to you in the Gospel; trusting in Him confidently for righteousness to your justification, and also for sanctification; seeing 'of God he is made unto us' both 'righteousness and sanctification' (1 Cor 1.30). Then, if you have as much credit to give to the Word of God, as you would allow to the word of an honest man, offering you a gift, and saying, Take it, and it is yours; you may believe that God is your God, Christ is yours, His salvation is yours, your sins are pardoned, you have strength in Him for repentance and for holiness; for all these are made over to you in the free offer of the gospel. Believing on the Son of God, you are justified, the curse is removed. And while it lies upon you, how is it possible you should bring forth the fruits of holiness? But, the curse removed, that death which seized on you with the first Adam, according to the threatening (Gen 2.17), is taken away. In consequence of which, you will find the bands of wickedness, now holding you fast in impenitence, broken asunder, as the bands of that death; so as you will be able to repent indeed from the heart: you will find the spirit of life returned to your soul, on whose departure that death ensued, so as thenceforth you will be enabled to live unto righteousness. No man's case is so bad, but it may be mended this way, in time, to be perfectly right in eternity: and no man's case is so good, but, another way being taken, it will be ruined for time and eternity too.

III: The damned shall have the society of devils in their miserable state in hell: for they must depart into 'fire prepared for the devil and his angels.' O horrible company! O frightful association! Who would choose to dwell in a palace haunted by devils? To be confined to the most pleasant spot of earth, with the devil and his infernal furies, would be a most terrible confinement. How would men's hearts fail them, and their hair stand up, finding themselves environed with the hellish crew! But, ah! how much more terrible must it be, to be cast with the devils into one fire, locked up with them in one dungeon, shut up with them in one pit! To be closed up in a den of roaring lions, girded about with serpents, surrounded with venomous asps, and to have the heart eaten out by vipers, altogether and at once, is a comparison too low to show the misery of the damned, shut up in hell with the devil and his angels. They go about now as roaring lions, seeking whom they may devour: but then they shall be confined in their den with their prey. They shall be filled with the wrath of God, and receive the full torment (Matt 8.29), which they tremble in expectation of (James 2.19), being cast into the fire prepared for them. How will these lions roar and tear! how will these serpents hiss! these dragons cast out fire! what horrible anguish will seize the damned, finding themselves in the lake of fire with the devil who deceived them; drawn thither with the silken cords of temptation by these wicked spirits; and bound with them in everlasting chains under darkness! (Rev 20.10), 'And the devil that deceived them was cast into the lake of fire and brimstone, where the beast and the false prophet are, and shall be tormented day and night for ever and ever.'

O that men would consider this in time, renounce the devil and his lusts, and join themselves to the Lord in faith and holiness! Why should men choose such company in this world, and delight in such society, as they would not desire to associate with in the other world? Those who like not the company of the saints on earth will get none of it in eternity; but, as godless company is their delight now, they will afterwards get enough of it, when they have eternity to pass in the roaring and blaspheming society of devils and reprobates in hell. Let those who use to invocate the devil to take them, soberly consider that the company so often invited will be terrible at last, when come.

IV: And, Lastly, Let us consider the eternity of the whole, the everlasting continuance of the miserable state of the damned in hell.

1: If I could, I would show what eternity is, I mean, the creature's eternity. But who can measure the waters of the ocean; or who can tell you the days, years, and ages of eternity, which are infinitely more than the drops of the ocean? None can comprehend eternity but the eternal God. Eternty is an ocean whereof we shall never see the shore; it is a deep where we can find no bottom; a labyrinth from whence we cannot extricate ourselves, and where we shall ever lose the door. There are two things we may say of it. 1. It has a beginning. God's eternity has no beginning, but the creature's has. Once there was no lake of fire; and those who have been there for some hundreds of years, were once in time, as we now are. But, 2. It shall never have an end. The first who entered into the eternity of woe is as far from the end of it as the last who shall go thither will be at his entry. They who have launched out furthest into that ocean are as far from land as they were the first moment they went into it: and, thousands of ages after this they will be as far from it as ever. Wherefore eternity, which is before us, is a duration that has a beginning but no end. It is a beginning without a middle, a beginning without an end. After millions of years passed in it, still it is a beginning. God's wrath in hell will ever be the wrath to come. But there is no middle in eternity. When millions of ages are past in eternity, what is past bears no proportion to what is to come: no, not so much as one drop of water, falling from the tip of one's finger, bears to all the waters of the ocean. There is no end of it: while God is, it shall be. It is an entry without an end to it, a continual succession of ages, a glass always running, which shall never run out.

Observe the continual succession of hours, days, months, and years, how one still follows upon another; and think of eternity, wherein there is a continual succession without end. When you go out at night and behold the stars of heaven, how they cannot be numbered for multitude, think of the ages of eternity; consider also, there is a certain definite number of stars, but no number of the ages of eternity. When you see water running, think how vain a thing it would be to sit down by it, and wait till it should run out, that you may pass over; observe how new water still succeeds to that which passes by you: and therein you have an image of eternity, which is a river that never dries up. They who wear rings have an image of eternity on their fingers; and they who handle the wheel have an emblem of eternity before them: for to whichever part of the ring or wheel we look, one will still see another part beyond it; and on whatever moment of eternity you meditate, there is still another beyond it. When you are abroad in the fields, and behold the blades of grass on the earth, which no man can reckon, think with yourselves, that, were as many thousands of years to come, as there are blades of grass on the ground, even those would have an end at length; but eternity will have none. When you look to a mountain, imagine in your hearts how long would it be before that mountain should be removed by a little bird coming but once every thousand years, and carrying away but one grain of the dust of it at once: the mountain would at length be removed that way, and brought to an end; but eternity will never end. Suppose this with respect to all the mountains of the earth, no, with respect to the whole globe itself: the grains of dust of which the whole of it is made up are not infinite; and therefore the last grain would, at length, come to be carried away, as above: yet eternity would be, in effect, but beginning.

These are some rude emblems of eternity: and now add misery and woe to this eternity, what tongue can express it? what heart can conceive it? in what balance can that misery and that woe be weighed?

2: Let us take a view of what is eternal, in the state of the damned in hell. Whatever is included in the fearful torments of their state, is everlasting: therefore, all the doleful ingredients of their miserable state will be everlasting; they will never end.

The text expressly declares the fire, into which they must depart, to be everlasting fire. And our Lord elsewhere tells us, that in hell, the fire never shall be quenched (Mark 9.43). He had an eye to the valley of Hinnom, in which, besides the before-mentioned fire for burning the children to Molech, there was also another fire burning continually, to consume the dead carcases and filth of Jerusalem: so the Scripture, representing hell-fire by the fire of that valley, speaks it not only to be most exquisite, but also everlasting. Seeing, then, the damned must depart, as cursed ones, into everlasting fire, it is evident that:

(1) The damned themselves shall be eternal; they will have a being for ever, and will never be substantially destroyed or annihilated. To what end is the fire eternal, if those who are cast into it be not eternally in it? It is plain, the everlasting continuance of the fire is an aggravation of the misery of the damned. But, surely, if they be annihilated, or substantially destroyed, it would be all one to them, whether the fire be everlasting or not. Nay, but they depart into everlasting fire, to be everlastingly punished in it. (Matt 25.46), 'These shall go away into everlasting punishment.' Thus the execution of the sentence is a certain discovery of the meaning of it. The worm, that dieth not, must have a subject to live in: they, who shall have no rest, day nor night (Rev 14.11), but shall be 'tormented day and night for ever and ever' (chap 20.10), will certainly have a being for ever and ever, and not be brought into a state of eternal rest in annihilation. Destroyed indeed they shall be: but their destruction will be an everlasting destruction (2 Thess 1.9); a destruction of their well-being, but not of their being. What is destroyed is not therefore annihilated: 'Art thou come to destroy us?' said the devil unto Jesus Christ (Luke 4.34). The devils are afraid of torment, not of annihilation (Matt 8.29), 'Art thou come hither to torment us before the time?' The state of the damned is indeed a state of death; but such a death it is as is opposite only to a happy life, as is clear from other notions of their state, which necessarily include eternal existence. As they who are dead in

sin are dead to God and holiness, yet live to sin, so dying in hell they live, but separated from God and His favour, in which is life (Psa 30.5). They shall ever be under the pangs of death; ever dying, but never dead, or absolutely void of life. How desirable would such a death be to them! but it will flee from them for ever. Could they kill one another there, or could they, with their own hands, tear themselves into lifeless pieces, their misery would quickly be at an end: but there they must live, whose chose death and refused life; for there death lives, and the end ever begins.

(2) The curse shall lie upon them eternally, as the everlasting chain to hold them in the everlasting fire, a chain that shall never be loosed, being fixed for ever about them by the dreadful sentence of the eternal judgment. This chain, which spurns the united force of devils held fast by it, is too strong to be broken by men, who being solemnly anathematized and devoted to destruction, can never be recovered to any other use.

(3) Their punishment shall be eternal; (Matt 25.46), 'These shall go away into everlasting punishment.' They will be for ever separated from God and Christ, and from the society of the holy angels and saints, between whom and them an impassable gulf will be fixed (Luke 16.26), 'Between us and you,' says Abraham, in the parable, to the rich man in hell, 'there is a great gulf fixed: so that they which would pass from hence to you, cannot; neither can they pass to us, that would come from thence.' They shall for ever have the horrible society of the devil and his angels. There will be no change of company for ever in that region of darkness. Their torment in the fire will be everlasting: they must live for ever in it. Several authors, both ancient and modern, tell us of earth-flax, or salamander's hairs, that cloth made of it, being cast into the fire, is so far from being burnt or consumed, that it is only made clean thereby, as other things are by washing. But however that is, it is certain the damned shall be tormented for ever and ever in hell-fire, and not substantially destroyed (Rev 20.10). And indeed nothing is annihilated by fire, but only dissolved. Of whatsoever nature hell-fire is, no question, the same

God who kept the bodies of the three children from burning in Nebuchadnezzar's fiery furnace, can also keep the bodies of the damned from any such dissolution by hell-fire as may infer privation of life.

(4) Their knowledge and sense of their misery shall be eternal, and they shall assuredly know that it will be eternal. How desirable would it be to them to have their sense for ever locked up, and to lose the consciousness of their own misery! as one may rationally suppose it to fare at length with some, in the punishment of death inflicted on them on earth, and as it is with some mad people; but that agrees not with the notion of torment for ever and ever, nor the worm that dieth not. No, they will ever have a lively feeling of their misery, and strongest impressions of the wrath of God against them. And that dreadful intimation of the eternity of their punishment, made to them by their Judge, in their sentence, will fix such impressions of the eternity of their miserable state upon their minds, as they will never be able to lay aside; but will continue with them evermore, to complete their misery. This will fill them with everlasting despair; a most tormenting passion, which will continually rend their hearts, as it were, in a thousand pieces. To see floods of wrath ever coming, and never to cease; to be ever in torment, and to know that there shall never, never be a release, will be the topstone put on the misery of the damned. If 'hope deferred maketh the heart sick' (Prov 13.12), how killing will it be for hope to be rooted up, slain outright, and buried for ever out of the creature's sight! This will fill them with hatred and rage against God, their known irreconcilable enemy; and under it, they will roar for ever, like wild bulls in a net, and fill the pit with blasphemies evermore.

I might here show the reasonableness of the eternity of the punishment of the damned: but, having already spoken of it, in vindicating the justice of God, in His subjecting men in their natural state to eternal wrath, I only remind you of three things: 1. The infinite dignity of the party offended by sin requires an infinite punishment to be inflicted for the vindication of His honour; since the demerit of sin rises according to the dignity and excellence of the person against whom it is committed. The party offended is the great God, the chief good, the offender a vile worm; in respect of perfection, infinitely distant from God, to whom he is indebted for all that he ever had, implying any good or perfection whatsoever. This then requires an infinite punishment to be inflicted on the sinner; which, since it cannot in him be infinite in value, must needs be infinite in duration, that is to say, eternal. Sin is a kind of infinite evil, as it wrongs an infinite God; and the guilt and defilement of it is never taken away, but endures for ever, unless the Lord Himself in mercy remove it. God, who is offended, is eternal; His being never comes to an end: the sinful soul is immortal, and the man shall live for ever. The sinner, being without strength (Rom 5.6) to expiate his guilt, can never put away the offence; therefore it ever remains, unless the Lord put it away Himself, as in the elect, by His Son's blood. Wherefore the party offended, the offender, and the offence, ever remaining, the punishment cannot but be eternal. 2. The sinner would have continued the course of his provocations against God for ever without end, if God had not put a check to it by death. As long as they were capable of acting against Him in this world, they did it: and therefore justly will He act against them, while He is; that is, for ever. God, who judges of the will, intents, and inclinations of the heart, may justly do against sinners, in punishing, as they would have done against Him in sinning. 3. Though I put not the stress of the matter here, yet it is just and reasonable that the damned suffer eternally, since they will sin eternally in hell, gnashing their teeth (Matt 8.12), under their pain, in rage, envy, and grudge (compare Acts 7.54; Psa 112.10; Luke 13.28), and blaspheming God there (Rev 16.21) while they are 'driven away in their wickedness' (Prov 14.32). That the wicked be punished for their wickedness is just, and it is in no way inconsistent with justice that the being of the creature be continued for ever: wherefore it is just that the damned, continuing wicked eternally, do suffer eternally for their wickedness. The misery, under

[500]

which they sin, can neither free them from the debt of obedience, nor excuse their sinning and make it blameless. The creature, as a creature, is bound unto obedience to his Creator; and no punishment inflicted on him can free him from it, any more than the malefactor's prison, irons, whipping, and the like, set him at liberty again, to commit the crimes for which he is imprisoned or whipped. Neither can the torments of the damned excuse, or make blameless, their horrible sinning under them, any more than exquisite pains, inflicted upon men on earth, can excuse their murmuring, fretting, and blaspheming against God under them. It is not the wrath of God, but their own wicked nature, that is the true cause of their sinning under it; for the holy Jesus bore the wrath of God without so much as one unbecoming thought of God, and far less any one unbecoming word.

Use 1: Here is a measuring reed: O that men would apply it. 1. Apply it to your own time in this world, and you will find your time to be very short. A prospect of much time to come proves the ruin of many souls. Men will be reckoning their time by years, like that rich man (Luke 12.19,20), when, it may be, there are not many hours of it to run. But reckon as you will, laying your time to the measuring reed of eternity, you will see your age is as nothing. What a small and inconsiderable point is sixty, eighty, or a hundred years, in respect of eternity! Compared with eternity, there is a greater disproportion than between a hair's breadth and the circumference of the whole earth. Why do we then sleep in such a short day, while we are in danger of losing rest through the long night of eternity? 2. Apply it to your endeavours for salvation, and they will be found very scanty. When men are pressed to diligence in their salvation work, they are ready to say, 'To what purpose is this waste?' Alas! if it were to be judged by our diligence, what it is that we have in view; as to the most part of us, no man could thereby conjecture that we have eternity in view. If we duly considered eternity, we could not but conclude, that, to leave no appointed means of God unessayed till we get our salvation secured, to refuse rest or comfort in anything, till we are sheltered under the wings of the Mediator, to pursue our great interest with the utmost vigour, to cut off lusts dear as right hands and right eyes, to set our faces resolutely against all difficulties, and fight our way through all opposition made by the devil, the world, and the flesh, these are, all of them together, little enough for eternity.

Use 2: Here is a balance of the sanctuary, by which we may understand the lightness of what is falsely thought weighty; and the weight of some things, by many reckoned to be very light.

1 : Some things seem very weighty, which, weighed in this balance, will be found very light. (1) Weigh the world, and all that is in it, the lust of the flesh, the lust of the eyes, and the pride of life, and the whole will be found light in the balance of eternity. Weigh herein all worldly profits, gains, and advantages; and you will quickly see, that a thousand worlds will not compensate for an eternity of woe. 'For what is a man profited, if he shall gain the whole world, and lose his own soul?' (Matt 16.26). Weigh the pleasures of sin, which are but for a season, with the fire that is everlasting, and you show yourself to be fools and madmen, to run the hazard of the one for the other. (2) Weigh your afflictions in this balance, and you will find the heaviest of them very light, in respect of the weight of eternal anguish. Impatience under affliction, especially when worldly troubles so embitter men's spirits that they cannot relish the glad tidings of the Gospel, speaks great regardlessness of eternity. As a small and inconsiderable loss will be very little at heart with him who sees himself in danger of losing his whole estate, so troubles in the world will appear but light to him who has a lively view of eternity. Such a one will stoop and take up his cross, whatever it be, thinking it enough to escape eternal wrath. (3) Weigh the most difficult and uneasy duties of religion here, and you will no more reckon the yoke of Christ insupportable. Repentance and bitter mourning for sin, on earth, are very light in comparison of eternal weeping, wailing, and gnashing of teeth in hell. To wrestle with God in prayer, weeping and making supplication for the

blessing in time, is far easier than to lie under the curse through all eternity. Mortification of the most beloved lust is a light thing in comparison with the second death in hell. (4) Weigh your convictions in this balance. O how heavy do those lie upon many till they get them shaken off! They are not disposed to continue with them, but strive to get clear of them, as of a mighty burden. But the worm of an ill conscience will neither die nor sleep in hell, though we may now lull it asleep for a time. And certainly it is easier to entertain the sharpest convictions in this life, so that they lead us to Christ, than to have them fixed for ever in the conscience, and to be in hell totally and finally separated from Him.

2 : But, on the other hand, (1) Weigh sin in this balance, and, though now it seems but a light thing to you, you will find it a weight sufficient to turn up an eternal weight of wrath upon you. Even idle words, vain thoughts, and unprofitable actions, weighed in this balance, and considered as following the sinner into eternity, will each of them be heavier than the sand of the sea; time idly spent will make a weary eternity. Now is your seed-time; thoughts, words, and actions, are the seed sown, eternity is the harvest. Though the seed now lies under the clod, disregarded by most men, even the least grain shall spring up at length; and the fruit will be according to the seed (Gal 6.8), 'For he that soweth to his flesh, shall of the flesh reap corruption, (that is, destruction), but he that soweth to the Spirit shall of the Spirit reap life everlasting.' (2) Weigh in this balance your time and opportunities of grace and salvation, and you will find them very weighty. Precious time and seasons of grace, Sabbaths, communions, prayers, sermons, and the like, are by many, now-a-days, made light of; but the day is coming when one of these will be reckoned more valuable than a thousand worlds by those who now have the least value for them. When they are gone for ever, and the loss cannot be retrieved, those will see the worth of them who will not now see it.

Use 3 *and last* : Be warned and stirred up to flee from the wrath to come. Mind eternity, and closely ply the work of your salvation. What are you doing, while you are not so doing? Is heaven a fable, or hell a false alarm? Must we live eternally, and shall we be at no more pains to escape everlasting misery? Will faint wishes take the kingdom of heaven by force? And will such drowsy endeavours as most men satisfy themselves with, be accounted fleeing from the wrath to come? You who have already fled to Christ, up, and be doing. You who have begun the work, go on and loiter not, but 'work out your salvation with fear and trembling' (Phil 2.12). 'Fear him which is able to destroy both soul and body in hell' (Matt 10.28). Remember you are not yet ascended into heaven; you are but in your middle state. The everlasting arms have drawn you out of the gulf of wrath you were plunged into, in your natural state; they are still underneath you, that you can never fall down into it again; nevertheless, you have not yet got up to the top of the rock; the deep below you is frightful, look at it, and hasten your ascent. You who are yet in your natural state, lift up your eyes and take a view of the eternal state. Arise, ye profane persons, ye ignorant ones, ye formal hypocrites, strangers to the power of godliness, flee from the wrath to come. Let not the young venture to delay a moment longer, nor the old put off this work any more: 'To-day if ye will hear his voice, harden not your hearts;' lest He swear in His wrath that you shall never enter into His rest. It is no time to linger in a state of sin, as in Sodom, when fire and brimstone are coming down on it from the Lord. Take warning in time. They who are in hell are not troubled with such warnings, but are enraged against themselves, because they slighted the warning when they had it.

Consider, I pray you, 1. How uneasy it is to lie one whole night on a soft bed in perfect health, when we fain would have sleep but cannot get it, sleep being departed from us. How often do we in that case, wish for rest! how full of tossings to and fro! But ah! how dreadful must it be to lie in sorrow, wrapped up in scorching flames throughout eternity, in that place where they have no rest day nor night! 2. How terrible would it be to live under violent pains of the cholic or gravel for forty or sixty years together without any intermission! Yet that is but a very small thing compared with eternal separation from God, the worm that never dieth, and the fire that is never quenched. 3. Eternity is an awful thought; O long, long endless eternity! But will not every moment in eternity of woe seem a month, and every hour a year, in that most wretched and desperate condition? Hence, 'ever and ever', as it were, a double eternity. The sick man in the night, tossing to and fro on his bed, says it will never be day; complains, that his pain ever continues, never, never abates. Are these petty time-eternities, which men form to themselves in their own imaginations, so very grievous? Alas! then, how grievous, how utterly insupportable, must a real eternity of woe, and all manner of miseries, be! 4. There will be space enough there to reflect on all the ills of our heart and life, which we cannot get time to think of now; and to see that all that was said of the impenitent sinner's hazard was true, and that the half was not told. There will be space enough in eternity to carry on delayed repentance, to rue one's follies when it is too late; and in a state past remedy to speak forth these fruitless wishes, 'O that I had never been born! that the womb had been my grave, and I had never seen the sun! O that I had taken warning in time, and fled from this wrath while the door of mercy was standing open to me! O that I had never heard the Gospel, that I had lived in some corner of the world where a Saviour and the great salvation were not once named!' But all in vain. What is done cannot be undone; the opportunity is lost, and can never be retrieved; time is gone, and can never be recalled. Wherefore, improve time while you have it, and do not wilfully ruin yourself by stopping your ear to the Gospel call.

And now, if you would be saved from the wrath to come, and never go into this place of torment, take no rest in your natural state; believe the sinfulness and misery of it, and labour to get out of it quickly, fleeing unto Jesus Christ by faith. Sin in you is the seed of hell: and if the guilt and reigning power of it be not removed in time, they will bring you to the second death in eternity. There is no way to get them removed, but by receiving Christ as He is offered in the Gospel, for justification and sanctification: and He is now offered to you with all His salvation (Rev 22.12,17), 'And behold, I come quickly, and my reward is with me, to give to every man according as his work shall be. And the Spirit and the bride say, Come; and let him that heareth say, Come; and let him that is athirst come. And whosoever will, let him take the water of life freely.' Jesus Christ is the Mediator of peace, and the fountain of holiness: He it is who delivers us from the wrath to come. 'There is no condemnation to them which are in Christ Jesus, who walk not after the flesh, but after the Spirit' (Rom 8.1). And the terrors of hell, as well as the joys of heaven, are set before you, to stir you up to a cordial receiving of Him, with all His salvation; and to incline you to the way of faith and holiness, in which alone you can escape the everlasting fire. May the Lord Himself make them effectual to that end!

Thus far of man's eternal state, which, because it is eternal, admits no succeeding one for ever.